INTRODUCTORY MICROECONOMICS

Kruger Brentt
Publishers

INTRODUCTORY MICROECONOMICS

VOLUME-1

Margaret Anderson
Bryan Clark
Matthew Qiu

Kruger Brentt
Publishers
2023

Kruger Brentt Publishers UK. LTD.
Company Number 9728962

Regd. Office: 68 St Margarets Road, Edgware, Middlesex HA8 9UU

ISBN: 978-1-78715-178-9

For information on all our publications visit our website at http://krugerbrentt.com/

PREFACE

The science of economics was born with the publication of Adam Smith's an Inquiry into the Nature and Causes of Wealth of Nations in the year 1776. Adam Smith is known as the father of Economics. At its birth, the name of economics was 'Political Economy'. Towards the end of the 19th century there was a definite change from use of word 'Political Economy' to 'Economics'. The word 'Economics' was derived from two Greek words oikou (a house) and nomos (to manage). Thus, the word economics was used to mean home management with limited funds available in the most economical manner possible. Lionel Robbins defines economics as a science of scarcity. Prof. Robbins in his book Nature and Significance of Economic Science states, "Economics is the science which studies human behaviour as a relationship between ends and scarce means which have alternative uses". Paul A. Samuelson defines economics as "the study of how men and society choose, withor without the use of money, to employ scarce productive resources which could have alternative uses, to produce various commodities over time and distribute them for consumption now and in future among various people and groups of society." This definition emphasises growth over time. It is modern and wider in scope. The definition takes into account consumption, production, distribution and exchange ofgoods. Hence, it is most satisfactory definition of economics.

Traditionally, the subject matter of economics has been studied under two broad branches: Microeconomics and Macroeconomics. In microeconomics, we study the behaviour of individual economic agents in the markets for different goods and services and try to figure out how prices and quantities of goods and services are determined through the interaction of individuals in these markets. In macroeconomics, on the other hand, we try to get an understanding of the economy as a whole by focusing our attention on aggregate measures such as total output, employment and aggregate price level. Here, we are interested in finding out how the levels of these aggregate measures are determined and how the levels of these aggregate measures change over time.

The present book contains 28-chapters namely welcome to economics!, a world of scarcity and choice, a pluralist approach to defining economics, concepts of demand and supply, labor and financial markets, elasticity an overview, consumer choices, challenging utilitarianism's impact, modern consumption: an institutional analysis, the cost and the industry structure, perfect competition in economics, the monopoly and its kind, competition in monopolists and oligopoly, the growth of big business, pricing and costs: the evidence, the megacorp: principle of economics, policy on monopoly and antitrust, negative externalities and environmental protection, public goods and positive externalities, economic inequality and poverty, major issues in labor markets: unions, discrimination, immigration, knowledge, risk, and insurance, financial markets and business, introduction to public economy, money and the firm's theory, introduction to international trade, globalization and protectionism and the globalization and trade economics: a pluralistic approach. This book covers the scope and sequence of most introductory microeconomics courses. The text includes many current examples, which are handled in a politically equitable way. The outcome is a balanced approach to the theory and application of economics concept. This book provides clear, accurate coverage of advanced microeconomic concepts while illustrating how theory applies to practical situations. This book is useful for undergraduate as well as postgraduate students of economics, commerce, marketing, management, finance, banking and for everybody interested in microeconomics.

We are grateful to all those persons as well as various books, manuals, periodicals, magazines, journals etc. that helped in the preparation of this book. In spite of the best efforts, it is possible that some errors may have occurred into the compilation and editing of the book. Further queries, constructive suggestions and criticisms for the improvement of the book are always welcomed and shall be thankfully acknowledged.

Margaret Anderson

Bryan Clark

Matthew Qiu

CONTENTS

CHAPTER 1 WELCOME TO ECONOMICS!

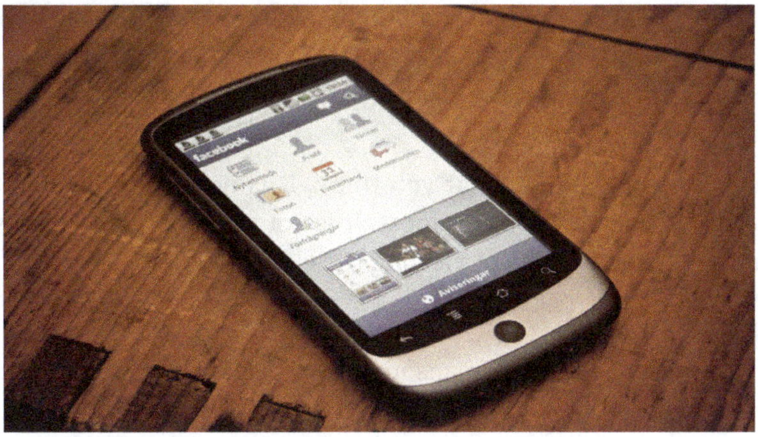

Do You Use Facebook? Economics is greatly impacted by how well information travels through society. Today, social media giants Twitter, Facebook, and Instagram are major forces on the information super highway. (Credit: Johan Larsson/Flickr)

DECISIONS ... DECISIONS IN THE SOCIAL MEDIA AGE

To post or not to post? Every day we are faced with a myriad of decisions, from what to have for breakfast, to which route to take to class, to the more complex—"Should I double major and add possibly another semester of study to my education?" Our response to these choices depends on the information we have available at any given moment; information economists call "imperfect" because we rarely have all the data we need to make perfect decisions. Despite the lack of perfect information, we still make hundreds of decisions a day.

And now, we have another avenue in which to gather information—social media. Outlets like Facebook and Twitter are altering the process by which we make choices, how we spend our time, which movies we see, which products we buy, and more. How many of you chose a university without checking out its Facebook page or Twitter stream first for information and feedback?

As you will see in this course, what happens in economics is affected by how well and how fast information is disseminated through a society, such as how quickly information travels through Facebook. "Economists love nothing better than when deep and liquid markets operate under conditions of perfect information," says Jessica Irvine, National Economics Editor for News Corp Australia.

This leads us to the topic of this chapter, an introduction to the world of making decisions, processing information, and understanding behavior in markets —the world of economics. Each chapter in this book will start with a discussion about current (or sometimes past) events and revisit it at chapter's end—to "bring home" the concepts in play.

What is economics and why should you spend your time learning it? After all, there are other disciplines you could be studying, and other ways you could be spending your time. As the Bring it Home feature just mentioned, making choices is at the heart of what economists study, and your decision to take this course is as much as economic decision as anything else.

Economics is probably not what you think. It is not primarily about money or finance. It is not primarily about business. It is not mathematics. What is it then? It is both a subject area and a way of viewing the world.

1.1 ECONOMICS, ANDITS IMPORTANCE?

Economics is the study of how humans make decisions in the face of scarcity. These can be individual decisions, family decisions, business decisions or societal decisions. If you look around carefully, you will see that scarcity is a fact of life. Scarcity means that human wants for goods, services and resources exceed what is available. Resources, such as labor, tools, land, and raw materials are necessary to produce the goods and services we want but they exist in limited supply. Of course, the ultimate scarce resource is time- everyone, rich or poor, has just 24 hours in the day to try to acquire the goods they want. At any point in time, there is only a finite amount of resources available.

Think about it this way: In 2015 the labor force in the United States contained over 158.6 million workers, according to the U.S. Bureau of Labor Statistics. Similarly, the total area of the United States is 3,794,101 square miles. These are large numbers for such crucial resources, however, they are limited. Because these resources are limited, so are the numbers of goods and services we produce with them. Combine this with the fact that human wants seem to be virtually infinite, and you can see why scarcity is a problem.

Figure 1. Scarcity of Resources. Homeless people are a stark reminder that scarcity of resources is real. (Credit: "daveynin"/Flickr Creative Commons)

If you still do not believe that scarcity is a problem, consider the following: Does everyone need food to eat? Does everyone need a decent place to live? Does everyone have access to healthcare? In every country in the world, there are people who are hungry, homeless (for example, those who call park benches their beds, as shown in Figure 1), and in need of healthcare, just to focus on a few critical goods and services. Why is this the case? It is because of scarcity. Let's delve into the concept of scarcity a little deeper, because it is crucial to understanding economics.

The Problem of Scarcity

Think about all the things you consume: food, shelter, clothing, transportation, healthcare, and entertainment. How do you acquire those items? You do not produce them yourself. You buy them. How do you afford the things you buy? You work for pay. Or if you do not, someone else does on your behalf. Yet most of us never have enough to buy all the things we want. This is because of scarcity. So how do we solve it?

Every society, at every level, must make choices about how to use its resources. Families must decide whether to spend their money on a new car or a fancy vacation. Towns must choose whether to put more of the budget into police and fire protection or into the school system. Nations must decide whether to devote more funds to national defense or to protecting the environment. In most cases, there just isn't enough money in the budget to do everything. So why do we not each just produce all of the things we consume? The simple answer is most of us do not know how, but that is not the main reason. (When you study economics, you will discover that the obvious choice is not always the right answer—or at least the complete answer.

Studying economics teaches you to think in a different of way.) Think back to pioneer days, when individuals knew how to do so much more than we do today, from building their homes, to growing their crops, to hunting for food, to repairing their equipment. Most of us do not know how to do all—or any—of those things. It is not because we could not learn. Rather, we do not have to. The reason why is something called *the division and specialization of labor*, a production innovation first put forth by **Adam Smith**, Figure 2, in his book, *The Wealth of Nations.*

Figure 2. Adam Smith. Adam Smith introduced the idea of dividing labor into discrete tasks. (Credit: Wikimedia Commons)

THE DIVISION OF AND SPECIALIZATION OF LABOR

The formal study of economics began when Adam Smith (1723–1790) published his famous book The Wealth of Nations in 1776. Many authors had written on economics in the centuries before Smith, but he was the first to address the subject in a comprehensive way. In the first chapter, Smith introduces the division of labor, which means that the way a good or service is produced is divided into a number of tasks that are performed by different workers, instead of all the tasks being done by the same person.

To illustrate the division of labor, Smith counted how many tasks went into making a pin: drawing out a piece of wire, cutting it to the right length, straightening it, putting a head on one end and a point on the other, and packaging pins for sale, to name just a few. Smith counted 18 distinct tasks that were often done by different people—all for a pin, believe it or not!

Modern businesses divide tasks as well. Even a relatively simple business like a restaurant divides up the task of serving meals into a range of jobs like top chef, sous chefs, less-skilled kitchen help, servers to wait on the tables, a greeter at the door, janitors to clean up, and a business manager to handle paychecks and bills—not to mention the economic connections a restaurant has with suppliers of food, furniture, kitchen equipment, and the building where it is located. A complex business like a large manufacturing factory, such as the shoe factory shown in Figure 3, or a hospital can have hundreds of job classifications.

Figure 3. Division of Labor. Workers on an assembly line are an example of the divisions of labor. (Credit: Nina Hale/Flickr Creative Commons)

Why the Division of Labor Increases Production

When the tasks involved with producing a good or service are divided and subdivided, workers and businesses can produce a greater quantity of output. In his observations of pin factories, Smith observed that one worker alone might make 20 pins in a day, but that a small business of 10 workers (some of whom would need to do two or three of the 18 tasks involved with pin-making), could make 48,000 pins in a day. How can a group of workers, each specializing in certain tasks, produce so much more than the same number of workers who try to produce the entire good or service by themselves? Smith offered three reasons.

First, specialization in a particular small job allows workers to focus on the parts of the production process where they have an advantage. (In later chapters, we will develop this idea by discussing comparative advantage.) People have different skills, talents, and interests, so they will be better at some jobs than at others. The particular advantages may be based on educational choices, which are in turn shaped by interests and talents. Only those with medical degrees qualify to become doctors, for instance. For some goods, specialization will be affected by geography—it is easier to be a wheat farmer in North Dakota than in Florida, but easier to run a tourist hotel in Florida than in North Dakota. If you live in or near a big city, it is easier to attract enough customers to operate a successful dry cleaning business or movie theater than if you live in a sparsely populated rural area. Whatever the reason, if people specialize in the production of what they do best, they will be more productive than if they produce a combination of things, some of which they are good at and some of which they are not.

Second, workers who specialize in certain tasks often learn to produce more quickly and with higher quality. This pattern holds true for many workers, including assembly line laborers who build cars, stylists who cut hair, and doctors who perform heart surgery. In fact, specialized workers often know their jobs well enough to suggest innovative ways to do their work faster and better.

A similar pattern often operates within businesses. In many cases, a business that focuses on one or a few products (sometimes called its "**core competency**") is more successful than firms that try to make a wide range of products.

Third, specialization allows businesses to take advantage of **economies of scale**, which means that for many goods, as the level of production increases, the average cost of producing each individual unit declines. For example, if a factory produces only 100 cars per year, each car will be quite expensive to make on average. However, if a factory produces 50,000 cars each year, then it can set up an assembly line with huge machines and workers performing specialized tasks, and the average cost of production per car will be lower. The ultimate result of workers who can focus on their preferences and talents, learn to do their specialized jobs better, and work in larger organizations is that society as a whole can produce and consume far more than if each person tried to produce all of their own goods and services. The division and specialization of labor has been a force against the problem of scarcity.

Trade and Markets

Specialization only makes sense, though, if workers can use the pay they receive for doing their jobs to purchase the other goods and services that they need. In short, specialization requires trade.

You do not have to know anything about electronics or sound systems to play music—you just buy an iPod or MP3 player, download the music and listen. You do not have to know anything about artificial fibers or the construction of sewing machines if you need a jacket—you just buy the jacket and wear it. You do not need to know anything about internal combustion engines to operate a car—you just get in and drive. Instead of trying to acquire all the knowledge and skills involved in producing all of the goods and services that you wish to consume, the market allows you to learn a specialized set of skills and then use the pay you receive to buy the goods and services you need or want. This is how our modern society has evolved into a strong economy.

Why Study Economics?

Now that we have gotten an overview on what economics studies, let's quickly discuss why you are right to study it. Economics is not primarily a collection of facts to be memorized, though there are plenty of important concepts to be learned. Instead, economics is better thought of as a collection of questions to be answered or puzzles to be worked out. Most important, economics provides the tools to work out those puzzles. If you have yet to be been bitten by the economics "bug," there are other reasons why you should study economics.

- Virtually every major problem facing the world today, from global warming, to world poverty, to the conflicts in Syria, Afghanistan, and Somalia, has an economic dimension. If you are going to be part of solving those problems, you need to be able to understand them. Economics is crucial.
- It is hard to overstate the importance of economics to good citizenship. You need to be able to vote intelligently on budgets, regulations, and laws in general. When the U.S. government came close to a standstill at the end of 2012 due to the "fiscal cliff," what were the issues involved? Did you know?
- A basic understanding of economics makes you a well-rounded thinker. When you read articles about economic issues, you will understand and be able to evaluate the writer's argument. When you hear classmates, co-workers, or political candidates talking about economics, you will be able to distinguish between common sense and nonsense. You will find new ways of thinking about current events and about personal and business decisions, as well as current events and politics.

The study of economics does not dictate the answers, but it can illuminate the different choices.

Key Concepts and Summary

Economics seeks to solve the problem of scarcity, which is when human wants for goods and services exceed the available supply. A modern economy displays a division of labor, in which people earn income by specializing in what they produce and then use that income to purchase the products they need or want. The division of labor allows individuals and firms to specialize and to produce more for several reasons: a) It allows the agents to focus on areas of advantage due to natural factors and skill levels; b) It encourages the agents to learn and invent; c) It allows agents to take advantage of economies of scale. Division and specialization of labor only work when individuals can purchase what they do not produce in markets. Learning about economics helps you understand the major problems facing the world today, prepares you to be a good citizen, and helps you become a well-rounded thinker.

1.2 MICROECONOMICS AND MACROECONOMICS

Economics is concerned with the well-being of all people, including those with jobs and those without jobs, as well as those with high incomes and those with low incomes. Economics acknowledges that production of useful goods and services can create problems of environmental pollution. It explores the question of how investing in education helps to develop workers' skills. It probes questions like how to tell when big businesses or big labor unions are operating in a way that benefits society as a whole and when they are operating in a way that benefits their owners or members at the expense of others. It looks at how government spending, taxes, and regulations affect decisions about production and consumption.

It should be clear by now that economics covers a lot of ground. That ground can be divided into two parts: Microeconomics focuses on the actions of individual agents within the economy, like households, workers, and businesses; Macroeconomics looks at the economy as a whole. It focuses on broad issues such as growth of production, the number of unemployed people, the inflationary increase in prices, government deficits, and levels of exports and imports. Microeconomics and macroeconomics are not separate subjects, but rather complementary perspectives on the overall subject of the economy.

To understand why both microeconomic and macroeconomic perspectives are useful, consider the problem of studying a biological ecosystem like a lake. One person who sets out to study the lake might focus on specific topics: certain kinds of algae or plant life; the characteristics of particular fish or snails; or the trees surrounding the lake. Another person might take an overall view and instead consider the entire ecosystem of the lake from top to bottom; what eats what, how the system stays in a rough balance, and what environmental stresses affect this balance. Both approaches are useful, and both examine the same lake, but the viewpoints are different. In a similar way, both microeconomics and macroeconomics study the same economy, but each has a different viewpoint.

Whether you are looking at lakes or economics, the micro and the macro insights should blend with each other. In studying a lake, the micro insights about particular plants and animals help to understand the overall food chain, while the macro insights about the overall food chain help to explain the environment in which individual plants and animals live.

In economics, the micro decisions of individual businesses are influenced by whether the macroeconomy is healthy; for example, firms will be more likely to hire workers if the overall economy is growing. In turn, the performance of the macroeconomy ultimately depends on the microeconomic decisions made by individual households and businesses.

Microeconomics

What determines how households and individuals spend their budgets? What combination of goods and services will best fit their needs and wants, given the budget they have to spend? How do people decide whether to work, and if so, whether to work full time or part time? How do people decide how much to save for the future, or whether they should borrow to spend beyond their current means?

What determines the products, and how many of each, a firm will produce and sell? What determines what prices a firm will charge? What determines how a firm will produce its products? What determines how many workers it will hire? How will a firm finance its business? When will a firm decide to expand, downsize, or even close? In the microeconomic part of this book, we will learn about the theory of consumer behavior and the theory of the firm.

Macroeconomics

What determines the level of economic activity in a society? In other words, what determines how many goods and services a nation actually produces? What determines how many jobs are available in an economy? What determines a nation's standard of living? What causes the economy to speed up or slow down? What causes firms to hire more workers or to lay workers off? Finally, what causes the economy to grow over the long term?

An economy's macroeconomic health can be defined by a number of goals: growth in the standard of living, low unemployment, and low inflation, to name the most important. How can macroeconomic policy be used to pursue these goals? **Monetary policy**, which involves policies that affect bank lending, interest rates, and financial capital markets, is conducted by a nation's central bank. For the United States, this is the Federal Reserve. **Fiscal policy**, which involves government spending and taxes, is determined by a nation's legislative body. For the United States, this is the Congress and the executive branch, which originates the federal budget. These are the main tools the government has to work with. Americans tend to expect that government can fix whatever economic problems we encounter, but to what extent is that expectation realistic? These are just some of the issues that will be explored in the macroeconomic chapters of this book.

Concepts and Summary

Microeconomics and macroeconomics are two different perspectives on the economy. The microeconomic perspective focuses on parts of the economy: individuals, firms, and industries. The macroeconomic perspective looks at the economy as a whole, focusing on goals like growth in the standard of living, unemployment, and inflation. Macroeconomics has two types of policies for pursuing these goals: monetary policy and fiscal policy.

1.3 HOW ECONOMISTS UNDERSTAND ECONOMIC ISSUES USES THEORIES AND MODELS

John Maynard Keynes (1883–1946), one of the greatest economists of the twentieth century, pointed out that economics is not just a subject area but also a way of thinking. Keynes, shown in Figure 1, famously wrote in the introduction to a fellow economist's book: "[Economics] is a method rather than a doctrine, an apparatus of the mind, a technique of thinking, which helps its possessor to draw correct conclusions." In other words, economics teaches you how to think, not what to think.

Figure 1. John Maynard Keynes. One of the most influential economists in modern times was John Maynard Keynes. (Credit: Wikimedia Commons)

Economists see the world through a different lens than anthropologists, biologists, classicists, or practitioners of any other discipline. They analyze issues and problems with economic theories that are based on particular assumptions about human behavior, that are different than the assumptions an anthropologist or psychologist might use. A theory is a simplified representation of how two or more variables interact with each other. The purpose of a theory is to take a complex, real-world issue and simplify it down to its essentials. If done well, this enables the analyst to understand the issue and any problems around it. A good theory is simple enough to be understood, while complex enough to capture the key features of the object or situation being studied.

Sometimes economists use the term model instead of theory. Strictly speaking, a theory is a more abstract representation, while a model is more applied or empirical representation. Models are used to test theories, but for this course we will use the terms interchangeably.

For example, an architect who is planning a major office building will often build a physical model that sits on a tabletop to show how the entire city block will look after the new building is constructed. Companies often build models of their new products, which are more rough and unfinished than the final product will be, but can still demonstrate how the new product will work.

A good model to start with in economics is the circular flow diagram, which is shown in Figure 2. It pictures the economy as consisting of two groups—households and firms—that interact in two markets: the goods and services market in which firms sell and households buy and the labor market in which households sell labor to business firms or other employees.

Figure 2. The Circular Flow Diagram. The circular flow diagram shows how households and firms interact in the goods and services market, and in the labor market.

The direction of the arrows shows that in the goods and services market, households receive goods and services and pay firms for them. In the labor market, households provide labor and receive payment from firms through wages, salaries, and benefits.

Of course, in the real world, there are many different markets for goods and services and markets for many different types of labor. The circular flow diagram simplifies this to make the picture easier to grasp. In the diagram, firms produce goods and services, which they sell to households in return for revenues. This is shown in the outer circle, and represents the two sides of the product market (for example, the market for goods and services) in which households demand and firms supply. Households sell their labor as workers to firms in return for wages, salaries and benefits. This is shown in the inner circle and represents the two sides of the labor market in which households supply and firms demand.

This version of the circular flow model is stripped down to the essentials, but it has enough features to explain how the product and labor markets work in the economy. We could easily add details to this basic model if we wanted to introduce more real-world elements, like financial markets, governments, and interactions with the rest of the globe (imports and exports).

Economists carry a set of theories in their heads like a carpenter carries around a toolkit. When they see an economic issue or problem, they go through the theories they know to see if they can find one that fits. Then they use the theory to derive insights about the issue or problem. In economics, theories are expressed as diagrams, graphs, or even as mathematical equations. (Do not worry. In this course, we will mostly use graphs.) Economists do not figure out the answer to the problem first and then draw the graph to illustrate. Rather, they use the graph of the theory to help them figure out the answer. Although at the introductory level, you can sometimes figure out the right answer without applying a model, if you keep studying economics, before too long you will run into issues and problems that you will need to graph to solve. Both micro and macroeconomics are explained in terms of theories and models. The most well-known theories are probably those of supply and demand, but you will learn a number of others.

Concepts and Summary

Economists analyze problems differently than do other disciplinary experts. The main tools economists use are economic theories or models. A theory is not an illustration of the answer to a problem. Rather, a theory is a tool for determining the answer.

1.4 HOW ECONOMIES CAN BE ORGANIZED: AN OVERVIEW OF ECONOMIC SYSTEMS

Think about what a complex system a modern economy is. It includes all production of goods and services, all buying and selling, all employment. The economic life of every individual is interrelated, at least to a small extent, with the economic lives of thousands or even millions of other individuals. Who organizes and coordinates this system? Who insures that, for example, the number of televisions a society provides is the same as the amount it needs and wants? Who insures that the right number of employees work in the electronics industry? Who insures that televisions are produced in the best way possible? How does it all get done?

There are at least three ways societies have found to organize an economy. The first is the traditional economy, which is the oldest economic system and can be found in parts of Asia, Africa, and South America. Traditional economies organize their economic affairs the way they have always done (i.e., tradition). Occupations stay in the family. Most families are farmers who grow the crops they have always grown using traditional methods. What you produce is what you get to consume. Because things are driven by tradition, there is little economic progress or development.

Figure 1. A Command Economy. Ancient Egypt was an example of a command economy. (Credit: Jay Bergesen/Flickr Creative Commons)

Command economies are very different. In a **command economy**, economic effort is devoted to goals passed down from a ruler or ruling class. Ancient Egypt was a good example: a large part of economic life was devoted to building pyramids, like those shown in Figure 1, for the pharaohs. Medieval manor life is another example: the lord provided the land for growing crops and protection in the event of war. In return, vassals provided labor and soldiers to do the lord's bidding. In the last century, communism emphasized command economies.

In a command economy, the government decides what goods and services will be produced and what prices will be charged for them. The government decides what methods of production will be used and how much workers will be paid. Many necessities like healthcare and education are provided for free. Currently, Cuba and North Korea have command economies.

Figure 2. A Market Economy. Nothing says "market" more than The New York Stock Exchange. (Credit: Erik Drost/Flickr Creative Commons)

Although command economies have a very centralized structure for economic decisions, market economies have a very decentralized structure. A **market** is an institution that brings together buyers and sellers of goods or services, who may be either individuals or businesses. The New York Stock Exchange, shown in Figure 2, is a prime example of market in which buyers and sellers are brought together. In a **market economy**, decision-making is decentralized. Market economies are based on **private enterprise**: the means of production (resources and businesses) are owned and operated by private individuals or groups of private individuals. Businesses supply goods and services based on demand. (In a command economy, by contrast, resources and businesses are owned by the government.) What goods and services are supplied depends on what is demanded. A person's income is based on his or her ability to convert resources (especially labor) into something that society values. The more society values the person's output, the higher the income (think Lady Gaga or LeBron James). In this scenario, economic decisions are determined by market forces, not governments.

Most economies in the real world are mixed; they combine elements of command and market (and even traditional) systems. The U.S. economy is positioned toward the market-oriented end of the spectrum. Many countries in Europe and Latin America, while primarily market-oriented, have a greater degree of government involvement in economic decisions than does the U.S. economy. China and Russia, while they are closer to having a market-oriented system now than several decades ago, remain closer to the command economy end of the spectrum. A rich resource of information about countries and their economies can be found on the Heritage Foundation's website, as the following Clear It Up feature discusses.

What countries are considered economically free?

Who is in control of economic decisions? Are people free to do what they want and to work where they want? Are businesses free to produce when they want and what they choose, and to hire and fire as they wish? Are banks free to choose who will receive loans? Or does the government control these kinds of choices? Each year, researchers at the Heritage Foundation and the Wall Street Journal look at 50 different categories of economic freedom for countries around the world. They give each nation a score based on the extent of economic freedom in each category.

The 2015 Heritage Foundation's Index of Economic Freedom report ranked 178 countries around the world: some examples of the most free and the least free countries are listed in Table 1. Several countries were not ranked because of extreme instability that made judgments about economic freedom impossible. These countries include Afghanistan, Iraq, Syria, and Somalia.

The assigned rankings are inevitably based on estimates, yet even these rough measures can be useful for discerning trends. In 2015, 101 of the 178 included countries shifted toward greater economic freedom, although 77 of the countries shifted toward less economic freedom. In recent decades, the overall trend has been a *higher level of economic freedom around the world.*

Table 1. Economic Freedoms, 2015 (Source: The Heritage Foundation, 2015 Index of Economic Freedom, Country Rankings, http://www.heritage.org/index/ranking)

Most Economic Freedom	Least Economic Freedom
1. Hong Kong	167. Timor-Leste
2. Singapore	168. Democratic Republic of Congo
3. New Zealand	169. Argentina
4. Australia	170. Republic of Congo
5. Switzerland	171. Iran
6. Canada	172. Turkmenistan
7. Chile	173. Equatorial Guinea
8. Estonia	174. Eritrea
9. Ireland	175. Zimbabwe
10. Mauritius	176. Venezuela
11. Denmark	177. Cuba
12. United States	178. North Korea

Regulations: The Rules of the Game

Markets and government regulations are always entangled. There is no such thing as an absolutely free market. Regulations always define the "rules of the game" in the economy. Economies that are primarily market-oriented have fewer regulations—ideally just enough to maintain an even playing field for participants. At a minimum, these laws govern matters like safeguarding private property against theft, protecting people from violence, enforcing legal contracts, preventing fraud, and collecting taxes. Conversely, even the most command-oriented economies operate using markets. How else would buying and selling occur? But the decisions of what will be produced and what prices will be charged are heavily regulated. Heavily regulated economies often have underground economies, which are markets where the buyers and sellers make transactions without the government's approval.

The question of how to organize economic institutions is typically not a black-or-white choice between all market or all government, but instead involves a balancing act over the appropriate combination of market freedom and government rules.

Figure 3. Globalization. Cargo ships are one mode of transportation for shipping goods in the global economy. (Credit: Raul Valdez/Flickr Creative Commons)

The Rise of Globalization

Recent decades have seen a trend toward globalization, which is the expanding cultural, political, and economic connections between people around the world. One measure of this is the increased buying and selling of goods, services, and assets across national borders—in other words, international trade and financial capital flows.

Globalization has occurred for a number of reasons. Improvements in shipping, as illustrated by the container ship shown in Figure 3, and air cargo have driven down transportation costs. Innovations in computing and telecommunications have made it easier and cheaper to manage long-distance economic connections of production and sales. Many valuable products and services in the modern economy can take the form of information—for example: computer software; financial advice; travel planning; music, books and movies; and blueprints for designing a building.

These products and many others can be transported over telephones and computer networks at ever-lower costs. Finally, international agreements and treaties between countries have encouraged greater trade.

Table 2 presents one measure of globalization. It shows the percentage of domestic economic production that was exported for a selection of countries from 2010 to 2013, according to an entity known as The World Bank. Exports are the goods and services that are produced domestically and sold abroad. Imports are the goods and services that are produced abroad and then sold domestically. The size of total production in an economy is measured by the gross domestic product (GDP). Thus, the ratio of exports divided by GDP measures what share of a country's total economic production is sold in other countries.

Table 2. The Extent of Globalization (exports/GDP) (Source: http://databank.worldbank.org/data/)

Country	2010	2011	2012	2013
Higher Income Countries				
United States	12.4	13.6	13.6	13.5
Belgium	76.2	81.4	82.2	82.8
Canada	29.1	30.7	30.0	30.1
France	26.0	27.8	28.1	28.3
Middle Income Countries				
Brazil	10.9	11.9	12.6	12.6
Mexico	29.9	31.2	32.6	31.7
South Korea	49.4	55.7	56.3	53.9
Lower Income Countries				
Chad	36.8	38.9	36.9	32.2
China	29.4	28.5	27.3	26.4
India	22.0	23.9	24.0	24.8
Nigeria	25.3	31.3	31.4	18.0

In recent decades, the export/GDP ratio has generally risen, both worldwide and for the U.S. economy. Interestingly, the share of U.S. exports in proportion to the U.S. economy is well below the global average, in part because large economies like the United States can contain more of the division of labor inside their national borders. However, smaller economies like Belgium, Korea, and Canada need to trade across their borders with other countries to take full advantage of division of labor, specialization, and economies of scale. In this sense, the enormous U.S. economy is less affected by globalization than most other countries.

Table 2 also shows that many medium and low income countries around the world, like Mexico and China, have also experienced a surge of globalization in recent decades. If an astronaut in orbit could put on special glasses that make all economic transactions visible as brightly colored lines and look down at Earth, the astronaut would see the planet covered with connections.

So, hopefully, you now have an idea of what economics is about. Before you move to any other chapter of study, be sure to read the very important appendix to this chapter called The Use of Mathematics in Principles of Economics. It is essential that you learn more about how to read and use models in economics.

Decisions ... Decisions in the Social Media Age

The world we live in today provides nearly instant access to a wealth of information. Consider that as recently as the late 1970s, the Farmer's Almanac, along with the Weather Bureau of the U.S. Department of Agriculture, were the primary sources American farmers used to determine when to plant and harvest their crops. Today, farmers are more likely to access, online, weather forecasts from the National Oceanic and Atmospheric Administration or watch the Weather Channel. After all, knowing the upcoming forecast could drive when to harvest crops. Consequently, knowing the upcoming weather could change the amount of crop harvested.

Some relatively new information forums, such as Facebook, are rapidly changing how information is distributed; hence, influencing decision making. In 2014, the Pew Research Center reported that 71% of online adults use Facebook. Facebook post topics range from the National Basketball Association, to celebrity singers and performers, to farmers.

Information helps us make decisions. Decisions as simple as what to wear today to how many reporters should be sent to cover a crash. Each of these decisions is an economic decision. After all, resources are scarce. If ten reporters are sent to cover an accident, they are not available to cover other stories or complete other tasks. Information provides the knowledge needed to make the best possible decisions on how to utilize scarce resources. Welcome to the world of economics!

Concepts and Summary

Societies can be organized as traditional, command, or market-oriented economies. Most societies are a mix. The last few decades have seen globalization evolve as a result of growth in commercial and financial networks that cross national borders, making businesses and workers from different economies increasingly interdependent.

CHAPTER

A WORLD OF SCARCITY AND CHOICE 2

INTRODUCTION TO CHOICE IN A WORLD OF SCARCITY

Choices and Tradeoffs. In general, the higher the degree, the higher the salary. So why aren't more people pursuing higher degrees? The short answer: choices and tradeoffs. (Credit: modification of work by "Jim, the Photographer"/Flickr Creative Commons)

Choices ... To What Degree?

In 2015, the median income for workers who hold master's degrees varies from males to females. The average of the two is $2,951 weekly. Multiply this average by 52 weeks, and you get an average salary of $153,452. Compare that to the median weekly earnings for a full-time worker over 25 with no higher than a bachelor's degree: $1,224 weekly and $63,648 a year. What about those with no higher than a high school diploma in 2015? They earn just $664 weekly and $34,528 over 12 months. In other words, says the Bureau of Labor Statistics (BLS), earning a bachelor's degree boosted salaries 54% over what you would have earned if you had stopped your education after high school. A master's degree yields a salary almost double that of a high school diploma.

Given these statistics, we might expect a lot of people to choose to go to college and at least earn a bachelor's degree. Assuming that people want to improve their material well-being, it seems like they would make those choices that give them the greatest opportunity to consume goods and services. As it turns out, the analysis is not nearly as simple as this. In fact, in 2014, the BLS reported that while almost 88% of the population in the United States had a high school diploma, only 33.6% of 25–65 year olds had bachelor's degrees, and only 7.4% of 25–65 year olds in 2014 had earned a master's.

This brings us to the subject of this chapter: why people make the choices they make and how economists go about explaining those choices.

2.1 HOW PEOPLE MAKE DECISIONS IN RELATION TO THEIR BUDGET CONSTRAINT

Consider the typical consumer's budget problem. Consumers have a limited amount of income to spend on the things they need and want. Suppose Alphonso has $10 in spending money each week that he can allocate between bus tickets for getting to work and the burgers that he eats for lunch. Burgers cost $2 each, and bus tickets are 50 cents each. Figure 1 shows Alphonso's budget constraint, that is, the outer boundary of his opportunity set. The opportunity set identifies all the opportunities for spending within his budget. The budget constraint indicates all the combinations of burgers and bus tickets Alphonso can afford when he exhausts his budget, given the prices of the two goods. (

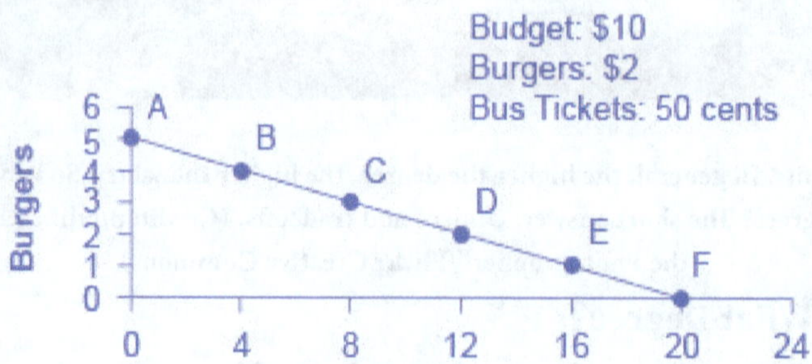

Figure 1. The Budget Constraint: Alphonso's Consumption Choice Opportunity Frontier. Each point on the budget constraint represents a combination of burgers and bus tickets whose total cost adds up to Alphonso's budget of ١٠$. The slope of the budget constraint is determined by the relative price of burgers and bus tickets. All along the budget set, giving up one burger means gaining four bus tickets.

The vertical axis in the figure shows burger purchases and the horizontal axis shows bus ticket purchases. If Alphonso spends all his money on burgers, he can afford five per week. ($10 per week/$2 per burger = 5 burgers per week.) But if he does this, he will not be able to afford any bus tickets. This choice (zero bus tickets and five burgers) is shown by point A in the figure. Alternatively, if Alphonso spends all his money on bus tickets, he can afford 20 per week. ($10 per week/$0.50 per bus ticket = 20 bus tickets per week.) Then, however, he will not be able to afford any burgers. This alternative choice (20 bus tickets and zero burgers) is shown by point F.

If Alphonso is like most people, he will choose some combination that includes both bus tickets and burgers. That is, he will choose some combination on the budget constraint that connects points A and F. Every point on (or inside) the constraint shows a combination of burgers and bus tickets that Alphonso can afford. Any point outside the constraint is not affordable, because it would cost more money than Alphonso has in his budget.

The budget constraint clearly shows the trade-off Alphonso faces in choosing between burgers and bus tickets. Suppose he is currently at point D, where he can afford 12 bus tickets and two burgers. What would it cost Alphonso for one more burger? It would be natural to answer $2, but that's not the way economists think. Instead they ask, how many bus tickets would Alphonso have to give up to get one more burger, while staying within his budget? The answer is four bus tickets. That is the true cost to Alphonso of one more burger.

The Concept of Opportunity Cost

Economists use the term opportunity cost to indicate what must be given up to obtain something that is desired. The idea behind opportunity cost is that the cost of one item is the lost opportunity to do or consume something else; in short, opportunity cost is the value of the next best alternative. For Alphonso, the opportunity cost of a burger is the four bus tickets he would have to give up. He would decide whether or not to choose the burger depending on whether the value of the burger exceeds the value of the forgone alternative—in this case, bus tickets. Since people must choose, they inevitably face trade-offs in which they have to give up things they desire to get other things they desire more.

A fundamental principle of economics is that every choice has an opportunity cost. If you sleep through your economics class (not recommended, by the way), the opportunity cost is the learning you miss from not attending class. If you spend your income on video games, you cannot spend it on movies. If you choose to marry one person, you give up the opportunity to marry anyone else. In short, opportunity cost is all around us and part of human existence.

Understanding Budget Constraints

Budget constraints are easy to understand if you apply a little math. The appendix The Use of Mathematics in Principles of Economics explains all the math you are likely to need in this book. So if math is not your strength, you might want to take a look at the appendix.

Step 1: The equation for any budget constraint is:

$$Budget = P_1 \times Q_1 + P_2 \times Q_2$$

where P and Q are the price and quantity of items purchased and Budget is the amount of income one has to spend.

Step 2. Apply the budget constraint equation to the scenario. In Alphonso's case, this works out to be:

$$Budget = P_1 \times Q_1 + P_2 \times Q_2$$

$10 budget $2 per burger x quantity of burgers + $0.50 per bus ticket x quantity of bus tickets

$\$10\ \$2 \text{ x } Q_{burgers} + \$0.50 \text{ x } Q_{bus}$ tickets

Step 3. Using a little algebra, we can turn this into the familiar equation of a line:

$$y = b + mx$$

For Alphonso, this is:

$$\$10 = \$2 \times Q_{burgers} + \$0.50 \times Q_{bus\ tickets}$$

Step 4. Simplify the equation. Begin by multiplying both sides of the equation by 2:

2 x 10 2 x 2 x Qburgers + 2 x 0.5 x Qbus tickets

20 4 x Qburgers + 1 x Qbus tickets

Step 5. Subtract one bus ticket from both sides:

$$20 - Q_{bus\ tickets} = 4 \times Q_{burgers}$$

Divide each side by 4 to yield the answer:

$5 - 0.25 \text{ x } Q_{bus}$ tickets $= Q_{burgers}$

or

$Q_{burgers} = 5\text{-}0.25 \text{ x } Q_{bus\ tickets}$

Step 6. Notice that this equation fits the budget constraint in Figure 1. The vertical intercept is 5 and the slope is –0.25, just as the equation says. If you plug 20 bus tickets into the equation, you get 0 burgers. If you plug other numbers of bus tickets into the equation, you get the results shown in Table 1, which are the points on Alphonso's budget constraint.

Table 1.

Point	Quantity of Burgers (at $2)	Quantity of Bus Tickets (at 50 cents)
A	5	0
B	4	4
C	3	8
D	2	12
E	1	16
F	0	20

Step 7. Notice that the slope of a budget constraint always shows the opportunity cost of the good which is on the horizontal axis. For Alphonso, the slope is -0.25, indicating that for every four bus tickets he buys, Alphonso must give up 1 burger.

There are two important observations here. First, the algebraic sign of the slope is negative, which means that the only way to get more of one good is to give up some of the other. Second, the slope is defined as the price of bus tickets (whatever is on the horizontal axis in the graph) divided by the price of burgers (whatever is on the vertical axis), in this case $0.50/$2 = 0.25. So if you want to determine the opportunity cost quickly, just divide the two prices.

Identifying Opportunity Cost

In many cases, it is reasonable to refer to the opportunity cost as the **price**. If your cousin buys a new bicycle for $300, then $300 measures the amount of "other consumption" that he has given up. For practical purposes, there may be no special need to identify the specific alternative product or products that could have been bought with that $300, but sometimes the price as measured in dollars may not accurately capture the true opportunity cost. This problem can loom especially large when costs of time are involved.

For example, consider a boss who decides that all employees will attend a two-day retreat to "build team spirit." The out-of-pocket monetary cost of the event may involve hiring an outside consulting firm to run the retreat, as well as room and board for all participants. But an opportunity cost exists as well: during the two days of the retreat, none of the employees are doing any other work.

Attending college is another case where the opportunity cost exceeds the monetary cost. The out-of-pocket costs of attending college include tuition, books, room and board, and other expenses. But in addition, during the hours that you are attending class and studying, it is impossible to work at a paying job. Thus, college imposes both an out-of-pocket cost and an opportunity cost of lost earnings.

What is the opportunity cost associated with increased airport security measures?

After the terrorist plane hijackings on September 11, 2001, many steps were proposed to improve air travel safety. For example, the federal government could provide armed "sky marshals" who would travel inconspicuously with the rest of the passengers. The cost of having a sky marshal on every flight would be roughly $3 billion per year. Retrofitting all U.S. planes with reinforced cockpit doors to make it harder for terrorists to take over the plane would have a price tag of $450 million. Buying more sophisticated security equipment for airports, like three-dimensional baggage scanners and cameras linked to face recognition software, could cost another $2 billion.

But the single biggest cost of greater airline security does not involve spending money. It is the opportunity cost of additional waiting time at the airport. According to the United States Department of Transportation (DOT), more than 800 million passengers took plane trips in the United States in 2012. Since the 9/11 hijackings, security screening has become more intensive, and consequently, the procedure takes longer than in the past. Say that, on average, each air passenger spends an extra 30 minutes in the airport per trip. Economists commonly place a value on time to convert an opportunity cost in time into a monetary figure. Because many air travelers are relatively high-paid business people, conservative estimates set the average price of time for air travelers at $20 per hour. By these back-of-the-envelope calculations, the opportunity cost of delays in airports could be as much as 800 million × 0.5 hours × $20/hour, or $8 billion per year. Clearly, the opportunity costs of waiting time can be just as important as costs that involve direct spending.

In some cases, realizing the opportunity cost can alter behavior. Imagine, for example, that you spend $8 on lunch every day at work. You may know perfectly well that bringing a lunch from home would cost only $3 a day, so the opportunity cost of buying lunch at the restaurant is $5 each day (that is, the $8 buying lunch costs minus the $3 your lunch from home would cost). $5 each day does not seem to be that much. However, if you project what that adds up to in a year—250 days a year × $5 per day equals $1,250, the cost, perhaps, of a decent vacation. If the opportunity cost is described as "a nice vacation" instead of "$5 a day," you might make different choices.

Marginal Decision-Making and Diminishing Marginal Utility

The budget constraint framework helps to emphasize that most choices in the real world are not about getting all of one thing or all of another; that is, they are not about choosing either the point at one end of the budget constraint or else the point all the way at the other end. Instead, most choices involve **marginal analysis**, which means comparing the benefits and costs of choosing a little more or a little less of a good.

People desire goods and services for the satisfaction or utility those goods and services provide. Utility, as we will see in the chapter on Consumer Choices, is subjective but that does not make it less real. Economists typically assume that the more of some good one consumes (for example, slices of pizza), the more utility one obtains. At the same time, the utility a person receives from consuming the first unit of a good is typically more than the utility received from consuming the fifth or the tenth unit of that same good. When Alphonso chooses between burgers and bus tickets, for example, the first few bus rides that he chooses might provide him with a great deal of utility—perhaps they help him get to a job interview or a doctor's appointment. But later bus rides might provide much less utility—they may only serve to kill time on a rainy day. Similarly, the first burger that Alphonso chooses to buy may be on a day when he missed breakfast and is ravenously hungry. However, if Alphonso has a burger every single day, the last few burgers may taste pretty boring. The general pattern that consumption of the first few units of any good tends to bring a higher level of utility to a person than consumption of later units is a common pattern. Economists refer to this pattern as the law of diminishing marginal utility, which means that as a person receives more of a good, the additional (or marginal) utility from each additional unit of the good declines. In other words, the first slice of pizza brings more satisfaction than the sixth.

The law of diminishing marginal utility explains why people and societies rarely make all-or-nothing choices. You would not say, "My favorite food is ice cream, so I will eat nothing but ice cream from now on." Instead, even if you get a very high level of utility from your favorite food, if you ate it exclusively, the additional or marginal utility from those last few servings would not be very high. Similarly, most workers do not say: "I enjoy leisure, so I'll never work." Instead, workers recognize that even though some leisure is very nice, a combination of all leisure and no income is not so attractive. The budget constraint framework suggests that when people make choices in a world of scarcity, they will use marginal analysis and think about whether they would prefer a little more or a little less.

Sunk Costs

In the budget constraint framework, all decisions involve what will happen next: that is, what quantities of goods will you consume, how many hours will you work, or how much will you save. These decisions do not look back to past choices. Thus, the budget constraint framework assumes that **sunk costs**, which are costs that were incurred in the past and cannot be recovered, should not affect the current decision.

Consider the case of Selena, who pays $8 to see a movie, but after watching the film for 30 minutes, she knows that it is truly terrible. Should she stay and watch the rest of the movie because she paid for the ticket, or should she leave? The money she spent is a sunk cost, and unless the theater manager is feeling kindly, Selena will not get a refund. But staying in the movie still means paying an opportunity cost in time. Her choice is whether to spend the next 90 minutes suffering through a cinematic disaster or to do something—anything—else. The lesson of sunk costs is to forget about the money and time that is irretrievably gone and instead to focus on the marginal costs and benefits of current and future options.

For people and firms alike, dealing with sunk costs can be frustrating. It often means admitting an earlier error in judgment. Many firms, for example, find it hard to give up on a new product that is doing poorly because they spent so much money in creating and launching the product. But the lesson of sunk costs is to ignore them and make decisions based on what will happen in the future.

From a Model with Two Goods to One of Many Goods

The budget constraint diagram containing just two goods, like most models used in this book, is not realistic. After all, in a modern economy people choose from thousands of goods. However, thinking about a model with many goods is a straightforward extension of what we discussed here. Instead of drawing just one budget constraint, showing the tradeoff between two goods, you can draw multiple budget constraints, showing the possible tradeoffs between many different pairs of goods. Or in more advanced classes in economics, you would use mathematical equations that include many possible goods and services that can be purchased, together with their quantities and prices, and show how the total spending on all goods and services is limited to the overall budget available. The graph with two goods that was presented here clearly illustrates that every choice has an opportunity cost, which is the point that does carry over to the real world.

Concepts and Summary

Economists see the real world as one of scarcity: that is, a world in which people's desires exceed what is possible. As a result, economic behavior involves tradeoffs in which individuals, firms, and society must give up something that they desire to obtain things that they desire more. Individuals face the tradeoff of what quantities of goods and services to consume. The budget constraint, which is the frontier of the opportunity set, illustrates the range of choices available. The slope of the budget constraint is determined by the relative price of the choices. Choices beyond the budget constraint are not affordable.

Opportunity cost measures cost by what is given up in exchange. Sometimes opportunity cost can be measured in money, but it is often useful to consider time as well, or to measure it in terms of the actual resources that must be given up.

Most economic decisions and tradeoffs are not all-or-nothing. Instead, they involve marginal analysis, which means they are about decisions on the margin, involving a little more or a little less. The law of diminishing marginal utility points out that as a person receives more of something—whether it is a specific good or another resource—the additional marginal gains tend to become smaller. Because sunk costs occurred in the past and cannot be recovered, they should be disregarded in making current decisions.

2.2 THE OPPORTUNITIES FOR PRODUCTION FRONTIER AND SOCIAL CHOICES

Just as individuals cannot have everything they want and must instead make choices, society as a whole cannot have everything it might want, either. This section of the chapter will explain the constraints faced by society, using a model called the **production possibilities frontier (PPF)**. There are more similarities than differences between individual choice and social choice. As you read this section, focus on the similarities.

Because society has limited resources (e.g., labor, land, capital, raw materials) at any point in time, there is a limit to the quantities of goods and services it can produce. Suppose a society desires two products, healthcare and education. This situation is illustrated by the production possibilities frontier in Figure 1.

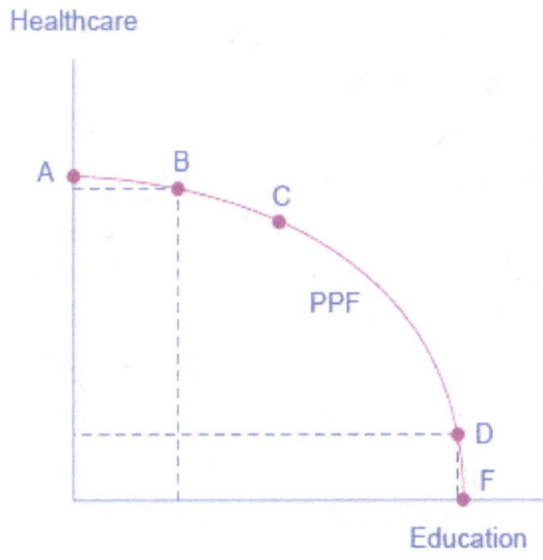

Figure 1. A Healthcare vs. Education Production Possibilities Frontier. This production possibilities frontier shows a tradeoff between devoting social resources to healthcare and devoting them to education. At A all resources go to healthcare and at B, most go to healthcare. At D most resources go to education, and at F, all go to education.

In Figure 1, healthcare is shown on the vertical axis and education is shown on the horizontal axis. If the society were to allocate all of its resources to healthcare, it could produce at point A. But it would not have any resources to produce education. If it were to allocate all of its resources to education, it could produce at point F. Alternatively, the society could choose to produce any combination of healthcare and education shown on the production possibilities frontier. In effect, the production possibilities frontier plays the same role for society as the budget constraint plays for Alphonso. Society can choose any combination of the two goods on or inside the PPF. But it does not have enough resources to produce outside the PPF.

Most important, the production possibilities frontier clearly shows the tradeoff between healthcare and education. Suppose society has chosen to operate at point B, and it is considering producing more education. Because the PPF is downward sloping from left to right, the only way society can obtain more education is by giving up some healthcare. That is the tradeoff society faces. Suppose it considers moving from point B to point C. What would the opportunity cost be for the additional education? The opportunity cost would be the healthcare society has to give up. Just as with Alphonso's budget constraint, the opportunity cost is shown by the slope of the production possibilities frontier. By now you might be saying, "Hey, this PPF is sounding like the budget constraint." If so, read the following Clear It Up feature.

How do a PPF and a budget constraint vary from one another?

There are two major differences between a budget constraint and a production possibilities frontier. The first is the fact that the budget constraint is a straight line. This is because its slope is given by the relative prices of the two goods. In contrast, the PPF has a curved shape because of the law of the diminishing returns. The second is the absence of specific numbers on the axes of the PPF. There are no specific numbers because we do not know the exact amount of resources this imaginary economy has, nor do we know how many resources it takes to produce healthcare and how many resources it takes to produce education. If this were a real world example, that data would be available. An additional reason for the lack of numbers is that there is no single way to measure levels of education and healthcare. However, when you think of improvements in education, you can think of accomplishments like more years of school completed, fewer high-school dropouts, and higher scores on standardized tests. When you think of improvements in healthcare, you can think of longer life expectancies, lower levels of infant mortality, and fewer outbreaks of disease.

Whether or not we have specific numbers, conceptually we can measure the opportunity cost of additional education as society moves from point B to point C on the PPF. The additional education is measured by the horizontal distance between B and C. The foregone healthcare is given by the vertical distance between B and C. The slope of the PPF between B and C is (approximately) the vertical distance (the "rise") over the horizontal distance (the "run"). This is the opportunity cost of the additional education.

The Shape of the PPF and the Law of Diminishing Returns

The budget constraints presented earlier in this chapter, showing individual choices about what quantities of goods to consume, were all straight lines. The reason for these straight lines was that the slope of the budget constraint was determined by relative prices of the two goods in the **consumption budget constraint**. However, the production possibilities frontier for healthcare and education was drawn as a curved line. Why does the PPF have a different shape?

To understand why the PPF is curved, start by considering point A at the top left-hand side of the PPF. At point A, all available resources are devoted to healthcare and none are left for education. This situation would be extreme and even ridiculous. For example, children are seeing a doctor every day, whether they are sick or not, but not attending school. People are having cosmetic surgery on every part of their bodies, but no high school or college education exists. Now imagine that some of these resources are diverted from healthcare to education, so that the economy is at point B instead of point A. Diverting some resources away from A to B causes relatively little reduction in health because the last few marginal dollars going into healthcare services are not producing much additional gain in health. However, putting those marginal dollars into education, which is completely without resources at point A, can produce relatively large gains. For this reason, the shape of the PPF from A to B is relatively flat, representing a relatively small drop-off in health and a relatively large gain in education.

Now consider the other end, at the lower right, of the production possibilities frontier. Imagine that society starts at choice D, which is devoting nearly all resources to education and very few to healthcare, and moves to point F, which is devoting all spending to education and none to healthcare. For the sake of concreteness, you can imagine that in the movement from D to F, the last few doctors must become high school science teachers, the last few nurses must become school librarians rather than dispensers of vaccinations, and the last few emergency rooms are turned into kindergartens. The gains to education from adding these last few resources to education are very small. However, the opportunity cost lost to health will be fairly large, and thus the slope of the PPF between D and F is steep, showing a large drop in health for only a small gain in education.

The lesson is not that society is likely to make an extreme choice like devoting no resources to education at point A or no resources to health at point F. Instead, the lesson is that the gains from committing additional marginal resources to education depend on how much is already being spent. If on the one hand, very few resources are currently committed to education, then an increase in resources used can bring relatively large gains. On the other hand, if a large number of resources are already committed to education, then committing additional resources will bring relatively smaller gains.

This pattern is common enough that it has been given a name: the **law of diminishing returns**, which holds that as additional increments of resources are added to a certain purpose, the marginal benefit from those additional increments will decline. When government spends a certain amount more on reducing crime, for example, the original gains in reducing crime could be relatively large. But additional increases typically cause relatively smaller reductions in crime, and paying for enough police and security to reduce crime to nothing at all would be tremendously expensive.

The curvature of the production possibilities frontier shows that as additional resources are added to education, moving from left to right along the horizontal axis, the original gains are fairly large, but gradually diminish. Similarly, as additional resources are added to healthcare, moving from bottom to top on the vertical axis, the original gains are fairly large, but again gradually diminish. In this way, the law of diminishing returns produces the outward-bending shape of the production possibilities frontier.

Productive Efficiency and Allocative Efficiency

The study of economics does not presume to tell a society what choice it should make along its production possibilities frontier. In a market-oriented economy with a democratic government, the choice will involve a mixture of decisions by individuals, firms, and government. However, economics can point out that some choices are unambiguously better than others. This observation is based on the concept of efficiency. In everyday usage, efficiency refers to lack of waste. An inefficient machine operates at high **cost**, while an efficient machine operates at lower cost, because it is not wasting energy or materials. An inefficient organization operates with long delays and high costs, while an efficient organization meets schedules, is focused, and performs within budget.

The production possibilities frontier can illustrate two kinds of efficiency: productive efficiency and allocative efficiency. Figure 2 illustrates these ideas using a production possibilities frontier between healthcare and education.

Productive efficiency means that, given the available inputs and technology, it is impossible to produce more of one good without decreasing the quantity that is produced of another good. All choices on the PPF in Figure 2, including A, B, C, D, and F, display productive efficiency. As a firm moves from any one of these choices to any other, either healthcare increases and education decreases or vice versa. However, any choice inside the production possibilities frontier is productively inefficient and wasteful because it is possible to produce more of one good, the other good, or some combination of both goods.

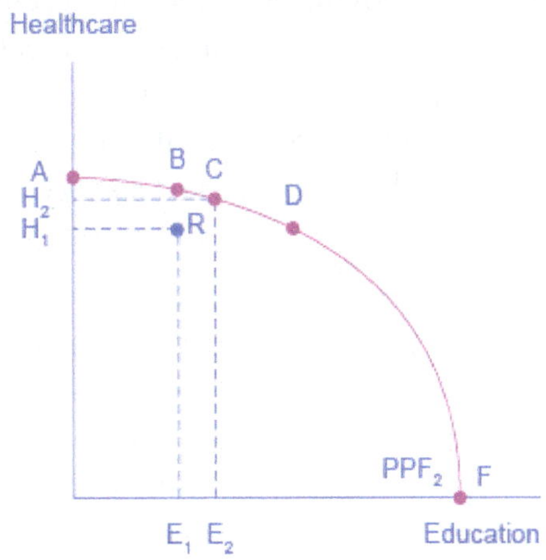

Figure 2. Productive and Allocative Efficiency. Productive efficiency means it is impossible to produce more of one good without decreasing the quantity that is produced of another good. Thus, all choices along a given PPF like B, C, and D display productive efficiency, but R does not. Allocative efficiency means that the particular mix of goods being produced—that is, the specific choice along the production possibilities frontier—represents the allocation that society most desires.

For example, point R is productively inefficient because it is possible at choice C to have more of both goods: education on the horizontal axis is higher at point C than point R (E_2 is greater than E_1), and healthcare on the vertical axis is also higher at point C than point R (H_2 is great than H_1).

The particular mix of goods and services being produced–that is, the specific combination of healthcare and education chosen along the production possibilities frontier–can be shown as a ray (line) from the origin to a specific point on the PPF. Output mixes that had more healthcare (and less education) would have a steeper ray, while those with more education (and less healthcare) would have a flatter ray.

Allocative efficiency means that the particular mix of goods a society produces represents the combination that society most desires. How to determine what a society desires can be a controversial question, and is usually discussed in political science, sociology, and philosophy classes as well as in economics. At its most basic, allocative efficiency means producers supply the quantity of each product that consumers demand. Only one of the productively efficient choices will be the allocatively efficient choice for society as a whole.

Why Society Must Choose

Every economy faces two situations in which it may be able to expand consumption of all goods. In the first case, a society may discover that it has been using its resources inefficiently, in which case by improving efficiency and producing on the production possibilities frontier, it can have more of all goods (or at least more of some and less of none). In the second case, as resources grow over a period of years (e.g., more labor and more capital), the economy grows. As it does, the production possibilities frontier for a society will tend to shift outward and society will be able to afford more of all goods.

But improvements in productive efficiency take time to discover and implement, and economic growth happens only gradually. So, a society must choose between tradeoffs in the present. For government, this process often involves trying to identify where additional spending could do the most good and where reductions in spending would do the least harm. At the individual and firm level, the market economy coordinates a process in which firms seek to produce goods and services in the quantity, quality, and price that people want. But for both the government and the market economy in the short term, increases in production of one good typically mean offsetting decreases somewhere else in the economy.

The PPF and Comparative Advantage

While every society must choose how much of each good it should produce, it does not need to produce every single good it consumes. Often how much of a good a country decides to produce depends on how expensive it is to produce it versus buying it from a different country. As we saw earlier, the curvature of a country's PPF gives us information about the tradeoff between devoting resources to producing one good versus another. In particular, its slope gives the opportunity cost of producing one more unit of the good in the x-axis in terms of the other good (in the y-axis). Countries tend to have different opportunity costs of producing a specific good, either because of different climates, geography, technology or skills.

Suppose two countries, the US and Brazil, need to decide how much they will produce of two crops: sugar cane and wheat. Due to its climatic conditions, Brazil can produce a lot of sugar cane per acre but not much wheat. Conversely, the U.S. can produce a lot of wheat per acre, but not much sugar cane. Clearly, Brazil has a lower opportunity cost of producing sugar cane (in terms of wheat) than the U.S. The reverse is also true; the U.S. has a lower opportunity cost of producing wheat than Brazil. This can be illustrated by the PPFs of the two countries in Figure 3.

When a country can produce a good at a lower opportunity cost than another country, we say that this country has a comparative advantage in that good. In our example, Brazil has a comparative advantage in sugar cane and the U.S. has a comparative advantage in wheat. One can easily see this with a simple observation of the extreme production points in the PPFs of the two countries. If Brazil devoted all of its resources to producing wheat, it would be producing at point A. If however it had devoted all of its resources to producing sugar cane instead, it would be producing a much larger amount, at point B. By moving from point A to point B Brazil would give up a relatively small quantity in wheat production to obtain a large production in sugar cane. The opposite is true for the U.S. If the U.S. moved from point A to B and produced only sugar cane, this would result in a large opportunity cost in terms of foregone wheat production.

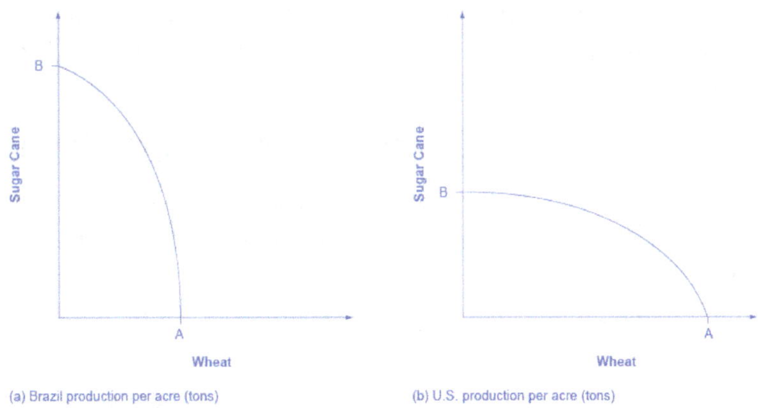

Figure 3. Production Possibility Frontier for the U.S. and Brazil. The U.S. PPF is flatter than the Brazil PPF implying that the opportunity cost of wheat in term of sugar cane is lower in the U.S. than in Brazil. Conversely, the opportunity cost of sugar cane is lower in Brazil. The U.S. has comparative advantage in wheat and Brazil has comparative advantage in sugar cane.

The slope of the PPF gives the opportunity cost of producing an additional unit of wheat. While the slope is not constant throughout the PPFs, it is quite apparent that the PPF in Brazil is much steeper than in the U.S., and therefore the opportunity cost of wheat generally higher in Brazil. In the chapter on International Trade you will learn that countries' differences in comparative advantage determine which goods they will choose to produce and trade. When countries engage in trade, they specialize in the production of the goods that they have comparative advantage in, and trade part of that production for goods they do not have comparative advantage in. With trade, goods are produced where the opportunity cost is lowest, so total production increases, benefiting both trading parties.

Concepts and Summary

A production possibilities frontier defines the set of choices society faces for the combinations of goods and services it can produce given the resources available. The shape of the PPF is typically curved outward, rather than straight. Choices outside the PPF are unattainable and choices inside the PPF are wasteful. Over time, a growing economy will tend to shift the PPF outwards.

The law of diminishing returns holds that as increments of additional resources are devoted to producing something, the marginal increase in output will become smaller and smaller. All choices along a production possibilities frontier display productive efficiency; that is, it is impossible to use society's resources to produce more of one good without decreasing production of the other good. The specific choice along a production possibilities frontier that reflects the mix of goods society prefers is the choice with allocative efficiency. The curvature of the PPF is likely to differ by country, which results in different countries having comparative advantage in different goods. Total production can increase if countries specialize in the goods they have comparative advantage in and trade some of their production for the remaining goods.

2.3 CONFRONTING OBJECTIONS TO THE ECONOMIC APPROACH

It is one thing to understand the economic approach to decision-making and another thing to feel comfortable applying it. The sources of discomfort typically fall into two categories: that people do not act in the way that fits the economic way of thinking, and that even if people did act that way, they should try not to. Let's consider these arguments in turn.

First Objection: People, Firms, and Society Do Not Act Like This

The economic approach to decision-making seems to require more information than most individuals possess and more careful decision-making than most individuals actually display. After all, do you or any of your friends draw a budget constraint and mutter to yourself about maximizing utility before you head to the shopping mall? Do members of the U.S. Congress contemplate production possibilities frontiers before they vote on the annual budget? The messy ways in which people and societies operate somehow doesn't look much like neat budget constraints or smoothly curving production possibilities frontiers.

However, the economics approach can be a useful way to analyze and understand the tradeoffs of economic decisions even so. To appreciate this point, imagine for a moment that you are playing basketball, dribbling to the right, and throwing a bounce-pass to the left to a teammate who is running toward the basket. A physicist or engineer could work out the correct speed and trajectory for the pass, given the different movements involved and the weight and bounciness of the ball. But when you are playing basketball, you do not perform any of these calculations. You just pass the ball, and if you are a good player, you will do so with high accuracy.

Someone might argue: "The scientist's formula of the bounce-pass requires a far greater knowledge of physics and far more specific information about speeds of movement and weights than the basketball player actually has, so it must be an unrealistic description of how basketball passes are actually made." This reaction would be wrongheaded. The fact that a good player can throw the ball accurately because of practice and skill, without making a physics calculation, does not mean that the physics calculation is wrong.

Similarly, from an economic point of view, someone who goes shopping for groceries every week has a great deal of practice with how to purchase the combination of goods that will provide that person with utility, even if the shopper does not phrase decisions in terms of a budget constraint. Government institutions may work imperfectly and slowly, but in general, a democratic form of government feels pressure from voters and social institutions to make the choices that are most widely preferred by people in that society. So, when thinking about the economic actions of groups of people, firms, and society, it is reasonable, as a first approximation, to analyze them with the tools of economic analysis. For more on this, read about behavioral economics in the chapter on Consumer Choices.

Second Objection: People, Firms, and Society Should Not Act This Way

The economics approach portrays people as self-interested. For some critics of this approach, even if self-interest is an accurate description of how people behave, these behaviors are not moral. Instead, the critics argue that people should be taught to care more deeply about others. Economists offer several answers to these concerns.

First, economics is not a form of moral instruction. Rather, it seeks to describe economic behavior as it actually exists. Philosophers draw a distinction between **positive statements**, which describe the world as it is, and **normative statements**, which describe how the world should be. For example, an economist could analyze a proposed subway system in a certain city. If the expected benefits exceed the costs, he concludes that the project is worth doing—an example of positive analysis. Another economist argues for extended unemployment compensation during the Great Depression because a rich country like the United States should take care of its less fortunate citizens—an example of normative analysis.

Even if the line between positive and normative statements is not always crystal clear, economic analysis does try to remain rooted in the study of the actual people who inhabit the actual economy. Fortunately however, the assumption that individuals are purely self-interested is a simplification about human nature. In fact, we need to look no further than to **Adam Smith**, the very father of modern economics to find evidence of this. The opening sentence of his book, *The Theory of Moral Sentiments*, puts it very clearly: "How selfish soever man may be supposed, there are evidently some principles in his nature, which interest him in the fortune of others, and render their happiness necessary to him, though he derives nothing from it except the pleasure of seeing it." Clearly, individuals are both self-interested and altruistic.

Second, self-interested behavior and profit-seeking can be labeled with other names, such as personal choice and freedom. The ability to make personal choices about buying, working, and saving is an important personal freedom. Some people may choose high-pressure, high-paying jobs so that they can earn and spend a lot of money on themselves. Others may earn a lot of money and give it to charity or spend it on their friends and family. Others may devote themselves to a career that can require a great deal of time, energy, and expertise but does not offer high financial rewards, like being an elementary school teacher or a social worker. Still others may choose a job that does not take lots of their time or provide a high level of income, but still leaves time for family, friends, and contemplation. Some people may prefer to work for a large company; others might want to start their own business. People's freedom to make their own economic choices has a moral value worth respecting.

Is a diagram by any other name the same?

When you study economics, you may feel buried under an avalanche of diagrams: diagrams in the text, diagrams in the lectures, diagrams in the problems, and diagrams on exams. Your goal should be to recognize the common underlying logic and pattern of the diagrams, not to memorize each of the individual diagrams.

This chapter uses only one basic diagram, although it is presented with different sets of labels. The consumption budget constraint and the production possibilities frontier for society, as a whole, are the same basic diagram. Figure 1 shows an individual budget constraint and a production possibilities frontier for two goods, Good 1 and Good 2. The tradeoff diagram always illustrates three basic themes: scarcity, tradeoffs, and economic efficiency.

The first theme is **scarcity**. It is not feasible to have unlimited amounts of both goods. But even if the budget constraint or a PPF shifts, scarcity remains—just at a different level. The second theme is **tradeoffs**. As depicted in the budget constraint or the production possibilities frontier, it is necessary to give up some of one good to gain more of the other good. The details of this tradeoff vary. In a budget constraint, the tradeoff is determined by the relative prices of the goods: that is, the relative price of two goods in the consumption choice budget constraint. These tradeoffs appear as a straight line. However, the tradeoffs in many production possibilities frontiers are represented by a curved line because the law of diminishing returns holds that as resources are added to an area, the marginal gains tend to diminish. Regardless of the specific shape, tradeoffs remain.

The third theme is **economic efficiency**, or getting the most benefit from scarce resources. All choices on the production possibilities frontier show productive efficiency because in such cases, there is no way to increase the quantity of one good without decreasing the quantity of the other. Similarly, when an individual makes a choice along a budget constraint, there is no way to increase the quantity of one good without decreasing the quantity of the other. The choice on a production possibilities set that is socially preferred, or the choice on an individual's budget constraint that is personally preferred, will display allocative efficiency.

The basic budget constraint/production possibilities frontier diagram will recur throughout this book. Some examples include using these tradeoff diagrams to analyze trade, labor supply versus leisure, saving versus consumption, environmental protection and economic output, equality of incomes and economic output, and the macroeconomic tradeoff between consumption and investment. Do not be confused by the different labels. The budget constraint/production possibilities frontier diagram is always just a tool for thinking carefully about scarcity, tradeoffs, and efficiency in a particular situation.

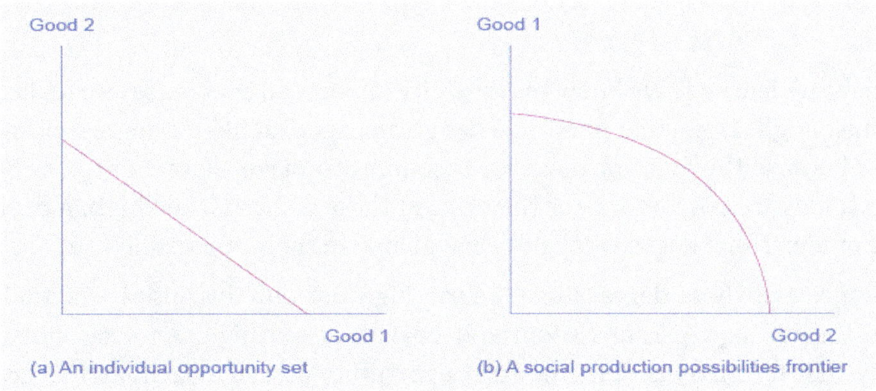

Figure 1. The Tradeoff Diagram. Both the individual opportunity set (or budget constraint) and the social production possibilities frontier show the constraints under which individual consumers and society as a whole operate. Both diagrams show the tradeoff in choosing more of one good at the cost of less of the other.

Third, self-interested behavior can lead to positive social results. For example, when people work hard to make a living, they create economic output. Consumers who are looking for the best deals will encourage businesses to offer goods and services that meet their needs. Adam Smith, writing in *The Wealth of Nations*, christened this property the **invisible hand**. In describing how consumers and producers interact in a market economy, Smith wrote:

Every individual...generally, indeed, neither intends to promote the public interest, nor knows how much he is promoting it. By preferring the support of domestic to that of foreign industry, he intends only his own security; and by directing that industry in such a manner as its produce may be of the greatest value, he intends only his own gain. And he is in this, as in many other cases, led by an invisible hand to promote an end which was no part of his intention...By pursuing his own interest he frequently promotes that of the society more effectually than when he really intends to promote it.

The metaphor of the invisible hand suggests the remarkable possibility that broader social good can emerge from selfish individual actions.

Fourth, even people who focus on their own self-interest in the economic part of their life often set aside their own narrow self-interest in other parts of life. For example, you might focus on your own self-interest when asking your employer for a raise or negotiating to buy a car. But then you might turn around and focus on other people when you volunteer to read stories at the local library, help a friend move to a new apartment, or donate money to a charity. Self-interest is a reasonable starting point for analyzing many economic decisions, without needing to imply that people never do anything that is not in their own immediate self-interest.

Choices ... To What Degree?

What have we learned? We know that scarcity impacts all the choices we make. So, an economist might argue that people do not go on to get bachelor's degrees or master's degrees because they do not have the resources to make those choices or because their incomes are too low and/or the price of these degrees is too high. A bachelor's degree or a master's degree may not be available in their opportunity set.

The price of these degrees may be too high not only because the actual price, college tuition (and perhaps room and board), is too high. An economist might also say that for many people, the full opportunity cost of a bachelor's degree or a master's degree is too high. For these people, they are unwilling or unable to make the tradeoff of giving up years of working, and earning an income, to earn a degree.

Finally, the statistics introduced at the start of the chapter reveal information about **intertemporal choices**. An economist might say that people choose not to get a college degree because they may have to borrow money to go to college, and the interest they have to pay on that loan in the future will affect their decisions today. Also, it could be that some people have a preference for current consumption over future consumption, so they choose to work at a lower salary and consume now, rather than putting that consumption off until after they graduate college.

Concepts and Summary

The economic way of thinking provides a useful approach to understanding human behavior. Economists make the careful distinction between positive statements, which describe the world as it is, and normative statements, which describe how the world should be. Even when economics analyzes the gains and losses from various events or policies, and thus draws normative conclusions about how the world should be, the analysis of economics is rooted in a positive analysis of how people, firms, and governments actually behave, not how they should behave.

CHAPTER

A PLURALIST APPROACH TO DEFINING ECONOMICS 3

3.1 DEFINITIONS' IMPORTANCE

The presentation of an alternative definition may appear generic, even unimportant. A definition often washes over a reader, leaving the reader influenced, but without any obvious new insight as to the intended meaning or implications of a word. Worse, without proper guidance, a reader may interpret a definition differently than what is intended by the author, or in the case of economics, different from how the discipline is actually employing the definition. Definitions are, however, important, potentially very important. A definition has the potential to provide clarity. At their best, definitions act like a compass, providing a lost reader with several potential directions from which to proceed.

3.2 A VARIETY OF PERSPECTIVES REQUIRES A VARIETY OF DEFINITIONS

The importance of clarity and directionality becomes heightened when a discipline has more than one potential definition. The discipline of economics, similar to the other social sciences, does not ascribe to only one definition. The definition of economics that is utilized by an economist will often depend on the paradigmatic perspective of the economist.

Paradigm – A school of thought. It represents the boundary of a discipline, framing the types of questions and phenomena that will be analyzed, and the approach or method of study a theorist will employ.

The discipline of economics has more than one paradigm. Not surprisingly, the discipline of economics also has more than one definition.

3.3 A SHORT SUMMARY OF VARIOUS ECONOMIC PERSPECTIVES

Multiple theoretical perspectives tend to create multiple ideas as to what economic questions, phenomena, and methods are most appropriate. With paradigmatic differences come ideological differences.

Ideology – The ideas, beliefs, subjective values, and prevailing world views that a person holds. One's ideology influences the way in which a person perceives what they believe is correct or incorrect about their social circumstance or the larger world in which they live.

Broadly speaking, the discipline of economics is occupied by theorists who tend to fall within one of three categories.

- Conservative economists
- Progressive economists
- Radical economists

In terms of beliefs, while there is some crossover, the differences between each of the ideological perspectives tends to be overwhelming.

Conservative Economists Believe...

- That markets works well on their own without outside interference.
- Because markets work well, a "Laissez-Faire" (Hands Off) view of markets is embraced.
- Given the belief in well-functioning markets, it is also believed, overwhelmingly, that markets should be responsible for how societies allocate resources
- Limited government involvement in markets is best because extensive government involvement is disruptive to market performance.

Progressive Economists Believe...

- Markets should generally be responsible for the allocation of resources
- Free markets generate inequality
- Free markets are often unstable
- Government intervention is necessary

Radical Economists Believe...

- Market economies are classed based economic systems.
- Class is determined by one's position in the economy: owner, laborer, etc.
- Market economies empower the wealthy, typically owners of assets.
- Market economies exploit labor
- Free market capitalism is unstable
- Capitalism needs to be replaced

Competing Paradigmatic Views

How might different economists address Different Microeconomic Issues?

- Consider the issue of Negative ***Externalities – When a third party suffers a loss from the actions of others. For example, consider the massive social costs associated with carbon emissions and climate change.***
- ***Conservative Economists***: Argue that the solution to market failure associated with externalities is to assign property rights. If the party causing or impacted by the externality has property rights, then markets and accurate prices emerge.
- ***Progressive Economists***: Argue that the government is needed to assist in correcting for externalities. Taxes and/or regulations can be instituted that require producers of externalities to account for the social costs they have generated.
- ***Radical Economists***: Argue that externalities are pervasive in market economies. Assigning property rights encourages producers of externalities to produce more negative externalities in an effort to extort payments from those afflicted. Also it is impossible to tax and/or regulate all externalities. An alternative to the market, as an allocative institution, is needed.

How might different economists address structural issues in economics?

- **Consider the issue of *Preferred Economic Institutional Structure(s)*,**
- ***Conservative Economists***: Argue that the free market is the ideal institution for allocating resources to their best (socially optimal) outcomes. Advocate that government should be limited to institutions useful toward the defense of private property and the enforcement of economic contracts.
- ***Progressive Economists***: Argue that as a result of market failure such as environmental pollution and significant unemployment, institutions, typically government institutions, are necessary in order to correct market failure and return markets to a more efficient allocation of resources.
- ***Radical Economists***: Argue that government institutions are an incomplete and ineffective mechanism for addressing market failure. Advocate for the creation of alternative institutions, such as worker cooperatives, that are designed to challenge and potentially supplant institutions favorable to the current operation of the economic system.

How might different economists address economic development issues?

- **Consider the issue of *Income Inequality*,**
- ***Conservative Economists***: Argue that income inequality arises from productivity differences that emerge between and among individuals.

Efforts to reduce inequality should be avoided as they distort incentives and market allocation.

- ***Progressive Economists***: Argue that income inequality results from social circumstances. Children born into higher income (higher wealth) families have more opportunities available to garner both the resources and skills necessary for higher incomes. Hence, these economists favor government programs that promote equality of opportunity.
- ***Radical Economists***: Argue that income inequality is a by product of a class-based economic system. Also inequality is exacerbated by social circumstances. Generally, they would support government programs that promote equality of opportunity, however, also argue that those programs cannot eliminate inequality in a system built upon inequality.

How might different economists address world economic issues?

- **Consider the issue of *Global Poverty,***
- ***Conservative Economists***: Argue that free trade between nations will drive specialization and the expansion of material production, thus gradually reducing global poverty.
- ***Progressive Economists***: Argue for a degree of government intervention in international trade. Suggest trade via such policies as infant industry, fair labor standards, and environmental protections. Trade is an economic development tool.
- ***Radical Economists***: Argue that international trade worsens class tensions. Low wages in developing countries cause wages to decline in developed countries. Poverty is a part of capitalism, free trade and/or managed trade cannot end global poverty.

3.4 ECONOMICS: DECONSTRUCTING THE ORTHODOX DEFINITION

Sometimes, in order to better understand how something works it is useful to break apart, or deconstruct (de-engineer), the object of examination. During periods of war, oppositional armies are known to commandeer their opponent's weaponry in order to de-engineer, or deconstruct, the equipment. The United States Army Air Forces Operation LUSTY (Luftwaffe Secret Technology) sought to capture German technology both during and after World War Two. By taking apart a piece of equipment piece by piece the examiner gains insight into both how the equipment operates as well as its weaknesses. In times of war, stealing good ideas and developing better ways to destroy an opponent's weapons can be invaluable. The object of deconstruction does not have to be physical or mechanical for the process to be useful; deconstructing an idea is also a valuable process for enriching understanding. Regarding the orthodox definition of economics, as it is the object of both examination and critique, this same type of deconstruction will also be useful.

In the first chapter of this text an example of the orthodox definition of economics was provided to the reader. The definition provided, similar to variations on the orthodox definition of economics in most textbooks, owes its origins to a famous early 20th century economist, Lionel Robbins. Robbins famously defined economics as, "the science which studies human behaviour as a relationship between ends and scarce means which have alternative uses." Contemporary orthodox economic textbooks tend to utilize a generic variation on Robbins' definition, often stipulating something akin to "Economics is the study of the allocation of limited resources over unlimited wants." In order to examine the appropriateness, or lack thereof, of the orthodox definition of economics, a closer examination of the definition is necessary.

One approach toward deconstructing the orthodox definition of economics is to define, specifically within the context of the orthodox economic meaning of the words, the other terms within the definition. Given the organization of the orthodox definition, with wants being conditioned by the availability of resources, one possible starting point for deconstruction is the orthodox definition of the term resources.

As should be noted from chapter two of this text, the orthodox economic definition of resources emphasizes that resources are those things that are needed for production. While other resources may be relevant, orthodox economics nearly exclusively focuses on Land,Labor, andCapital as the essential resources necessary for production. When more resources are present, more production is possible and when fewer resources are present, less production is possible. Obviously, if resources are unlimited, then production would be unlimited and all wants, and presumably needs, could be met. Of course, as noted by the definition, resources are assumed to be limited, otherwise referred to as scarce.

The terms "limited" or "scarce" are fairly self-explanatory. By definition, if something is scarce or limited, then there is only so much of the thing in question. In this case, orthodox economists are assuming that Land, Labor, and Capital are in some way constrained. In many ways this is a sensible assumption as the planet we reside upon has only so much available land, human population, albeit significant, is limited to 7.4 billion people, and capital, consisting of tools and equipment, are limited because only so many machines are available at any one time. Given limited or scarce resources, the ability for wants to be met must be limited.

Limits to wants are an important consideration. Given the orthodox definition of economics, the term wants could, presumably, represent any and all things people could want. However, because wants are deemed to be conditioned by resources and what resources are capable of producing, it stands to reason that what orthodox economics means by its use of the term "wants" are those things that are produced by resources. Since resources are factors of production, land, labor, and capital, then "wants" must be those things that are produced by land, labor, and capital—essentially products (goods and services).

But why do people want products? According to orthodox economics people want products because people garner satisfaction or utility (happiness) from their consumption of products. Given that wants are considered to be unlimited, which is to say endless or infinite, then, by logical continuation, people must have an endless desire for utility or happiness. Importantly, considering that wants must be the byproduct of the products produced by resources, orthodox economics is arguing that people have an endless desire for happiness and that happiness is derived, apparently exclusively, from the products that people acquire. Additionally, consistent with the circular logic of orthodox economics, if human beings have unlimited wants, then resources must be scarce. All wants can never be met, rendering resources on a finite planet scarce, if wants are endless.

In summary, given the above set of definitions the following if-then statement provides a summary of the belief of orthodox economists. If wants are unlimited and resources are used to produce the things that people want, those things being products for consumption, then economists assume people have an insatiable desire to acquire products (aka. inherently greedy). Additionally, if, presumably, products bring happiness and people have an endless desire for products, then it must be that people have an endless desire to be happy.

3.5 A CRITICAL EXAMINATION OF THE ORTHODOX DEFINITION OF ECONOMICS AND THE IMPLICATIONS THAT FOLLOW

ARE UNLIMITED WANTS (AND THEREFORE SCARCE RESOURCES) A FACT OF LIFE OR A BELIEF?

A fact is something immutable, it just is, whereas a belief is something that a person or people think, whether there is evidence to support their contention or not. An atheist or a theist cannot prove their beliefs, God may or may not exist, but there is no way to empirically prove either view. Atheism and theism are beliefs, not facts. In terms of belief-based versus fact-based analyses in the realm of economics, noted 20th century political economist Karl Polanyi criticized the orthodox (neoclassical) scarcity story as scarcity assumed within the mind of the orthodox economist. In other words, scarcity is a belief of the orthodox economist, not a fact.

Outside of orthodox economics, such as within heterodox (alternative) economic circles as well as the other social science disciplines, the issue of scarcity as induced by unlimited wants has been extensively evaluated and re-evaluated. For many theorists, the concept of unlimited/endless want of material items is simply not an immutable fact present in all times and places among all human beings. Among anthropologists, for example, there is a rich history of ethnographic studies documenting ways in which small-scale, non-market oriented economies appear to behave differently than orthodox economists predict. One such anthropologist, Marshall Sahlins, explicitly notes that people residing in hunter-gatherer societies, while viewed as deeply impoverished by the standards of people residing in advanced industrial economies, are actually quite affluent because "all the people's wants are easily satisfied." For Sahlins and other anthropologists, the hunter-gatherer's affluence is not one of vast material abundance, but rather a happiness shaped by being contented with having basic needs and wants met. By having little and demanding little, a successful hunt can yield great want satisfaction.

Borrowing from psychology, there is also a sub-discipline of economics known as Happiness Economics. Utilizing survey data, theorists pursuing the study of happiness have repeatedly found that people that focus on the goals of monetary gain and material benefits tend to be less happy than people who are less focused or not focused on those goals. It seems that for every endless maximizer of products, there are many more people that are apt to be content and satisfied with far fewer material items, particularly if fewer material items mean a greater level of interpersonal satisfaction like love, the respect of peers, affection, family fulfillment, and relationship fulfillment. Apparently, these and other equally non-material but important psychological factors are more important to the pursuit of happiness than is monetary wealth.

Can Facts and Values Really be Separated?

Utilizing beliefs, ideas, or subjective values is not, however, an unacceptable practice for most social scientists. Orthodox economics insists that facts and values are to remain separate, otherwise known as positive economics. The orthodox fact/value dichotomy is, however, misleading. Nearly all theorists apply some sort of pre-analytical value to their analysis. The very use of assumptions implies that some kind of value-based decision making process was utilized by the theorist. The irony in this instance is that orthodox economics insists that it is a fact-based science when, in *fact*, it utilizes value based (normative) propositions.

Within their very definition, orthodox economists employ subjective values, such as the desire to maximize acquisition (an assumption, or belief, not a fact), to frame their vision of the discipline of economics. Once again, the use of subjective values on their own is not the problem or even a problem (contrary to the orthodox perspective that economics should be a positive science), but it becomes a problem when a definition states something as "is" as opposed to "believed." Compare the following phrases, "the study of economics is" and "one belief is that economics studies." The first phrase leads the reader to believe that economists deal in absolute facts while the second phrase implies that some economists may have settled on an accepted set of ideas, but those ideas remain up for debate. An honest presentation of the orthodox definition of economics would note its subjective, normative, non-positive nature.

Scarcity or Surplus?

There is another fundamental question that Polanyi's critique alludes to: does scarcity as perceived by the mind actually mean that there is a scarcity of resources? For Polanyi, the orthodox definition of economics is circular, it has neither a beginning nor an end, just continuous scarcity because of limitless want. After all, if human beings have unlimited wants, then resources have to be scarce, there is simply no way for all wants to be met if wants are endless. Close inspection of the orthodox definition of economics makes it clear that the picture of the homeless man on the bench presented in chapter one is not actually a result of scarcity, at least not as scarcity is defined within the orthodox tradition.

Again, recall that the orthodox definition of economics describes scarcity as resulting from endless "**want**." Endless want does not mean that there are not enough resources available to fulfill all of humanities basic **needs**. Nor does endless "want" mean that many wants cannot be met given available resources. Obviously the man on the park bench may have some very legitimate wants (certainly needs, like adequate shelter), but is he on the bench because there are not enough resources available to make sure his basic needs, such as a home, or other wants, are met? At least in terms of available housing, the answer to this question is an overwhelming no. According to the U.S. Department of Housing and Urban Development on any given night in January of 2015, 564,708 people were homeless. At the same time, the number of vacant residential properties in the United States numbered approximately 1.4 million.

The homeless man's lack of housing is not the byproduct of scarcity, at least not by the definition of scarcity that many people are accustomed. Rather, the homeless man on the bench is the byproduct of either misallocated resources or a maldistribution of production.

Homelessness (or house-less-ness) is not the only instance in which the orthodox economic scarcity story breaks down. There are other well documented instances. One particularly disturbing instance relates to malnourishment and general starvation. According to the World Hunger Education Service (WHES) around the world there is enough food produced on an annualized basis to ensure that every person is adequately nourished. In fact, the sheer amount of calories per person generated by global food production has risen since the early 1960s through the mid-2000s, with the amount of per capita calories produced being enough to adequately feed an adult in both developed and developing economies. At the same time, "The

United Nations Food and Agriculture Organization estimates that about 795 million people of the 7.3 billion people in the world, or one in nine, were suffering from chronic undernourishment in 2014-2016."

Again, this instance of basic needs not being met may be perceived as a situation of scarcity. However, as reported by the WHES, poverty is the overwhelming driver of global malnourishment. While poverty implies a scarcity of income, possibly due to a scarcity of employment possibilities, the actual product that resolves malnourishment, food is produced in enough abundance to adequately feed everyone. Once again, basic human needs are going unmet and this has nothing at all to do with the scarcity of resources.

An interesting outcome of reorienting the definition of economics away from the scarcity story, when evaluated on what is actually available, is not that resources are endless or that all wants can necessarily be met, but that it is apparent that there are often more than enough resources to meet all of humanity's material needs as well as many, many, many of humanities wants. Reoriented this way the story of economics becomes a story of surplus and abundance, rather than shortfall and hardship. A much less dismal, and likely more realistic, science indeed!

Needs versus Wants

A distinction must be made between needs and wants, as they are decidedly not the same.

Need – Reflects something that is necessary for a human being to sustain basic physical and psychological health.

One fairly well known measure defining needs is Maslow's hierarchy of needs. In Maslow's hierarchy basic physiological needs, like food, water, air, shelter, safety, must be met first, followed by psychological needs, such as love and affection, with self-actualizing needs being met last. Importantly, while Maslow's hierarchy provides a framework, it must also be understood that the concept of need evolves depending on the social circumstances and technological make up of a given economy. In the absence of basic physiological needs being met, a person's life will suffer to the degree that in many instances their life may be shortened. For example, homeless people have shorter life spans, 42 to 52 years, than non-homeless people, 78 years.

A want is different from a need.

Want – is something that is desired, but also not necessary for an individual to live and function in a society.

For example, while basic shelter with appropriate utilities such as gas, electric, water, sanitation, and basic cooking, cleaning, and food storage appliances will generally fulfill basic needs, additional products such as dishwashers, large screen televisions, hot tubs, and many, many other products are wants.

To further distinguish between needs and wants, consider the following example. In some communities the existing transportation infrastructure is nearly completely and exclusively automobile dependent. In order for a person to have a reasonable expectation of functioning, physically, socially, and economically in this socioeconomic environment, a person will need access to an automobile. In this case, a functional automobile is, in fact, a need, but a high end SUV is not a need, it is a want.

Based on the orthodox definition of economics it is clear that the orthodoxy is interested in wants rather than needs. The absence of needs from the orthodox definition is a curiosity. There are several possible reasons why needs are not explicitly referenced in the orthodox definition. Two possible reasons will be addressed here. First, it is possible that orthodox economists do not differentiate between needs and wants, thus all needs really are just wants. Second, orthodox economists may be assuming that needs are already being met. If basic needs are met, then it is not only possible but reasonable to study what people want.

In critique, the orthodox merger of needs and wants seems to produce potentially misleading insights. While one can certainly make the argument that all people want their needs to be met, such that a need is nothing more than a type of want, basic needs must be met or the study of additional wants becomes useless as there can be no other wants. Additionally, even if it is assumed that needs are being met, this does not actually mean that needs are being met in the world where people really live. If needs are not being met, can orthodox economics be trusted to study the situation and then prescribe a solution that might ease human suffering? The answer to this question is unclear as the orthodox definition of economics does not provide direction toward the study of needs.

Individual perspective or social perspective?

As a discipline, economics is categorized as a social science. The social sciences, in general, seek to develop understandings about human interactions on a social level. For example, an anthropologist may be interested in understanding the role of culture as it influences human behavior. Culture can be represented as social norms, rituals, and/or customs that different groups of people, mostly collectively, participate in performing. Another example of a social science is political science. A political scientist may be interested in examining political institutions and legal structures. In order to better understand why individuals or larger social groups of people exhibit certain behaviors, an understanding of how a society structures its laws, the rewards or penalties people encounter as a result of socially derived rules, is essential.

For the orthodox economist, however, the social element of economics is secondary to that of the individual. Again, the orthodox definition of economics gives the orthodox economist direction. Recall, the focus of the orthodox economist is on want fulfillment with wants being satisfied by goods and services produced by resources. The reason products are wanted is because products, presumably, provide the recipient with happiness, or utility. Since people are presumed to have endless wants, people are also presumed to have an endless desire for utility. In many ways orthodox economics is really just the study of the maximization of utility. But how is utility measured? Well, it's not. Utility is subjective, it is in the eye of the beholder. As such, the study of utility maximization is the study of individual choices. After all, the only way to know what makes a person happy, or bringing the most utility is to evaluate the consumption choices that people make. As such, the focus of orthodox economics is that of individual choice making.

For some in the orthodox economic community, the focus on the individual is a conscious choice, purposeful and known, and often times affectionately referred to as "**methodological individualism**." A methodology is an approach for addressing concerns that a discipline believes are essential. Methodological individualism is a method anchored to examining the individual, placing front and center the issue most essential to that of the orthodox economist: individual decision-making. But if the individual is of utmost importance, then the role of social is much less clear within orthodox economics. This is not to say that the larger society is ignored by orthodox economists. For orthodox economics the social does emerge but, consistent with their dedication to studying individual choice, it is as a byproduct of individual maximizing behavior. Once individuals pursue their own self-interest, the orthodox economist is tasked with simply summing or aggregating the individual behavior and the result is the larger social outcome.

For those outside of the orthodox economic tradition, many important considerations are seemingly lost by the direction of orthodox economic analysis. Take for example the question of how broader societal norms as a function of social institutions may have influenced the behavior of individuals. By assuming away the social and focusing exclusively on the individual, the orthodox economist will be apt to ignore such issues as how social institutions may have influenced individual behavior such that it is now not prone to maximizing individual acquisition. In other words, let's say people really don't just look out for themselves all of the time, seeking to acquire as many products for themselves as they can, but instead, people behave such that they are concerned for the well-being of others, maybe because the norms of their society encourage a less than self-centered set of behaviors. Non-acquisitive, non-self-interested individual behavior tends to be outside of the scope of orthodox economics, but it is not outside the scope of actual human economic interactions.

For many non-orthodox economists, the absence of a clear social perspective limits the understandings available to the practitioner of methodological individualism.

Utility as everything, utility as nothing

Some orthodox economists have objected to the idea that they are assuming that people are greedy, only wanting products or those things that can get products, namely resources or money as money is what is used to perform purchases. One orthodox economic argument that has emerged claims that the orthodox economic model can be extended to include the story of "**enlightened self-interest**." Enlightened self-interest is the idea that it can be in one's self-interest to act to benefit others. In some regards enlightened self-interest can be interpreted as someone serving society such that through their service society is better-off and, subsequently, as a member of society, the individual then benefits.

A common example of enlightened self-interest is charitable giving. Charitable giving is the opposite of individual acquisition as the person giving to charity is presumably giving away something of personal value for themselves so that someone else can benefit. Orthodox economists argue that the reason a person engages in charity, or another type of enlightened self-interest, is because they gain utility from knowing that they have done something that is perceived as "good" for society.

There are two problems that become evident when the orthodox enlightened self-interest argument is compared to the orthodox definition of economics. First, enlightened self-interest is inconsistent with the basic premise described by the orthodox definition of economics. To once again reiterate, the orthodox definition of economics is stipulating that people's unlimited wants are fulfilled by resources and resources are utilized to produce products, thus want fulfillment is synonymous with product acquisition. Returning to the charitable giving example, it is clear that charitable giving is not product acquisition but rather product dissipation. Thus orthodox economics cannot, without contradicting itself, apply its definition of economics to a story of enlightened self-interest. Another definition of economics would be necessary to account for human behavioral actions associated with what is perceived as enlightened self-interest, or really any human action that is not associated with the acquisition of products.

Some thoughtful orthodox economists have recognized the contradiction between their definition of economics and the idea of enlightened self-interest. As a result, some orthodox economists have re-cast their position arguing that utility can be derived from anything, not just material products. In other words, for the orthodox economist all human actions and behaviors are driven around utility maximization and thus the study of economics is really the study of utility maximization. When re-cast in this light, however, the second problem appears. If all actions provide a person with utility, and all people are utility maximizers, then any action can be said to be utility maximizing, otherwise the person would not engage in the action. Based on this construction, the orthodox economist would be reduced to observing what people do and then proclaiming that it must be in their best interest. As a critical thinking exercise an important question now emerges: when exactly does orthodox economics become a social science? Saying that people do as they do because otherwise they wouldn't do it does not represent science, it has very little empirical function. It is also not focused on the social as it does not account for any social factors that may influence or disrupt individual behavior. And it provides almost no predictive possibilities other than identifying what might happen in the future based on what has happened in the past. Once again, confronted with such limitations many economists suggest that another definition of economics may be more substantive and useful.

Breakout box – what about behavioral economics?

Because people frequently engage in behaviors that are not considered rational, that is to say individually acquisitive, orthodox economics has been targeted for criticism that their models do not accurately depict the real world. In response a sub-field of orthodox economics, behavioral economics, has developed that seeks to utilize experiments and psychology to better understand actual human behavior. Behavioral economics tends to start from the position that otherwise-rational, optimizing people will deviate from standard orthodox economic actions because people can be influenced by non-economic factors, such as religious beliefs or cultural norms

A common approach to identifying the factors that condition individual choice-making is to run experiments that test human response to incentives. A controlled experiment provides researchers with empirical, data-driven evidence as to how and why people may not respond to opportunities for individual gain in the ways that orthodox economics predicts.

For many outside of orthodox economics, the development of behavioral economics is a step in right direction for the larger science of economics. Having evidence and being able to explain a wider range of phenomena rather than simply stipulating that people do as they do otherwise they wouldn't do it, appears to move the discipline of economics toward more realistic insights. At the same time, critiques of orthodox economics are also apt to note that behavioral economics still does not go far enough with its approach. Behavioral economics emphasizes an analysis that begins with the standard orthodox isolated maximizing individual and then searches for deviations from this behavior. By the very nature of their focus, behavioral economics under-emphasizes social considerations. As such, data may be derived that draws out the idea that an individual is making choices that are influenced by social institutions, but absent the study of those social institutions, the theorist is possibly still in the dark as to why the social institutions elicit the response that they do on the part of the individual. The result is that behavioral economics broadens the scope of economic inquiry but, for those outside of orthodox economics, it is still too narrow of an approach.

Limitless versus limits: the implications for the health of the planetary environment

The final critique presented here may be the most important in terms of its implications for the future of humanity. The Earth is a finite biosphere. There is simply only so much atmosphere, land, water, minerals, ores, and other natural resources within the bounds of the planet. In this way, the Earth really is representative of a circumstance of scarcity. Certainly improved efficiency is capable of extending the productive capability of the available natural resources, but this does not change the fact that there is a limit to how much is actually available.

Regardless, for many orthodox economists, the principle of endless growth is unquestionably desirable and it is downright sacrilegious to doubt the merits of endless economic growth. Consider the orthodox definition of economics and its emphasis on the desirability of endless happiness and that happiness being derived from the endless consumption of products. Given the premise of unlimited wants, the need for endless production is obvious and, by continuation, endless production is a synonym for endless, exponential, economic growth. In the simplest sense, more products produced means that the material well-being of society is improved. For orthodox economists, the improved material well-being of society cannot be understated. For example, it is not uncommon for orthodox economists to argue that given enough growth, social maladies such as poverty can be alleviated and, in time, eliminated. Of course, the orthodox economic perspective leaves aside incredibly important considerations such as whether or not new material products are equitably distributed. But, as orthodox economists would note, an unequal distribution of products is a separate problem from inadequate production and overt want, so the existence of inequality does not undermine the importance of economic growth.

The issue of endless growth in a finite biosphere presents orthodox economics with interesting conundrums. If resources are finite, how is endless growth possible? Again, orthodox economics does provide an answer in form of the advancement of knowledge and technology that allow for improvements in productivity and efficiencies creating opportunities for endless growth. But what if endless growth then yields waste that pollutes the natural environment making human life on the planet ever more difficult to sustain? The answer to this question is more difficult and the failure to answer is more perilous. Even if knowledge and technological advancement can improve productive efficiencies, absent the elimination of waste, exponential economic growth will add waste to the land, sea, and air. Just as lily pads can overrun a pond, with exponential economic growth and its associated waste, the effluent byproducts of industrial production can inundate and overwhelm a finite biosphere.

The mass annihilation of the Plain's Bison in the 19th century is a grave depiction of the ability of humanity to inflict harm upon the natural environment.

Figure 1. A large pile of bison skulls c. 1870s. (Wikimedia, Public Domain)

Figure 2. Endless economic growth necessitates endless production. At the expense of rich, biodiverse, rainforest human beings burn and clear cut the forest in order expand agricultural capacity. (Credit: Jami Dwyer, Wikimedia, Public Domain)

It is clear that human economic activity nearly inevitably leads to the creation of waste byproducts, pollution. Not only is the Earth's biosphere limited in terms of what it can provide in the way of natural resources toward productive output, it is also limited in terms of how much waste it is capable of absorbing on land, in the sea, and in the air. For example, the Stockholm Resilience Centre has identified nine planetary boundaries (environmental thresholds) that must not be eclipsed if human life is to safely exist. The nine planetary boundaries are stratospheric ozone depletion, biodiversity loss, chemical pollution, climate change, ocean acidification, freshwater consumption, land system change, nitrogen and phosphorous flows to the biosphere and oceans, and atmospheric aerosol loading. Of these nine boundaries, three in particular, climate change, ocean acidification, and stratospheric ozone depletion, are of such consequence that if the threshold is surpassed, then the planet's basic ecology will likely be fundamentally destabilized. In the case of climate change and ocean acidification, the two issues are caused by human economic activity and are inherently interrelated. Climate change is caused by carbon dioxide emissions and ocean acidification is triggered when the oceans absorb and process carbon dioxide. Strikingly, at least in the case of climate change, the proposed boundary for atmospheric carbon dioxide has been surpassed as 350 parts per million (ppm) is the boundary while actual carbon dioxide levels now exceed 400 ppm. Clearly, human economic activity, and the associated environmental destruction of the Earth's biosphere as a result of economic growth, does present a powerful challenge to the importance of economic growth.

Given the above-stated considerations, going forward humanity must consider the possibility of orienting its economic activity within the context of limits. The direction of orthodox economics, as guided by its definition, is not, however, oriented toward accepting limits. In the face of the abundance of scientific evidence pointing toward human factors as the cause of a de-stabilizing natural environment, the orthodox definition of economics appears to point economic analysis in a direction counter-productive to health and well-being of life on this planet. As a result, it stands to reason that another definition of economics, one less rigid and one-dimensional, may be of use.

Environmental Resource Economics

Orthodox economics is not entirely oblivious to environmental concerns. Nearly a century ago orthodox economic thinkers such as A. C. Pigou recognized the potential for a concept known as **externalities**. Discussed in chapter 18: Environmental Protection and Negative Externalities, negative externalities represent the idea that sometimes economic activities create unaccounted for costs that impact third parties, or those people who are not directly involved in the economic activity. Any failure to properly account for a negative externality means that the market system has failed to efficiently allocate resources. For Pigou and orthodox economics, the solution to negative externalities is the development of institutional mechanisms that assign penalties to those that create negative externalities.

A common orthodox example of an institutional mechanism designed to address negative externalities is the government being granted the regulatory task of environmental protection. From the standpoint of orthodox economics, pollution and environmental degradation represent a negative externality, an unaccounted for cost on the larger society. As a regulator, the government can utilize any number of regulatory tools to try and mitigate pollution. For example, one choice preferred by many, but not all, orthodox economists, is the use of taxation as a way to increase costs to polluters. Overall, orthodox environmental resource economics places the environment as sub-ordinate to the economy, and argues that marginal analysis should be utilized to measure the economic costs and benefits of environmental changes.

As will be later illustrated in chapter 18: Environmental Protection and Negative Externalities, by invoking a tax on polluters in a market economy, costs to producers rise. As costs rise the producer will produce less of the product the production of which is creating pollution. Additionally, with less production of the product, the supply of the product will decline generating an increase in price of the product. The outcome is three-fold. First, with less production comes less pollution. Second, with less production the product now sells at a higher price, with the price capturing more of the negative externality and reflecting something closer to the true cost of the product. Third, the tax revenue generated from the tax has the potential to be used to compensate the victims of the negative externality. On the face of it, it appears as though the taxation solution to an externality is providing a final outcome that is close to ideal.

Critics of the orthodox economic externality resolution argument have their doubts about the efficacy of the orthodox approach. The following questions represent a small sample of possible concerns. For starters, it is possible to conceive of an economy with a seemingly endless variety of negative externalities, does this mean that all externalities will be taxed? Failure to properly tax negative externalities means that the economy is rife with inefficiencies. Additionally, how large of a government bureaucratic structure would be needed to adequately address all externalities? Might the solution be worse than the cure? Also, even if all products to be taxed could be identified, how can a regulator be certain to precisely calculate the size of the tax in order to correct for the costs of the negative externality.

Of course, even if all of the questions above could be sorted out and resolved, there are still basic fundamental issues and contradictions, associated with the orthodox definition of economics, which the orthodox argument fails to address. For example, all efforts to address negative environmental externalities call for the reduction of waste and some kind of constraint on economic activity and growth. Any check on growth clearly and obviously runs afoul of the basic tenet of orthodox economics, as is clear in their definition, of endless want of products and the associated desirability to try and meet those wants. Also, any reduction in production will also act to reduce consumption, presumably limiting consumers' abilities to increase their utility by acquiring products. The primary conclusion being that orthodox economics' own solution for externalities runs counter to the foundations of their definition of economics.

Some critics of the standard orthodox environmental resource economics arguments, through their application and advocacy for **ecological economics**, have sought to re-orient the relationship between the economy and the environment. Whereas orthodox economics views the natural environment as an external factor that may be impacted by economic activity, ecological economists place the economy in a sub-ordinate role to the natural environment. Ecological economics generally tends to support the notion that the natural environment must be nurtured and protected, as, without it, an economy and human life cannot function. As such ecological economics has a more cautious perspective regarding economic activity and how it impacts the natural environment. As a result, standard orthodox economic concepts such as endless economic growth and want fulfillment are of secondary importance to long term sustained living made possible through the protection of the natural environment. As such, ecological economics operates outside of the orthodox definition of economics.

3.6 A DIFFERENT WAY OF DEFINING ECONOMICS

The preceding presentation centered on deconstructing and then challenging the orthodox definition of economics. Of central concern throughout is the way in which the orthodox definition of economics potentially handcuffs the economist into viewing economic activity through a very narrow and specific lens. Given the problems associated with the orthodox definition of economics, a concerned student may be apt to ask, what does an alternative definition of economics look like? The answer to this question is that there are many possible alternative definitional variations.

The structure of an alternative definition of economics can take many forms, although the overall essence of alternative definitions is frequently similar. With regard to structure, some alternative definitions are apt to simplify economic activity to its most basic form. For example, economics can be the study of how human beings must work together, and with nature, to produce those things that fulfill the material needs and wants of society. In other instances alternative definitions of economics seek to reduce the definition to the essential characteristics of an economy. For example, economics can be defined as the study of how human beings organize production, distribution, and consumption. Still in other instances alternative definitions of economics focus on interdisciplinary facets of the structure of economic decision making. For instance, economics can be defined as the study of how cultural norms, social institutions, political structures, and general decision making processes influence human behavior toward economic ends.

Importantly, each of the possible definitional structures stipulated above appear to avoid the pitfalls that plague the orthodox definition of economics. First, none of the above alternative definitional possibilities assumes scarcity. Rather, each definition is open to the possibility of differing forms of economic organization and a diversity of ways to meet societal needs and wants. Second, none of the above alternative definitional structures make unprovable assumptions about individual human behavior and motivation. Rather, the social elements of the organization of economic activity are emphasized, opening the door to analyzing how individuals respond to social conditions. Third, none of the above alternative definitional structures predicates endless want and the need and desirability for endless economic growth. Rather, each is open to the possibility of alternative economic structures that can be coordinated to operate within the limits of the natural biosphere.

Going forward, within the context of the alternative perspectives developed within this textbook, and in addition to the above definitional structures, the following definition of economics is suggested.

Economics – Is the study of social provisioning, in which an understanding of the development of political economies is rooted in social, political, natural, and cultural processes.

CHAPTER

CONCEPTS OF DEMAND AND SUPPLY

4

INTRODUCTION TO DEMAND AND SUPPLY

Farmer's Market. Organic vegetables and fruits that are grown and sold within a specific geographical region should, in theory, cost less than conventional produce because the transportation costs are less. That is not, however, usually the case. (Credit: modification of work by Natalie Maynor/Flickr Creative Commons)

Why Can We Not Get Enough of Organic?

Organic food is increasingly popular, not just in the United States, but worldwide. At one time, consumers had to go to specialty stores or farmer's markets to find organic produce. Now it is available in most grocery stores. In short, organic is part of the mainstream.

Ever wonder why organic food costs more than conventional food? Why, say, does an organic Fuji apple cost $1.99 a pound, while its conventional counterpart costs $1.49 a pound? The same price relationship is true for just about every organic product on the market. If many organic foods are locally grown, would they not take less time to get to market and therefore be cheaper? What are the forces that keep those prices from coming down? Turns out those forces have a lot to do with this chapter's topic: demand and supply.

4.1 DEMAND, SUPPLY, AND EQUILIBRIUM IN MARKETS FOR GOODS AND SERVICES

Demand for Goods and Services

Economists use the term demand to refer to the amount of some good or service consumers are willing and able to purchase at each price. Demand is based on needs and wants—a consumer may be able to differentiate between a need and a want, but from an economist's perspective they are the same thing. Demand is also based on ability to pay. If you cannot pay for it, you have no effective demand.

What a buyer pays for a unit of the specific good or service is called **price**. The total number of units purchased at that price is called the **quantity demanded**. A rise in price of a good or service almost always decreases the quantity demanded of that good or service. Conversely, a fall in price will increase the quantity demanded. When the price of a gallon of gasoline goes up, for example, people look for ways to reduce their consumption by combining several errands, commuting by carpool or mass transit, or taking weekend or vacation trips closer to home. Economists call this inverse relationship between price and quantity demanded the **law of demand**. The law of demand assumes that all other variables that affect demand (to be explained in the next module) are held constant.

An example from the market for gasoline can be shown in the form of a table or a graph. A table that shows the quantity demanded at each price, such as Table 1, is called a demand schedule. Price in this case is measured in dollars per gallon of gasoline. The quantity demanded is measured in millions of gallons over some time period (for example, per day or per year) and over some geographic area (like a state or a country). A demand curve shows the relationship between price and quantity demanded on a graph like Figure 1, with quantity on the horizontal axis and the price per gallon on the vertical axis. (Note that this is an exception to the normal rule in mathematics that the independent variable (x) goes on the horizontal axis and the dependent variable (y) goes on the vertical. Economics is not math.)

The demand schedule shown by Table 1 and the demand curve shown by the graph in Figure 1 are two ways of describing the same relationship between price and quantity demanded.

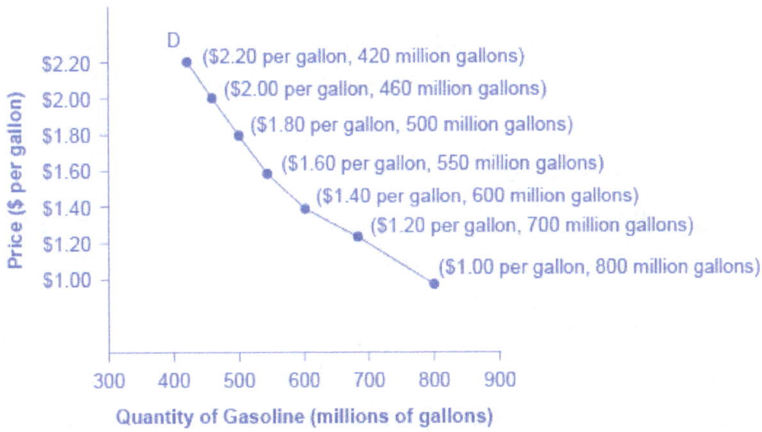

Figure 1. A Demand Curve for Gasoline. The demand schedule shows that as price rises, quantity demanded decreases, and vice versa. These points are then graphed, and the line connecting them is the demand curve (D). The downward slope of the demand curve again illustrates the law of demand—the inverse relationship between prices and quantity demanded.

Table 1. Price and Quantity Demanded of Gasoline

Price (per gallon)	Quantity Demanded (millions of gallons)
$1.00	800
$1.20	700
$1.40	600
$1.60	550
$1.80	500
$2.00	460
$2.20	420

Demand curves will appear somewhat different for each product. They may appear relatively steep or flat, or they may be straight or curved. Nearly all demand curves share the fundamental similarity that they slope down from left to right. So demand curves embody the law of demand: As the price increases, the quantity demanded decreases, and conversely, as the price decreases, the quantity demanded increases.

Confused about these different types of demand? Read the next Clear It Up feature.

Is demand the same as quantity demanded?

In economic terminology, demand is not the same as quantity demanded. When economists talk about demand, they mean the relationship between a range of prices and the quantities demanded at those prices, as illustrated by a demand curve or a demand schedule. When economists talk about quantity demanded, they mean only a certain point on the demand curve, or one quantity on the demand schedule. In short, demand refers to the curve and quantity demanded refers to the (specific) point on the curve.

Supply of Goods and Services

When economists talk about supply, they mean the amount of some good or service a producer is willing to supply at each price. Price is what the producer receives for selling one unit of a good or service. A rise in price almost always leads to an increase in the quantity supplied of that good or service, while a fall in price will decrease the quantity supplied. When the price of gasoline rises, for example, it encourages profit-seeking firms to take several actions: expand exploration for oil reserves; drill for more oil; invest in more pipelines and oil tankers to bring the oil to plants where it can be refined into gasoline; build new oil refineries; purchase additional pipelines and trucks to ship the gasoline to gas stations; and open more gas stations or keep existing gas stations open longer hours. Economists call this positive relationship between price and quantity supplied—that a higher price leads to a higher quantity supplied and a lower price leads to a lower quantity supplied—the law of supply. The law of supply assumes that all other variables that affect supply (to be explained in the next module) are held constant.

Still unsure about the different types of supply? See the following Clear It Up feature.

Is supply the same as quantity supplied?

In economic terminology, supply is not the same as quantity supplied. When economists refer to supply, they mean the relationship between a range of prices and the quantities supplied at those prices, a relationship that can be illustrated with a supply curve or a supply schedule. When economists refer to quantity supplied, they mean only a certain point on the supply curve, or one quantity on the supply schedule. In short, supply refers to the curve and quantity supplied refers to the (specific) point on the curve.

Figure 2 illustrates the law of supply, again using the market for gasoline as an example. Like demand, supply can be illustrated using a table or a graph. A supply schedule is a table, like Table 2, that shows the quantity supplied at a range of different prices. Again, price is measured in dollars per gallon of gasoline and quantity supplied is measured in millions of gallons. A supply curve is a graphic illustration of the relationship between price, shown on the vertical axis, and quantity, shown on the horizontal axis. The supply schedule and the supply curve are just two different ways of showing the same information. Notice that the horizontal and vertical axes on the graph for the supply curve are the same as for the demand curve.

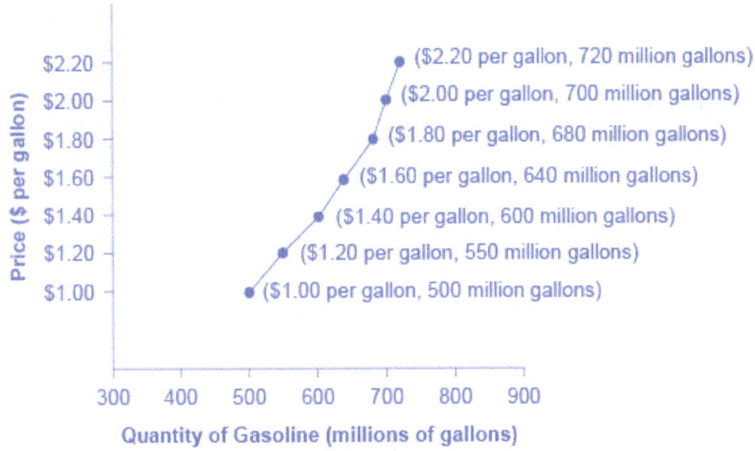

Figure 2. A Supply Curve for Gasoline. The supply schedule is the table that shows quantity supplied of gasoline at each price. As price rises, quantity supplied also increases, and vice versa. The supply curve (S) is created by graphing the points from the supply schedule and then connecting them. The upward slope of the supply curve illustrates the law of supply—that a higher price leads to a higher quantity supplied, and vice versa.

Table 2. Price and Supply of Gasoline

Price (per gallon)	Quantity Supplied (millions of gallons)
$1.00	500
$1.20	550
$1.40	600
$1.60	640
$1.80	680
$2.00	700
$2.20	720

The shape of supply curves will vary somewhat according to the product: steeper, flatter, straighter, or curved. Nearly all supply curves, however, share a basic similarity: they slope up from left to right and illustrate the law of supply: as the price rises, say, from $1.00 per gallon to $2.20 per gallon, the quantity supplied increases from 500 gallons to 720 gallons. Conversely, as the price falls, the quantity supplied decreases.

Equilibrium—Where Demand and Supply Intersect

Because the graphs for demand and supply curves both have price on the vertical axis and quantity on the horizontal axis, the demand curve and supply curve for a particular good or service can appear on the same graph. Together, demand and supply determine the price and the quantity that will be bought and sold in a market.

Figure 3 illustrates the interaction of demand and supply in the market for gasoline. The demand curve (D) is identical to Figure 1. The supply curve (S) is identical to Figure 2. Table 3 contains the same information in tabular form.

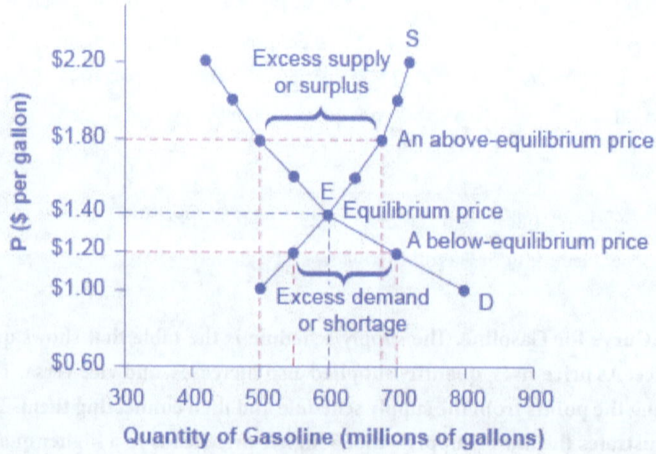

Figure 3. Demand and Supply for Gasoline. The demand curve (D) and the supply curve (S) intersect at the equilibrium point E, with a price of $1.40 and a quantity of 600. The equilibrium is the only price where quantity demanded is equal to quantity supplied. At a price above equilibrium like $1.80, quantity supplied exceeds the quantity demanded, so there is excess supply. At a price below equilibrium such as $1.20, quantity demanded exceeds quantity supplied, so there is excess demand.

Table 3. Price, Quantity Demanded, and Quantity Supplied

Price (per gallon)	Quantity demanded (millions of gallons)	Quantity supplied (millions of gallons)
$1.00	800	500
$1.20	700	550
$1.40	600	600
$1.60	550	640
$1.80	500	680
$2.00	460	700
$2.20	420	720

Remember this: When two lines on a diagram cross, this intersection usually means something. The point where the supply curve (S) and the demand curve (D) cross, designated by point E in Figure 3, is called the equilibrium. The equilibrium price is the only price where the plans of consumers and the plans of producers agree—that is, where the amount of the product consumers want to buy (quantity demanded) is equal to the amount producers want to sell (quantity supplied). This common quantity is called the equilibrium quantity. At any other price, the quantity demanded does not equal the quantity supplied, so the market is not in equilibrium at that price.

In Figure 3, the equilibrium price is $1.40 per gallon of gasoline and the equilibrium quantity is 600 million gallons. If you had only the demand and supply schedules, and not the graph, you could find the equilibrium by looking for the price level on the tables where the quantity demanded and the quantity supplied are equal.

The word "equilibrium" means "balance." If a market is at its equilibrium price and quantity, then it has no reason to move away from that point. However, if a market is not at equilibrium, then economic pressures arise to move the market toward the equilibrium price and the equilibrium quantity.

Imagine, for example, that the price of a gallon of gasoline was above the equilibrium price—that is, instead of $1.40 per gallon, the price is $1.80 per gallon. This above-equilibrium price is illustrated by the dashed horizontal line at the price of $1.80 in Figure 3. At this higher price, the quantity demanded drops from 600 to 500. This decline in quantity reflects how consumers react to the higher price by finding ways to use less gasoline.

Moreover, at this higher price of $1.80, the quantity of gasoline supplied rises from the 600 to 680, as the higher price makes it more profitable for gasoline producers to expand their output. Now, consider how quantity demanded and quantity supplied are related at this above-equilibrium price. Quantity demanded has fallen to 500 gallons, while quantity supplied has risen to 680 gallons. In fact, at any above-equilibrium price, the quantity supplied exceeds the quantity demanded. We call this an **excess supply** or a **surplus**.

With a surplus, gasoline accumulates at gas stations, in tanker trucks, in pipelines, and at oil refineries. This accumulation puts pressure on gasoline sellers. If a surplus remains unsold, those firms involved in making and selling gasoline are not receiving enough cash to pay their workers and to cover their expenses. In this situation, some producers and sellers will want to cut prices, because it is better to sell at a lower price than not to sell at all. Once some sellers start cutting prices, others will follow to avoid losing sales. These price reductions in turn will stimulate a higher quantity demanded. So, if the price is above the equilibrium level, incentives built into the structure of demand and supply will create pressures for the price to fall toward the equilibrium.

Now suppose that the price is below its equilibrium level at $1.20 per gallon, as the dashed horizontal line at this price in Figure 3 shows. At this lower price, the quantity demanded increases from 600 to 700 as drivers take longer trips, spend more minutes warming up the car in the driveway in wintertime, stop sharing rides to work, and buy larger cars that get fewer miles to the gallon. However, the below-equilibrium price reduces gasoline producers' incentives to produce and sell gasoline, and the quantity supplied falls from 600 to 550.

When the price is below equilibrium, there is excess demand, or a shortage—that is, at the given price the quantity demanded, which has been stimulated by the lower price, now exceeds the quantity supplied, which had been depressed by the lower price. In this situation, eager gasoline buyers mob the gas stations, only to find many stations running short of fuel. Oil companies and gas stations recognize that they have an opportunity to make higher profits by selling what gasoline they have at a higher price. As a result, the price rises toward the equilibrium level. Read Demand, Supply, and Efficiency for more discussion on the importance of the demand and supply model.

Concepts and Summary

A demand schedule is a table that shows the quantity demanded at different prices in the market. A demand curve shows the relationship between quantity demanded and price in a given market on a graph. The law of demand states that a higher price typically leads to a lower quantity demanded.

A supply schedule is a table that shows the quantity supplied at different prices in the market. A supply curve shows the relationship between quantity supplied and price on a graph. The law of supply says that a higher price typically leads to a higher quantity supplied.

The equilibrium price and equilibrium quantity occur where the supply and demand curves cross. The equilibrium occurs where the quantity demanded is equal to the quantity supplied. If the price is below the equilibrium level, then the quantity demanded will exceed the quantity supplied. Excess demand or a shortage will exist. If the price is above the equilibrium level, then the quantity supplied will exceed the quantity demanded. Excess supply or a surplus will exist. In either case, economic pressures will push the price toward the equilibrium level.

4.2 CHANGES IN THE SUPPLY AND DEMAND OF GOODS AND SERVICES

What Factors Affect Demand?

We defined demand as the amount of some product a consumer is willing and able to purchase at each price. That suggests at least two factors in addition to price that affect demand. Willingness to purchase suggests a desire, based on what economists call tastes and preferences. If you neither need nor want something, you will not buy it. Ability to purchase suggests that income is important. Professors are usually able to afford better housing and transportation than students, because they have more income. Prices of related goods can affect demand also. If you need a new car, the price of a Honda may affect your demand for a Ford. Finally, the size or composition of the population can affect demand. The more children a family has, the greater their demand for clothing. The more driving-age children a family has, the greater their demand for car insurance, and the less for diapers and baby formula.

These factors matter both for demand by an individual and demand by the market as a whole. Exactly how do these various factors affect demand, and how do we show the effects graphically? To answer those questions, we need the *ceteris paribus* assumption.

The *Ceteris Paribus* Assumption

A demand curve or a supply curve is a relationship between two, and only two, variables: quantity on the horizontal axis and price on the vertical axis. The assumption behind a demand curve or a supply curve is that no relevant economic factors, other than the product's price, are changing. Economists call this assumption ceteris paribus, a Latin phrase meaning "other things being equal." Any given demand or supply curve is based on the ceteris paribus assumption that all else is held equal. A demand curve or a supply curve is a relationship between two, and only two, variables when all other variables are kept constant. If all else is not held equal, then the laws of supply and demand will not necessarily hold, as the following Clear It Up feature shows.

When does *ceteris paribus* apply?

Ceteris paribus is typically applied when we look at how changes in price affect demand or supply, but ceteris paribus can be applied more generally. In the real world, demand and supply depend on more factors than just price. For example, a consumer's demand depends on income and a producer's supply depends on the cost of producing the product. How can we analyze the effect on demand or supply if multiple factors are changing at the same time—say price rises and income falls? The answer is that we examine the changes one at a time, assuming the other factors are held constant.

For example, we can say that an increase in the price reduces the amount consumers will buy (assuming income, and anything else that affects demand, is unchanged). Additionally, a decrease in income reduces the amount consumers can afford to buy (assuming price, and anything else that affects demand, is unchanged). This is what the ceteris paribus assumption really means. In this particular case, after we analyze each factor separately, we can combine the results. The amount consumers buy falls for two reasons: first because of the higher price and second because of the lower income.

How Does Income Affect Demand?

Let's use income as an example of how factors other than price affect demand. Figure 1 shows the initial demand for automobiles as D0. At point Q, for example, if the price is $20,000 per car, the quantity of cars demanded is 18 million. D0 also shows how the quantity of cars demanded would change as a result of a higher or lower price. For example, if the price of a car rose to $22,000, the quantity demanded would decrease to 17 million, at point R.

The original demand curve D0, like every demand curve, is based on the ceteris paribus assumption that no other economically relevant factors change. Now imagine that the economy expands in a way that raises the incomes of many people, making cars more affordable. How will this affect demand? How can we show this graphically?

Return to Figure 1. The price of cars is still $20,000, but with higher incomes, the quantity demanded has now increased to 20 million cars, shown at point S. As a result of the higher income levels, the demand curve shifts to the right to the new demand curve D1, indicating an increase in demand. Table 4 shows clearly that this increased demand would occur at every price, not just the original one.

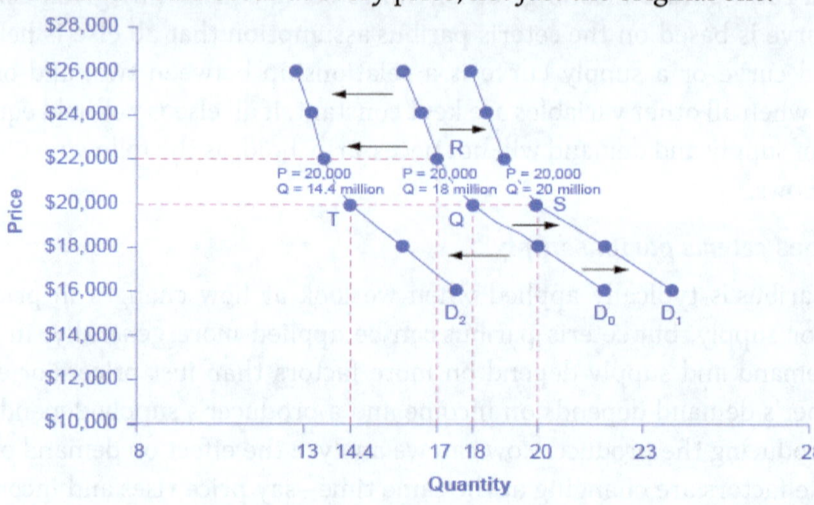

Figure 1. Shifts in Demand: A Car Example. Increased demand means that at every given price, the quantity demanded is higher, so that the demand curve shifts to the right from D0 to D1. Decreased demand means that at every given price, the quantity demanded is lower, so that the demand curve shifts to the left from D0 to D2.

Table 4. Price and Demand Shifts: A Car Example

Price	Decrease to D2	Original Quantity Demanded D0	Increase to D1
$16,000	17.6 million	22.0 million	24.0 million
$18,000	16.0 million	20.0 million	22.0 million
$20,000	14.4 million	18.0 million	20.0 million
$22,000	13.6 million	17.0 million	19.0 million
$24,000	13.2 million	16.5 million	18.5 million
$26,000	12.8 million	16.0 million	18.0 million

Now, imagine that the economy slows down so that many people lose their jobs or work fewer hours, reducing their incomes. In this case, the decrease in income would lead to a lower quantity of cars demanded at every given price, and the original demand curve D_0 would shift left to D_2. The shift from D_0 to D_2 represents such a decrease in demand: At any given price level, the quantity demanded is now lower. In this example, a price of 20,000$ means 18 million cars sold along the original demand curve, but only 14.4 million sold after demand fell.

When a demand curve shifts, it does not mean that the quantity demanded by every individual buyer changes by the same amount. In this example, not everyone would have higher or lower income and not everyone would buy or not buy an additional car. Instead, a shift in a demand curve captures an pattern for the market as a whole.

In the previous section, we argued that higher income causes greater demand at every price. This is true for most goods and services. For some—luxury cars, vacations in Europe, and fine jewelry—the effect of a rise in income can be especially pronounced. A product whose demand rises when income rises, and vice versa, is called a **normal good**. A few exceptions to this pattern do exist. As incomes rise, many people will buy fewer generic brand groceries and more name brand groceries. They are less likely to buy used cars and more likely to buy new cars. They will be less likely to rent an apartment and more likely to own a home, and so on. A product whose demand falls when income rises, and vice versa, is called an **inferior good**. In other words, when income increases, the demand curve shifts to the left.

Other Factors That Shift Demand Curves

Income is not the only factor that causes a shift in demand. Other things that change demand include tastes and preferences, the composition or size of the population, the prices of related goods, and even expectations. A change in any one of the underlying factors that determine what quantity people are willing to buy at a given price will cause a shift in demand. Graphically, the new demand curve lies either to the right (an increase) or to the left (a decrease) of the original demand curve. Let's look at these factors.

Changing Tastes or Preferences

From 1980 to 2014, the per-person consumption of chicken by Americans rose from 48 pounds per year to 85 pounds per year, and consumption of beef fell from 77 pounds per year to 54 pounds per year, according to the U.S. Department of Agriculture (USDA). Changes like these are largely due to movements in taste, which change the quantity of a good demanded at every price: that is, they shift the demand curve for that good, rightward for chicken and leftward for beef.

Changes in the Composition of the Population

The proportion of elderly citizens in the United States population is rising. It rose from 9.8% in 1970 to 12.6% in 2000, and will be a projected (by the **U.S. Census Bureau**) 20% of the population by 2030. A society with relatively more children, like the United States in the 1960s, will have greater demand for goods and services like tricycles and day care facilities. A society with relatively more elderly persons, as the United States is projected to have by 2030, has a higher demand for nursing homes and hearing aids. Similarly, changes in the size of the population can affect the demand for housing and many other goods. Each of these changes in demand will be shown as a shift in the demand curve.

The demand for a product can also be affected by changes in the prices of related goods such as substitutes or complements. A substitute is a good or service that can be used in place of another good or service. As electronic books, like this one, become more available, you would expect to see a decrease in demand for traditional printed books. A lower price for a substitute decreases demand for the other product. For example, in recent years as the price of tablet computers has fallen, the quantity demanded has increased (because of the law of demand). Since people are purchasing tablets, there has been a decrease in demand for laptops, which can be shown graphically as a leftward shift in the demand curve for laptops. A higher price for a substitute good has the reverse effect.

Other goods are complements for each other, meaning that the goods are often used together, because consumption of one good tends to enhance consumption of the other. Examples include breakfast cereal and milk; notebooks and pens or pencils, golf balls and golf clubs; gasoline and sport utility vehicles; and the five-way combination of bacon, lettuce, tomato, mayonnaise, and bread. If the price of golf clubs rises, since the quantity demanded of golf clubs falls (because of the law of demand), demand for a complement good like golf balls decreases, too. Similarly, a higher price for skis would shift the demand curve for a complement good like ski resort trips to the left, while a lower price for a complement has the reverse effect.

Changes in Expectations about Future Prices or Other Factors that Affect Demand

While it is clear that the price of a good affects the quantity demanded, it is also true that expectations about the future price (or expectations about tastes and preferences, income, and so on) can affect demand. For example, if people hear that a hurricane is coming, they may rush to the store to buy flashlight batteries and bottled water. If people learn that the price of a good like coffee is likely to rise in the future, they may head for the store to stock up on coffee now. These changes in demand are shown as shifts in the curve. Therefore, a shift in demand happens when a change in some economic factor (other than price) causes a different quantity to be demanded at every price. The following Work It Out feature shows how this happens.

Shift in Demand

A shift in demand means that at any price (and at every price), the quantity demanded will be different than it was before. Following is an example of a shift in demand due to an income increase.

Step 1. Draw the graph of a demand curve for a normal good like pizza. Pick a price (like P_0). Identify the corresponding Q_0. An example is shown in Figure 2.

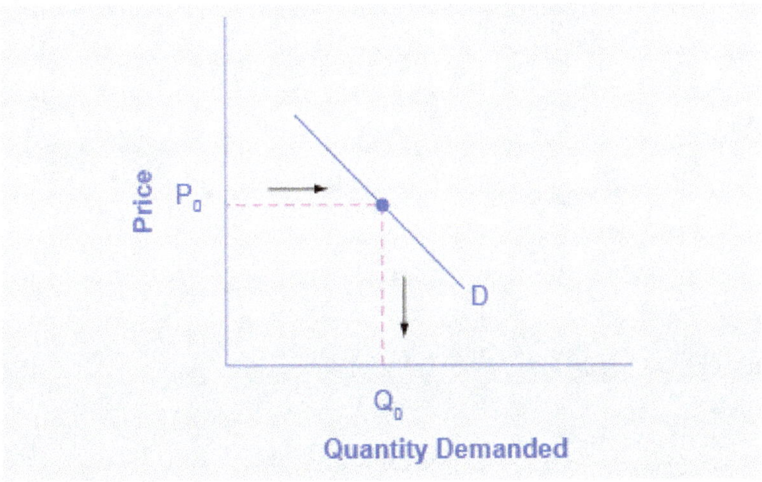

Figure 2. Demand Curve. The demand curve can be used to identify how much consumers would buy at any given price.

Step 2. Suppose income increases. As a result of the change, are consumers going to buy more or less pizza? The answer is more. Draw a dotted horizontal line from the chosen price, through the original quantity demanded, to the new point with the new Q_1. Draw a dotted vertical line down to the horizontal axis and label the new Q_1. An example is provided in Figure 3.

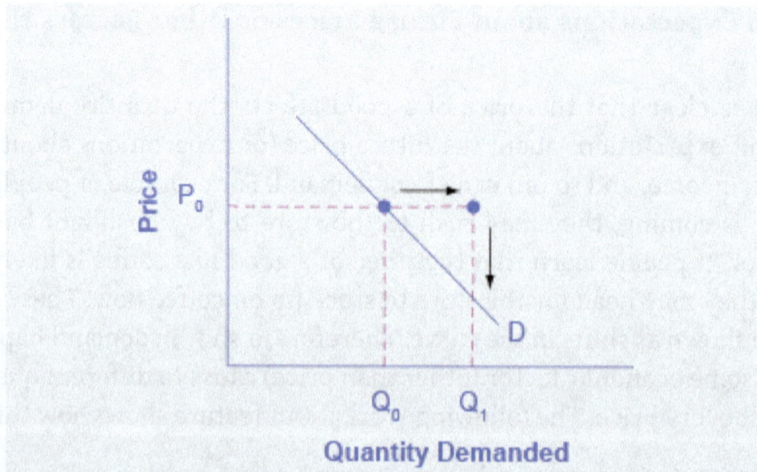

Figure 3. Demand Curve with Income Increase. With an increase in income, consumers will purchase larger quantities, pushing demand to the right.

Step 3. Now, shift the curve through the new point. You will see that an increase in income causes an upward (or rightward) shift in the demand curve, so that at any price the quantities demanded will be higher, as shown in Figure 4.

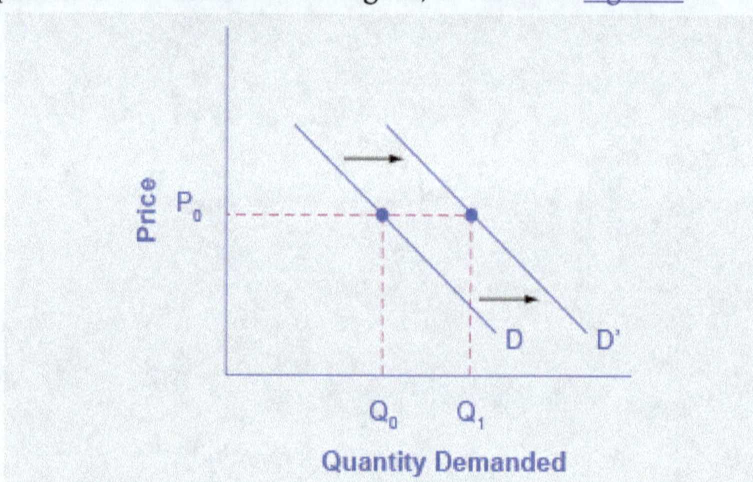

Figure 4. Demand Curve Shifted Right. With an increase in income, consumers will purchase larger quantities, pushing demand to the right, and causing the demand curve to shift right.

Summing Up Factors That Change Demand

Six factors that can shift demand curves are summarized in Figure 5. The direction of the arrows indicates whether the demand curve shifts represent an increase in demand or a decrease in demand. Notice that a change in the price of the good or service itself is not listed among the factors that can shift a demand curve. A change in the price of a good or service causes a movement along a specific demand curve, and it typically leads to some change in the quantity demanded, but it does not shift the demand curve.

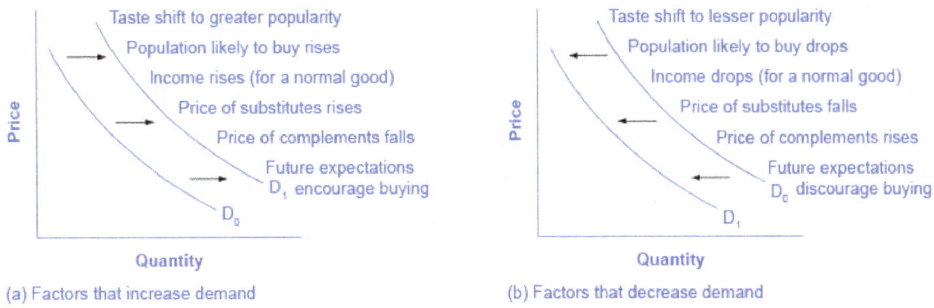

Figure 5. Factors That Shift Demand Curves. (a) A list of factors that can cause an increase in demand from D_0 to D_1. (b) The same factors, if their direction is reversed, can cause a decrease in demand from D_0 to D_1.

When a demand curve shifts, it will then intersect with a given supply curve at a different equilibrium price and quantity. We are, however, getting ahead of our story. Before discussing how changes in demand can affect equilibrium price and quantity, we first need to discuss shifts in supply curves.

How Production Costs Affect Supply

A supply curve shows how quantity supplied will change as the price rises and falls, assuming ceteris paribus so that no other economically relevant factors are changing. If other factors relevant to supply do change, then the entire supply curve will shift. Just as a shift in demand is represented by a change in the quantity demanded at every price, a shift in supply means a change in the quantity supplied at every price.

In thinking about the factors that affect supply, remember what motivates firms: profits, which are the difference between revenues and costs. Goods and services are produced using combinations of labor, materials, and machinery, or what we call **inputs** or **factors of production.** If a firm faces lower costs of production, while the prices for the good or service the firm produces remain unchanged, a firm's profits go up. When a firm's profits increase, it is more motivated to produce output, since the more it produces the more profit it will earn. So, when costs of production fall, a firm will tend to supply a larger quantity at any given price for its output. This can be shown by the supply curve shifting to the right.

Take, for example, a messenger company that delivers packages around a city. The company may find that buying gasoline is one of its main costs. If the price of gasoline falls, then the company will find it can deliver messages more cheaply than before. Since lower costs correspond to higher profits, the messenger company may now supply more of its services at any given price. For example, given the lower gasoline prices, the company can now serve a greater area, and increase its supply.

Conversely, if a firm faces higher costs of production, then it will earn lower profits at any given selling price for its products. As a result, a higher cost of production typically causes a firm to supply a smaller quantity at any given price. In this case, the supply curve shifts to the left.

Consider the supply for cars, shown by curve S0 in Figure 6. Point J indicates that if the price is $20,000, the quantity supplied will be 18 million cars. If the price rises to $22,000 per car, ceteris paribus, the quantity supplied will rise to 20 million cars, as point K on the S0 curve shows. The same information can be shown in table form, as in Table 5.

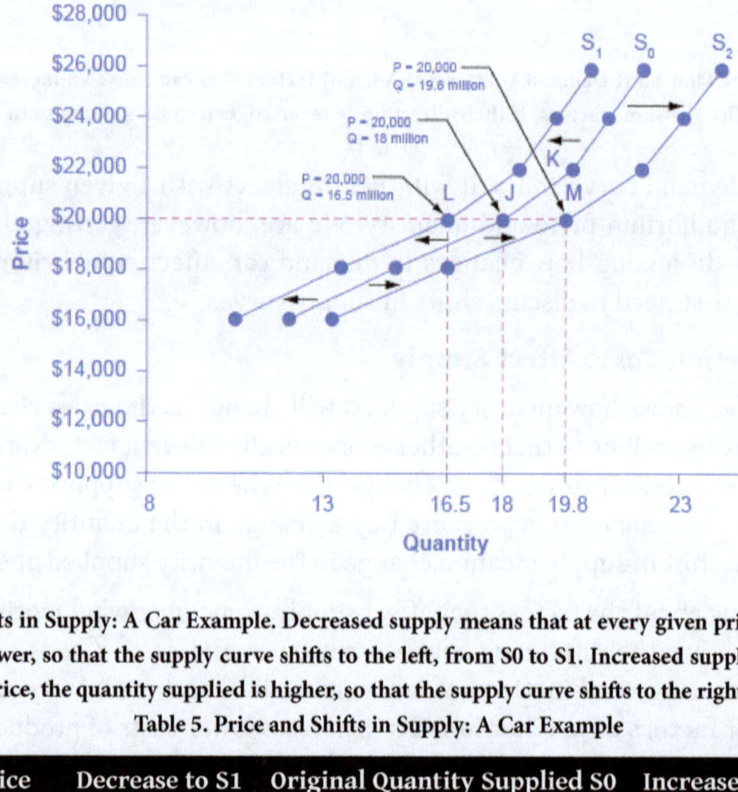

Figure 6. Shifts in Supply: A Car Example. Decreased supply means that at every given price, the quantity supplied is lower, so that the supply curve shifts to the left, from S0 to S1. Increased supply means that at every given price, the quantity supplied is higher, so that the supply curve shifts to the right, from S0 to S2.

Table 5. Price and Shifts in Supply: A Car Example

Price	Decrease to S1	Original Quantity Supplied S0	Increase to S2
$16,000	10.5 million	12.0 million	13.2 million
$18,000	13.5 million	15.0 million	16.5 million
$20,000	16.5 million	18.0 million	19.8 million
$22,000	18.5 million	20.0 million	22.0 million
$24,000	19.5 million	21.0 million	23.1 million
$26,000	20.5 million	22.0 million	24.2 million

Now, imagine that the price of steel, an important ingredient in manufacturing cars, rises, so that producing a car has become more expensive. At any given price for selling cars, car manufacturers will react by supplying a lower quantity. This can be shown graphically as a leftward shift of supply, from S_0 to S_1, which indicates that at any given price, the quantity supplied decreases. In this example, at a price of $20,000, the quantity supplied decreases from 18 million on the original supply curve (S_0) to 16.5 million on the supply curve S_1, which is labeled as point L.

Conversely, if the price of steel decreases, producing a car becomes less expensive. At any given price for selling cars, car manufacturers can now expect to earn higher profits, so they will supply a higher quantity. The shift of supply to the right, from S_0 to S_2, means that at all prices, the quantity supplied has increased. In this example, at a price of $20,000, the quantity supplied increases from 18 million on the original supply curve (S_0) to 19.8 million on the supply curve S_2, which is labeled M.

Other Factors That Affect Supply

In the example above, we saw that changes in the prices of inputs in the production process will affect the cost of production and thus the supply. Several other things affect the cost of production, too, such as changes in weather or other natural conditions, new technologies for production, and some government policies.

The cost of production for many agricultural products will be affected by changes in natural conditions. For example, in 2014 the Manchurian Plain in Northeastern China, which produces most of the country's wheat, corn, and soybeans, experienced its most severe drought in 50 years. A drought decreases the supply of agricultural products, which means that at any given price, a lower quantity will be supplied; conversely, especially good weather would shift the supply curve to the right.

When a firm discovers a new technology that allows the firm to produce at a lower cost, the supply curve will shift to the right, as well. For instance, in the 1960s a major scientific effort nicknamed the Green Revolution focused on breeding improved seeds for basic crops like wheat and rice. By the early 1990s, more than two-thirds of the wheat and rice in low-income countries around the world was grown with these Green Revolution seeds—and the harvest was twice as high per acre. A technological improvement that reduces costs of production will shift supply to the right, so that a greater quantity will be produced at any given price.

Government policies can affect the cost of production and the supply curve through taxes, regulations, and subsidies. For example, the U.S. government imposes a tax on alcoholic beverages that collects about $8 billion per year from producers. Taxes are treated as costs by businesses. Higher costs decrease supply for the reasons discussed above. Other examples of policy that can affect cost are the wide array of government regulations that require firms to spend money to provide a cleaner environment or a safer workplace; complying with regulations increases costs.

A government subsidy, on the other hand, is the opposite of a tax. A subsidy occurs when the government pays a firm directly or reduces the firm's taxes if the firm carries out certain actions. From the firm's perspective, taxes or regulations are an additional cost of production that shifts supply to the left, leading the firm to produce a lower quantity at every given price. Government subsidies reduce the cost of production and increase supply at every given price, shifting supply to the right. The following Work It Out feature shows how this shift happens.

Shift in Supply

We know that a supply curve shows the minimum price a firm will accept to produce a given quantity of output. What happens to the supply curve when the cost of production goes up? Following is an example of a shift in supply due to a production cost increase.

Step 1. Draw a graph of a supply curve for pizza. Pick a quantity (like Q0). If you draw a vertical line up from Q0 to the supply curve, you will see the price the firm chooses. An example is shown in Figure 7.

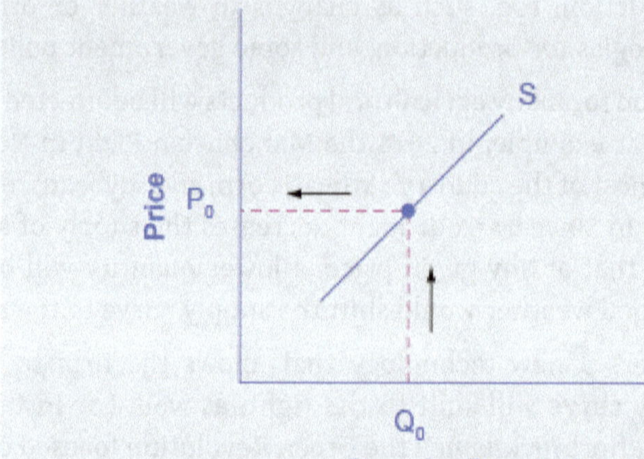

Figure 7. Supply Curve. The supply curve can be used to show the minimum price a firm will accept to produce a given quantity of output.

Step 2. Why did the firm choose that price and not some other? One way to think about this is that the price is composed of two parts. The first part is the average cost of production, in this case, the cost of the pizza ingredients (dough, sauce, cheese, pepperoni, and so on), the cost of the pizza oven, the rent on the shop, and the wages of the workers. The second part is the firm's desired profit, which is determined, among other factors, by the profit margins in that particular business. If you add these two parts together, you get the price the firm wishes to charge. The quantity Q0 and associated price P0 give you one point on the firm's supply curve, as shown in Figure 8.

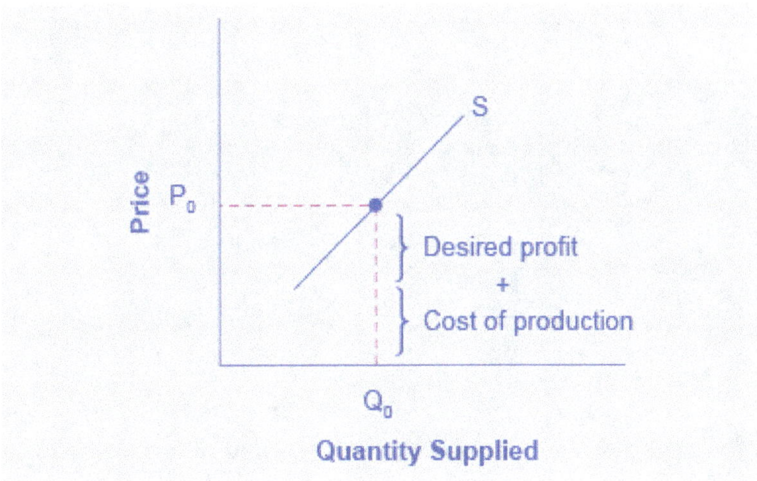

Figure 8. Setting Prices. The cost of production and the desired profit equal the price a firm will set for a product.

Step 3. Now, suppose that the cost of production goes up. Perhaps cheese has become more expensive by $0.75 per pizza. If that is true, the firm will want to raise its price by the amount of the increase in cost ($0.75). Draw this point on the supply curve directly above the initial point on the curve, but $0.75 higher, as shown in Figure 9.

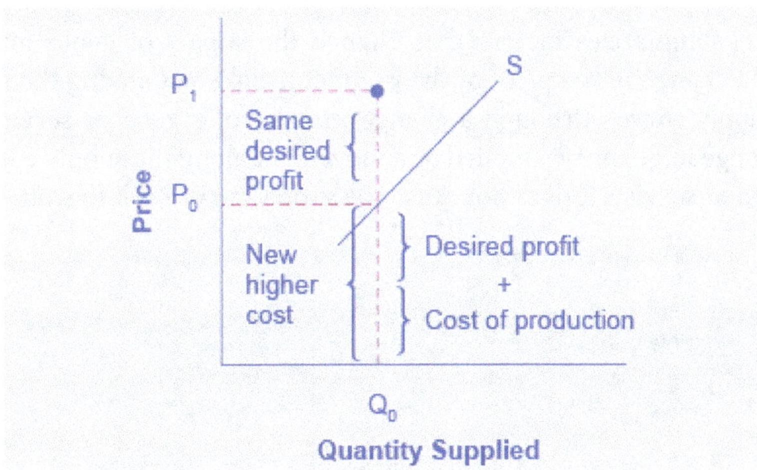

Figure 9. Increasing Costs Leads to Increasing Price. Because the cost of production and the desired profit equal the price a firm will set for a product, if the cost of production increases, the price for the product will also need to increase.

Step 4. Shift the supply curve through this point. You will see that an increase in cost causes an upward (or a leftward) shift of the supply curve so that at any price, the quantities supplied will be smaller, as shown in Figure 10.

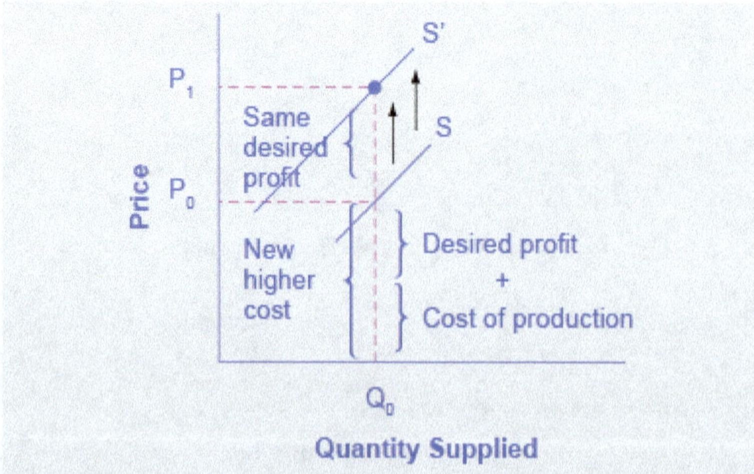

Figure 10. Supply Curve Shifts. When the cost of production increases, the supply curve shifts upwardly to a new price level.

Summing Up Factors That Change Supply

Changes in the cost of inputs, natural disasters, new technologies, and the impact of government decisions all affect the cost of production. In turn, these factors affect how much firms are willing to supply at any given price.

Figure 11 summarizes factors that change the supply of goods and services. Notice that a change in the price of the product itself is not among the factors that shift the supply curve. Although a change in price of a good or service typically causes a change in quantity supplied or a movement along the supply curve for that specific good or service, it does not cause the supply curve itself to shift.

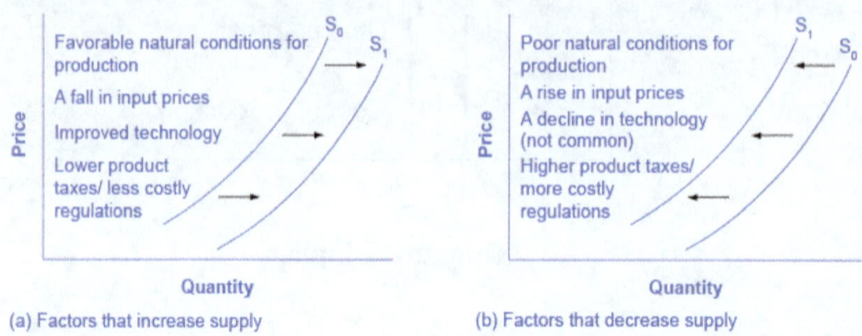

Figure 11. Factors That Shift Supply Curves. (a) A list of factors that can cause an increase in supply from S_0 to S_1. (b) The same factors, if their direction is reversed, can cause a decrease in supply from S_0 to S_1.

Because demand and supply curves appear on a two-dimensional diagram with only price and quantity on the axes, an unwary visitor to the land of economics might be fooled into believing that economics is about only four topics: demand, supply, price, and quantity. However, demand and supply are really "umbrella" concepts: demand covers all the factors that affect demand, and supply covers all the factors that affect supply. Factors other than price that affect demand and supply are included by using shifts in the demand or the supply curve. In this way, the two-dimensional demand and supply model becomes a powerful tool for analyzing a wide range of economic circumstances.

Concepts and Summary

Economists often use the ceteris paribus or "other things being equal" assumption: while examining the economic impact of one event, all other factors remain unchanged for the purpose of the analysis. Factors that can shift the demand curve for goods and services, causing a different quantity to be demanded at any given price, include changes in tastes, population, income, prices of substitute or complement goods, and expectations about future conditions and prices. Factors that can shift the supply curve for goods and services, causing a different quantity to be supplied at any given price, include input prices, natural conditions, changes in technology, and government taxes, regulations, or subsidies.

4.3 THE FOUR-STEP PROCESS FOR CHANGES IN EQUILIBRIUM PRICE AND QUANTITY

Let's begin this discussion with a single economic event. It might be an event that affects demand, like a change in income, population, tastes, prices of substitutes or complements, or expectations about future prices. It might be an event that affects supply, like a change in natural conditions, input prices, or technology, or government policies that affect production. How does this economic event affect equilibrium price and quantity? We will analyze this question using a four-step process.

Step 1. Draw a demand and supply model before the economic change took place. To establish the model requires four standard pieces of information: The law of demand, which tells us the slope of the demand curve; the law of supply, which gives us the slope of the supply curve; the shift variables for demand; and the shift variables for supply. From this model, find the initial equilibrium values for price and quantity.

Step 2. Decide whether the economic change being analyzed affects demand or supply. In other words, does the event refer to something in the list of demand factors or supply factors?

Step 3. Decide whether the effect on demand or supply causes the curve to shift to the right or to the left, and sketch the new demand or supply curve on the diagram. In other words, does the event increase or decrease the amount consumers want to buy or producers want to sell?

Step 4. Identify the new equilibrium and then compare the original equilibrium price and quantity to the new equilibrium price and quantity.

Let's consider one example that involves a shift in supply and one that involves a shift in demand. Then we will consider an example where both supply and demand shift.

Good Weather for Salmon Fishing

In the summer of 2000, weather conditions were excellent for commercial salmon fishing off the California coast. Heavy rains meant higher than normal levels of water in the rivers, which helps the salmon to breed. Slightly cooler ocean temperatures stimulated the growth of plankton, the microscopic organisms at the bottom of the ocean food chain, providing everything in the ocean with a hearty food supply. The ocean stayed calm during fishing season, so commercial fishing operations did not lose many days to bad weather. How did these climate conditions affect the quantity and price of salmon? Figure 1 illustrates the four-step approach, which is explained below, to work through this problem. Table 7 provides the information to work the problem as well.

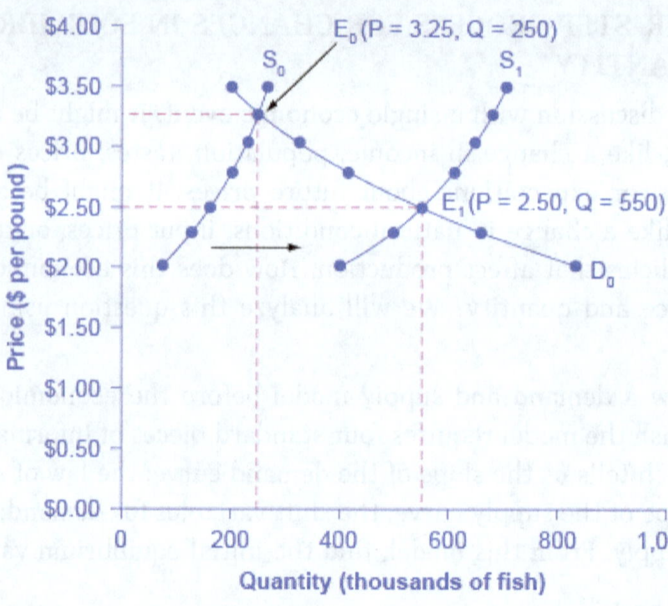

Figure 1. Good Weather for Salmon Fishing: The Four-Step Process. Unusually good weather leads to changes in the price and quantity of salmon.

Table 7. Salmon Fishing

Price per Pound	Quantity Supplied in 1999	Quantity Supplied in 2000	Quantity Demanded
$2.00	80	400	840
$2.25	120	480	680
$2.50	160	550	550
$2.75	200	600	450
$3.00	230	640	350
$3.25	250	670	250
$3.50	270	700	200

Step 1. Draw a demand and supply model to illustrate the market for salmon in the year before the good weather conditions began. The demand curve D0 and the supply curve S0 show that the original equilibrium price is $3.25 per pound and the original equilibrium quantity is 250,000 fish. (This price per pound is what commercial buyers pay at the fishing docks; what consumers pay at the grocery is higher.)

Step 2. Did the economic event affect supply or demand? Good weather is an example of a natural condition that affects supply.

Step 3. Was the effect on supply an increase or a decrease? Good weather is a change in natural conditions that increases the quantity supplied at any given price. The supply curve shifts to the right, moving from the original supply curve S_0 to the new supply curve S_1, which is shown in both the table and the figure.

Step 4. Compare the new equilibrium price and quantity to the original equilibrium. At the new equilibrium E_1, the equilibrium price falls from $3.25 to $2.50, but the equilibrium quantity increases from 250,000 to 550,000 salmon. Notice that the equilibrium quantity demanded increased, even though the demand curve did not move.

In short, good weather conditions increased supply of the California commercial salmon. The result was a higher equilibrium quantity of salmon bought and sold in the market at a lower price.

Newspapers and the Internet

According to the **Pew Research Center for People and the Press**, more and more people, especially younger people, are getting their news from online and digital sources. The majority of U.S. adults now own smartphones or tablets, and most of those Americans say they use them in part to get the news. From 2004 to 2012, the share of Americans who reported getting their news from digital sources increased from 24% to 39%. How has this affected consumption of print news media, and radio and television news? Figure 2 and the text below illustrates using the four-step analysis to answer this question.

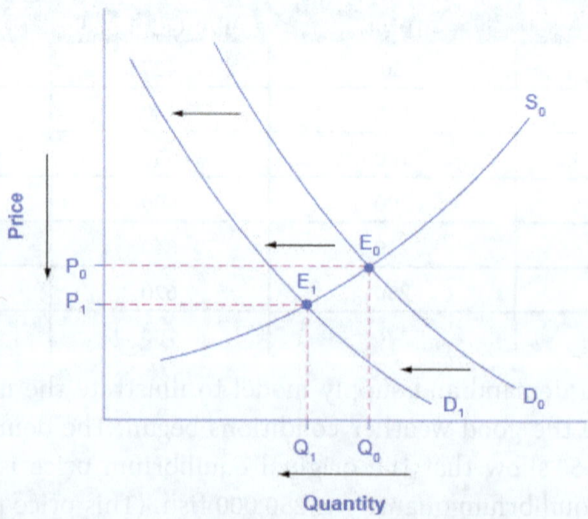

Figure 2. The Print News Market: A Four-Step Analysis. A change in tastes from print news sources to digital sources results in a leftward shift in demand for the former. The result is a decrease in both equilibrium price and quantity.

Step 1. Develop a demand and supply model to think about what the market looked like before the event. The demand curve D0 and the supply curve S0 show the original relationships. In this case, the analysis is performed without specific numbers on the price and quantity axis.

Step 2. Did the change described affect supply or demand? A change in tastes, from traditional news sources (print, radio, and television) to digital sources, caused a change in demand for the former.

Step 3. Was the effect on demand positive or negative? A shift to digital news sources will tend to mean a lower quantity demanded of traditional news sources at every given price, causing the demand curve for print and other traditional news sources to shift to the left, from D_0 to D_1.

Step 4. Compare the new equilibrium price and quantity to the original equilibrium price. The new equilibrium (E_1) occurs at a lower quantity and a lower price than the original equilibrium (E_0).

The decline in print news reading predates 2004. Print newspaper circulation peaked in 1973 and has declined since then due to competition from television and radio news. In 1991, 55% of Americans indicated they got their news from print sources, while only 29% did so in 2012. Radio news has followed a similar path in recent decades, with the share of Americans getting their news from radio declining from 54% in 1991 to 33% in 2012. Television news has held its own over the last 15 years, with a market share staying in the mid to upper fifties. What does this suggest for the future, given that two-thirds of Americans under 30 years old say they do not get their news from television at all?

The Interconnections and Speed of Adjustment in Real Markets

In the real world, many factors that affect demand and supply can change all at once. For example, the demand for cars might increase because of rising incomes and population, and it might decrease because of rising gasoline prices (a complementary good). Likewise, the supply of cars might increase because of innovative new technologies that reduce the cost of car production, and it might decrease as a result of new government regulations requiring the installation of costly pollution-control technology.

Moreover, rising incomes and population or changes in gasoline prices will affect many markets, not just cars. How can an economist sort out all these interconnected events? The answer lies in the ceteris paribus assumption. Look at how each economic event affects each market, one event at a time, holding all else constant. Then combine the analyses to see the net effect.

A Combined Example

The U.S. Postal Service is facing difficult challenges. Compensation for postal workers tends to increase most years due to cost-of-living increases. At the same time, more and more people are using email, text, and other digital message forms such as Facebook and Twitter to communicate with friends and others. What does this suggest about the continued viability of the Postal Service? Figure 3 and the text below illustrates using the four-step analysis to answer this question.

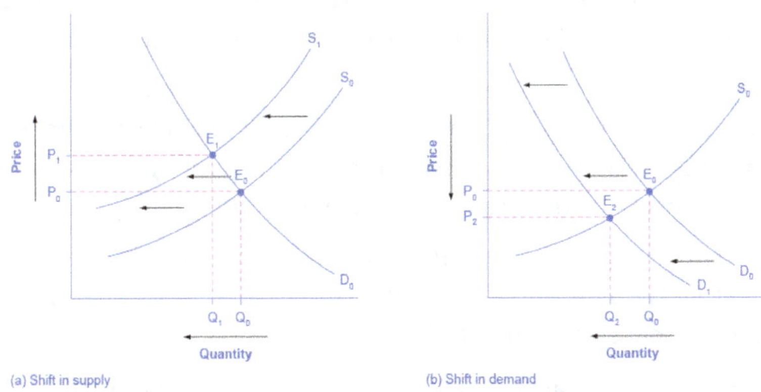

Figure 3. Higher Compensation for Postal Workers: A Four-Step Analysis. (a) Higher labor compensation causes a leftward shift in the supply curve, a decrease in the equilibrium quantity, and an increase in the equilibrium price. (b) A change in tastes away from Postal Services causes a leftward shift in the demand curve, a decrease in the equilibrium quantity, and a decrease in the equilibrium price.

Since this problem involves two disturbances, we need two four-step analyses, the first to analyze the effects of higher compensation for postal workers, the second to analyze the effects of many people switching from "snailmail" to email and other digital messages.

Figure 3 (a) shows the shift in supply discussed in the following steps.

Step 1. Draw a demand and supply model to illustrate what the market for the U.S. Postal Service looked like before this scenario starts. The demand curve D_0 and the supply curve S_0 show the original relationships.

Step 2. Did the change described affect supply or demand? Labor compensation is a cost of production. A change in production costs caused a change in supply for the Postal Service.

Step 3. Was the effect on supply positive or negative? Higher labor compensation leads to a lower quantity supplied of postal services at every given price, causing the supply curve for postal services to shift to the left, from S_0 to S_1.

Step 4. Compare the new equilibrium price and quantity to the original equilibrium price. The new equilibrium (E_1) occurs at a lower quantity and a higher price than the original equilibrium (E_0).

Figure 3 (b) shows the shift in demand discussed in the following steps.

Step 1. Draw a demand and supply model to illustrate what the market for U.S. Postal Services looked like before this scenario starts. The demand curve D0 and the supply curve S0 show the original relationships. Note that this diagram is independent from the diagram in panel (a).

Step 2. Did the change described affect supply or demand? A change in tastes away from snailmail toward digital messages will cause a change in demand for the Postal Service.

Step 3. Was the effect on supply positive or negative? Higher labor compensation leads to a lower quantity supplied of postal services at every given price, causing the supply curve for postal services to shift to the left, from D_0 to D_1.

Step 4. Compare the new equilibrium price and quantity to the original equilibrium price. The new equilibrium (E_2) occurs at a lower quantity and a lower price than the original equilibrium (E_0).

The final step in a scenario where both supply and demand shift is to combine the two individual analyses to determine what happens to the equilibrium quantity and price. Graphically, we superimpose the previous two diagrams one on top of the other, as in Figure 4.

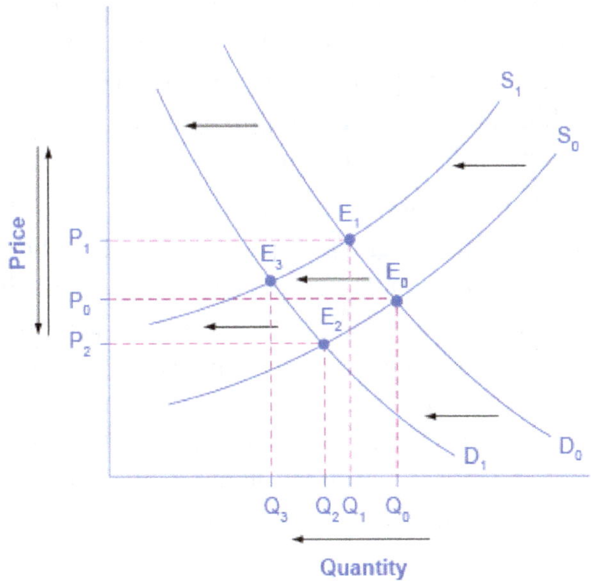

Figure 4. Combined Effect of Decreased Demand and Decreased Supply. Supply and demand shifts cause changes in equilibrium price and quantity.

Following are the results:

Effect on Quantity: The effect of higher labor compensation on Postal Services because it raises the cost of production is to decrease the equilibrium quantity. The effect of a change in tastes away from snailmail is to decrease the equilibrium quantity. Since both shifts are to the left, the overall impact is a decrease in the equilibrium quantity of Postal Services (Q_3). This is easy to see graphically, since Q_3 is to the left of Q_0.

Effect on Price: The overall effect on price is more complicated. The effect of higher labor compensation on Postal Services, because it raises the cost of production, is to increase the equilibrium price. The effect of a change in tastes away from snailmail is to decrease the equilibrium price. Since the two effects are in opposite directions, unless we know the magnitudes of the two effects, the overall effect is unclear. This is not unusual. When both curves shift, typically we can determine the overall effect on price or on quantity, but not on both. In this case, we determined the overall effect on the equilibrium quantity, but not on the equilibrium price. In other cases, it might be the opposite.

The next Clear It Up feature focuses on the difference between shifts of supply or demand and movements along a curve.

Difference between shifts of demand or supply versus movements along a demand or supply curve

One common mistake in applying the demand and supply framework is to confuse the shift of a demand or a supply curve with movement along a demand or supply curve. As an example, consider a problem that asks whether a drought will increase or decrease the equilibrium quantity and equilibrium price of wheat. Lee, a student in an introductory economics class, might reason:

"Well, it is clear that a drought reduces supply, so I will shift back the supply curve, as in the shift from the original supply curve S_0 to S_1 shown on the diagram (called Shift 1). So the equilibrium moves from E_0 to E_1, the **equilibrium quantity** is lower and the equilibrium price is higher. Then, a higher price makes farmers more likely to supply the good, so the supply curve shifts right, as shown by the shift from S_1 to S_2, on the diagram (shown as Shift 2), so that the equilibrium now moves from E_1 to E_2. The higher price, however, also reduces demand and so causes demand to shift back, like the shift from the original demand curve, D_0 to D_1 on the diagram (labeled Shift 3), and the equilibrium moves from E_2 to E_3."

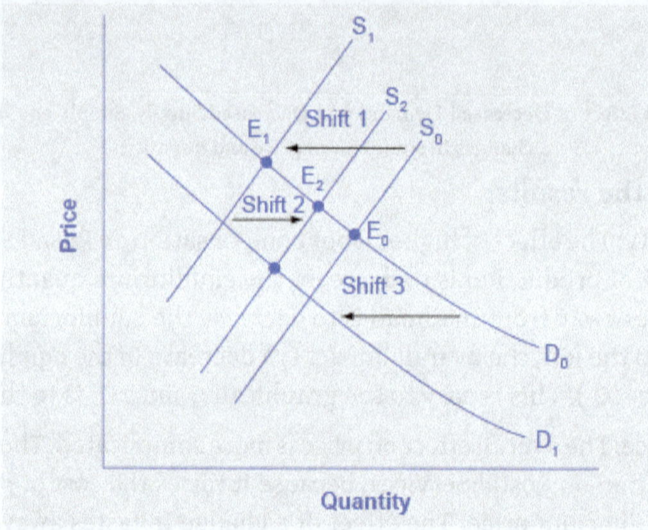

Figure 5. Shifts of Demand or Supply versus Movements along a Demand or Supply Curve. A shift in one curve never causes a shift in the other curve. Rather, a shift in one curve causes a movement along the second curve.

At about this point, Lee suspects that this answer is headed down the wrong path. Think about what might be wrong with Lee's logic, and then read the answer that follows.

Answer: Lee's first step is correct: that is, a drought shifts back the supply curve of wheat and leads to a prediction of a lower equilibrium quantity and a higher equilibrium price. This corresponds to a movement along the original demand curve (D0), from E0 to E1. The rest of Lee's argument is wrong, because it mixes up shifts in supply with quantity supplied, and shifts in demand with quantity demanded.

A higher or lower price never shifts the supply curve, as suggested by the shift in supply from S1 to S2. Instead, a price change leads to a movement along a given supply curve. Similarly, a higher or lower price never shifts a demand curve, as suggested in the shift from D0 to D1. Instead, a price change leads to a movement along a given demand curve. Remember, a change in the price of a good never causes the demand or supply curve for that good to shift.

Think carefully about the timeline of events: What happens first, what happens next? What is cause, what is effect? If you keep the order right, you are more likely to get the analysis correct.

In the four-step analysis of how economic events affect equilibrium price and quantity, the movement from the old to the new equilibrium seems immediate. As a practical matter, however, prices and quantities often do not zoom straight to equilibrium. More realistically, when an economic event causes demand or supply to shift, prices and quantities set off in the general direction of equilibrium. Indeed, even as they are moving toward one new equilibrium, prices are often then pushed by another change in demand or supply toward another equilibrium.

Concepts and Summary

When using the supply and demand framework to think about how an event will affect the equilibrium price and quantity, proceed through four steps: (1) sketch a supply and demand diagram to think about what the market looked like before the event; (2) decide whether the event will affect supply or demand; (3) decide whether the effect on supply or demand is negative or positive, and draw the appropriate shifted supply or demand curve; (4) compare the new equilibrium price and quantity to the original ones.

4.4 PRICE FLOORS AND CEILINGS

Controversy sometimes surrounds the prices and quantities established by demand and supply, especially for products that are considered necessities. In some cases, discontent over prices turns into public pressure on politicians, who may then pass legislation to prevent a certain price from climbing "too high" or falling "too low."

The demand and supply model shows how people and firms will react to the incentives provided by these laws to control prices, in ways that will often lead to undesirable consequences. Alternative policy tools can often achieve the desired goals of price control laws, while avoiding at least some of their costs and tradeoffs.

Price Ceilings

Laws that government enacts to regulate prices are called Price controls. Price controls come in two flavors. A price ceiling keeps a price from rising above a certain level (the "ceiling"), while a price floor keeps a price from falling below a certain level (the "floor"). This section uses the demand and supply framework to analyze price ceilings. The next section discusses price floors.

In many markets for goods and services, demanders outnumber suppliers. Consumers, who are also potential voters, sometimes unite behind a political proposal to hold down a certain price. In some cities, such as Albany, renters have pressed political leaders to pass rent control laws, a price ceiling that usually works by stating that rents can be raised by only a certain maximum percentage each year.

Rent control becomes a politically hot topic when rents begin to rise rapidly. Everyone needs an affordable place to live. Perhaps a change in tastes makes a certain suburb or town a more popular place to live. Perhaps locally-based businesses expand, bringing higher incomes and more people into the area. Changes of this sort can cause a change in the demand for rental housing, as Figure 1 illustrates. The original equilibrium (E_0) lies at the intersection of supply curve S_0 and demand curve D_0, corresponding to an equilibrium price of $500 and an equilibrium quantity of 15,000 units of rental housing. The effect of greater income or a change in tastes is to shift the demand curve for rental housing to the right, as shown by the data in Table 10 and the shift from D_0 to D_1 on the graph. In this market, at the new equilibrium E_1, the price of a rental unit would rise to $600 and the equilibrium quantity would increase to 17,000 units.

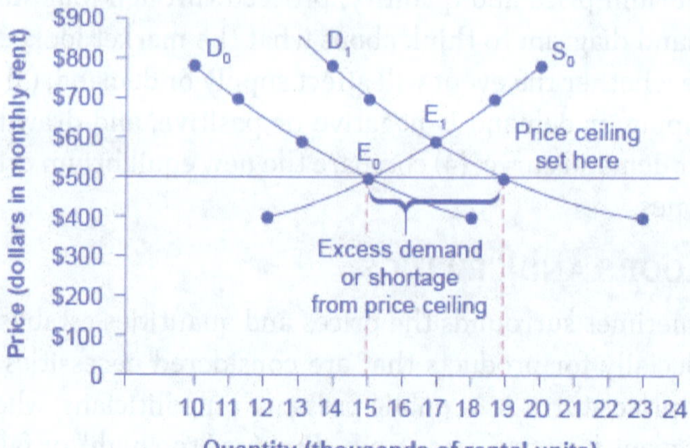

Figure 1. A Price Ceiling Example—Rent Control. The original intersection of demand and supply occurs at E0. If demand shifts from D0 to D1, the new equilibrium would be at E1—unless a price ceiling prevents the price from rising. If the price is not permitted to rise, the quantity supplied remains at 15,000. However, after the change in demand, the quantity demanded rises to 19,000, resulting in a shortage.

Table 10. Rent Control

Price	Original Quantity Supplied	Original Quantity Demanded	New Quantity Demanded
$400	12,000	18,000	23,000
$500	15,000	15,000	19,000
$600	17,000	13,000	17,000
$700	19,000	11,000	15,000
$800	20,000	10,000	14,000

Suppose that a rent control law is passed to keep the price at the original equilibrium of $500 for a typical apartment. In Figure 1, the horizontal line at the price of $500 shows the legally fixed maximum price set by the rent control law. However, the underlying forces that shifted the demand curve to the right are still there. At that price ($500), the quantity supplied remains at the same 15,000 rental units, but the quantity demanded is 19,000 rental units. In other words, the quantity demanded exceeds the quantity supplied, so there is a shortage of rental housing. One of the ironies of price ceilings is that while the price ceiling was intended to help renters, there are actually fewer apartments rented out under the price ceiling (15,000 rental units) than would be the case at the market rent of $600 (17,000 rental units).

Price ceilings do not simply benefit renters at the expense of landlords. Rather, some renters (or potential renters) lose their housing as landlords convert apartments to co-ops and condos. Even when the housing remains in the rental market, landlords tend to spend less on maintenance and on essentials like heating, cooling, hot water, and lighting. The first rule of economics is you do not get something for nothing—everything has an opportunity cost. So if renters get "cheaper" housing than the market requires, they tend to also end up with lower quality housing.

Price ceilings have been proposed for other products. For example, price ceilings to limit what producers can charge have been proposed in recent years for prescription drugs, doctor and hospital fees, the charges made by some automatic teller bank machines, and auto insurance rates. Price ceilings are enacted in an attempt to keep prices low for those who demand the product. But when the market price is not allowed to rise to the equilibrium level, quantity demanded exceeds quantity supplied, and thus a shortage occurs. Those who manage to purchase the product at the lower price given by the price ceiling will benefit, but sellers of the product will suffer, along with those who are not able to purchase the product at all. Quality is also likely to deteriorate.

Price Floors

A price floor is the lowest legal price that can be paid in markets for goods and services, labor, or financial capital. Perhaps the best-known example of a price floor is the minimum wage, which is based on the normative view that someone working full time ought to be able to afford a basic standard of living. The federal minimum wage at the end of 2014 was $7.25 per hour, which yields an income for a single person slightly higher than the poverty line. As the cost of living rises over time, the Congress periodically raises the federal minimum wage.

Price floors are sometimes called "price supports," because they support a price by preventing it from falling below a certain level. Around the world, many countries have passed laws to create agricultural price supports. Farm prices and thus farm incomes fluctuate, sometimes widely. So even if, on average, farm incomes are adequate, some years they can be quite low. The purpose of price supports is to prevent these swings.

The most common way price supports work is that the government enters the market and buys up the product, adding to demand to keep prices higher than they otherwise would be. According to the Common Agricultural Policy reform passed in 2013, the European Union (EU) will spend about 60 billion euros per year, or 67 billion dollars per year, or roughly 38% of the EU budget, on price supports for Europe's farmers from 2014 to 2020.

Figure 2 illustrates the effects of a government program that assures a price above the equilibrium by focusing on the market for wheat in Europe. In the absence of government intervention, the price would adjust so that the quantity supplied would equal the quantity demanded at the equilibrium point E0, with price P0 and quantity Q0. However, policies to keep prices high for farmers keeps the price above what would have been the market equilibrium level—the price Pf shown by the dashed horizontal line in the diagram. The result is a quantity supplied in excess of the quantity demanded (Qd). When quantity supplied exceeds quantity demanded, a surplus exists.

The high-income areas of the world, including the United States, Europe, and Japan, are estimated to spend roughly $1 billion per day in supporting their farmers. If the government is willing to purchase the excess supply (or to provide payments for others to purchase it), then farmers will benefit from the price floor, but taxpayers and consumers of food will pay the costs. Numerous proposals have been offered for reducing farm subsidies. In many countries, however, political support for subsidies for farmers remains strong. Either because this is viewed by the population as supporting the traditional rural way of life or because of the lobbying power of the agro-business industry.

For more detail on the effects price ceilings and floors have on demand and supply, see the following Clear It Up feature.

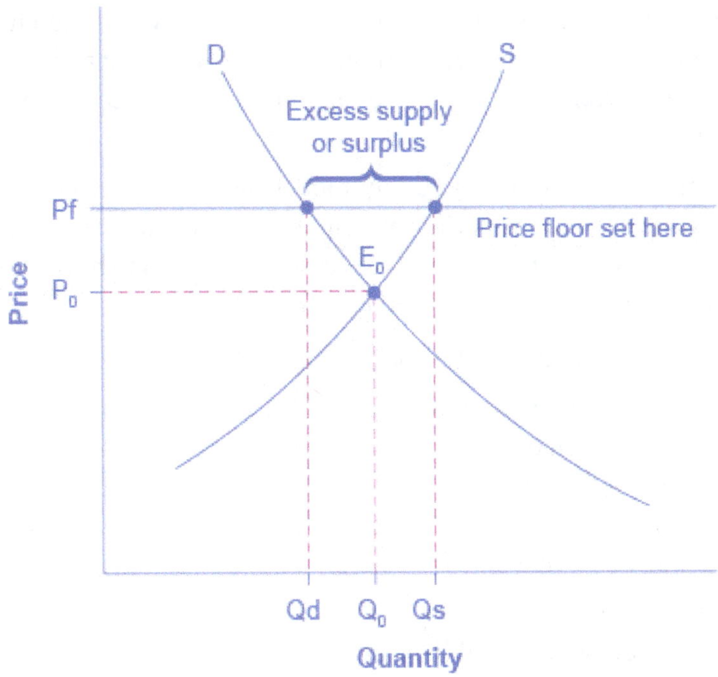

Figure 2. European Wheat Prices: A Price Floor Example. The intersection of demand (D) and supply (S) would be at the equilibrium point E0. However, a price floor set at Pf holds the price above E0 and prevents it from falling. The result of the price floor is that the quantity supplied Qs exceeds the quantity demanded Qd. There is excess supply, also called a surplus.

Do price ceilings and floors change demand or supply?

Neither price ceilings nor price floors cause demand or supply to change. They simply set a price that limits what can be legally charged in the market. Remember, changes in price do not cause demand or supply to change. Price ceilings and price floors can cause a different choice of quantity demanded along a demand curve, but they do not move the demand curve. Price controls can cause a different choice of quantity supplied along a supply curve, but they do not shift the supply curve.

Concepts and Summary

Price ceilings prevent a price from rising above a certain level. When a price ceiling is set below the equilibrium price, quantity demanded will exceed quantity supplied, and excess demand or shortages will result. Price floors prevent a price from falling below a certain level. When a price floor is set above the equilibrium price, quantity supplied will exceed quantity demanded, and excess supply or surpluses will result. Price floors and price ceilings often lead to unintended consequences.

4.5 DEMAND, SUPPLY, AND EFFICIENCY

The familiar demand and supply diagram holds within it the concept of economic efficiency. One typical way that economists define efficiency is when it is impossible to improve the situation of one party without imposing a cost on another. Conversely, if a situation is inefficient, it becomes possible to benefit at least one party without imposing costs on others.

Efficiency in the demand and supply model has the same basic meaning: The economy is getting as much benefit as possible from its scarce resources and all the possible gains from trade have been achieved. In other words, the optimal amount of each good and service is being produced and consumed.

Consumer Surplus, Producer Surplus, Social Surplus

Consider a market for tablet computers, as shown in Figure 1. The equilibrium price is $80 and the equilibrium quantity is 28 million. To see the benefits to consumers, look at the segment of the demand curve above the equilibrium point and to the left. This portion of the demand curve shows that at least some demanders would have been willing to pay more than $80 for a tablet.

For example, point J shows that if the price was $90, 20 million tablets would be sold. Those consumers who would have been willing to pay $90 for a tablet based on the utility they expect to receive from it, but who were able to pay the equilibrium price of $80, clearly received a benefit beyond what they had to pay for. Remember, the demand curve traces consumers' willingness to pay for different quantities. The amount that individuals would have been willing to pay, minus the amount that they actually paid, is called **consumer surplus.** Consumer surplus is the area labeled F—that is, the area above the market price and below the demand curve.

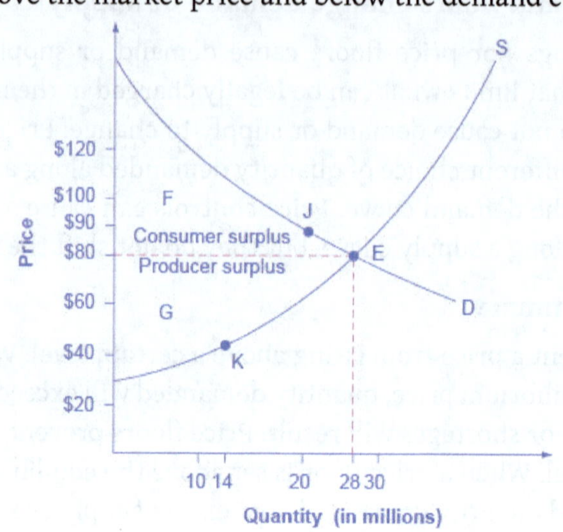

Figure 1. Consumer and Producer Surplus. The somewhat triangular area labeled by F shows the area of consumer surplus, which shows that the equilibrium price in the market was less than what many of the

consumers were willing to pay. Point J on the demand curve shows that, even at the price of $90, consumers would have been willing to purchase a quantity of 20 million. The somewhat triangular area labeled by G shows the area of producer surplus, which shows that the equilibrium price received in the market was more than what many of the producers were willing to accept for their products. For example, point K on the supply curve shows that at a price of $45, firms would have been willing to supply a quantity of 14 million.

The supply curve shows the quantity that firms are willing to supply at each price. For example, point K in Figure 1 illustrates that, at $45, firms would still have been willing to supply a quantity of 14 million. Those producers who would have been willing to supply the tablets at $45, but who were instead able to charge the equilibrium price of $80, clearly received an extra benefit beyond what they required to supply the product. The amount that a seller is paid for a good minus the seller's actual cost is called producer surplus. In Figure 1, producer surplus is the area labeled G—that is, the area between the market price and the segment of the supply curve below the equilibrium.

The sum of consumer surplus and producer surplus is **social surplus**, also referred to as **economic surplus** or **total surplus.** In Figure 1, social surplus would be shown as the area F + G. Social surplus is larger at equilibrium quantity and price than it would be at any other quantity. This demonstrates the economic efficiency of the market equilibrium. In addition, at the efficient level of output, it is impossible to produce greater consumer surplus without reducing producer surplus, and it is impossible to produce greater producer surplus without reducing consumer surplus.

INEFFICIENCY OF PRICE FLOORS AND PRICE CEILINGS

The imposition of a price floor or a price ceiling will prevent a market from adjusting to its equilibrium price and quantity, and thus will create an inefficient outcome. But there is an additional twist here. Along with creating inefficiency, price floors and ceilings will also transfer some consumer surplus to producers, or some producer surplus to consumers.

Imagine that several firms develop a promising but expensive new drug for treating back pain. If this therapy is left to the market, the equilibrium price will be $600 per month and 20,000 people will use the drug, as shown in Figure 2 (a). The original level of consumer surplus is T + U and producer surplus is V + W + X. However, the government decides to impose a price ceiling of $400 to make the drug more affordable. At this price ceiling, firms in the market now produce only 15,000.

As a result, two changes occur. First, an inefficient outcome occurs and the total surplus of society is reduced. The loss in social surplus that occurs when the economy produces at an inefficient quantity is called deadweight loss. In a very real sense, it is like money thrown away that benefits no one. In Figure 2 (a), the deadweight loss is the area U + W. When deadweight loss exists, it is possible for both consumer and producer surplus to be higher, in this case because the price control is blocking some suppliers and demanders from transactions they would both be willing to make.

A second change from the price ceiling is that some of the producer surplus is transferred to consumers. After the price ceiling is imposed, the new consumer surplus is T + V, while the new producer surplus is X. In other words, the price ceiling transfers the area of surplus (V) from producers to consumers. Note that the gain to consumers is less than the loss to producers, which is just another way of seeing the deadweight loss.

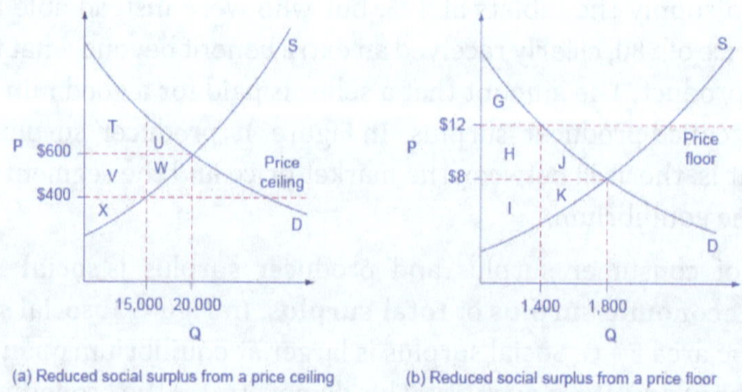

Figure 2. (a) Efficiency and Price Floors and Ceilings. The original equilibrium price is $600 with a quantity of 20,000. Consumer surplus is T + U, and producer surplus is V + W + X. A price ceiling is imposed at $400, so firms in the market now produce only a quantity of 15,000. As a result, the new consumer surplus is T + V, while the new producer surplus is X. (b) The original equilibrium is $8 at a quantity of 1,800. Consumer surplus is G + H + J, and producer surplus is I + K. A price floor is imposed at $12, which means that quantity demanded falls to 1,400. As a result, the new consumer surplus is G, and the new producer surplus is H + I.

Figure 2 (b) shows a price floor example using a string of struggling movie theaters, all in the same city. The current equilibrium is $8 per movie ticket, with 1,800 people attending movies. The original consumer surplus is G + H + J, and producer surplus is I + K. The city government is worried that movie theaters will go out of business, reducing the entertainment options available to citizens, so it decides to impose a price floor of $12 per ticket. As a result, the quantity demanded of movie tickets falls to 1,400. The new consumer surplus is G, and the new producer surplus is H + I. In effect, the price floor causes the area H to be transferred from consumer to producer surplus, but also causes a deadweight loss of J + K.

This analysis shows that a price ceiling, like a law establishing rent controls, will transfer some producer surplus to consumers—which helps to explain why consumers often favor them. Conversely, a price floor like a guarantee that farmers will receive a certain price for their crops will transfer some consumer surplus to producers, which explains why producers often favor them. However, both price floors and price ceilings block some transactions that buyers and sellers would have been willing to make, and creates deadweight loss. Removing such barriers, so that prices and quantities can adjust to their equilibrium level, will increase the economy's social surplus.

Demand and Supply as a Social Adjustment Mechanism

The demand and supply model emphasizes that prices are not set only by demand or only by supply, but by the interaction between the two. In 1890, the famous economist Alfred Marshall wrote that asking whether supply or demand determined a price was like arguing "whether it is the upper or the under blade of a pair of scissors that cuts a piece of paper." The answer is that both blades of the demand and supply scissors are always involved.

The adjustments of equilibrium price and quantity in a market-oriented economy often occur without much government direction or oversight. If the coffee crop in Brazil suffers a terrible frost, then the supply curve of coffee shifts to the left and the price of coffee rises. Some people—call them the coffee addicts—continue to drink coffee and pay the higher price. Others switch to tea or soft drinks. No government commission is needed to figure out how to adjust coffee prices, which companies will be allowed to process the remaining supply, which supermarkets in which cities will get how much coffee to sell, or which consumers will ultimately be allowed to drink the brew. Such adjustments in response to price changes happen all the time in a market economy, often so smoothly and rapidly that we barely notice them.

Think for a moment of all the seasonal foods that are available and inexpensive at certain times of the year, like fresh corn in midsummer, but more expensive at other times of the year. People alter their diets and restaurants alter their menus in response to these fluctuations in prices without fuss or fanfare. For both the U.S. economy and the world economy as a whole, markets—that is, demand and supply—are the primary social mechanism for answering the basic questions about what is produced, how it is produced, and for whom it is produced.

Why Can We Not Get Enough of Organic?

Organic food is grown without synthetic pesticides, chemical fertilizers or genetically modified seeds. In recent decades, the demand for organic products has increased dramatically. The Organic Trade Association reported sales increased from $1 billion in 1990 to $35.1 billion in 2013, more than 90% of which were sales of food products.

Why, then, are organic foods more expensive than their conventional counterparts? The answer is a clear application of the theories of supply and demand. As people have learned more about the harmful effects of chemical fertilizers, growth hormones, pesticides and the like from large-scale factory farming, our tastes and preferences for safer, organic foods have increased. This change in tastes has been reinforced by increases in income, which allow people to purchase pricier products, and has made organic foods more mainstream. This has led to an increased demand for organic foods. Graphically, the demand curve has shifted right, and we have moved up the supply curve as producers have responded to the higher prices by supplying a greater quantity.

In addition to the movement along the supply curve, we have also had an increase in the number of farmers converting to organic farming over time. This is represented by a shift to the right of the supply curve. Since both demand and supply have shifted to the right, the resulting equilibrium quantity of organic foods is definitely higher, but the price will only fall when the increase in supply is larger than the increase in demand. We may need more time before we see lower prices in organic foods. Since the production costs of these foods may remain higher than conventional farming, because organic fertilizers and pest management techniques are more expensive, they may never fully catch up with the lower prices of non-organic foods.

As a final, specific example: The Environmental Working Group's "Dirty Dozen" list of fruits and vegetables, which test high for pesticide residue even after washing, was released in April 2013. The inclusion of strawberries on the list has led to an increase in demand for organic strawberries, resulting in both a higher equilibrium price and quantity of sales.

Concepts and Summary

Consumer surplus is the gap between the price that consumers are willing to pay, based on their preferences, and the market equilibrium price. Producer surplus is the gap between the price for which producers are willing to sell a product, based on their costs, and the market equilibrium price. Social surplus is the sum of consumer surplus and producer surplus. Total surplus is larger at the equilibrium quantity and price than it will be at any other quantity and price. Deadweight loss is loss in total surplus that occurs when the economy produces at an inefficient quantity.

CHAPTER

LABOR AND FINANCIAL MARKETS 5

Introduction to Labor and Financial Markets

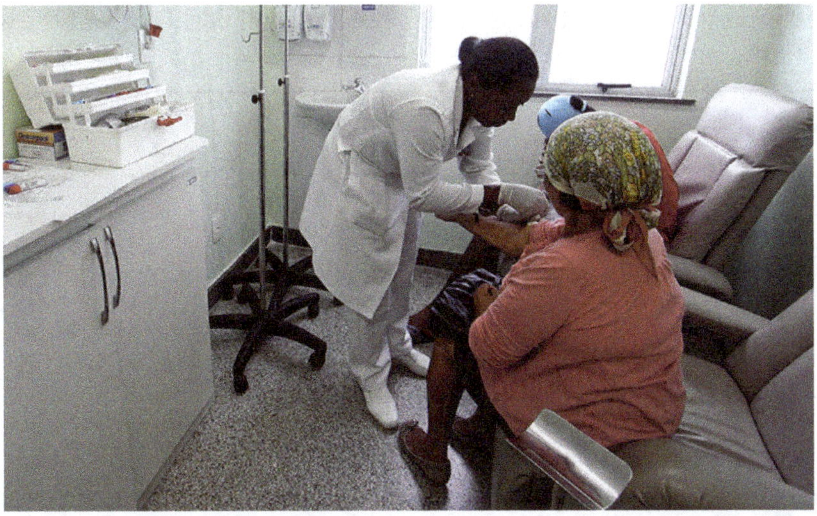

People often think of demand and supply in relation to goods, but labor markets, such as the nursing profession, can also apply to this analysis. (Credit: modification of work by "Fotos GOVBA"/Flickr Creative Commons)

Baby Boomers Come of Age

The Census Bureau reports that as of 2013, 20% of the U.S. population was over 60 years old, which means that almost 63 million people are reaching an age when they will need increased medical care.

The baby boomer population, the group born between 1946 and 1964, is comprised of approximately 74 million people who have just reached retirement age. As this population grows older, they will be faced with common healthcare issues such as heart conditions, arthritis, and Alzheimer's that may require hospitalization, long-term, or at-home nursing care. Aging baby boomers and advances in life-saving and life-extending technologies will increase the demand for healthcare and nursing. Additionally, the Affordable Care Act, which expands access to healthcare for millions of Americans, will further increase the demand.

According to the Bureau of Labor Statistics, registered nursing jobs are expected to increase by 19% between 2012 and 2022. The median annual wage of $67,930 (in 2012) is also expected to increase. The BLS forecasts that 526,000 new nurses will be needed by 2022. One concern is the low rate of enrollment in nursing programs to help meet the growing demand. According to the American Association of Colleges of Nursing (AACN), enrollment in 2011 increased by only 5.1% due to a shortage of nursing educators and teaching facilities.

These data tell us, as economists, that the market for healthcare professionals, and nurses in particular, will face several challenges. Our study of supply and demand will help us to analyze what might happen in the labor market for nursing and other healthcare professionals, as discussed in the second half of this case at the end of the chapter.

Chapter Objectives

Introduction to Labor and Financial Markets

In this chapter, you will learn about:

- Demand and Supply at Work in Labor Markets
- Demand and Supply in Financial Markets
- The Market System as an Efficient Mechanism for Information

The theories of supply and demand do not apply just to markets for goods. They apply to any market, even markets for labor and financial services. Labor markets are markets for employees or jobs. Financial services markets are markets for saving or borrowing.

When we think about demand and supply curves in goods and services markets, it is easy to picture who the demanders and suppliers are: businesses produce the products and households buy them. Who are the demanders and suppliers in labor and financial service markets? In labor markets job seekers (individuals) are the suppliers of labor, while firms and other employers who hire labor are the demanders for labor. In financial markets, any individual or firm who saves contributes to the supply of money, and any who borrows (person, firm, or government) contributes to the demand for money.

As a college student, you most likely participate in both labor and financial markets. Employment is a fact of life for most college students: In 2011, says the BLS, 52% of undergraduates worked part time and another 20% worked full time. Most college students are also heavily involved in financial markets, primarily as borrowers. Among full-time students, about half take out a loan to help finance their education each year, and those loans average about $6,000 per year. Many students also borrow for other expenses, like purchasing a car. As this chapter will illustrate, we can analyze labor markets and financial markets with the same tools we use to analyze demand and supply in the goods markets.

5.1 DEMAND AND SUPPLY AT WORK IN LABOR MARKETS

Markets for labor have demand and supply curves, just like markets for goods. The law of demand applies in labor markets this way: A higher **salary** or **wage**—that is, a higher price in the labor market—leads to a decrease in the quantity of labor demanded by employers, while a lower salary or wage leads to an increase in the quantity of labor demanded. The law of supply functions in labor markets, too: A higher price for labor leads to a higher quantity of labor supplied; a lower price leads to a lower quantity supplied.

Equilibrium in the Labor Market

In 2013, about 34,000 registered nurses worked in the Minneapolis-St. Paul-Bloomington, Minnesota-Wisconsin metropolitan area, according to the BLS. They worked for a variety of employers: hospitals, doctors' offices, schools, health clinics, and nursing homes. Figure 1 illustrates how demand and supply determine equilibrium in this labor market. The demand and supply schedules in Table 1 list the quantity supplied and quantity demanded of nurses at different salaries.

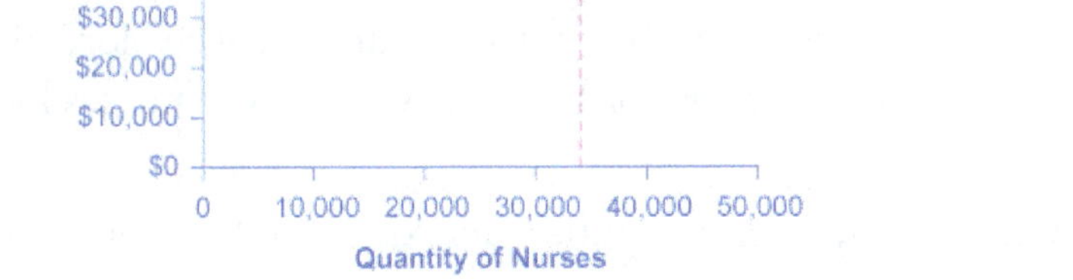

Figure 1. Labor Market Example: Demand and Supply for Nurses in Minneapolis-St. Paul-Bloomington. The demand curve (D) of those employers who want to hire nurses intersects with the supply curve (S) of those who are qualified and willing to work as nurses at the equilibrium point (E). The equilibrium salary is $70,000 and the equilibrium quantity is 34,000 nurses. At an above-equilibrium salary of $75,000, quantity supplied increases to 38,000, but the quantity of nurses demanded at the higher pay declines to 33,000. At this above-equilibrium salary, an excess supply or surplus of nurses would exist. At a below-equilibrium salary of $60,000, quantity supplied declines to 27,000, while the quantity demanded at the lower wage increases to 40,000 nurses. At this below-equilibrium salary, excess demand or a surplus exists.

Table 1. Demand and Supply of Nurses in Minneapolis-St. Paul-Bloomington

Annual Salary	Quantity Demanded	Quantity Supplied
$55,000	45,000	20,000
$60,000	40,000	27,000
$65,000	37,000	31,000
$70,000	34,000	34,000
$75,000	33,000	38,000
$80,000	32,000	41,000

The horizontal axis shows the quantity of nurses hired. In this example, labor is measured by number of workers, but another common way to measure the quantity of labor is by the number of hours worked. The vertical axis shows the price for nurses' labor—that is, how much they are paid. In the real world, this "price" would be total labor compensation: salary plus benefits. It is not obvious, but benefits are a significant part (as high as 30 percent) of labor compensation. In this example, the price of labor is measured by salary on an annual basis, although in other cases the price of labor could be measured by monthly or weekly pay, or even the wage paid per hour. As the salary for nurses rises, the quantity demanded will fall. Some hospitals and nursing homes may cut back on the number of nurses they hire, or they may lay off some of their existing nurses, rather than pay them higher salaries. Employers who face higher nurses' salaries may also try to replace some nursing functions by investing in physical equipment, like computer monitoring and diagnostic systems to monitor patients, or by using lower-paid health care aides to reduce the number of nurses they need.

As the salary for nurses rises, the quantity supplied will rise. If nurses' salaries in Minneapolis-St. Paul-Bloomington are higher than in other cities, more nurses will move to Minneapolis-St. Paul-Bloomington to find jobs, more people will be willing to train as nurses, and those currently trained as nurses will be more likely to pursue nursing as a full-time job. In other words, there will be more nurses looking for jobs in the area.

At **equilibrium**, the quantity supplied and the quantity demanded are equal. Thus, every employer who wants to hire a nurse at this equilibrium wage can find a willing worker, and every nurse who wants to work at this equilibrium salary can find a job. In Figure 1, the supply curve (S) and demand curve (D) intersect at the equilibrium point (E). The equilibrium quantity of nurses in the Minneapolis-St. Paul-Bloomington area is 34,000, and the equilibrium salary is $70,000 per year. This example simplifies the nursing market by focusing on the "average" nurse. In reality, of course, the market for nurses is actually made up of many smaller markets, like markets for nurses with varying degrees of experience and credentials. Many markets contain closely related products that differ in quality; for instance, even a simple product like gasoline comes in regular, premium, and super-premium, each with a different price. Even in such cases, discussing the average price of gasoline, like the average salary for nurses, can still be useful because it reflects what is happening in most of the submarkets.

When the price of labor is not at the equilibrium, economic incentives tend to move salaries toward the equilibrium. For example, if salaries for nurses in Minneapolis-St. Paul-Bloomington were above the equilibrium at $75,000 per year, then 38,000 people want to work as nurses, but employers want to hire only 33,000 nurses. At that above-equilibrium salary, excess supply or a surplus results. In a situation of excess supply in the **labor market**, with many applicants for every job opening, employers will have an incentive to offer lower wages than they otherwise would have. Nurses' salary will move down toward equilibrium.

In contrast, if the salary is below the equilibrium at, say, $60,000 per year, then a situation of excess demand or a shortage arises. In this case, employers encouraged by the relatively lower wage want to hire 40,000 nurses, but only 27,000 individuals want to work as nurses at that salary in Minneapolis-St. Paul-Bloomington. In response to the shortage, some employers will offer higher pay to attract the nurses. Other employers will have to match the higher pay to keep their own employees. The higher salaries will encourage more nurses to train or work in Minneapolis-St. Paul-Bloomington. Again, price and quantity in the labor market will move toward equilibrium.

Shifts in Labor Demand

The demand curve for labor shows the quantity of labor employers wish to hire at any given salary or wage rate, under the ceteris paribus assumption. A change in the wage or salary will result in a change in the quantity demanded of labor. If the wage rate increases, employers will want to hire fewer employees. The quantity of labor demanded will decrease, and there will be a movement upward along the demand curve. If the wages and salaries decrease, employers are more likely to hire a greater number of workers. The quantity of labor demanded will increase, resulting in a downward movement along the demand curve.

Shifts in the demand curve for labor occur for many reasons. One key reason is that the demand for labor is based on the demand for the good or service that is being produced. For example, the more new automobiles consumers demand, the greater the number of workers automakers will need to hire. Therefore the demand for labor is called a "derived demand." Here are some examples of derived demand for labor:

- The demand for chefs is dependent on the demand for restaurant meals.
- The demand for pharmacists is dependent on the demand for prescription drugs.
- The demand for attorneys is dependent on the demand for legal services.

As the demand for the goods and services increases, the demand for labor will increase, or shift to the right, to meet employers' production requirements. As the demand for the goods and services decreases, the demand for labor will decrease, or shift to the left. Table 2 shows that in addition to the derived demand for labor, demand can also increase or decrease (shift) in response to several factors.

Table 2. Factors That Can Shift Demand

Factors	Results
Demand for Output	When the demand for the good produced (output) increases, both the output price and profitability increase. As a result, producers demand more labor to ramp up production.
Education and Training	A well-trained and educated workforce causes an increase in the demand for that labor by employers. Increased levels of productivity within the workforce will cause the demand for labor to shift to the right. If the workforce is not well-trained or educated, employers will not hire from within that labor pool, since they will need to spend a significant amount of time and money training that workforce. Demand for such will shift to the left.
Technology	Technology changes can act as either substitutes for or complements to labor. When technology acts as a substitute, it replaces the need for the number of workers an employer needs to hire. For example, word processing decreased the number of typists needed in the workplace. This shifted the demand curve for typists left. An increase in the availability of certain technologies may increase the demand for labor. Technology that acts as a complement to labor will increase the demand for certain types of labor, resulting in a rightward shift of the demand curve. For example, the increased use of word processing and other software has increased the demand for information technology professionals who can resolve software and hardware issues related to a firm's network. More and better technology will increase demand for skilled workers who know how to use technology to enhance workplace productivity. Those workers who do not adapt to changes in technology will experience a decrease in demand.
Number of Companies	An increase in the number of companies producing a given product will increase the demand for labor resulting in a shift to the right. A decrease in the number of companies producing a given product will decrease the demand for labor resulting in a shift to the left.

Factors	Results
Government Regulations	Complying with government regulations can increase or decrease the demand for labor at any given wage. In the healthcare industry, government rules may require that nurses be hired to carry out certain medical procedures. This will increase the demand for nurses. Less-trained healthcare workers would be prohibited from carrying out these procedures, and the demand for these workers will shift to the left.
Price and Availability of Other Inputs	Labor is not the only input into the production process. For example, a salesperson at a call center needs a telephone and a computer terminal to enter data and record sales. The demand for salespersons at the call center will increase if the number of telephones and computer terminals available increases. This will cause a rightward shift of the demand curve. As the amount of inputs increases, the demand for labor will increase. If the terminal or the telephones malfunction, then the demand for that labor force will decrease. As the quantity of other inputs decreases, the demand for labor will decrease. Similarly, if prices of other inputs fall, production will become more profitable and suppliers will demand more labor to increase production. The opposite is also true. Higher input prices lower demand for labor

Shifts in Labor Supply

The supply of labor is upward-sloping and adheres to the law of supply: The higher the price, the greater the quantity supplied and the lower the price, the less quantity supplied. The supply curve models the tradeoff between supplying labor into the market or using time in leisure activities at every given price level. The higher the wage, the more labor is willing to work and forego leisure activities. Table 3 lists some of the factors that will cause the supply to increase or decrease.

Table 3. Factors that Can Shift Supply

Factors	Results
Number of Workers	An increased number of workers will cause the supply curve to shift to the right. An increased number of workers can be due to several factors, such as immigration, increasing population, an aging population, and changing demographics. Policies that encourage immigration will increase the supply of labor, and vice versa. Population grows when birth rates exceed death rates; this eventually increases supply of labor when the former reach working age. An aging and therefore retiring population will decrease the supply of labor. Another example of changing demographics is more women working outside of the home, which increases the supply of labor.

Factors	Results
Required Education	The more required education, the lower the supply. There is a lower supply of PhD mathematicians than of high school mathematics teachers; there is a lower supply of cardiologists than of primary care physicians; and there is a lower supply of physicians than of nurses.
Government Policies	Government policies can also affect the supply of labor for jobs. On the one hand, the government may support rules that set high qualifications for certain jobs: academic training, certificates or licenses, or experience. When these qualifications are made tougher, the number of qualified workers will decrease at any given wage. On the other hand, the government may also subsidize training or even reduce the required level of qualifications. For example, government might offer subsidies for nursing schools or nursing students. Such provisions would shift the supply curve of nurses to the right. In addition, government policies that change the relative desirability of working versus not working also affect the labor supply. These include unemployment benefits, maternity leave, child care benefits and welfare policy. For example, child care benefits may increase the labor supply of working mothers. Long term unemployment benefits may discourage job searching for unemployed workers. All these policies must therefore be carefully designed to minimize any negative labor supply effects.

A change in salary will lead to a movement along labor demand or labor supply curves, but it will not shift those curves. However, other events like those outlined here will cause either the demand or the supply of labor to shift, and thus will move the labor market to a new equilibrium salary and quantity.

Technology and Wage Inequality: The Four-Step Process

Economic events can change the equilibrium salary (or wage) and quantity of labor. Consider how the wave of new information technologies, like computer and telecommunications networks, has affected low-skill and high-skill workers in the U.S. economy. From the perspective of employers who demand labor, these new technologies are often a substitute for low-skill laborers like file clerks who used to keep file cabinets full of paper records of transactions. However, the same new technologies are a complement to high-skill workers like managers, who benefit from the technological advances by being able to monitor more information, communicate more easily, and juggle a wider array of responsibilities. So, how will the new technologies affect the wages of high-skill and low-skill workers? For this question, the four-step process of analyzing how shifts in supply or demand affect a market (introduced in Demand and Supply) works in this way:

Step 1. What did the markets for low-skill labor and high-skill labor look like before the arrival of the new technologies? In Figure 2 (a) and Figure 2 (b), S_0 is the original supply curve for labor and D_0 is the original demand curve for labor in each market. In each graph, the original point of equilibrium, E_0, occurs at the price W_0 and the quantity Q_0.

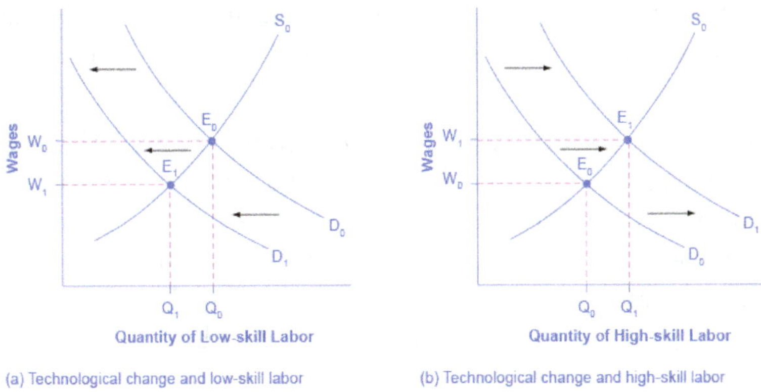

Figure 2. Technology and Wages: Applying Demand and Supply (a) The demand for low-skill labor shifts to the left when technology can do the job previously done by these workers. (b) New technologies can also increase the demand for high-skill labor in fields such as information technology and network administration.

Step 2. Does the new technology affect the supply of labor from households or the demand for labor from firms? The technology change described here affects demand for labor by firms that hire workers.

Step 3. Will the new technology increase or decrease demand? Based on the description earlier, as the substitute for low-skill labor becomes available, demand for low-skill labor will shift to the left, from D_0 to D_1. As the technology complement for high-skill labor becomes cheaper, demand for high-skill labor will shift to the right, from D_0 to D_1.

Step 4. The new equilibrium for low-skill labor, shown as point E_1 with price W_1 and quantity Q_1, has a lower wage and quantity hired than the original equilibrium, E_0. The new equilibrium for high-skill labor, shown as point E_1 with price W_1 and quantity Q_1, has a higher wage and quantity hired than the original equilibrium (E_0).

So, the demand and supply model predicts that the new computer and communications technologies will raise the pay of high-skill workers but reduce the pay of low-skill workers. Indeed, from the 1970s to the mid-2000s, the wage gap widened between high-skill and low-skill labor. According to the National Center for Education Statistics, in 1980, for example, a college graduate earned about 30% more than a high school graduate with comparable job experience, but by 2012, a college graduate earned about 60% more than an otherwise comparable high school graduate. Many economists believe that the trend toward greater wage inequality across the U.S. economy was primarily caused by the new technologies.

PRICE FLOORS IN THE LABOR MARKET: LIVING WAGES AND MINIMUM WAGES

In contrast to goods and services markets, price ceilings are rare in labor markets, because rules that prevent people from earning income are not politically popular. There is one exception: sometimes limits are proposed on the high incomes of top business executives.

The labor market, however, presents some prominent examples of price floors, which are often used as an attempt to increase the wages of low-paid workers. The U.S. government sets a **minimum wage**, a price floor that makes it illegal for an employer to pay employees less than a certain hourly rate. In mid-2009, the U.S. minimum wage was raised to $7.25 per hour. Local political movements in a number of U.S. cities have pushed for a higher minimum wage, which they call a **living wage.** Promoters of living wage laws maintain that the minimum wage is too low to ensure a reasonable standard of living. They base this conclusion on the calculation that, if you work 40 hours a week at a minimum wage of $7.25 per hour for 50 weeks a year, your annual income is $14,500, which is less than the official U.S. government definition of what it means for a family to be in poverty. (A family with two adults earning minimum wage and two young children will find it more cost efficient for one parent to provide childcare while the other works for income. So the family income would be $14,500, which is significantly lower than the federal poverty line for a family of four, which was $23,850 in 2014.)

Supporters of the living wage argue that full-time workers should be assured a high enough wage so that they can afford the essentials of life: food, clothing, shelter, and healthcare. Since Baltimore passed the first living wage law in 1994, several dozen cities enacted similar laws in the late 1990s and the 2000s. The living wage ordinances do not apply to all employers, but they have specified that all employees of the city or employees of firms that are hired by the city be paid at least a certain wage that is usually a few dollars per hour above the U.S. minimum wage.

Figure 3 illustrates the situation of a city considering a living wage law. For simplicity, we assume that there is no federal minimum wage. The wage appears on the vertical axis, because the wage is the price in the labor market. Before the passage of the living wage law, the equilibrium wage is $10 per hour and the city hires 1,200 workers at this wage. However, a group of concerned citizens persuades the city council to enact a living wage law requiring employers to pay no less than $12 per hour. In response to the higher wage, 1,600 workers look for jobs with the city. At this higher wage, the city, as an employer, is willing to hire only 700 workers. At the price floor, the quantity supplied exceeds the quantity demanded, and a surplus of labor exists in this market. For workers who continue to have a job at a higher salary, life has improved. For those who were willing to work at the old wage rate but lost their jobs with the wage increase, life has not improved. Table 4 shows the differences in supply and demand at different wages.

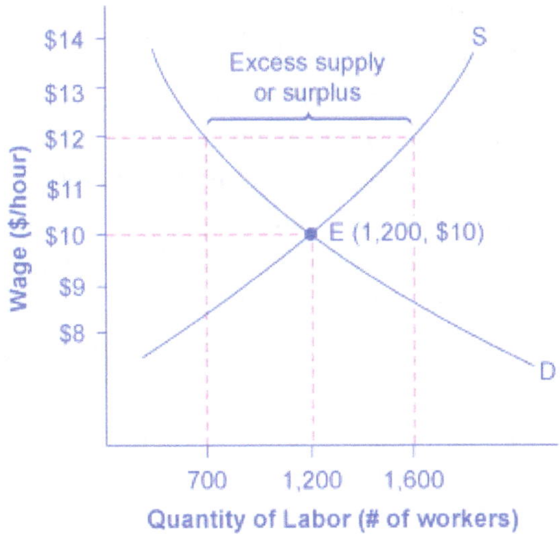

Figure 3. A Living Wage: Example of a Price Floor The original equilibrium in this labor market is a wage of $10/hour and a quantity of 1,200 workers, shown at point E. Imposing a wage floor at $12/hour leads to an excess supply of labor. At that wage, the quantity of labor supplied is 1,600 and the quantity of labor demanded is only 700.

Table 4. Living Wage: Example of a Price Floor

Wage	Quantity Labor Demanded	Quantity Labor Supplied
$8/hr	1,900	500
$9/hr	1,500	900
$10/hr	1,200	1,200
$11/hr	900	1,400
$12/hr	700	1,600
$13/hr	500	1,800
$14/hr	400	1,900

The Minimum Wage as an Example of a Price Floor

The U.S. minimum wage is a price floor that is set either very close to the equilibrium wage or even slightly below it. About 1% of American workers are actually paid the minimum wage. In other words, the vast majority of the U.S. labor force has its wages determined in the labor market, not as a result of the government price floor. But for workers with low skills and little experience, like those without a high school diploma or teenagers, the minimum wage is quite important. In many cities, the federal minimum wage is apparently below the market price for unskilled labor, because employers offer more than the minimum wage to checkout clerks and other low-skill workers without any government prodding.

Economists have attempted to estimate how much the minimum wage reduces the quantity demanded of low-skill labor. A typical result of such studies is that a 10% increase in the minimum wage would decrease the hiring of unskilled workers by 1 to 2%, which seems a relatively small reduction. In fact, some studies have even found no effect of a higher minimum wage on employment at certain times and places—although these studies are controversial.

Let's suppose that the minimum wage lies just slightly below the equilibrium wage level. Wages could fluctuate according to market forces above this price floor, but they would not be allowed to move beneath the floor. In this situation, the price floor minimum wage is said to be nonbinding —that is, the price floor is not determining the market outcome. Even if the minimum wage moves just a little higher, it will still have no effect on the quantity of employment in the economy, as long as it remains below the equilibrium wage. Even if the minimum wage is increased by enough so that it rises slightly above the equilibrium wage and becomes binding, there will be only a small excess supply gap between the quantity demanded and quantity supplied.

These insights help to explain why U.S. minimum wage laws have historically had only a small impact on employment. Since the minimum wage has typically been set close to the equilibrium wage for low-skill labor and sometimes even below it, it has not had a large effect in creating an excess supply of labor. However, if the minimum wage were increased dramatically—say, if it were doubled to match the living wages that some U.S. cities have considered—then its impact on reducing the quantity demanded of employment would be far greater. The following Clear It Up feature describes in greater detail some of the arguments for and against changes to minimum wage.

WHAT'S THE HARM IN RAISING THE MINIMUM WAGE?

Because of the law of demand, a higher required wage will reduce the amount of low-skill employment either in terms of employees or in terms of work hours. Although there is controversy over the numbers, let's say for the sake of the argument that a 10% rise in the minimum wage will reduce the employment of low-skill workers by 2%. Does this outcome mean that raising the minimum wage by 10% is bad public policy? Not necessarily.

If 98% of those receiving the minimum wage have a pay increase of 10%, but 2% of those receiving the minimum wage lose their jobs, are the gains for society as a whole greater than the losses? The answer is not clear, because job losses, even for a small group, may cause more pain than modest income gains for others. For one thing, we need to consider which minimum wage workers are losing their jobs. If the 2% of minimum wage workers who lose their jobs are struggling to support families, that is one thing. If those who lose their job are high school students picking up spending money over summer vacation, that is something else.

Another complexity is that many minimum wage workers do not work full-time for an entire year. Imagine a minimum wage worker who holds different part-time jobs for a few months at a time, with bouts of unemployment in between. The worker in this situation receives the 10% raise in the minimum wage when working, but also ends up working 2% fewer hours during the year because the higher minimum wage reduces how much employers want people to work. Overall, this worker's income would rise because the 10% pay raise would more than offset the 2% fewer hours worked.

Of course, these arguments do not prove that raising the minimum wage is necessarily a good idea either. There may well be other, better public policy options for helping low-wage workers. (The Poverty and Economic Inequality chapter discusses some possibilities.) The lesson from this maze of minimum wage arguments is that complex social problems rarely have simple answers. Even those who agree on how a proposed economic policy affects quantity demanded and quantity supplied may still disagree on whether the policy is a good idea.

Key Concepts and Summary

In the labor market, households are on the supply side of the market and firms are on the demand side. In the market for financial capital, households and firms can be on either side of the market: they are suppliers of financial capital when they save or make financial investments, and demanders of financial capital when they borrow or receive financial investments.

In the demand and supply analysis of labor markets, the price can be measured by the annual salary or hourly wage received. The quantity of labor can be measured in various ways, like number of workers or the number of hours worked.

Factors that can shift the demand curve for labor include: a change in the quantity demanded of the product that the labor produces; a change in the production process that uses more or less labor; and a change in government policy that affects the quantity of labor that firms wish to hire at a given wage. Demand can also increase or decrease (shift) in response to: workers' level of education and training, technology, the number of companies, and availability and price of other inputs.

The main factors that can shift the supply curve for labor are: how desirable a job appears to workers relative to the alternatives, government policy that either restricts or encourages the quantity of workers trained for the job, the number of workers in the economy, and required education.

5.2 DEMAND AND SUPPLY IN FINANCIAL MARKETS

United States' households, institutions, and domestic businesses saved almost $1.9 trillion in 2013. Where did that savings go and what was it used for? Some of the savings ended up in banks, which in turn loaned the money to individuals or businesses that wanted to borrow money. Some was invested in private companies or loaned to government agencies that wanted to borrow money to raise funds for purposes like building roads or mass transit. Some firms reinvested their savings in their own businesses.

In this section, we will determine how the demand and supply model links those who wish to supply financial capital (i.e., savings) with those who demand financial capital (i.e., borrowing). Those who save money (or make financial investments, which is the same thing), whether individuals or businesses, are on the supply side of the financial market. Those who borrow money are on the demand side of the financial market. For a more detailed treatment of the different kinds of financial investments like bank accounts, stocks and bonds, see the Financial Markets chapter.

Who Demands and Who Supplies in Financial Markets?

In any market, the price is what suppliers receive and what demanders pay. In financial markets, those who supply financial capital through saving expect to receive a rate of return, while those who demand financial capital by receiving funds expect to pay a rate of return. This rate of return can come in a variety of forms, depending on the type of investment.

The simplest example of a rate of return is the **interest rate**. For example, when you supply money into a savings account at a bank, you receive interest on your deposit. The interest paid to you as a percent of your deposits is the interest rate. Similarly, if you demand a loan to buy a car or a computer, you will need to pay interest on the money you borrow.

Let's consider the market for borrowing money with credit cards. In 2014, almost 200 million Americans were cardholders. Credit cards allow you to borrow money from the card's issuer, and pay back the borrowed amount plus interest, though most allow you a period of time in which you can repay the loan without paying interest. A typical credit card interest rate ranges from 12% to 18% per year. In 2014, Americans had about $793 billion outstanding in credit card debts. About half of U.S. families with credit cards report that they almost always pay the full balance on time, but one-quarter of U.S. families with credit cards say that they "hardly ever" pay off the card in full. In fact, in 2014, 56% of consumers carried an unpaid balance in the last 12 months. Let's say that, on average, the annual interest rate for credit card borrowing is 15% per year. So, Americans pay tens of billions of dollars every year in interest on their credit cards—plus basic fees for the credit card or fees for late payments.

Figure 1 illustrates demand and supply in the financial market for credit cards. The horizontal axis of the financial market shows the quantity of money that is loaned or borrowed in this market. The vertical or price axis shows the rate of return, which in the case of credit card borrowing can be measured with an interest rate. Table 5 shows the quantity of financial capital that consumers demand at various interest rates and the quantity that credit card firms (often banks) are willing to supply.

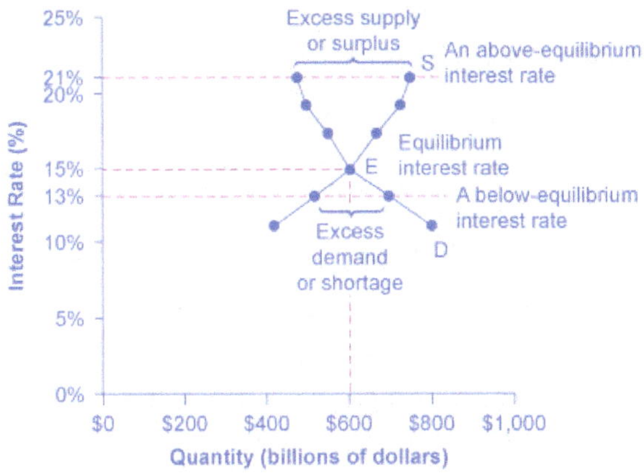

Figure 1. Demand and Supply for Borrowing Money with Credit Cards. In this market for credit card borrowing, the demand curve (D) for borrowing financial capital intersects the supply curve (S) for lending financial capital at equilibrium €. At the equilibrium, the interest rate (the "price" in this market) is 15% and the quantity of financial capital being loaned and borrowed is $600 billion. The equilibrium price is where the quantity demanded and the quantity supplied are equal. At an above-equilibrium interest rate like 21%, the quantity of financial capital supplied would increase to $750 billion, but the quantity demanded would decrease to $480 billion. At a below-equilibrium interest rate like 13%, the quantity of financial capital demanded would increase to $700 billion, but the quantity of financial capital supplied would decrease to $510 billion.

Table 5. Demand and Supply for Borrowing Money with Credit Cards

Interest Rate (%)	Quantity of Financial Capital Demanded (Borrowing) ($ billions)	Quantity of Financial Capital Supplied (Lending) ($ billions)
11	$800	$420
13	$700	$510
15	$600	$600
17	$550	$660
19	$500	$720
21	$480	$750

The laws of demand and supply continue to apply in the financial markets. According to the **law of demand**, a higher rate of return (that is, a higher price) will decrease the quantity demanded. As the interest rate rises, consumers will reduce the quantity that they borrow. According to the law of supply, a higher price increases the quantity supplied. Consequently, as the interest rate paid on credit card borrowing rises, more firms will be eager to issue credit cards and to encourage customers to use them. Conversely, if the interest rate on credit cards falls, the quantity of financial capital supplied in the credit card market will decrease and the quantity demanded will fall.

Equilibrium in Financial Markets

In the financial market for credit cards shown in Figure 1, the supply curve (S) and the demand curve (D) cross at the equilibrium point (E). The equilibrium occurs at an interest rate of 15%, where the quantity of funds demanded and the quantity supplied are equal at an equilibrium quantity of $600 billion.

If the interest rate (remember, this measures the "price" in the financial market) is above the equilibrium level, then an excess supply, or a surplus, of financial capital will arise in this market. For example, at an interest rate of 21%, the quantity of funds supplied increases to $750 billion, while the quantity demanded decreases to $480 billion. At this above-equilibrium interest rate, firms are eager to supply loans to credit card borrowers, but relatively few people or businesses wish to borrow. As a result, some credit card firms will lower the interest rates (or other fees) they charge to attract more business. This strategy will push the interest rate down toward the equilibrium level.

If the interest rate is below the equilibrium, then excess demand or a shortage of funds occurs in this market. At an interest rate of 13%, the quantity of funds credit card borrowers demand increases to $700 billion; but the quantity credit card firms are willing to supply is only $510 billion. In this situation, credit card firms will perceive that they are overloaded with eager borrowers and conclude that they have an opportunity to raise interest rates or fees. The interest rate will face economic pressures to creep up toward the equilibrium level.

SHIFTS IN DEMAND AND SUPPLY IN FINANCIAL MARKETS

Those who supply financial capital face two broad decisions: how much to save, and how to divide up their savings among different forms of financial investments. We will discuss each of these in turn.

Participants in financial markets must decide when they prefer to consume goods: now or in the future. Economists call this intertemporal decision making because it involves decisions across time. Unlike a decision about what to buy from the grocery store, decisions about investment or saving are made across a period of time, sometimes a long period.

Most workers save for retirement because their income in the present is greater than their needs, while the opposite will be true once they retire. So they save today and supply financial markets. If their income increases, they save more. If their perceived situation in the future changes, they change the amount of their saving. For example, there is some evidence that Social Security, the program that workers pay into in order to qualify for government checks after retirement, has tended to reduce the quantity of financial capital that workers save. If this is true, Social Security has shifted the supply of financial capital at any interest rate to the left.

By contrast, many college students need money today when their income is low (or nonexistent) to pay their college expenses. As a result, they borrow today and demand from financial markets. Once they graduate and become employed, they will pay back the loans. Individuals borrow money to purchase homes or cars. A business seeks financial investment so that it has the funds to build a factory or invest in a research and development project that will not pay off for five years, ten years, or even more. So when consumers and businesses have greater confidence that they will be able to repay in the future, the quantity demanded of financial capital at any given interest rate will shift to the right.

For example, in the technology boom of the late 1990s, many businesses became extremely confident that investments in new technology would have a high rate of return, and their demand for financial capital shifted to the right. Conversely, during the Great Recession of 2008 and 2009, their demand for financial capital at any given interest rate shifted to the left.

To this point, we have been looking at saving in total. Now let us consider what affects saving in different types of financial investments. In deciding between different forms of financial investments, suppliers of financial capital will have to consider the rates of return and the risks involved. Rate of return is a positive attribute of investments, but risk is a negative. If Investment A becomes more risky, or the return diminishes, then savers will shift their funds to Investment B—and the supply curve of financial capital for Investment A will shift back to the left while the supply curve of capital for Investment B shifts to the right.

The United States as a Global Borrower

In the global economy, trillions of dollars of financial investment cross national borders every year. In the early 2000s, financial investors from foreign countries were investing several hundred billion dollars per year more in the U.S. economy than U.S. financial investors were investing abroad. The following Work It Out deals with one of the macroeconomic concerns for the U.S. economy in recent years.

The Effect of Growing U.S. Debt

Imagine that the U.S. economy became viewed as a less desirable place for foreign investors to put their money because of fears about the growth of the U.S. public debt. Using the four-step process for analyzing how changes in supply and demand affect equilibrium outcomes, how would increased U.S. public debt affect the equilibrium price and quantity for capital in U.S. financial markets?

Step 1. Draw a diagram showing demand and supply for financial capital that represents the original scenario in which foreign investors are pouring money into the U.S. economy. Figure 2 shows a demand curve, D, and a supply curve, S, where the supply of capital includes the funds arriving from foreign investors. The original equilibrium E0 occurs at interest rate R0 and quantity of financial investment Q0.

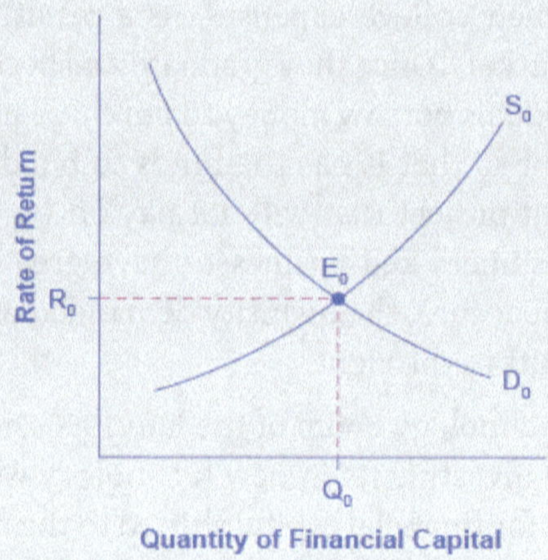

Figure 2. The United States as a Global Borrower Before U.S. Debt Uncertainty. The graph shows the demand for financial capital from and supply of financial capital into the U.S. financial markets by the foreign sector before the increase in uncertainty regarding U.S. public debt. The original equilibrium (E0) occurs at an equilibrium rate of return (R0) and the equilibrium quantity is at Q0.

Step 2. Will the diminished confidence in the U.S. economy as a place to invest affect demand or supply of financial capital? Yes, it will affect supply. Many foreign investors look to the U.S. financial markets to store their money in safe financial vehicles with low risk and stable returns. As the U.S. debt increases, debt servicing will increase—that is, more current income will be used to pay the interest rate on past debt. Increasing U.S. debt also means that businesses may have to pay higher interest rates to borrow money, because business is now competing with the government for financial resources.

Step 3. Will supply increase or decrease? When the enthusiasm of foreign investors' for investing their money in the U.S. economy diminishes, the supply of financial capital shifts to the left. Figure 3 shows the supply curve shift from S0 to S1.

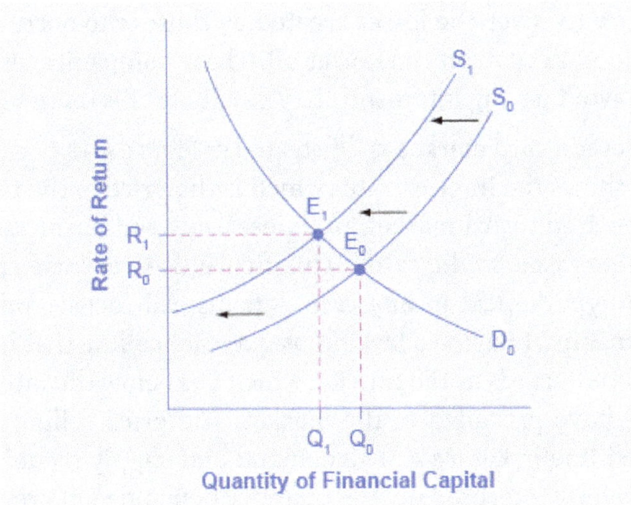

Figure 3. The United States as a Global Borrower Before and After U.S. Debt Uncertainty. The graph shows the demand for financial capital and supply of financial capital into the U.S. financial markets by the foreign sector before and after the increase in uncertainty regarding U.S. public debt. The original equilibrium (E0) occurs at an equilibrium rate of return (R0) and the equilibrium quantity is at Q0.

Step 4. Thus, foreign investors' diminished enthusiasm leads to a new equilibrium, E_1, which occurs at the higher interest rate, R_1, and the lower quantity of financial investment, Q_1.

The economy has experienced an enormous inflow of foreign capital. According to the U.S. Bureau of Economic Analysis, by the third quarter of 2014, U.S. investors had accumulated $24.6 trillion of foreign assets, but foreign investors owned a total of $30.8 trillion of U.S. assets. If foreign investors were to pull their money out of the U.S. economy and invest elsewhere in the world, the result could be a significantly lower quantity of financial investment in the United States, available only at a higher interest rate. This reduced inflow of foreign financial investment could impose hardship on U.S. consumers and firms interested in borrowing.

In a modern, developed economy, financial capital often moves invisibly through electronic transfers between one bank account and another. Yet these flows of funds can be analyzed with the same tools of demand and supply as markets for goods or labor.

PRICE CEILINGS IN FINANCIAL MARKETS: USURY LAWS

As we noted earlier, about 200 million Americans own credit cards, and their interest payments and fees total tens of billions of dollars each year. It is little wonder that political pressures sometimes arise for setting limits on the interest rates or fees that credit card companies charge. The firms that issue credit cards, including banks, oil companies, phone companies, and retail stores, respond that the higher interest rates are necessary to cover the losses created by those who borrow on their credit cards and who do not repay on time or at all. These companies also point out that cardholders can avoid paying interest if they pay their bills on time.

Consider the credit card market as illustrated in Figure 4. In this financial market, the vertical axis shows the interest rate (which is the price in the financial market). Demanders in the credit card market are households and businesses; suppliers are the companies that issue credit cards. This figure does not use specific numbers, which would be hypothetical in any case, but instead focuses on the underlying economic relationships. Imagine a law imposes a price ceiling that holds the interest rate charged on credit cards at the rate Rc, which lies below the interest rate R0 that would otherwise have prevailed in the market. The price ceiling is shown by the horizontal dashed line in Figure 4. The demand and supply model predicts that at the lower price ceiling interest rate, the quantity demanded of credit card debt will increase from its original level of Q0 to Qd; however, the quantity supplied of credit card debt will decrease from the original Q0 to Qs. At the price ceiling (Rc), quantity demanded will exceed quantity supplied. Consequently, a number of people who want to have credit cards and are willing to pay the prevailing interest rate will find that companies are unwilling to issue cards to them. The result will be a credit shortage.

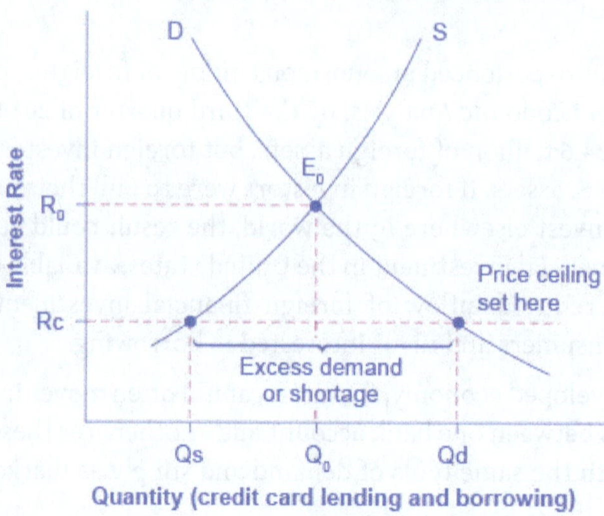

Figure 4. Credit Card Interest Rates: Another Price Ceiling Example. The original intersection of demand D and supply S occurs at equilibrium E0. However, a price ceiling is set at the interest rate Rc, below the equilibrium interest rate R0, and so the interest rate cannot adjust upward to the equilibrium. At the price ceiling, the quantity demanded, Qd, exceeds the quantity supplied, Qs. There is excess demand, also called a shortage.

Many states do have **usury laws**, which impose an upper limit on the interest rate that lenders can charge. However, in many cases these upper limits are well above the market interest rate. For example, if the interest rate is not allowed to rise above 30% per year, it can still fluctuate below that level according to market forces. A price ceiling that is set at a relatively high level is nonbinding, and it will have no practical effect unless the equilibrium price soars high enough to exceed the price ceiling.

KEY CONCEPTS AND SUMMARY

In the demand and supply analysis of financial markets, the "price" is the rate of return or the interest rate received. The quantity is measured by the money that flows from those who supply financial capital to those who demand it.

Two factors can shift the supply of financial capital to a certain investment: if people want to alter their existing levels of consumption, and if the riskiness or return on one investment changes relative to other investments. Factors that can shift demand for capital include business confidence and consumer confidence in the future—since financial investments received in the present are typically repaid in the future.

5.3 THE MARKET SYSTEM AS AN EFFICIENT MECHANISM FOR INFORMATION

Prices exist in markets for goods and services, for labor, and for financial capital. In all of these markets, prices serve as a remarkable social mechanism for collecting, combining, and transmitting information that is relevant to the market—namely, the relationship between demand and supply—and then serving as messengers to convey that information to buyers and sellers. In a market-oriented economy, no government agency or guiding intelligence oversees the set of responses and interconnections that result from a change in price. Instead, each consumer reacts according to that person's preferences and budget set, and each profit-seeking producer reacts to the impact on its expected profits. The following Clear It Up feature examines the **demand and supply models**.

Why are demand and supply curves important?

The demand and supply model is the second fundamental diagram for this course. (The opportunity set model introduced in the Choice in a World of Scarcity chapter was the first.) Just as it would be foolish to try to learn the arithmetic of long division by memorizing every possible combination of numbers that can be divided by each other, it would be foolish to try to memorize every specific example of demand and supply in this chapter, this textbook, or this course. Demand and supply is not primarily a list of examples; it is a model to analyze prices and quantities. Even though demand and supply diagrams have many labels, they are fundamentally the same in their logic. Your goal should be to understand the underlying model so you can use it to analyze any market.

Figure 1 displays a generic demand and supply curve. The horizontal axis shows the different measures of quantity: a quantity of a good or service, or a quantity of labor for a given job, or a quantity of financial capital. The vertical axis shows a measure of price: the price of a good or service, the wage in the labor market, or the rate of return (like the interest rate) in the financial market.

The demand and supply model can explain the existing levels of prices, wages, and rates of return. To carry out such an analysis, think about the quantity that will be demanded at each price and the quantity that will be supplied at each price—that is, think about the shape of the demand and supply curves—and how these forces will combine to produce equilibrium.

Demand and supply can also be used to explain how economic events will cause changes in prices, wages, and rates of return. There are only four possibilities: the change in any single event may cause the demand curve to shift right or to shift left; or it may cause the supply curve to shift right or to shift left. The key to analyzing the effect of an economic event on equilibrium prices and quantities is to determine which of these four possibilities occurred. The way to do this correctly is to think back to the list of factors that shift the demand and supply curves. Note that if more than one variable is changing at the same time, the overall impact will depend on the degree of the shifts; when there are multiple variables, economists isolate each change and analyze it independently.

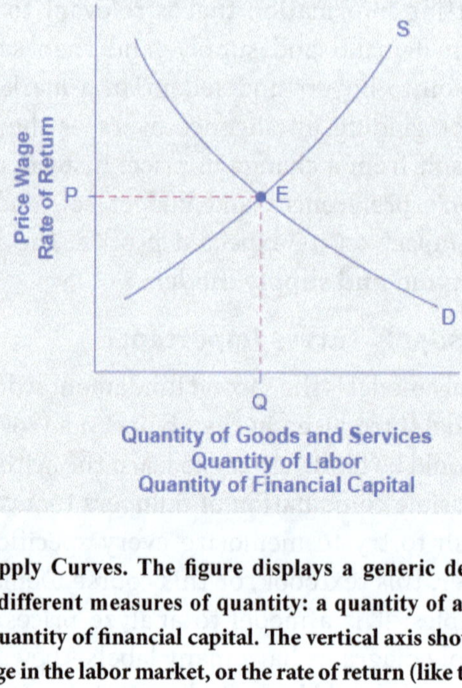

Figure 1. Demand and Supply Curves. The figure displays a generic demand and supply curve. The horizontal axis shows the different measures of quantity: a quantity of a good or service, a quantity of labor for a given job, or a quantity of financial capital. The vertical axis shows a measure of price: the price of a good or service, the wage in the labor market, or the rate of return (like the interest rate) in the financial market. The demand and supply curves can be used to explain how economic events will cause changes in prices, wages, and rates of return.

An increase in the price of some product signals consumers that there is a shortage and the product should perhaps be economized on. For example, if you are thinking about taking a plane trip to Hawaii, but the ticket turns out to be expensive during the week you intend to go, you might consider other weeks when the ticket might be cheaper. The price could be high because you were planning to travel during a holiday when demand for traveling is high. Or, maybe the cost of an input like jet fuel increased or the airline has raised the price temporarily to see how many people are willing to pay it. Perhaps all of these factors are present at the same time. You do not need to analyze the market and break down the price change into its underlying factors. You just have to look at the price of a ticket and decide whether and when to fly.

In the same way, price changes provide useful information to producers. Imagine the situation of a farmer who grows oats and learns that the price of oats has risen. The higher price could be due to an increase in demand caused by a new scientific study proclaiming that eating oats is especially healthful. Or perhaps the price of a substitute grain, like corn, has risen, and people have responded by buying more oats. But the oat farmer does not need to know the details. The farmer only needs to know that the price of oats has risen and that it will be profitable to expand production as a result.

The actions of individual consumers and producers as they react to prices overlap and interlock in markets for goods, labor, and financial capital. A change in any single market is transmitted through these multiple interconnections to other markets. The vision of the role of flexible prices helping markets to reach equilibrium and linking different markets together helps to explain why price controls can be so counterproductive. Price controls are government laws that serve to regulate prices rather than allow the various markets to determine prices. There is an old proverb: "Don't kill the messenger." In ancient times, messengers carried information between distant cities and kingdoms. When they brought bad news, there was an emotional impulse to kill the messenger. But killing the messenger did not kill the bad news. Moreover, killing the messenger had an undesirable side effect: Other messengers would refuse to bring news to that city or kingdom, depriving its citizens of vital information.

Those who seek price controls are trying to kill the messenger—or at least to stifle an unwelcome message that prices are bringing about the equilibrium level of price and quantity. But price controls do nothing to affect the underlying forces of demand and supply, and this can have serious repercussions. During China's "Great Leap Forward" in the late 1950s, food prices were kept artificially low, with the result that 30 to 40 million people died of starvation because the low prices depressed farm production. Changes in demand and supply will continue to reveal themselves through consumers' and producers' behavior. Immobilizing the price messenger through price controls will deprive everyone in the economy of critical information. Without this information, it becomes difficult for everyone—buyers and sellers alike—to react in a flexible and appropriate manner as changes occur throughout the economy.

Baby Boomers Come of Age

The theory of supply and demand can explain what happens in the labor markets and suggests that the demand for nurses will increase as healthcare needs of baby boomers increase, as Figure 2 shows. The impact of that increase will result in an average salary higher than the $67,930 earned in 2012 referenced in the first part of this case. The new equilibrium (E1) will be at the new equilibrium price (Pe1). Equilibrium quantity will also increase from Qe0 to Qe1.

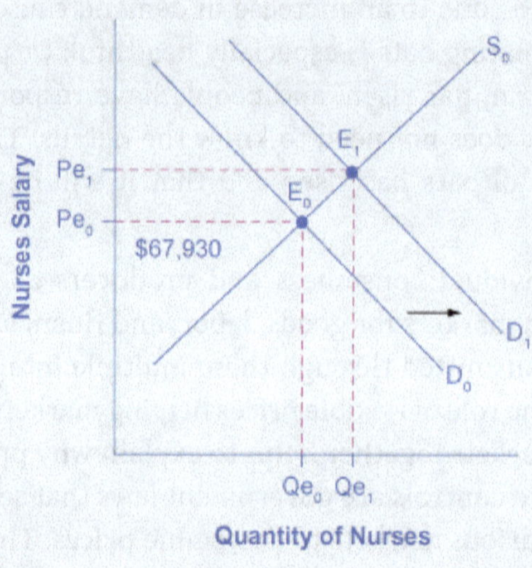

Figure 2. Impact of Increasing Demand for Nurses 2012-2022. In 2012, the median salary for nurses was $67,930. As demand for services increases, the demand curve shifts to the right (from D0 to D1) and the equilibrium quantity of nurses increases from Qe0 to Qe1. The equilibrium salary increases from Pe0 to Pe1.

Suppose that as the demand for nurses increases, the supply shrinks due to an increasing number of nurses entering retirement and increases in the tuition of nursing degrees. The impact of a decreasing supply of nurses is captured by the leftward shift of the supply curve in Figure 3 The shifts in the two curves result in higher salaries for nurses, but the overall impact in the quantity of nurses is uncertain, as it depends on the relative shifts of supply and demand.

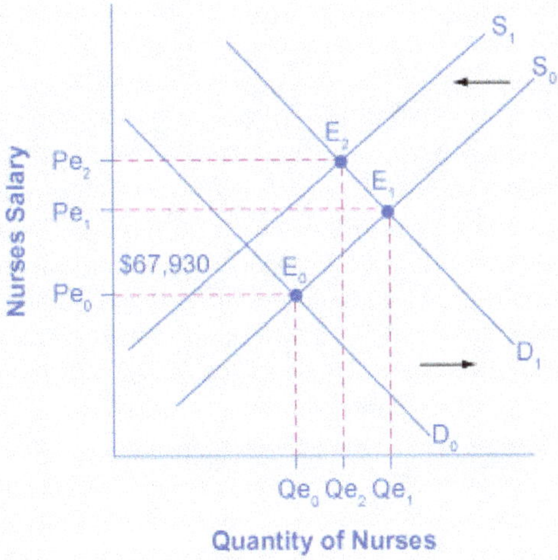

Figure 3. Impact of Decreasing Supply of Nurses between 2012 and 2022. Initially, salaries increase as demand for nursing increases to Pe1. When demand increases, so too does the equilibrium quantity, from Qe0 to Qe1. The decrease in the supply of nurses due to nurses retiring from the workforce and fewer nursing graduates (ceterus paribus), causes a leftward shift of the supply curve resulting in even higher salaries for nurses, at Pe2, but an uncertain outcome for the equilibrium quantity of nurses, which in this representation is less than Qe1, but more than the initial Qe0.

While we do not know if the number of nurses will increase or decrease relative to their initial employment, we know they will have higher salaries. The situation of the labor market for nurses described in the beginning of the chapter is different from this example, because instead of a shrinking supply, we had the supply growing at a lower rate than the growth in demand. Since both curves were shifting to the right, we would have an unequivocal increase in the quantity of nurses. And because the shift in the demand curve was larger than the one in the supply, we would expect higher wages as a result.

Key Concepts and Summary

The market price system provides a highly efficient mechanism for disseminating information about relative scarcities of goods, services, labor, and financial capital. Market participants do not need to know why prices have changed, only that the changes require them to revisit previous decisions they made about supply and demand. Price controls hide information about the true scarcity of products and thereby cause misallocation of resources.

CHAPTER

ELASTICITY AN OVERVIEW 6

Introduction to Elasticity

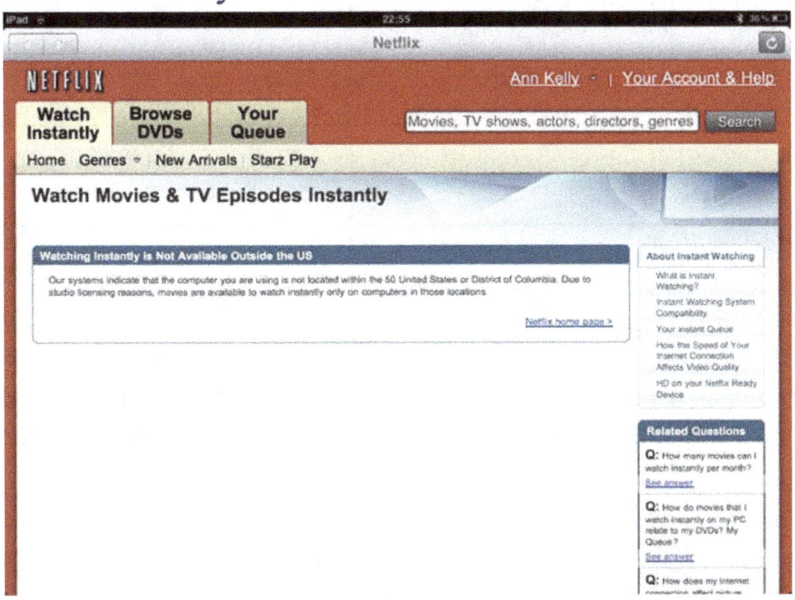

Netflix On-Demand Media. Netflix, Inc. is an American provider of on-demand Internet streaming media to many countries around the world, including the United States, and of flat rate DVD-by-mail in the United States. (Credit: modification of work by Traci Lawson/Flickr Creative Commons)

6.1 PRICE ELASTICITY OF SUPPLY AND DEMAND

Both the demand and supply curve show the relationship between price and the number of units demanded or supplied. Price elasticity is the ratio between the percentage change in the quantity demanded (Qd) or supplied (Qs) and the corresponding percent change in price. The price elasticity of demand is the percentage change in the quantity demanded of a good or service divided by the percentage change in the price. The price elasticity of supply is the percentage change in quantity supplied divided by the percentage change in price.

Elasticities can be usefully divided into three broad categories: elastic, inelastic, and unitary. An elastic demand or elastic supply is one in which the elasticity is greater than one, indicating a high responsiveness to changes in price. Elasticities that are less than one indicate low responsiveness to price changes and correspond to inelastic demand or inelastic supply. Unitary elasticities indicate proportional responsiveness of either demand or supply, as summarized in Table 1.

Table 1. Elastic, Inelastic, and Unitary: Three Cases of Elasticity

If:	Then:	And It Is Called:
$\%\ change\ in\ quantity > \%\ change\ in\ price$ \%\;change\;in\;price» title=»\%\;change\;in\;quantity > \%\;change\;in\;price» class=»latex mathjax">	$\frac{\%\ change\ in\ quantity}{\%\ change\ in\ price)} > 1$ 1» title=»\frac{\%\;change\;in\;quantity}{\%\;change\;in\;price)} > 1» class=»latex mathjax">	Elastic
$\%\ change\ in\ quantity = \%\ change\ in\ price$	$\frac{\%\ change\ in\ quantity}{\%\ change\ in\ price)} = 1$	Unitary
$\%\ change\ in\ quantity < \%\ change\ in\ price$	$\frac{\%\ change\ in\ quantity}{\%\ change\ in\ price)} < 1$	Inelastic

To calculate elasticity, instead of using simple percentage changes in quantity and price, economists use the average percent change in both quantity and price. This is called the Midpoint Method for Elasticity, and is represented in the following equations:

$$\%\ change\ in\ quantity \quad \frac{Q_2-Q_1}{(Q_2+Q_1)/2} \times 100$$

$$\%\ change\ in\ price \quad \frac{P_2-P_1}{(P_2+P_1)/2} \times 100$$

The advantage of the is Midpoint Method is that one obtains the same elasticity between two price points whether there is a price increase or decrease. This is because the formula uses the same base for both cases.

Calculating Price Elasticity of Demand

Let's calculate the elasticity between points A and B and between points G and H shown in Figure 1.

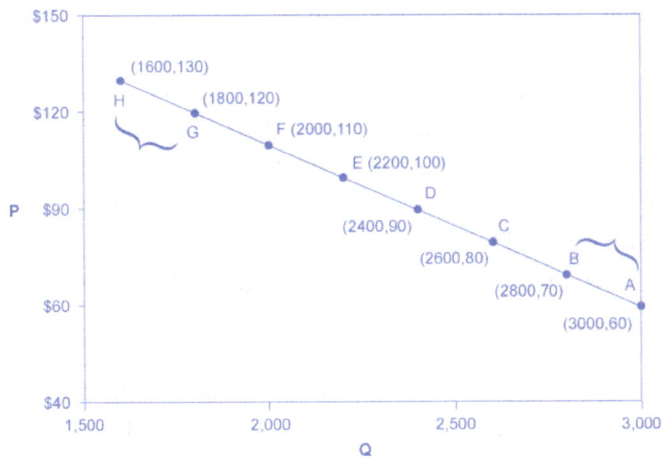

Figure 1. Calculating the Price Elasticity of Demand. The price elasticity of demand is calculated as the percentage change in quantity divided by the percentage change in price.

$$\% \; change \; in \; quantity \quad \frac{3{,}000-2{,}800}{(3{,}000+2{,}800)/2} \times 100$$

$$\frac{200}{2{,}900} \times 100$$

$$= 6.9$$

$$\% \; change \; in \; price \quad \frac{60-70}{(60+70)/2} \times 100$$

$$\frac{-10}{65} \times 100$$

$$-15.4$$

$$Price \; Elasticity \; of \; Demand \quad \frac{6.9\%}{-15.4\%}$$

$$0.45$$

First, apply the formula to calculate the elasticity as price decreases from $70 at point B to $60 at point A:

Therefore, the elasticity of demand between these two points is $\frac{6.9\%}{-15.4\%}$ which is 0.45, an amount smaller than one, showing that the demand is inelastic in this interval. Price elasticities of demand are always negative since price and quantity demanded always move in opposite directions (on the demand curve). By convention, we always talk about elasticities as positive numbers. So mathematically, we take the absolute value of the result. We will ignore this detail from now on, while remembering to interpret elasticities as positive numbers.

This means that, along the demand curve between point B and A, if the price changes by 1%, the quantity demanded will change by 0.45%. A change in the price will result in a smaller percentage change in the quantity demanded. For example, a 10% increase in the price will result in only a 4.5% decrease in quantity demanded. A 10% decrease in the price will result in only a 4.5% increase in the quantity demanded. Price elasticities of demand are negative numbers indicating that the demand curve is downward sloping, but are read as absolute values. The following Work It Out feature will walk you through calculating the price elasticity of demand.

Finding the Price Elasticity of Demand

Calculate the price elasticity of demand using the data in Figure 1 for an increase in price from G to H. Has the elasticity increased or decreased?

Step 1. We know that:

$$\textit{Price Elasticity of Demand} = \frac{\%\ \textit{change in quantity}}{\%\ \textit{change in price}}$$

Step 2. From the **Midpoint Formula** we know that:

$$\%\ \textit{change in quantity} \quad \frac{Q_2 - Q_1}{(Q_2 + Q_1)/2} \times 100$$

$$\%\ \textit{change in price} \quad \frac{P_2 - P_1}{(P_2 + P_1)/2} \times 100$$

Step 3. So we can use the values provided in the figure in each equation:

$$\%\ \textit{change in quantity} \quad \frac{1{,}600 - 1{,}800}{(1{,}600 + 1{,}800)/2} \times 100$$

$$\frac{-200}{1{,}700} \times 100$$

$$-11.76$$

$$\%\ \textit{change in price} \quad \frac{130 - 120}{(130 + 120)/2} \times 100$$

$$\frac{10}{125} \times 100$$

$$8.0$$

Step 4. Then, those values can be used to determine the price elasticity of demand:

$$\textit{Price Elasticity of Demand} \quad \frac{\%\ \textit{change in quantity}}{\%\ \textit{change in price}}$$

$$\frac{-11.76}{8}$$

$$1.47$$

Therefore, the elasticity of demand from G to H 1.47. The magnitude of the elasticity has increased (in absolute value) as we moved up along the demand curve from points A to B. Recall that the elasticity between these two points was 0.45. Demand was inelastic between points A and B and elastic between points G and H. This shows us that price elasticity of demand changes at different points along a straight-line demand curve.

Calculating the Price Elasticity of Supply

Assume that an apartment rents for \$650 per month and at that price 10,000 units are rented as shown in Figure 2. When the price increases to \$700 per month, 13,000 units are supplied into the market. By what percentage does apartment supply increase? What is the price sensitivity?

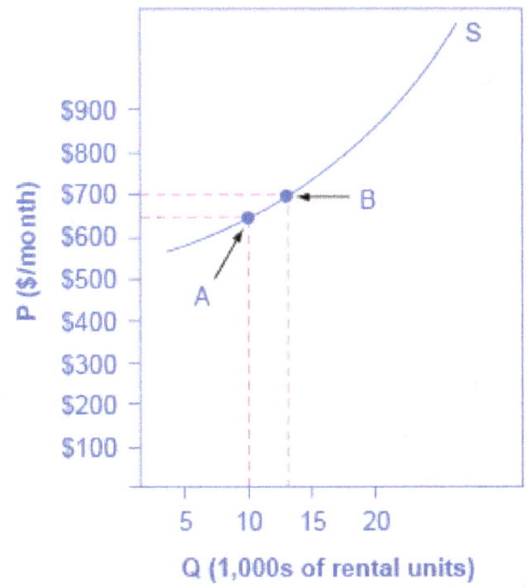

Figure 2. Price Elasticity of Supply. The price elasticity of supply is calculated as the percentage change in quantity divided by the percentage change in price.

$$\textit{\% change in quantity} \quad \frac{13{,}000-10{,}000}{(13{,}000+10{,}000)/2} \times 100$$

$$\frac{3{,}000}{11{,}500} \times 100$$

$$26.1$$

$$\textit{\% change in price} \quad \frac{\$700-\$650}{(\$700+\$650)/2} \times 100$$

$$\frac{50}{675} \times 100$$

$$7.4$$

$$\textit{Price Elasticity of Demand} \quad \frac{26.1\%}{7.4\%}$$

$$3.53$$

Using the Midpoint Method,

Again, as with the elasticity of demand, the elasticity of supply is not followed by any units. Elasticity is a ratio of one percentage change to another percentage change—nothing more—and is read as an absolute value. In this case, a 1% rise in price causes an increase in quantity supplied of 3.5%. The greater than one elasticity of supply means that the percentage change in quantity supplied will be greater than a one percent price change. If you're starting to wonder if the concept of slope fits into this calculation, read the following Clear It Up box.

Is the elasticity the slope?

It is a common mistake to confuse the slope of either the supply or demand curve with its elasticity. The slope is the rate of change in units along the curve, or the rise/run (change in y over the change in x). For example, in Figure 1, each point shown on the demand curve, price drops by $10 and the number of units demanded increases by 200. So the slope is –10/200 along the entire demand curve and does not change. The price elasticity, however, changes along the curve. Elasticity between points A and B was 0.45 and increased to 1.47 between points G and H. Elasticity is the percentage change, which is a different calculation from the slope and has a different meaning.

When we are at the upper end of a demand curve, where price is high and the quantity demanded is low, a small change in the quantity demanded, even in, say, one unit, is pretty big in percentage terms. A change in price of, say, a dollar, is going to be much less important in percentage terms than it would have been at the bottom of the demand curve. Likewise, at the bottom of the demand curve, that one unit change when the quantity demanded is high will be small as a percentage.

So, at one end of the demand curve, where we have a large percentage change in quantity demanded over a small percentage change in price, the elasticity value would be high, or demand would be relatively elastic. Even with the same change in the price and the same change in the quantity demanded, at the other end of the demand curve the quantity is much higher, and the price is much lower, so the percentage change in quantity demanded is smaller and the percentage change in price is much higher. That means at the bottom of the curve we'd have a small numerator over a large denominator, so the elasticity measure would be much lower, or inelastic.

As we move along the demand curve, the values for quantity and price go up or down, depending on which way we are moving, so the percentages for, say, a $1 difference in price or a one unit difference in quantity, will change as well, which means the ratios of those percentages will change.

Concepts and Summary

Price elasticity measures the responsiveness of the quantity demanded or supplied of a good to a change in its price. It is computed as the percentage change in quantity demanded (or supplied) divided by the percentage change in price. Elasticity can be described as elastic (or very responsive), unit elastic, or inelastic (not very responsive). Elastic demand or supply curves indicate that quantity demanded or supplied respond to price changes in a greater than proportional manner. An inelastic demand or supply curve is one where a given percentage change in price will cause a smaller percentage change in quantity demanded or supplied. A unitary elasticity means that a given percentage change in price leads to an equal percentage change in quantity demanded or supplied.

6.2 ELASTICITY IN POLAR CASES AND CONSTANT ELASTICITY

Infinite elasticity or perfect elasticity refers to the extreme case where either the quantity demanded (Qd) or supplied (Qs) changes by an infinite amount in response to any change in price at all. In both cases, the supply and the demand curve are horizontal as shown in Figure 1. While perfectly elastic supply curves are unrealistic, goods with readily available inputs and whose production can be easily expanded will feature highly elastic supply curves. Examples include pizza, bread, books and pencils. Similarly, perfectly elastic demand is an extreme example. But luxury goods, goods that take a large share of individuals' income, and goods with many substitutes are likely to have highly elastic demand curves. Examples of such goods are Caribbean cruises and sports vehicles.

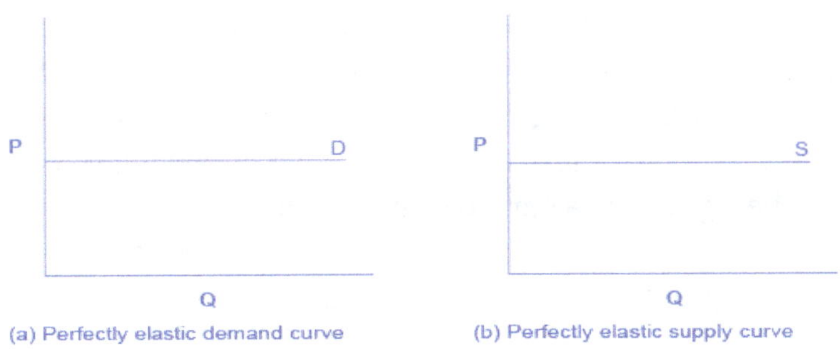

Figure 1. Infinite Elasticity. The horizontal lines show that an infinite quantity will be demanded or supplied at a specific price. This illustrates the cases of a perfectly (or infinitely) elastic demand curve and supply curve. The quantity supplied or demanded is extremely responsive to price changes, moving from zero for prices close to P to infinite when price reach P.

Zero elasticity or perfect inelasticity, as depicted in Figure 2 refers to the extreme case in which a percentage change in price, no matter how large, results in zero change in quantity. While a perfectly inelastic supply is an extreme example, goods with limited supply of inputs are likely to feature highly inelastic supply curves. Examples include diamond rings or housing in prime locations such as apartments facing Central Park in New York City. Similarly, while perfectly inelastic demand is an extreme case, necessities with no close substitutes are likely to have highly inelastic demand curves. This is the case of life-saving drugs and gasoline.

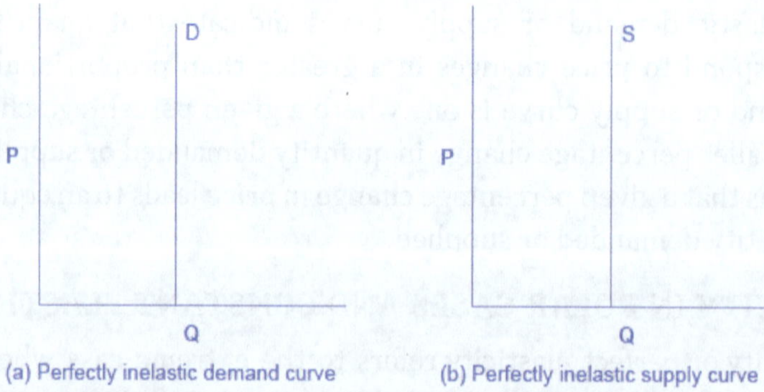

Figure 2. Zero Elasticity. The vertical supply curve and vertical demand curve show that there will be zero percentage change in quantity (a) demanded or (b) supplied, regardless of the price.

Constant unitary elasticity, in either a supply or demand curve, occurs when a price change of one percent results in a quantity change of one percent. Figure 3 shows a demand curve with constant unit elasticity. As we move down the demand curve from A to B, the price falls by 33% and quantity demanded rises by 33%; as you move from B to C, the price falls by 25% and the quantity demanded rises by 25%; as you move from C to D, the price falls by 16% and the quantity rises by 16%. Notice that in absolute value, the declines in price, as you step down the demand curve, are not identical. Instead, the price falls by $3 from A to B, by a smaller amount of $1.50 from B to C, and by a still smaller amount of $0.75 from C to D. As a result, a demand curve with constant unitary elasticity moves from a steeper slope on the left and a flatter slope on the right—and a curved shape overall.

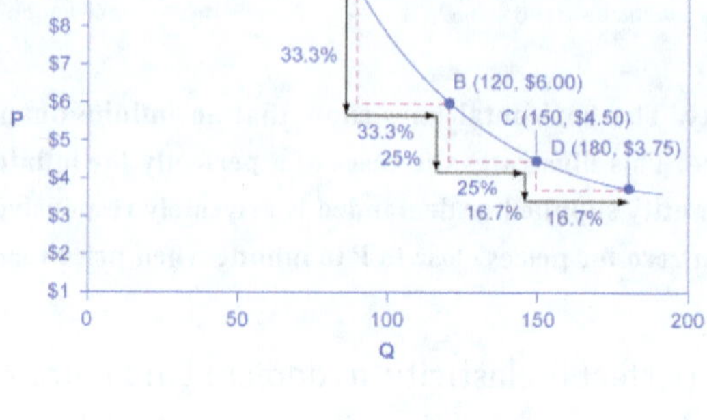

Figure 3. A Constant Unitary Elasticity Demand Curve. A demand curve with constant unitary elasticity will be a curved line. Notice how price and quantity demanded change by an identical amount in each step down the demand curve.

Unlike the demand curve with unitary elasticity, the supply curve with unitary elasticity is represented by a straight line. In moving up the supply curve from left to right, each increase in quantity of 30, from 90 to 120 to 150 to 180, is equal in absolute value. However, in percentage value, the steps are decreasing, from 33.3% to 25% to 16.7%, because the original quantity points in each percentage calculation are getting larger and larger, which expands the denominator in the elasticity calculation.

Consider the price changes moving up the supply curve in Figure 4. From points D to E to F and to G on the supply curve, each step of $1.50 is the same in absolute value. However, if the price changes are measured in percentage change terms, they are also decreasing, from 33.3% to 25% to 16.7%, because the original price points in each percentage calculation are getting larger and larger in value. Along the constant unitary elasticity supply curve, the percentage quantity increases on the horizontal axis exactly match the percentage price increases on the vertical axis—so this supply curve has a constant unitary elasticity at all points.

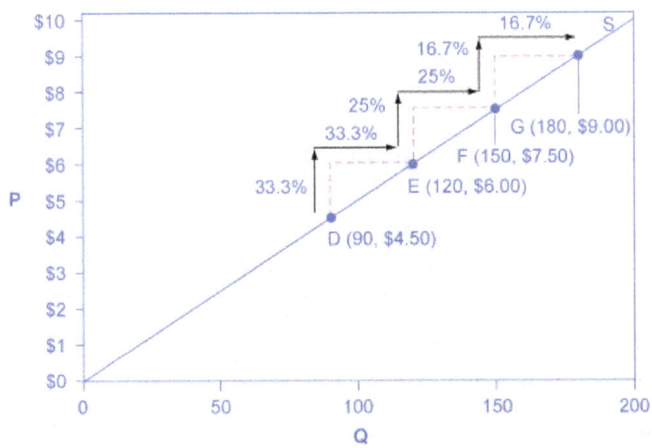

Figure 4. A Constant Unitary Elasticity Supply Curve. A constant unitary elasticity supply curve is a straight line reaching up from the origin. Between each point, the percentage increase in quantity supplied is the same as the percentage increase in price.

Concepts and Summary

Infinite or perfect elasticity refers to the extreme case where either the quantity demanded or supplied changes by an infinite amount in response to any change in price at all. Zero elasticity refers to the extreme case in which a percentage change in price, no matter how large, results in zero change in quantity. Constant unitary elasticity in either a supply or demand curve refers to a situation where a price change of one percent results in a quantity change of one percent.

6.3 PRICING AND ELASTICITY

Studying elasticities is useful for a number of reasons, pricing being most important. Let's explore how elasticity relates to revenue and pricing, both in the long run and short run. But first, let's look at the elasticities of some common goods and services.

Table 4 shows a selection of demand elasticities for different goods and services drawn from a variety of different studies by economists, listed in order of increasing elasticity.

Table 4. Some Selected Elasticities of Demand

Goods and Services	Elasticity of Price
Housing	0.12
Transatlantic air travel (economy class)	0.12
Rail transit (rush hour)	0.15
Electricity	0.20
Taxi cabs	0.22
Gasoline	0.35
Transatlantic air travel (first class)	0.40
Wine	0.55
Beef	0.59
Transatlantic air travel (business class)	0.62
Kitchen and household appliances	0.63
Cable TV (basic rural)	0.69
Chicken	0.64
Soft drinks	0.70
Beer	0.80
New vehicle	0.87
Rail transit (off-peak)	1.00
Computer	1.44
Cable TV (basic urban)	1.51
Cable TV (premium)	1.77
Restaurant meals	2.27

Note that necessities such as housing and electricity are inelastic, while items that are not necessities such as restaurant meals are more price-sensitive. If the price of the restaurant meal increases by 10%, the quantity demanded will decrease by

22.7%. A 10% increase in the price of housing will cause a slight decrease of 1.2% in the quantity of housing demanded.

Does Raising Price Bring in More Revenue?

Imagine that a band on tour is playing in an indoor arena with 15,000 seats. To keep this example simple, assume that the band keeps all the money from ticket sales. Assume further that the band pays the costs for its appearance, but that these costs, like travel, setting up the stage, and so on, are the same regardless of how many people are in the audience. Finally, assume that all the tickets have the same price. (The same insights apply if ticket prices are more expensive for some seats than for others, but the calculations become more complicated.) The band knows that it faces a downward-sloping demand curve; that is, if the band raises the price of tickets, it will sell fewer tickets. How should the band set the price for tickets to bring in the most total revenue, which in this example, because costs are fixed, will also mean the highest profits for the band? Should the band sell more tickets at a lower price or fewer tickets at a higher price?

The key concept in thinking about collecting the most revenue is the price elasticity of demand. Total revenue is price times the quantity of tickets sold. Imagine that the band starts off thinking about a certain price, which will result in the sale of a certain quantity of tickets. The three possibilities are laid out in Table 5. If demand is elastic at that price level, then the band should cut the price, because the percentage drop in price will result in an even larger percentage increase in the quantity sold—thus raising total revenue. However, if demand is inelastic at that original quantity level, then the band should raise the price of tickets, because a certain percentage increase in price will result in a smaller percentage decrease in the quantity sold—and total revenue will rise. If demand has a unitary elasticity at that quantity, then a moderate percentage change in the price will be offset by an equal percentage change in quantity—so the band will earn the same revenue whether it (moderately) increases or decreases the price of tickets.

Table 5. Will the Band Earn More Revenue by Changing Ticket Prices?

If Demand Is . . .	Then . . .	Therefore . . .
Elastic	% change in Qd > % change in P	A given % rise in P will be more than offset by a larger % fall in Q so that total revenue (P × Q) falls.
Unitary	% change in Qd = % change in P	A given % rise in P will be exactly offset by an equal % fall in Q so that total revenue (P × Q) is unchanged.
Inelastic	% change in Qd < % change in P	A given % rise in P will cause a smaller % fall in Q so that total revenue (P × Q) rises.

What if the band keeps cutting price, because demand is elastic, until it reaches a level where all 15,000 seats in the available arena are sold? If demand remains elastic at that quantity, the band might try to move to a bigger arena, so that it could cut ticket prices further and see a larger percentage increase in the quantity of tickets sold. Of course, if the 15,000-seat arena is all that is available or if a larger arena would add substantially to costs, then this option may not work.

Conversely, a few bands are so famous, or have such fanatical followings, that demand for tickets may be inelastic right up to the point where the arena is full. These bands can, if they wish, keep raising the price of tickets. Ironically, some of the most popular bands could make more revenue by setting prices so high that the arena is not filled—but those who buy the tickets would have to pay very high prices. However, bands sometimes choose to sell tickets for less than the absolute maximum they might be able to charge, often in the hope that fans will feel happier and spend more on recordings, T-shirts, and other paraphernalia.

Can Costs Be Passed on to Consumers?

Most businesses face a day-to-day struggle to figure out ways to produce at a lower cost, as one pathway to their goal of earning higher profits. However, in some cases, the price of a key input over which the firm has no control may rise. For example, many chemical companies use petroleum as a **key input**, but they have no control over the world market price for crude oil. Coffee shops use coffee as a key input, but they have no control over the world market price of coffee. If the cost of a key input rises, can the firm pass those higher costs along to consumers in the form of higher prices? Conversely, if new and less expensive ways of producing are invented, can the firm keep the benefits in the form of higher profits, or will the market pressure them to pass the gains along to consumers in the form of lower prices? The price elasticity of demand plays a key role in answering these questions.

Imagine that as a consumer of legal pharmaceutical products, you read a newspaper story that a technological breakthrough in the production of aspirin has occurred, so that every aspirin factory can now make aspirin more cheaply than it did before. What does this discovery mean to you? Figure 1 illustrates two possibilities. In Figure 1 (a), the demand curve is drawn as highly inelastic. In this case, a technological breakthrough that shifts supply to the right, from S0 to S1, so that the equilibrium shifts from E0 to E1, creates a substantially lower price for the product with relatively little impact on the quantity sold. In Figure 1 (b), the demand curve is drawn as highly elastic. In this case, the technological breakthrough leads to a much greater quantity being sold in the market at very close to the original price. Consumers benefit more, in general, when the demand curve is more inelastic because the shift in the supply results in a much lower price for consumers.

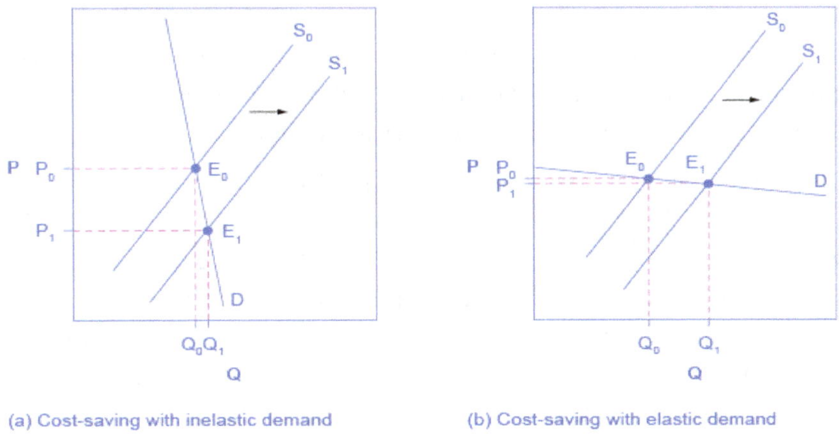

Figure 1. Passing along Cost Savings to Consumers. Cost-saving gains cause supply to shift out to the right from S0 to S1; that is, at any given price, firms will be willing to supply a greater quantity. If demand is inelastic, as in (a), the result of this cost-saving technological improvement will be substantially lower prices. If demand is elastic, as in (b), the result will be only slightly lower prices. Consumers benefit in either case, from a greater quantity at a lower price, but the benefit is greater when demand is inelastic, as in (a).

Producers of aspirin may find themselves in a nasty bind here. The situation shown in Figure 1, with extremely inelastic demand, means that a new invention may cause the price to drop dramatically while quantity changes little. As a result, the new production technology can lead to a drop in the revenue that firms earn from sales of aspirin. However, if strong competition exists between producers of aspirin, each producer may have little choice but to search for and implement any breakthrough that allows it to reduce production costs. After all, if one firm decides not to implement such a cost-saving technology, it can be driven out of business by other firms that do.

Since demand for food is generally inelastic, farmers may often face the situation in Figure 1 (a). That is, a surge in production leads to a severe drop in price that can actually decrease the total revenue received by farmers. Conversely, poor weather or other conditions that cause a terrible year for farm production can sharply raise prices so that the total revenue received increases. The Clear It Up box discusses how these issues relate to coffee.

How do coffee prices fluctuate?

Coffee is an international crop. The top five coffee-exporting nations are Brazil, Vietnam, Colombia, Indonesia, and Ethiopia. In these nations and others, 20 million families depend on selling coffee beans as their main source of income. These families are exposed to enormous risk, because the world price of coffee bounces up and down. For example, in 1993, the world price of coffee was about 50 cents per pound;

in 1995 it was four times as high, at $2 per pound. By 1997 it had fallen by half to $1.00 per pound. In 1998 it leaped back up to $2 per pound. By 2001 it had fallen back to 46 cents a pound; by early 2011 it went back up to about $2.31 per pound. By the end of 2012, the price had fallen back to about $1.31 per pound.

The reason for these price bounces lies in a combination of inelastic demand and shifts in supply. The elasticity of coffee demand is only about 0.3; that is, a 10% rise in the price of coffee leads to a decline of about 3% in the quantity of coffee consumed. When a major frost hit the Brazilian coffee crop in 1994, coffee supply shifted to the left with an inelastic demand curve, leading to much higher prices. Conversely, when Vietnam entered the world coffee market as a major producer in the late 1990s, the supply curve shifted out to the right. With a highly inelastic demand curve, coffee prices fell dramatically. This situation is shown in Figure 1 (a).

Elasticity also reveals whether firms can pass higher costs that they incur on to consumers. Addictive substances tend to fall into this category. For example, the demand for cigarettes is relatively inelastic among regular smokers who are somewhat addicted; economic research suggests that increasing the price of cigarettes by 10% leads to about a 3% reduction in the quantity of cigarettes smoked by adults, so the elasticity of demand for cigarettes is 0.3. If society increases taxes on companies that make cigarettes, the result will be, as in Figure 2 (a), that the supply curve shifts from S0 to S1. However, as the equilibrium moves from E0 to E1, these taxes are mainly passed along to consumers in the form of higher prices. These higher taxes on cigarettes will raise tax revenue for the government, but they will not much affect the quantity of smoking.

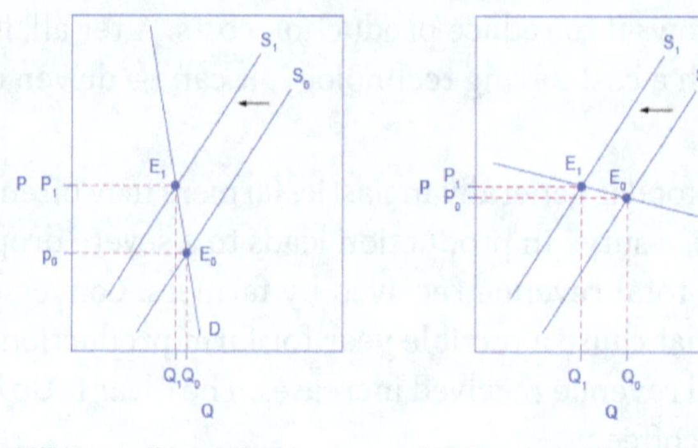

Figure 2. Passing along Higher Costs to Consumers. Higher costs, like a higher tax on cigarette companies for the example given in the text, lead supply to shift to the left. This shift is identical in (a) and (b). However, in (a), where demand is inelastic, the cost increase can largely be passed along to consumers in the form of higher prices, without much of a decline in equilibrium quantity. In (b), demand is elastic, so the shift in supply results primarily in a lower equilibrium quantity. Consumers suffer in either case, but in (a), they suffer from paying a higher price for the same quantity, while in (b), they suffer from buying a lower quantity (and presumably needing to shift their consumption elsewhere).

If the goal is to reduce the quantity of cigarettes demanded, it must be achieved by shifting this inelastic demand back to the left, perhaps with public programs to discourage the use of cigarettes or to help people to quit. For example, anti-smoking advertising campaigns have shown some ability to reduce smoking. However, if demand for cigarettes was more elastic, as in Figure 2 (b), then an increase in taxes that shifts supply from S0 to S1 and equilibrium from E0 to E1 would reduce the quantity of cigarettes smoked substantially. Youth smoking seems to be more elastic than adult smoking—that is, the quantity of youth smoking will fall by a greater percentage than the quantity of adult smoking in response to a given percentage increase in price.

Elasticity and Tax Incidence

The example of cigarette taxes showed that because demand is inelastic, taxes are not effective at reducing the equilibrium quantity of smoking, and they are mainly passed along to consumers in the form of higher prices. The analysis, or manner, of how the burden of a tax is divided between consumers and producers is called **tax incidence**. Typically, the incidence, or burden, of a tax falls both on the consumers and producers of the taxed good. But if one wants to predict which group will bear most of the burden, all one needs to do is examine the elasticity of demand and supply. In the tobacco example, the tax burden falls on the most inelastic side of the market.

If demand is more inelastic than supply, consumers bear most of the tax burden, and if supply is more inelastic than demand, sellers bear most of the tax burden.

The intuition for this is simple. When the demand is inelastic, consumers are not very responsive to price changes, and the quantity demanded remains relatively constant when the tax is introduced. In the case of smoking, the demand is inelastic because consumers are addicted to the product. The government can then pass the tax burden along to consumers in the form of higher prices, without much of a decline in the equilibrium quantity.

Similarly, when a tax is introduced in a market with an inelastic supply, such as, for example, beachfront hotels, and sellers have no alternative than to accept lower prices for their business, taxes do not greatly affect the equilibrium quantity. The tax burden is now passed on to the sellers. If the supply was elastic and sellers had the possibility of reorganizing their businesses to avoid supplying the taxed good, the tax burden on the sellers would be much smaller. The tax would result in a much lower quantity sold instead of lower prices received. Figure 3 illustrates this relationship between the tax incidence and elasticity of demand and supply.

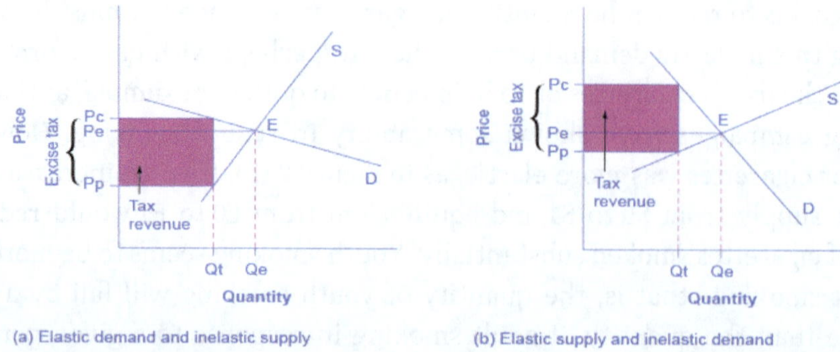

Figure 3. Elasticity and Tax Incidence. An excise tax introduces a wedge between the price paid by consumers (Pc) and the price received by producers (Pp). (a) When the demand is more elastic than supply, the tax incidence on consumers Pc – Pe is lower than the tax incidence on producers Pe – Pp. (b) When the supply is more elastic than demand, the tax incidence on consumers Pc – Pe is larger than the tax incidence on producers Pe – Pp. The more elastic the demand and supply curves are, the lower the tax revenue.

In Figure 3 (a), the supply is inelastic and the demand is elastic, such as in the example of beachfront hotels. While consumers may have other vacation choices, sellers can't easily move their businesses. By introducing a tax, the government essentially creates a wedge between the price paid by consumers Pc and the price received by producers Pp. In other words, of the total price paid by consumers, part is retained by the sellers and part is paid to the government in the form of a tax. The distance between Pc and Pp is the tax rate. The new market price is Pc, but sellers receive only Pp per unit sold, as they pay Pc-Pp to the government. Since a tax can be viewed as raising the costs of production, this could also be represented by a leftward shift of the supply curve, where the new supply curve would intercept the demand at the new quantity Qt. For simplicity, Figure 3 omits the shift in the supply curve.

The tax revenue is given by the shaded area, which is obtained by multiplying the tax per unit by the total quantity sold Qt. The tax incidence on the consumers is given by the difference between the price paid Pc and the initial equilibrium price Pe. The tax incidence on the sellers is given by the difference between the initial equilibrium price Pe and the price they receive after the tax is introduced Pp. In Figure 3 (a), the tax burden falls disproportionately on the sellers, and a larger proportion of the tax revenue (the shaded area) is due to the resulting lower price received by the sellers than by the resulting higher prices paid by the buyers. The example of the tobacco excise tax could be described by Figure 3 (b) where the supply is more elastic than demand. The tax incidence now falls disproportionately on consumers, as shown by the large difference between the price they pay, Pc, and the initial equilibrium price, Pe. Sellers receive a lower price than before the tax, but this difference is much smaller than the change in consumers' price. From this analysis one can also predict whether a tax is likely to create a large revenue or not. The more elastic the demand curve, the easier it is for consumers to reduce quantity instead of paying higher prices. The more elastic the supply curve, the easier it is for sellers to reduce the quantity sold, instead of taking lower prices. In a market where both the demand and supply are very elastic, the imposition of an excise tax generates low revenue.

Excise taxes tend to be thought to hurt mainly the specific industries they target. For example, the medical device excise tax, in effect since 2013, has been controversial for it can delay industry profitability and therefore hamper start-ups and medical innovation. But ultimately, whether the tax burden falls mostly on the medical device industry or on the patients depends simply on the elasticity of demand and supply.

Long-Run vs. Short-Run Impact

Elasticities are often lower in the short run than in the long run. On the demand side of the market, it can sometimes be difficult to change Qd in the short run, but easier in the long run. Consumption of energy is a clear example. In the short run, it is not easy for a person to make substantial changes in the energy consumption. Maybe you can carpool to work sometimes or adjust your home thermostat by a few degrees if the cost of energy rises, but that is about all. However, in the long-run you can purchase a car that gets more miles to the gallon, choose a job that is closer to where you live, buy more energy-efficient home appliances, or install more insulation in your home. As a result, the elasticity of demand for energy is somewhat inelastic in the short run, but much more elastic in the long run.

Figure 4 is an example, based roughly on historical experience, for the responsiveness of Qd to price changes. In 1973, the price of crude oil was $12 per barrel and total consumption in the U.S. economy was 17 million barrels per day. That year, the nations who were members of the Organization of Petroleum Exporting Countries (OPEC) cut off oil exports to the United States for six months because the Arab members of OPEC disagreed with the U.S. support for Israel. OPEC did not bring exports back to their earlier levels until 1975—a policy that can be interpreted as a shift of the supply curve to the left in the U.S. petroleum market. Figure 4 (a) and Figure 4 (b) show the same original equilibrium point and the same identical shift of a supply curve to the left from S0 to S1.

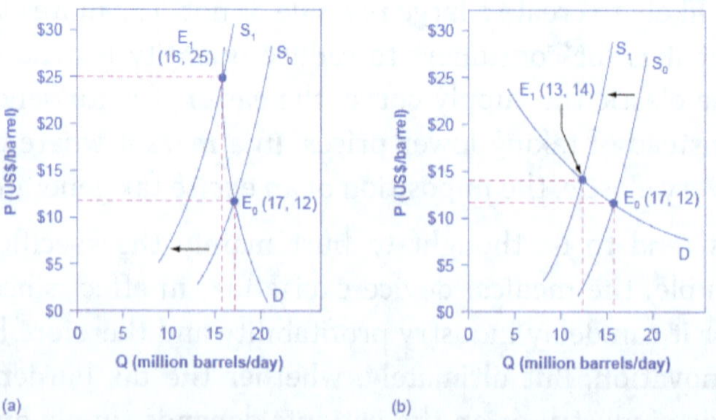

Figure 4. How a Shift in Supply Can Affect Price or Quantity. The intersection (E0) between demand curve D and supply curve S0 is the same in both (a) and (b). The shift of supply to the left from S0 to S1 is identical in both (a) and (b). The new equilibrium (E1) has a higher price and a lower quantity than the original equilibrium (E0) in both (a) and (b). However, the shape of the demand curve D is different in (a) and (b). As a result, the shift in supply can result either in a new equilibrium with a much higher price and an only slightly smaller quantity, as in (a), or in a new equilibrium with only a small increase in price and a relatively larger reduction in quantity, as in (b).

Figure 4 (a) shows inelastic demand for oil in the short run similar to that which existed for the United States in 1973. In Figure 4 (a), the new equilibrium (E1) occurs at a price of $25 per barrel, roughly double the price before the OPEC shock, and an equilibrium quantity of 16 million barrels per day. Figure 4 (b) shows what the outcome would have been if the U.S. demand for oil had been more elastic, a result more likely over the long term. This alternative equilibrium (E1) would have resulted in a smaller price increase to $14 per barrel and larger reduction in equilibrium quantity to 13 million barrels per day. In 1983, for example, U.S. petroleum consumption was 15.3 million barrels a day, which was lower than in 1973 or 1975. U.S. petroleum consumption was down even though the U.S. economy was about one-fourth larger in 1983 than it had been in 1973. The primary reason for the lower quantity was that higher energy prices spurred conservation efforts, and after a decade of home insulation, more fuel-efficient cars, more efficient appliances and machinery, and other fuel-conserving choices, the demand curve for energy had become more elastic.

On the supply side of markets, producers of goods and services typically find it easier to expand production in the long term of several years rather than in the short run of a few months. After all, in the short run it can be costly or difficult to build a new factory, hire many new workers, or open new stores. But over a few years, all of these are possible.

Indeed, in most markets for goods and services, prices bounce up and down more than quantities in the short run, but quantities often move more than prices in the long run. The underlying reason for this pattern is that supply and demand are often inelastic in the short run, so that shifts in either demand or supply can cause a relatively greater change in prices. But since supply and demand are more elastic in the long run, the long-run movements in prices are more muted, while quantity adjusts more easily in the long run.

Concepts and Summary

In the market for goods and services, quantity supplied and quantity demanded are often relatively slow to react to changes in price in the short run, but react more substantially in the long run. As a result, demand and supply often (but not always) tend to be relatively inelastic in the short run and relatively elastic in the long run. The tax incidence depends on the relative price elasticity of supply and demand. When supply is more elastic than demand, buyers bear most of the tax burden, and when demand is more elastic than supply, producers bear most of the cost of the tax. Tax revenue is larger the more inelastic the demand and supply are.

6.4 ELASTICITY OTHER THAN IN PRICES

The basic idea of elasticity—how a percentage change in one variable causes a percentage change in another variable—does not just apply to the responsiveness of supply and demand to changes in the price of a product. Recall that quantity demanded (Qd) depends on income, tastes and preferences, the prices of related goods, and so on, as well as price. Similarly, quantity supplied (Qs) depends on the cost of production, and so on, as well as price. Elasticity can be measured for any determinant of supply and demand, not just the price.

Income Elasticity of Demand

The income elasticity of demand is the percentage change in quantity demanded divided by the percentage change in income.

$$Income\ elasticity\ of\ demand = \frac{\%\ change\ in\ quantity\ demanded}{\%\ change\ in\ income}$$

For most products, most of the time, the income elasticity of demand is positive: that is, a rise in income will cause an increase in the quantity demanded. This pattern is common enough that these goods are referred to as **normal goods**. However, for a few goods, an increase in income means that one might purchase less of the good; for example, those with a higher income might buy fewer hamburgers, because they are buying more steak instead, or those with a higher income might buy less cheap wine and more imported beer. When the income elasticity of demand is negative, the good is called an **inferior good**.

The concepts of normal and inferior goods were introduced in Demand and Supply. A higher level of income for a normal good causes a demand curve to shift to the right for a normal good, which means that the income elasticity of demand is positive. How far the demand shifts depends on the income elasticity of demand. A higher income elasticity means a larger shift. However, for an inferior good, that is, when the income elasticity of demand is negative, a higher level of income would cause the demand curve for that good to shift to the left. Again, how much it shifts depends on how large the (negative) income elasticity is.

Cross-Price Elasticity of Demand

A change in the price of one good can shift the quantity demanded for another good. If the two goods are complements, like bread and peanut butter, then a drop in the price of one good will lead to an increase in the quantity demanded of the other good. However, if the two goods are substitutes, like plane tickets and train tickets, then a drop in the price of one good will cause people to substitute toward that good, and to reduce consumption of the other good. Cheaper plane tickets lead to fewer train tickets, and vice versa.

The cross-price elasticity of demand puts some meat on the bones of these ideas. The term "cross-price" refers to the idea that the price of one good is affecting the quantity demanded of a different good. Specifically, the cross-price elasticity of demand is the percentage change in the quantity of good A that is demanded as a result of a percentage change in the price of good B.

Substitute goods have positive cross-price elasticities of demand: if good A is a substitute for good B, like coffee and tea, then a higher price for B will mean a greater quantity consumed of A. Complement goods have negative cross-price elasticities: if good A is a complement for good B, like coffee and sugar, then a higher price for B will mean a lower quantity consumed of A.

Elasticity in Labor and Financial Capital Markets

The concept of elasticity applies to any market, not just markets for goods and services. In the labor market, for example, the **wage elasticity of labor supply**—that is, the percentage change in hours worked divided by the percentage change in wages—will determine the shape of the labor supply curve. Specifically:

$$\textit{Cross} - \textit{price elasticity of demand} = \frac{\textit{\% change in Qd of good A}}{\textit{\% change in price of good B}}$$

The wage elasticity of labor supply for teenage workers is generally thought to be fairly elastic: that is, a certain percentage change in wages will lead to a larger percentage change in the quantity of hours worked. Conversely, the wage elasticity of labor supply for adult workers in their thirties and forties is thought to be fairly inelastic. When wages move up or down by a certain percentage amount, the quantity of hours that adults in their prime earning years are willing to supply changes but by a lesser percentage amount.

$$\textit{Elasticity of labor supply} = \frac{\textit{\% change in quantity of labor supplied}}{\textit{\% change in wage}}$$

In markets for financial capital, the **elasticity of savings**—that is, the percentage change in the quantity of savings divided by the percentage change in interest rates—will describe the shape of the supply curve for financial capital. That is:

$$\textit{Elasticity of savings} = \frac{\textit{\% change in quantity of financial savings}}{\textit{\% change in interest rate}}$$

Sometimes laws are proposed that seek to increase the quantity of savings by offering tax breaks so that the return on savings is higher. Such a policy will increase the quantity if the supply curve for financial capital is elastic, because then a given percentage increase in the return to savings will cause a higher percentage increase in the quantity of savings. However, if the supply curve for financial capital is highly inelastic, then a percentage increase in the return to savings will cause only a small increase in the quantity of savings. The evidence on the supply curve of financial capital is controversial but, at least in the short run, the elasticity of savings with respect to the interest rate appears fairly inelastic.

Expanding the Concept of Elasticity

The elasticity concept does not even need to relate to a typical supply or demand curve at all. For example, imagine that you are studying whether the Internal Revenue Service should spend more money on auditing tax returns. The question can be framed in terms of the elasticity of tax collections with respect to spending on tax enforcement; that is, what is the percentage change in tax collections derived from a percentage change in spending on tax enforcement?

With all of the elasticity concepts that have just been described, some of which are listed in Table 6, the possibility of confusion arises. When you hear the phrases "elasticity of demand" or "elasticity of supply," they refer to the elasticity with respect to price. Sometimes, either to be extremely clear or because a wide variety of elasticities are being discussed, the elasticity of demand or the demand elasticity will be called the price elasticity of demand or the "elasticity of demand with respect to price." Similarly, elasticity of supply or the supply elasticity is sometimes called, to avoid any possibility of confusion, the price elasticity of supply or "the elasticity of supply with respect to price." But in whatever context elasticity is invoked, the idea always refers to percentage change in one variable, almost always a price or money variable, and how it causes a percentage change in another variable, typically a quantity variable of some kind.

Table 6. Formulas for Calculating Elasticity

$$Income\ elasticity\ of\ demand = \frac{\%\ change\ in\ Qd}{\%\ change\ in\ income}$$

$$Cross-price\ elasticity\ of\ demand = \frac{\%\ change\ in\ Qd\ of\ good\ A}{\%\ change\ in\ price\ of\ good\ B}$$

$$Wage\ elasticity\ of\ labor\ supply = \frac{\%\ change\ in\ quantity\ of\ labor\ supplied}{\%\ change\ in\ wage}$$

$$Wage\ elasticity\ of\ labor\ demand = \frac{\%\ change\ in\ quantity\ of\ labor\ demanded}{\%\ change\ in\ wage}$$

$$Interest\ rate\ elasticity\ of\ savings = \frac{\%\ change\ in\ quantity\ of\ savings}{\%\ change\ in\ interest\ rate}$$

$$Interest\ rate\ elasticity\ of\ borrowing = \frac{\%\ change\ in\ quantity\ of\ borrowing}{\%\ change\ in\ interest\ rate}$$

That Will Be How Much?

How did the 60% price increase in 2011 end up for Netflix? It has been a very bumpy ride.

Before the price increase, there were about 24.6 million U.S. subscribers. After the price increase, 810,000 infuriated U.S. consumers canceled their Netflix subscriptions, dropping the total number of subscribers to 23.79 million. Fast forward to June 2013, when there were 36 million streaming Netflix subscribers in the United States. This was an increase of 11.4 million subscribers since the price increase—an average per quarter growth of about 1.6 million. This growth is less than the 2 million per quarter increases Netflix experienced in the fourth quarter of 2010 and the first quarter of 2011.

During the first year after the price increase, the firm's stock price (a measure of future expectations for the firm) fell from about $300 per share to just under $54. In 2015, however, the stock price is at $448 per share. Today, Netflix has 57 million subscribers in fifty countries.

What happened? Obviously, Netflix company officials understood the law of demand. Company officials reported, when announcing the price increase, this could result in the loss of about 600,000 existing subscribers. Using the elasticity of demand formula, it is easy to see company officials expected an inelastic response:

$$\frac{-600{,}000/[(24\ million+24.6\ million)/2]}{\$6/[(\$10+\$16)/2]}$$

$$\frac{-600{,}000/24.3\ million}{\$6/\$13}$$

$$\frac{-0.025}{0.46}$$

$$-0.05$$

In addition, Netflix officials had anticipated the price increase would have little impact on attracting new customers. Netflix anticipated adding up to 1.29 million new subscribers in the third quarter of 2011. It is true this was slower growth than the firm had experienced—about 2 million per quarter.

Why was the estimate of customers leaving so far off? In the 18 years since Netflix had been founded, there was an increase in the number of close, but not perfect, substitutes. Consumers now had choices ranging from Vudu, Amazon Prime, Hulu, and Redbox, to retail stores. Jaime Weinman reported in Maclean's that Redbox kiosks are "a five-minute drive for less from 68 percent of Americans, and it seems that many people still find a five-minute drive more convenient than loading up a movie online." It seems that in 2012, many consumers still preferred a physical DVD disk over streaming video.

What missteps did the Netflix management make? In addition to misjudging the elasticity of demand, by failing to account for close substitutes, it seems they may have also misjudged customers' preferences and tastes. Yet, as the population increases, the preference for streaming video may overtake physical DVD disks. Netflix, the source of numerous late night talk show laughs and jabs in 2011, may yet have the last laugh.

Concepts and Summary

Elasticity is a general term, referring to percentage change of one variable divided by percentage change of a related variable that can be applied to many economic connections. For instance, the income elasticity of demand is the percentage change in quantity demanded divided by the percentage change in income. The cross-price elasticity of demand is the percentage change in the quantity demanded of a good divided by the percentage change in the price of another good. Elasticity applies in labor markets and financial capital markets just as it does in markets for goods and services. The wage elasticity of labor supply is the percentage change in the quantity of hours supplied divided by the percentage change in the wage. The elasticity of savings with respect to interest rates is the percentage change in the quantity of savings divided by the percentage change in interest rates.

CHAPTER

CONSUMER CHOICES 7

INTRODUCTION TO CONSUMER CHOICES

Microeconomics seeks to understand the behavior of individual economic agents such as individuals and businesses. Economists believe that individuals' decisions, such as what goods and services to buy, can be analyzed as choices made within certain budget constraints. Generally, consumers are trying to get the most for their limited budget. In economic terms they are trying to maximize total utility, or satisfaction, given their budget constraint.

Everyone has their own personal tastes and preferences. The French say: Chacun à son goût, or "Each to his own taste." An old Latin saying states, De gustibus non est disputandum or "There's no disputing about taste." If people's decisions are based on their own tastes and personal preferences, however, then how can economists hope to analyze the choices consumers make?

An economic explanation for why people make different choices begins with accepting the proverbial wisdom that tastes are a matter of personal preference. But economists also believe that the choices people make are influenced by their incomes, by the prices of goods and services they consume, and by factors like where they live. This chapter introduces the economic theory of how consumers make choices about what to buy, how much to work, and how much to save.

The analysis in this chapter will build on the three budget constraints introduced in the Choice in a World of Scarcity chapter. These were the consumption choice budget constraint, the labor-leisure budget constraint, and the intertemporal budget constraint. This chapter will also illustrate how economic theory provides a tool to systematically look at the full range of possible consumption choices to predict how consumption responds to changes in prices or incomes. After reading this chapter, consult the appendix Indifference Curves to learn more about representing utility and choice through indifference curves.

7.1 CONSUMPTION OPTIONS

Information on the consumption choices of Americans is available from the Consumer Expenditure Survey carried out by the U.S. Bureau of Labor Statistics. Table 1 shows spending patterns for the average U.S. household. The first row shows income and, after taxes and personal savings are subtracted, it shows that, in 2015, the average U.S. household spent $48,109 on consumption. The table then breaks down consumption into various categories. The average U.S. household spent roughly one-third of its consumption on shelter and other housing expenses, another one-third on food and vehicle expenses, and the rest on a variety of items, as shown. Of course, these patterns will vary for specific households by differing levels of family income, by geography, and by preferences.

Table 1. U.S. Consumption Choices in 2015 (Source: http://www.bls.gov/cex/csxann13.pdf)

Average Household Income before Taxes	$62,481
Average Annual Expenditures	$48.109
Food at home	$3,264
Food away from home	$2,505
Housing	$16,557
Apparel and services	$1,700
Transportation	$7,677
Healthcare	$3,157
Entertainment	$2,504
Education	$1,074
Personal insurance and pensions	$5,357
All else: alcohol, tobacco, reading, personal care, cash contributions, miscellaneous	$3,356

Total Utility and Diminishing Marginal Utility

To understand how a household will make its choices, economists look at what consumers can afford, as shown in a budget constraint line, and the total utility or satisfaction derived from those choices. In a budget constraint line, the quantity of one good is measured on the horizontal axis and the quantity of the other good is measured on the vertical axis. The budget constraint line shows the various combinations of two goods that are affordable given consumer income. Consider the situation of José, shown in Figure 1. José likes to collect T-shirts and watch movies.

In Figure 1, the quantity of T-shirts is shown on the horizontal axis, while the quantity of movies is shown on the vertical axis. If José had unlimited income or goods were free, then he could consume without limit. But José, like all of us, faces a **budget constraint**. José has a total of $56 to spend. The price of T-shirts is $14 and the price of movies is $7. Notice that the vertical intercept of the budget constraint line is at eight movies and zero T-shirts ($56/$7=8). The horizontal intercept of the budget constraint is four, where José spends of all of his money on T-shirts and no movies ($56/14=4). The slope of the budget constraint line is rise/run or –8/4=–2. The specific choices along the budget constraint line show the combinations of T-shirts and movies that are affordable.

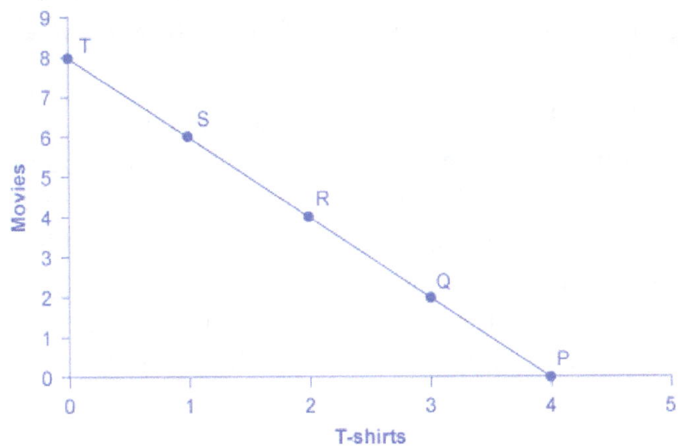

Figure 1. A Choice between Consumption Goods. José has income of $56. Movies cost $7 and T-shirts cost $14. The points on the budget constraint line show the combinations of movies and T-shirts that are affordable.

José wishes to choose the combination that will provide him with the greatest **utility**, which is the term economists use to describe a person's level of satisfaction or happiness with his or her choices.

Let's begin with an assumption, which will be discussed in more detail later, that José can measure his own utility with something called utils. (It is important to note that you cannot make comparisons between the utils of individuals; if one person gets 20 utils from a cup of coffee and another gets 10 utils, this does not mean than the first person gets more enjoyment from the coffee than the other or that they enjoy the coffee twice as much.) Table 2 shows how José's utility is connected with his consumption of T-shirts or movies. The first column of the table shows the quantity of T-shirts consumed. The second column shows the total utility, or total amount of satisfaction, that José receives from consuming that number of T-shirts. The most common pattern of total utility, as shown here, is that consuming additional goods leads to greater total utility, but at a decreasing rate. The third column shows marginal utility, which is the additional utility provided by one additional unit of consumption. This equation for marginal utility is:

$$MU = \frac{change\ in\ total\ utility}{change\ in\ quantity}$$

Notice that marginal utility diminishes as additional units are consumed, which means that each subsequent unit of a good consumed provides less *additional* utility. For example, the first T-shirt José picks is his favorite and it gives him an addition of 22 utils. The fourth T-shirt is just to something to wear when all his other clothes are in the wash and yields only 18 additional utils. This is an example of the law of **diminishing marginal utility**, which holds that the additional utility decreases with each unit added.

The rest of Table 2 shows the quantity of movies that José attends, and his total and marginal utility from seeing each movie. Total utility follows the expected pattern: it increases as the number of movies seen rises. Marginal utility also follows the expected pattern: each additional movie brings a smaller gain in utility than the previous one. The first movie José attends is the one he wanted to see the most, and thus provides him with the highest level of utility or satisfaction. The fifth movie he attends is just to kill time. Notice that total utility is also the sum of the marginal utilities. Read the next Work It Out feature for instructions on how to calculate total utility.

Table 2. Total and Marginal Utility

T-Shirts (Quantity)	Total Utility	Marginal Utility	Movies (Quantity)	Total Utility	Marginal Utility
1	22	22	1	16	16
2	43	21	2	31	15
3	63	20	3	45	14
4	81	18	4	58	13
5	97	16	5	70	12
6	111	14	6	81	11
7	123	12	7	91	10
8	133	10	8	100	9

Table 3 looks at each point on the budget constraint in Figure 1, and adds up José's total utility for five possible combinations of T-shirts and movies.

Table 3. Finding the Choice with the Highest Utility

Point	T-Shirts	Movies	Total Utility
P	4	0	81 + 0 = 81
Q	3	2	63 + 31 = 94

Point	T-Shirts	Movies	Total Utility
R	2	4	43 + 58 = 101
S	1	6	22 + 81 = 103
T	0	8	0 + 100 = 100

Calculating Total Utility

Let's look at how José makes his decision in more detail.

Step 1. Observe that, at point Q (for example), José consumes three T-shirts and two movies.

Step 2. Look at Table 2. You can see from the fourth row/second column that three T-shirts are worth 63 utils. Similarly, the second row/fifth column shows that two movies are worth 31 utils.

Step 3. From this information, you can calculate that point Q has a total utility of 94 (63 + 31).

Step 4. You can repeat the same calculations for each point on Table 3, in which the total utility numbers are shown in the last column.

For José, the highest total utility for all possible combinations of goods occurs at point S, with a total utility of 103 from consuming one T-shirt and six movies.

Choosing with Marginal Utility

Most people approach their utility-maximizing combination of choices in a step-by-step way. This step-by-step approach is based on looking at the trade-offs, measured in terms of marginal utility, of consuming less of one good and more of another.

For example, say that José starts off thinking about spending all his money on T-shirts and choosing point P, which corresponds to four T-shirts and no movies, as illustrated in Figure 1. José chooses this starting point randomly; he has to start somewhere. Then he considers giving up the last T-shirt, the one that provides him the least marginal utility, and using the money he saves to buy two movies instead. Table 4 tracks the step-by-step series of decisions José needs to make (Key: T-shirts are $14, movies are $7, and income is $56). The following Work It Out feature explains how marginal utility can effect decision making.

Table 4. A Step-by-Step Approach to Maximizing Utility

Try	Which Has	Total Utility	Marginal Gain and Loss of Utility, Compared with Previous Choice	Conclusion
Choice 1: P	4 T-shirts and 0 movies	81 from 4 T-shirts + 0 from 0 movies = 81	–	–
Choice 2: Q	3 T-shirts and 2 movies	63 from 3 T-shirts + 31 from 0 movies = 94	Loss of 18 from 1 less T-shirt, but gain of 31 from 2 more movies, for a net utility gain of 13	Q is preferred over P
Choice 3: R	2 T-shirts and 4 movies	43 from 2 T-shirts + 58 from 4 movies = 101	Loss of 20 from 1 less T-shirt, but gain of 27 from two more movies for a net utility gain of 7	R is preferred over Q
Choice 4: S	1 T-shirt and 6 movies	22 from 1 T-shirt + 81 from 6 movies = 103	Loss of 21 from 1 less T-shirt, but gain of 23 from two more movies, for a net utility gain of 2	S is preferred over R
Choice 5: T	0 T-shirts and 8 movies	0 from 0 T-shirts + 100 from 8 movies = 100	Loss of 22 from 1 less T-shirt, but gain of 19 from two more movies, for a net utility loss of 3	S is preferred over T

Decision Making by Comparing Marginal Utility

José could use the following thought process (if he thought in utils) to make his decision regarding how many T-shirts and movies to purchase:

Step 1. From Table 2, José can see that the marginal utility of the fourth T-shirt is 18. If José gives up the fourth T-shirt, then he loses 18 utils.

Step 2. Giving up the fourth T-shirt, however, frees up $14 (the price of a T-shirt), allowing José to buy the first two movies (at $7 each).

Step 3. José knows that the marginal utility of the first movie is 16 and the marginal utility of the second movie is 15. Thus, if José moves from point P to point Q, he gives up 18 utils (from the T-shirt), but gains 31 utils (from the movies).

Step 4. Gaining 31 utils and losing 18 utils is a net gain of 13. This is just another way of saying that the total utility at Q (94 according to the last column in Table 3) is 13 more than the total utility at P (81).

Step 5. So, for José, it makes sense to give up the fourth T-shirt in order to buy two movies.

José clearly prefers point Q to point P. Now repeat this step-by-step process of decision making with marginal utilities. José thinks about giving up the third T-shirt and surrendering a marginal utility of 20, in exchange for purchasing two more movies that promise a combined marginal utility of 27. José prefers point R to point Q. What if José thinks about going beyond R to point S? Giving up the second T-shirt means a marginal utility loss of 21, and the marginal utility gain from the fifth and sixth movies would combine to make a marginal utility gain of 23, so José prefers point S to R.

However, if José seeks to go beyond point S to point T, he finds that the loss of marginal utility from giving up the first T-shirt is 22, while the marginal utility gain from the last two movies is only a total of 19. If José were to choose point T, his utility would fall to 100. Through these stages of thinking about marginal tradeoffs, José again concludes that S, with one T-shirt and six movies, is the choice that will provide him with the highest level of total utility. This step-by-step approach will reach the same conclusion regardless of José's starting point.

Another way to look at this is by focusing on satisfaction per dollar. Marginal utility per dollar is the amount of additional utility José receives given the price of the product. For José's T-shirts and movies, the marginal utility per dollar is shown in Table 5.

$$marginal\ utility\ per\ dollar = \frac{marginal\ utility}{price}$$

José's first purchase will be a movie. Why? Because it gives him the highest marginal utility per dollar and it is affordable. José will continue to purchase the good which gives him the highest marginal utility per dollar until he exhausts the budget. José will keep purchasing movies because they give him a greater "bang or the buck" until the sixth movie is equivalent to a T-shirt purchase. José can afford to purchase that T-shirt. So José will choose to purchase six movies and one T-shirt.

Table 5. Marginal Utility per Dollar

Quantity of T-Shirts	Total Utility	Marginal Utility	Marginal Utility per Dollar	Quantity of Movies	Total Utility	Marginal Utility	Marginal Utility per Dollar
1	22	22	22/$14=1.6	1	16	16	16/$7=2.3
2	43	21	21/$14=1.5	2	31	15	15/$7=2.14
3	63	20	20/$14=1.4	3	45	14	14/$7=2
4	81	18	18/$14=1.3	4	58	13	13/$7=1.9
5	97	16	16/$14=1.1	5	70	12	12/$7=1.7
6	111	14	14/$14=1	6	81	11	11/$7=1.6
7	123	12	12/$14=1.2	7	91	10	10/$7=1.4

A Rule for Maximizing Utility

This process of decision making suggests a rule to follow when **maximizing utility**. Since the price of T-shirts is twice as high as the price of movies, to maximize utility the last T-shirt chosen needs to provide exactly twice the marginal utility (MU) of the last movie. If the last T-shirt provides less than twice the marginal utility of the last movie, then the T-shirt is providing less "bang for the buck" (i.e., marginal utility per dollar spent) than if the same money were spent on movies. If this is so, José should trade the T-shirt for more movies to increase his total utility. Marginal utility per dollar measures the additional utility that José will enjoy given what he has to pay for the good.

If the last T-shirt provides more than twice the marginal utility of the last movie, then the T-shirt is providing more "bang for the buck" or marginal utility per dollar, than if the money were spent on movies. As a result, José should buy more T-shirts. Notice that at José's optimal choice of point S, the marginal utility from the first T-shirt, of 22 is exactly twice the marginal utility of the sixth movie, which is 11. At this choice, the marginal utility per dollar is the same for both goods. This is a tell-tale signal that José has found the point with highest total utility.

This argument can be written as a general rule: the utility-maximizing choice between consumption goods occurs where the marginal utility per dollar is the same for both goods.

$$\frac{MU_1}{P_1} = \frac{MU_2}{P_2}$$

A sensible economizer will pay twice as much for something only if, in the marginal comparison, the item confers twice as much utility. Notice that the formula for the table above is:

$$\frac{22}{\$14} = \frac{11}{\$7}$$
$$1.6 = 1.6$$

The following Work It Out feature provides step by step guidance for this concept of utility-maximizing choices.

Maximizing Utility

The general rule, $\frac{MU_1}{P_1} = \frac{MU_2}{P_2}$, means that the last dollar spent on each good provides exactly the same marginal utility. So:

Step 1. If we traded a dollar more of movies for a dollar more of T-shirts, the marginal utility gained from T-shirts would exactly offset the marginal utility lost from fewer movies. In other words, the net gain would be zero.

Step 2. Products, however, usually cost more than a dollar, so we cannot trade a dollar's worth of movies. The best we can do is trade two movies for another T-shirt, since in this example T-shirts cost twice what a movie does.

Step 3. If we trade two movies for one T-shirt, we would end up at point R (two T-shirts and four movies).

Step 4. Choice 4 in Table 4 shows that if we move to point S, we would lose 21 utils from one less T-shirt, but gain 23 utils from two more movies, so we would end up with more total utility at point S.

In short, the general rule shows us the utility-maximizing choice.

There is another, equivalent way to think about this. The general rule can also be expressed as the ratio of the prices of the two goods should be equal to the ratio of the marginal utilities. When the price of good 1 is divided by the price of good 2, at the utility-maximizing point this will equal the marginal utility of good 1 divided by the marginal utility of good 2. This rule, known as the consumer equilibrium, can be written in algebraic form:

$$\frac{P_1}{P_2} = \frac{MU_1}{MU_2}$$

Along the budget constraint, the total price of the two goods remains the same, so the ratio of the prices does not change. However, the marginal utility of the two goods changes with the quantities consumed. At the optimal choice of one T-shirt and six movies, point S, the ratio of marginal utility to price for T-shirts (22:14) matches the ratio of marginal utility to price for movies (of 11:7).

Measuring Utility with Numbers

This discussion of utility started off with an assumption that it is possible to place numerical values on utility, an assumption that may seem questionable. You can buy a thermometer for measuring temperature at the hardware store, but what store sells an "utilimometer" for measuring utility? However, while measuring utility with numbers is a convenient assumption to clarify the explanation, the key assumption is not that utility can be measured by an outside party, but only that individuals can decide which of two alternatives they prefer.

To understand this point, think back to the step-by-step process of finding the choice with highest total utility by comparing the marginal utility that is gained and lost from different choices along the budget constraint. As José compares each choice along his budget constraint to the previous choice, what matters is not the specific numbers that he places on his utility—or whether he uses any numbers at all—but only that he personally can identify which choices he prefers.

In this way, the step-by-step process of choosing the highest level of utility resembles rather closely how many people make consumption decisions. We think about what will make us the happiest; we think about what things cost; we think about buying a little more of one item and giving up a little of something else; we choose what provides us with the greatest level of satisfaction. The vocabulary of comparing the points along a budget constraint and total and marginal utility is just a set of tools for discussing this everyday process in a clear and specific manner. It is welcome news that specific utility numbers are not central to the argument, since a good utilimometer is hard to find. Do not worry—while we cannot measure utils, by the end of the next module, we will have transformed our analysis into something we can measure—demand.

Concepts and Summary

Economic analysis of household behavior is based on the assumption that people seek the highest level of utility or satisfaction. Individuals are the only judge of their own utility. In general, greater consumption of a good brings higher total utility. However, the additional utility received from each unit of greater consumption tends to decline in a pattern of diminishing marginal utility.

The utility-maximizing choice on a consumption budget constraint can be found in several ways. You can add up total utility of each choice on the budget line and choose the highest total. You can choose a starting point at random and compare the marginal utility gains and losses of moving to neighboring points—and thus eventually seek out the preferred choice. Alternatively, you can compare the ratio of the marginal utility to price of good 1 with the marginal utility to price of good 2 and apply the rule that at the optimal choice, the two ratios should be equal:

$$\frac{MU_1}{P_1} = \frac{MU_2}{P_2}$$

7.2 HOW CONSUMPTION CHOICES ARE AFFECTED BY CHANGES IN INCOME AND PRICES

Just as utility and marginal utility can be used to discuss making consumer choices along a budget constraint, these ideas can also be used to think about how consumer choices change when the budget constraint shifts in response to changes in income or price. Indeed, because the budget constraint framework can be used to analyze how quantities demanded change because of price movements, the budget constraint model can illustrate the underlying logic behind demand curves.

HOW CHANGES IN INCOME AFFECT CONSUMER CHOICES

Let's begin with a concrete example illustrating how changes in income level affect consumer choices. Figure 1 shows a budget constraint that represents Kimberly's choice between concert tickets at $50 each and getting away overnight to a bed-and-breakfast for $200 per night. Kimberly has $1,000 per year to spend between these two choices. After thinking about her total utility and marginal utility and applying the decision rule that the ratio of the marginal utilities to the prices should be equal between the two products, Kimberly chooses point M, with eight concerts and three overnight getaways as her utility-maximizing choice.

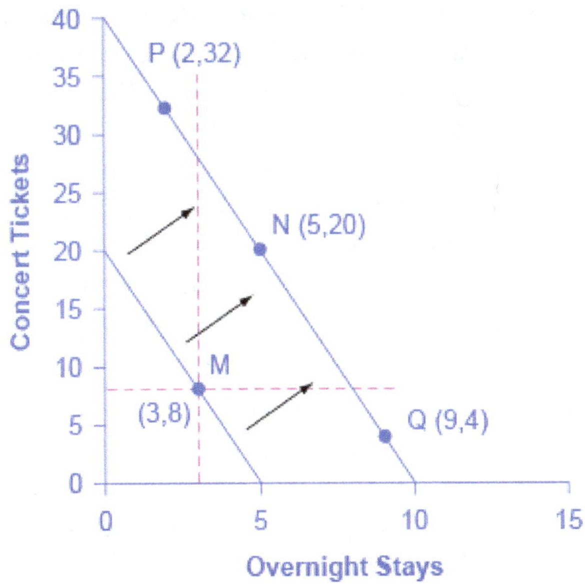

Figure 1. How a Change in Income Affects Consumption Choices. The utility-maximizing choice on the original budget constraint is M. The dashed horizontal and vertical lines extending through point M allow you to see at a glance whether the quantity consumed of goods on the new budget constraint is higher or lower than on the original budget constraint. On the new budget constraint, a choice like N will be made if both goods are normal goods. If overnight stays is an inferior good, a choice like P will be made. If concert tickets are an inferior good, a choice like Q will be made.

Now, assume that the income Kimberly has to spend on these two items rises to $2,000 per year, causing her budget constraint to shift out to the right. How does this rise in income alter her utility-maximizing choice? Kimberly will again consider the utility and marginal utility that she receives from concert tickets and overnight getaways and seek her **utility-maximizing choice** on the new budget line. But how will her new choice relate to her original choice?

The possible choices along the new budget constraint can be divided into three groups, which are divided up by the dashed horizontal and vertical lines that pass through the original choice M in the figure. All choices on the upper left of the new budget constraint that are to the left of the vertical dashed line, like choice P with two overnight stays and 32 concert tickets, involve less of the good on the horizontal axis but much more of the good on the vertical axis. All choices to the right of the vertical dashed line and above the horizontal dashed line—like choice N with five overnight getaways and 20 concert tickets—have more consumption of both goods. Finally, all choices that are to the right of the vertical dashed line but below the horizontal dashed line, like choice Q with four concerts and nine overnight getaways, involve less of the good on the vertical axis but much more of the good on the horizontal axis.

All of these choices are theoretically possible, depending on Kimberly's personal preferences as expressed through the total and marginal utility she would receive from consuming these two goods. When income rises, the most common reaction is to purchase more of both goods, like choice N, which is to the upper right relative to Kimberly's original choice M, although exactly how much more of each good will vary according to personal taste. Conversely, when income falls, the most typical reaction is to purchase less of both goods. As defined in the chapter on Demand and Supply and again in the chapter on Elasticity, goods and services are called normal goods when a rise in income leads to a rise in the quantity consumed of that good and a fall in income leads to a fall in quantity consumed.

However, depending on Kimberly's preferences, a rise in income could cause consumption of one good to increase while consumption of the other good declines. A choice like P means that a rise in income caused her quantity consumed of overnight stays to decline, while a choice like Q would mean that a rise in income caused her quantity of concerts to decline. Goods where demand declines as income rises (or conversely, where the demand rises as income falls) are called "inferior goods." An inferior good occurs when people trim back on a good as income rises, because they can now afford the more expensive choices that they prefer. For example, a higher-income household might eat fewer hamburgers or be less likely to buy a used car, and instead eat more steak and buy a new car.

HOW PRICE CHANGES AFFECT CONSUMER CHOICES

For analyzing the possible effect of a change in price on consumption, let's again use a concrete example. Figure 2 represents the consumer choice of Sergei, who chooses between purchasing baseball bats and cameras. A price increase for baseball bats would have no effect on the ability to purchase cameras, but it would reduce the number of bats Sergei could afford to buy. Thus a price increase for baseball bats, the good on the horizontal axis, causes the budget constraint to rotate inward, as if on a hinge, from the vertical axis. As in the previous section, the point labeled M represents the originally preferred point on the original budget constraint, which Sergei has chosen after contemplating his total utility and marginal utility and the tradeoffs involved along the budget constraint. In this example, the units along the horizontal and vertical axes are not numbered, so the discussion must focus on whether more or less of certain goods will be consumed, not on numerical amounts.

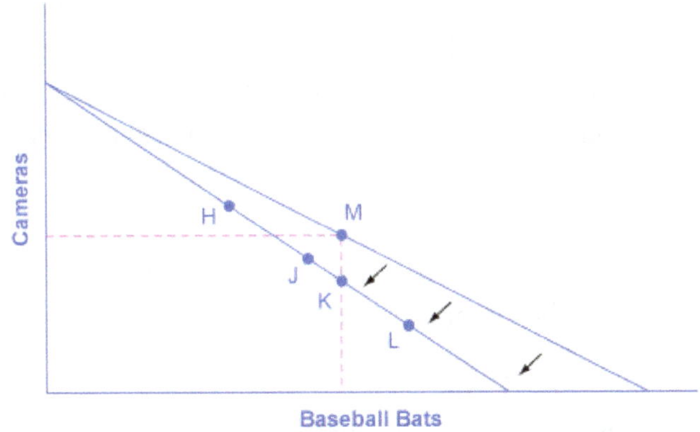

Figure 2. How a Change in Price Affects Consumption Choices. The original utility-maximizing choice is M. When the price rises, the budget constraint shifts in to the left. The dashed lines make it possible to see at a glance whether the new consumption choice involves less of both goods, or less of one good and more of the other. The new possible choices would be fewer baseball bats and more cameras, like point H, or less of both goods, as at point J. Choice K would mean that the higher price of bats led to exactly the same quantity of bats being consumed, but fewer cameras. Choices like L are ruled out as theoretically possible but highly unlikely in the real world, because they would mean that a higher price for baseball bats means a greater quantity consumed of baseball bats.

After the price increase, Sergei will make a choice along the new budget constraint. Again, his choices can be divided into three segments by the dashed vertical and horizontal lines. In the upper left portion of the new budget constraint, at a choice like H, Sergei consumes more cameras and fewer bats. In the central portion of the new budget constraint, at a choice like J, he consumes less of both goods. At the right-hand end, at a choice like L, he consumes more bats but fewer cameras.

The typical response to higher prices is that a person chooses to consume less of the product with the higher price. This occurs for two reasons, and both effects can occur simultaneously. The substitution effect occurs when a price changes and consumers have an incentive to consume less of the good with a relatively higher price and more of the good with a relatively lower price. The income effect is that a higher price means, in effect, the buying power of income has been reduced (even though actual income has not changed), which leads to buying less of the good (when the good is normal). In this example, the higher price for baseball bats would cause Sergei to buy a fewer bats for both reasons. Exactly how much will a higher price for bats cause Sergei consumption of bats to fall? Figure 2 suggests a range of possibilities. Sergei might react to a higher price for baseball bats by purchasing the same quantity of bats, but cutting his consumption of cameras. This choice is the point K on the new budget constraint, straight below the original choice M. Alternatively, Sergei might react by dramatically reducing his purchases of bats and instead buy more cameras.

The key is that it would be imprudent to assume that a change in the price of baseball bats will only or primarily affect the good whose price is changed, while the quantity consumed of other goods remains the same. Since Sergei purchases all his products out of the same budget, a change in the price of one good can also have a range of effects, either positive or negative, on the quantity consumed of other goods.

In short, a higher price typically causes reduced consumption of the good in question, but it can affect the consumption of other goods as well.

The Foundations of Demand Curves

Changes in the price of a good lead the budget constraint to shift. A shift in the budget constraint means that when individuals are seeking their highest utility, the quantity that is demanded of that good will change. In this way, the logical foundations of demand curves—which show a connection between prices and quantity demanded—are based on the underlying idea of individuals seeking utility. Figure 3 (a) shows a budget constraint with a choice between housing and "everything else." (Putting "everything else" on the vertical axis can be a useful approach in some cases, especially when the focus of the analysis is on one particular good.) The preferred choice on the original budget constraint that provides the highest possible utility is labeled M0. The other three budget constraints represent successively higher prices for housing of P1, P2, and P3. As the budget constraint rotates in, and in, and in again, the utility-maximizing choices are labeled M1, M2, and M3, and the quantity demanded of housing falls from Q0 to Q1 to Q2 to Q3.

So, as the price of housing rises, the budget constraint shifts to the left, and the quantity consumed of housing falls, *ceteris paribus* (meaning, with all other things being the same). This relationship—the price of housing rising from P_0 to P_1 to P_2 to P_3, while the quantity of housing demanded falls from Q_0 to Q_1 to Q_2 to Q_3—is graphed on the demand curve in Figure 3 (b). Indeed, the vertical dashed lines stretching between the top and bottom of Figure 3 show that the quantity of housing demanded at each point is the same in both (a) and (b). The shape of a demand curve is ultimately determined by the underlying choices about maximizing utility subject to a budget constraint. And while economists may not be able to measure "utils," they can certainly measure price and quantity demanded.

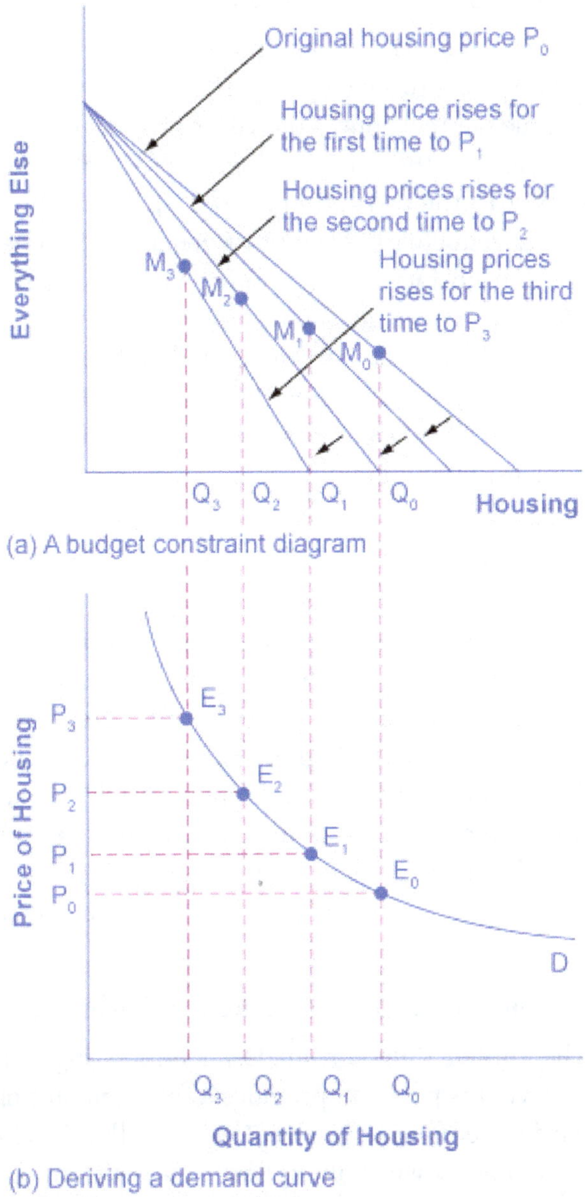

Figure 3. The Foundations of a Demand Curve: An Example of Housing. (a) As the price increases from P_0 to P_1 to P_2 to P_3, the budget constraint on the upper part of the diagram shifts to the left. The utility-maximizing choice changes from M_0 to M_1 to M_2 to M_3. As a result, the quantity demanded of housing shifts from Q_0 to Q_1 to Q_2 to Q_3, *ceteris paribus*. (b) The demand curve graphs each combination of the price of housing and the quantity of housing demanded, *ceteris paribus*. Indeed, the quantities of housing are the same at the points on both (a) and (b). Thus, the original price of housing (P_0) and the original quantity of housing (Q_0) appear on the demand curve as point E_0. The higher price of housing (P_1) and the corresponding lower quantity demanded of housing (Q_1) appear on the demand curve as point E_1.

Applications in Government and Business

The budget constraint framework for making utility-maximizing choices offers a reminder that people can react to a change in price or income in a range of different ways. For example, in the winter months of 2005, costs for heating homes increased significantly in many parts of the country as prices for natural gas and electricity soared, due in large part to the disruption caused by Hurricanes Katrina and Rita. Some people reacted by reducing the quantity demanded of energy; for example, by turning down the thermostats in their homes by a few degrees and wearing a heavier sweater inside. Even so, many home heating bills rose, so people adjusted their consumption in other ways, too. As you learned in the chapter on Elasticity, the short run demand for home heating is generally inelastic. Each household cut back on what it valued least on the margin; for some it might have been some dinners out, or a vacation, or postponing buying a new refrigerator or a new car. Indeed, sharply higher energy prices can have effects beyond the energy market, leading to a widespread reduction in purchasing throughout the rest of the economy.

A similar issue arises when the government imposes taxes on certain products, like it does on gasoline, cigarettes, and alcohol. Say that a tax on alcohol leads to a higher price at the liquor store, the higher price of alcohol causes the budget constraint to pivot left, and consumption of alcoholic beverages is likely to decrease. However, people may also react to the higher price of alcoholic beverages by cutting back on other purchases. For example, they might cut back on snacks at restaurants like chicken wings and nachos. It would be unwise to assume that the liquor industry is the only one affected by the tax on alcoholic beverages. Read the next Clear It Up to learn about how buying decisions are influenced by who controls the household income.

Does who controls household income make a difference?

In the mid-1970s, the United Kingdom made an interesting policy change in its "child allowance" policy. This program provides a fixed amount of money per child to every family, regardless of family income. Traditionally, the child allowance had been distributed to families by withholding less in taxes from the paycheck of the family wage earner—typically the father in this time period. The new policy instead provided the child allowance as a cash payment to the mother. As a result of this change, households have the same level of income and face the same prices in the market, but the money is more likely to be in the purse of the mother than in the wallet of the father.

Should this change in policy alter household consumption patterns? Basic models of consumption decisions, of the sort examined in this chapter, assume that it does not matter whether the mother or the father receives the money, because both parents seek to maximize the utility of the family as a whole. In effect, this model assumes that everyone in the family has the same preferences.

In reality, the share of income controlled by the father or the mother does affect what the household consumes. When the mother controls a larger share of family income a number of studies, in the United Kingdom and in a wide variety of other countries, have found that the family tends to spend more on restaurant meals, child care, and women's clothing, and less on alcohol and tobacco. As the mother controls a larger share of household resources, children's health improves, too. These findings suggest that when providing assistance to poor families, in high-income countries and low-income countries alike, the monetary amount of assistance is not all that matters: it also matters which member of the family actually receives the money.

The budget constraint framework serves as a constant reminder to think about the full range of effects that can arise from changes in income or price, not just effects on the one product that might seem most immediately affected.

Concepts and Summary

The budget constraint framework suggest that when income or price changes, a range of responses are possible. When income rises, households will demand a higher quantity of normal goods, but a lower quantity of inferior goods. When the price of a good rises, households will typically demand less of that good—but whether they will demand a much lower quantity or only a slightly lower quantity will depend on personal preferences. Also, a higher price for one good can lead to more or less of the other good being demanded.

7.3 LABOR-LEISURE CHOICES

People do not obtain utility just from products they purchase. They also obtain utility from leisure time. Leisure time is time not spent at work. The decision-making process of a utility-maximizing household applies to what quantity of hours to work in much the same way that it applies to purchases of goods and services. Choices made along the **labor-leisure budget constraint**, as wages shift, provide the logical underpinning for the labor supply curve. The discussion also offers some insights about the range of possible reactions when people receive higher wages, and specifically about the claim that if people are paid higher wages, they will work a greater quantity of hours—assuming that they have a say in the matter.

According to the Bureau of Labor Statistics, U.S. workers averaged 38.6 hours per week on the job in 2014. This average includes part-time workers; for full-time workers only, the average was 42.5 hours per week. Table 10 shows that more than half of all workers are on the job 35 to 48 hours per week, but significant proportions work more or less than this amount.

Table 11 breaks down the average hourly compensation received by private industry workers, including wages and benefits. Wages and salaries are about three-quarters of total compensation received by workers; the rest is in the form of health insurance, vacation pay, and other benefits. The compensation workers receive differs for many reasons, including experience, education, skill, talent, membership in a labor union, and the presence of discrimination against certain groups in the labor market. Issues surrounding the inequality of incomes in a market-oriented economy are explored in the chapters on Poverty and Economic Inequality and Issues in Labor Markets: Unions, Discrimination, Immigration.

Table 10. Persons at Work, by Average Hours Worked per Week in 2013 (Total number of workers: 137.7 million). (Source: http://www.bls.gov/news.release/empsit.t18.htm)

Hours Worked per Week	Number of Workers	Percentage of Workforce
1–14 hours	6.9 million	5.0%
15–34 hours	27.6 million	20.1%
35–40 hours	68.5 million	49.9%
41–48 hours	11.9 million	8.6%
49–59 hours	13.3 million	9.6%
60 hours and over	9.3 million	6.8%

Table 11. Hourly Compensation: Wages, Benefits, and Taxes in 2014. (Source: http://www.bls.gov/news.release/pdf/ecec.pdf)

Compensation, Wage, Salary, and Benefits	$30.92 per hour
Wages and Salaries	$20.92
Benefits	
Vacation	$2.09
Supplemental Pay	$0.84
Insurance	$2.15
Health Benefits	$2.36
Retirement and Savings	$1.24
Defined Benefit	$0.57
Defined Contribution	$0.064
Legally Required	$2.46

The Labor-Leisure Budget Constraint

How do workers make decisions about the number of hours to work? Again, let's proceed with a concrete example. The economic logic is precisely the same as in the case of a **consumption choice budget constraint**, but the labels are different on a labor-leisure budget constraint.

Vivian has 70 hours per week that she could devote either to work or to leisure, and her wage is $10/hour. The lower budget constraint in Figure 1 shows Vivian's possible choices. The horizontal axis of this diagram measures both leisure and labor, by showing how Vivian's time is divided between leisure and labor. Hours of leisure are measured from left to right on the horizontal axis, while hours of labor are measured from right to left. Vivian will compare choices along this budget constraint, ranging from 70 hours of leisure and no income at point S to zero hours of leisure and $700 of income at point L. She will choose the point that provides her with the highest total utility. For this example, let's assume that Vivian's utility-maximizing choice occurs at O, with 30 hours of leisure, 40 hours of work, and $400 in weekly income.

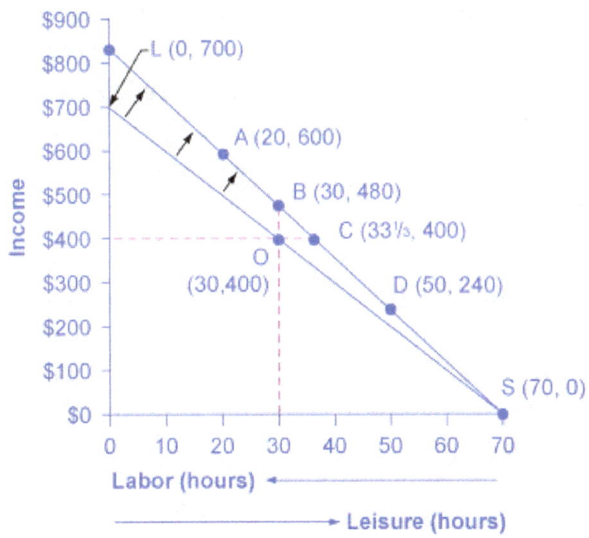

Figure 1. How a Rise in Wages Alters the Utility-Maximizing Choice. Vivian's original choice is point O on the lower opportunity set. A rise in her wage causes her opportunity set to swing upward. In response to the increase in wages, Vivian can make a range of different choices available to her: a choice like D, which involves less work; and a choice like B, which involves the same amount of work but more income; or a choice like A, which involves more work and considerably more income. Vivian's personal preferences will determine which choice she makes.

For Vivian to discover the labor-leisure choice that will maximize her utility, she does not have to place numerical values on the total and marginal utility that she would receive from every level of income and leisure. All that really matters is that Vivian can compare, in her own mind, whether she would prefer more leisure or more income, given the tradeoffs she faces. If Vivian can say to herself: "I'd really rather work a little less and have more leisure, even if it means less income," or "I'd be willing to work more hours to make some extra income," then as she gradually moves in the direction of her preferences, she will seek out the utility-maximizing choice on her labor-leisure budget constraint.

Now imagine that Vivian's wage level increases to $12/hour. A higher wage will mean a new budget constraint that tilts up more steeply; conversely, a lower wage would have led to a new budget constraint that was flatter. How will a change in the wage and the corresponding shift in the budget constraint affect Vivian's decisions about how many hours to work?

Vivian's choices of quantity of hours to work and income along her new budget constraint can be divided into several categories, using the dashed horizontal and vertical lines in Figure 1 that go through her original choice (O). One set of choices in the upper-left portion of the new budget constraint involves more hours of work (that is, less leisure) and more income, at a point like A with 20 hours of leisure, 50 hours of work, and $600 of income (that is, 50 hours of work multiplied by the new wage of $12 per hour). A second choice would be to work exactly the same 40 hours, and to take the benefits of the higher wage in the form of income that would now be $480, at choice B. A third choice would involve more leisure and the same income at point C (that is, 33-1/3 hours of work multiplied by the new wage of $12 per hour equals $400 of total income). A fourth choice would involve less income and much more leisure at a point like D, with a choice like 50 hours of leisure, 20 hours of work, and $240 in income.

In effect, Vivian can choose whether to receive the benefits of her wage increase in the form of more income, or more leisure, or some mixture of these two. With this range of possibilities, it would be unwise to assume that Vivian (or anyone else) will necessarily react to a wage increase by working substantially more hours. Maybe they will; maybe they will not.

Applications of Utility Maximizing with the Labor-Leisure Budget Constraint

The theoretical insight that higher wages will sometimes cause an increase in hours worked, sometimes cause hours worked not to change by much, and sometimes cause hours worked to decline, has led to labor supply curves that look like the one in Figure 2. The bottom-left portion of the labor supply curve slopes upward, which reflects the situation of a person who reacts to a higher wage by supplying a greater quantity of labor. The middle, close-to-vertical portion of the labor supply curve reflects the situation of a person who reacts to a higher wage by supplying about the same quantity of labor. The very top portion of the labor supply curve is called a **backward-bending supply curve for labor**, which is the situation of high-wage people who can earn so much that they respond to a still-higher wage by working fewer hours. Read the following Clear It Up feature for more on the number of hours the average person works each year.

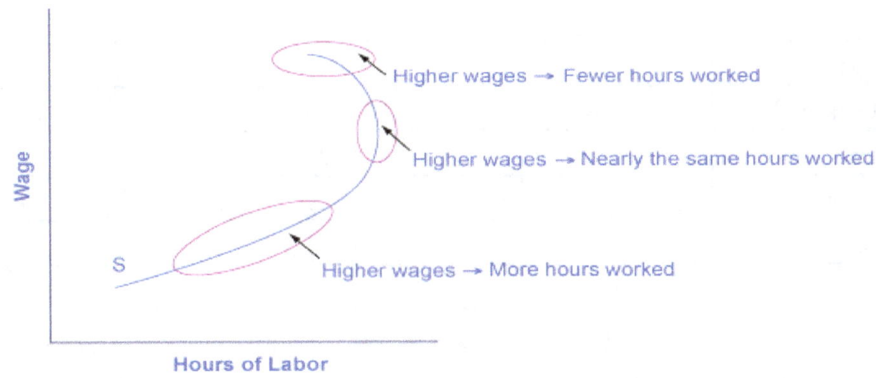

Figure 2. A Backward-Bending Supply Curve of Labor. The bottom upward-sloping portion of the labor supply curve shows that as wages increase over this range, the quantity of hours worked also increases. The middle, nearly vertical portion of the labor supply curve shows that as wages increase over this range, the quantity of hours worked changes very little. The backward-bending portion of the labor supply curve at the top shows that as wages increase over this range, the quantity of hours worked actually decreases. All three of these possibilities can be derived from how a change in wages causes movement in the labor-leisure budget constraint, and thus different choices by individuals.

Is America a nation of workaholics?

Americans work a lot. Table 12 shows average hours worked per year in the United States, Canada, Japan, and several European countries, with data from 2013. To get a perspective on these numbers, someone who works 40 hours per week for 50 weeks per year, with two weeks off, would work 2,000 hours per year. The gap in hours worked is a little astonishing; the 250 to 300 hour gap between how much Americans work and how much Germans or the French work amounts to roughly six to seven weeks less of work per year. Economists who study these international patterns debate the extent to which average Americans and Japanese have a preference for working more than, say, Germans, or whether German workers and employers face particular kinds of taxes and regulations that lead to fewer hours worked. Many countries have laws that regulate the work week and dictate holidays and the standards of "normal" vacation time vary from country to country. It is also interesting to take the amount of time spent working in context; it is estimated that in the late nineteenth century in the United States, the average work week was over 60 hours per week—leaving little to no time for leisure.

Table 12. Average Hours Worked Per Year in Select Countries. (Source: http://stats.oecd.org/Index.aspx?DataSetCode=ANHRS)

Country	Average Annual Hours Actually Worked per Employed Person
United States	1,824
Spain	1,799

Japan	1,759
Canada	1,751
United Kingdom	1,669
Sweden	1,585
Germany	1,443
France	1,441

The different responses to a rise in wages—more hours worked, the same hours worked, or fewer hours worked—are patterns exhibited by different groups of workers in the U.S. economy. Many full-time workers have jobs where the number of hours is held relatively fixed, partly by their own choice and partly by their employer's practices. These workers do not much change their hours worked as wages rise or fall, so their supply curve of labor is inelastic. However, part-time workers and younger workers tend to be more flexible in their hours, and more ready to increase hours worked when wages are high or cut back when wages fall.

The backward-bending supply curve for labor, when workers react to higher wages by working fewer hours and having more income, is not observed often in the short run. However, some well-paid professionals, like dentists or accountants, may react to higher wages by choosing to limit the number of hours, perhaps by taking especially long vacations, or taking every other Friday off. Over a long-term perspective, the backward-bending supply curve for labor is common. Over the last century, Americans have reacted to gradually rising wages by working fewer hours; for example, the length of the average work-week has fallen from about 60 hours per week in 1900 to the present average of less than 40 hours per week.

Recognizing that workers have a range of possible reactions to a change in wages casts some fresh insight on a perennial political debate: the claim that a reduction in income taxes—which would, in effect, allow people to earn more per hour—will encourage people to work more. The leisure-income budget set points out that this connection will not hold true for all workers. Some people, especially part-timers, may react to higher wages by working more. Many will work the same number of hours. Some people, especially those whose incomes are already high, may react to the tax cut by working fewer hours. Of course, cutting taxes may be a good or a bad idea for a variety of reasons, not just because of its impact on work incentives, but the specific claim that tax cuts will lead people to work more hours is only likely to hold for specific groups of workers and will depend on how and for whom taxes are cut.

Concepts and Summary

When making a choice along the labor-leisure budget constraint, a household will choose the combination of labor, leisure, and income that provides the most utility. The result of a change in wage levels can be higher work hours, the same work hours, or lower work hours.

7.4 INTERTEMPORAL CHOICES IN FINANCIAL CAPITAL MARKETS

Rates of saving in America have never been especially high, but they seem to have dipped even lower in recent years, as the data from the Bureau of Economic Analysis in Figure 1 show. A decision about how much to save can be represented using an intertemporal budget constraint. Household decisions about the quantity of financial savings show the same underlying pattern of logic as the consumption choice decision and the labor-leisure decision.

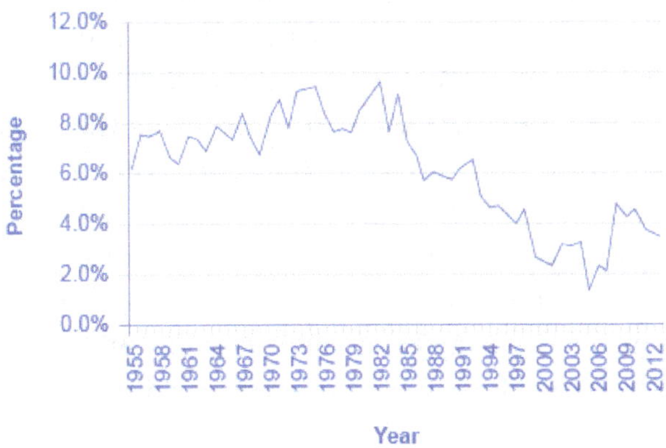

Figure 1. Personal Savings as a Percentage of Personal Income. Personal savings were about 7 to 11% of personal income for most of the years from the late 1950s up to the early 1990s. Since then, the rate of personal savings has fallen substantially, although it seems to have bounced back a bit since 2008. (Source: http://www.bea.gov/newsreleases/national/pi/pinewsrelease.htm)

The discussion of financial saving here will not focus on the specific financial investment choices, like bank accounts, stocks, bonds, mutual funds, or owning a house or gold coins. The characteristics of these specific financial investments, along with the risks and tradeoffs they pose, are detailed in the Labor and Financial Markets chapter. Here, the focus is saving in total—that is, on how a household determines how much to consume in the present and how much to save, given the expected rate of return (or interest rate), and how the quantity of saving alters when the rate of return changes.

Using Marginal Utility to Make Intertemporal Choices

Savings behavior varies considerably across households. One factor is that households with higher incomes tend to save a larger percentage of their income. This pattern makes intuitive sense; a well-to-do family has the flexibility in its budget to save 20–25% of income, while a poor family struggling to keep food on the table will find it harder to put money aside.

Another factor that causes personal saving to vary is personal preferences. Some people may prefer to consume more now, and let the future look after itself. Others may wish to enjoy a lavish retirement, complete with expensive vacations, or to pile up money that they can pass along to their grandchildren. There are savers and spendthrifts among the young, middle-aged, and old, and among those with high, middle, and low income levels.

Consider this example: Yelberton is a young man starting off at his first job. He thinks of the "present" as his working life and the "future" as after retirement. Yelberton's plan is to save money from ages 30 to 60, retire at age 60, and then live off his retirement money from ages 60 to 85. On average, therefore, he will be saving for 30 years. If the rate of return that he can receive is 6% per year, then \$1 saved in the present would build up to \$5.74 after 30 years (using the formula for compound interest, \$1(1 + 0.06)30 = \$5.74). Say that Yelberton will earn \$1,000,000 over the 30 years from age 30 to age 60 (this amount is approximately an annual salary of \$33,333 multiplied by 30 years). The question for Yelberton is how much of those lifetime earnings to consume during his working life, and how much to put aside until after retirement. This example is obviously built on simplifying assumptions, but it does convey the basic life-cycle choice of saving during working life for future consumption after retirement.

Figure 2 and Table 16 show Yelberton's intertemporal budget constraint. Yelberton's choice involves comparing the utility of present consumption during his working life and future consumption after retirement. The rate of return that determines the slope of the intertemporal budget line between present consumption and future consumption in this example is the annual interest rate that he would earn on his savings, compounded over the 30 years of his working life. (For simplicity, we are assuming that any savings from current income will compound for 30 years.) Thus, in the lower budget constraint line on the figure, future consumption grows by increments of \$574,000, because each time \$100,000 is saved in the present, it compounds to \$574,000 after 30 years at a 6% interest rate. If some of the numbers on the future consumption axis look bizarrely large, remember that this occurs because of the power of compound interest over substantial periods of time, and because the figure is grouping together all of Yelberton's saving for retirement over his lifetime.

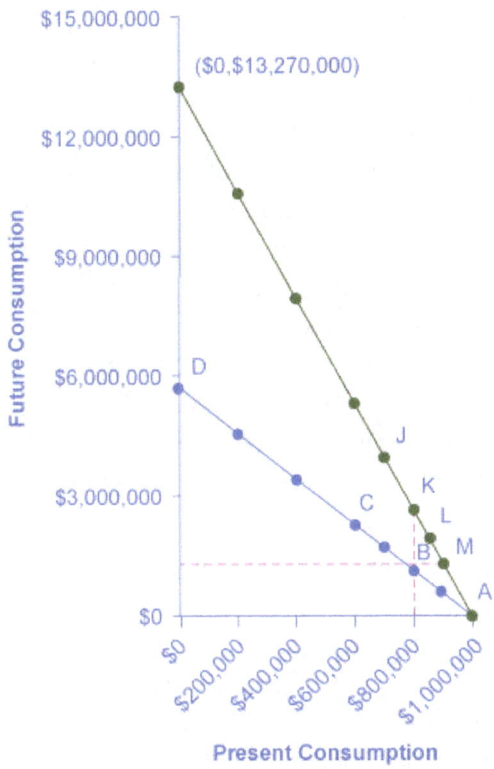

Figure 2. Yelberton's Choice: The Intertemporal Budget Set. Yelberton will make a choice between present and future consumption. With an annual rate of return of 6%, he decides that his utility will be highest at point B, which represents a choice of $800,000 in present consumption and $1,148,000 in future consumption. When the annual rate of return rises to 9%, the intertemporal budget constraint pivots up. Yelberton could choose to take the gains from this higher rate of return in several forms: more present saving and much higher future consumption (J), the same present saving and higher future consumption (K), more present consumption and more future consumption (L), or more present consumption and the same future consumption (M).

Table 16. Yelburton's Intertemporal Budget Constraint

Present Consumption	Present Savings	Future Consumption (6% annual return)	Future Consumption (9% annual return)
$1,000,000	0	0	0
$900,000	$100,000	$574,000	$1,327,000
$800,000	$200,000	$1,148,000	$2,654,000
$700,000	$300,000	$1,722,000	$3,981,000
$600,000	$400,000	$2,296,000	$5,308,000
$400,000	$600,000	$3,444,000	$7,962,000
$200,000	$800,000	$4,592,000	$10,616,000
0	$1,000,000	$5,740,000	$13,270,000

Yelberton will compare the different choices along the budget constraint and choose the one that provides him with the highest utility. For example, he will compare the utility he would receive from a choice like point A, with consumption of $1 million in the present, zero savings, and zero future consumption; point B, with present consumption of $800,000, savings of $200,000, and future consumption of $1,148,000; point C, with present consumption of $600,000, savings of $400,000, and future consumption of $2,296,000; or even choice D, with present consumption of zero, savings of $1,000,000, and future consumption of $5,740,000. Yelberton will also ask himself questions like these: "Would I prefer to consume a little less in the present, save more, and have more future consumption?" or "Would I prefer to consume a little more in the present, save less, and have less future consumption?" By considering marginal changes toward more or less consumption, he can seek out the choice that will provide him with the highest level of utility.

Let us say that Yelberton's preferred choice is B. Imagine that Yelberton's annual rate of return raises from 6% to 9%. In this case, each time he saves $100,000 in the present, it will be worth $1,327,000 in 30 years from now (using the formula for compound interest that $100,000 (1 + 0.09)30 = $1,327,000). A change in rate of return alters the slope of the intertemporal budget constraint: a higher rate of return or interest rate will cause the budget line to pivot upward, while a lower rate of return will cause it to pivot downward. If Yelberton were to consume nothing in the present and save all $1,000,000, with a 9% rate of return, his future consumption would be $13,270,000, as shown on Figure 2.

As the rate of return rises, Yelberton considers a range of choices on the new intertemporal budget constraint. The dashed vertical and horizontal lines running through the original choice B help to illustrate his range of options. One choice is to reduce present consumption (that is, to save more) and to have considerably higher future consumption at a point like J above and to the left of his original choice B. A second choice would be to keep the level of present consumption and savings the same, and to receive the benefits of the higher rate of return entirely in the form of higher future consumption, which would be choice K.

As a third choice Yelberton could have both more present consumption—that is, less savings—but still have higher future consumption because of the higher interest rate, which would be choice like L, above and to the right of his original choice B. Thus, the higher rate of return might cause Yelberton to save more, or less, or the same amount, depending on his own preferences. A fourth choice would be that Yelberton could react to the higher rate of return by increasing his current consumption and leaving his future consumption unchanged, as at point M directly to the right of his original choice B. The actual choice of what quantity to save and how saving will respond to changes in the rate of return will vary from person to person, according to the choice that will maximize each person's utility.

Applications of the Model of Intertemporal Choice

The theoretical model of the intertemporal budget constraint suggests that when the rate of return rises, the quantity of saving may rise, fall, or remain the same, depending on the preferences of individuals. For the U.S. economy as a whole, the most common pattern seems to be that the quantity of savings does not adjust much to changes in the rate of return. As a practical matter, many households either save at a fairly steady pace, by putting regular contributions into a retirement account or by making regular payments as they buy a house, or they do not save much at all. Of course, some people will have preferences that cause them to react to a higher rate of return by increasing their quantity of saving; others will react to a higher rate of return by noticing that with a higher rate of return, they can save less in the present and still have higher future consumption.

One prominent example in which a higher rate of return leads to a lower savings rate occurs when firms save money because they have promised to pay workers a certain fixed level of pension benefits after retirement. When rates of return rise, those companies can save less money in the present in their pension fund and still have enough to pay the promised retirement benefits in the future.

This insight suggests some skepticism about political proposals to encourage higher savings by providing savers with a higher rate of return. For example, Individual Retirement Accounts (IRAs) and 401(k) accounts are special savings accounts where the money going into the account is not taxed until it is taken out many years later, after retirement. The main difference between these accounts is that an IRA is usually set up by an individual, while a 401(k) needs to be set up through an employer. By not taxing savings in the present, the effect of an IRA or a 401(k) is to increase the return to saving in these accounts.

IRA and 401(k) accounts have attracted a large quantity of savings since they became common in the late 1980s and early 1990s. In fact, the amount of IRAs rose from $239 million in 1992 to $3.7 billion in 2005 to over $5 billion in 2012, as per the Investment Company Institute, a national association of U.S. investment companies. However, overall U.S. personal savings, as discussed earlier, actually dropped from low to lower in the late 1990s and into the 2000s. Evidently, the larger amounts in these retirement accounts are being offset, in the economy as a whole, either by less savings in other kinds of accounts, or by a larger amount of borrowing (that is, negative savings). The following Clear It Up further explores America's saving rates.

A rise in interest rates makes it easier for people to enjoy higher future consumption. But it also allows them to enjoy higher present consumption, if that is what these individuals desire. Again, a change in prices—in this case, in interest rates—leads to a range of possible outcomes.

How does America's saving rates compare to other countries?

By international standards, Americans do not save a high proportion of their income, as Table 17 shows. The rate of gross national saving includes saving by individuals, businesses, and government. By this measure, U.S. national savings amount to 17% of the size of the U.S. GDP, which measures the size of the U.S. economy. The comparable world average rate of savings is 22%.

Table 17. National Savings in Select Countries.

Country	Gross Domestic Savings as a Percentage of GDP
China	51%
India	30%
Russia	28%
Mexico	22%
Germany	26%
Japan	22%
Canada	21%
France	21%
Brazil	15%
United States	17%
United Kingdom	13%

The Unifying Power of the Utility-Maximizing Budget Set Framework

The choices of households are determined by an interaction between prices, budget constraints, and personal preferences. The flexible and powerful terminology of utility-maximizing gives economists a vocabulary for bringing these elements together.

Not even economists believe that people walk around mumbling about their marginal utilities before they walk into a shopping mall, accept a job, or make a deposit in a savings account. However, economists do believe that individuals seek their own satisfaction or utility and that people often decide to try a little less of one thing and a little more of another. If these assumptions are accepted, then the idea of utility-maximizing households facing budget constraints becomes highly plausible.

Behavioral Economics: An Alternative Viewpoint

As we know, people sometimes make decisions that seem "irrational" and not in their own best interest. People's decisions can seem inconsistent from one day to the next and they even deliberately ignore ways to save money or time. The traditional economic models assume rationality, which means that people take all available information and make consistent and informed decisions that are in their best interest. (In fact, economics professors often delight in pointing out so-called "irrational behavior" each semester to their new students, and present economics as a way to become more rational.)

But a new group of economists, known as behavioral economists, argue that the traditional method leaves out something important: people's state of mind. For example, one can think differently about money if one is feeling revenge, optimism, or loss. These are not necessarily irrational states of mind, but part of a range of emotions that can affect anyone on a given day. And what's more, actions under these conditions are indeed predictable, if the underlying environment is better understood. So, behavioral economics seeks to enrich the understanding of decision-making by integrating the insights of psychology into economics. It does this by investigating how given dollar amounts can mean different things to individuals depending on the situation. This can lead to decisions that appear outwardly inconsistent, or irrational, to the outside observer.

The way the mind works, according to this view, may seem inconsistent to traditional economists but is actually far more complex than an unemotional cost-benefit adding machine. For example, a traditional economist would say that if you lost a $10 bill today, and also got an extra $10 in your paycheck, you should feel perfectly neutral. After all, –$10 + $10 = $0. You are the same financially as you were before. However, behavioral economists have done research that shows many people will feel some negative emotion—anger, frustration, and so forth—after those two things happen. We tend to focus more on the loss than the gain. This is known as loss aversion, where a $1 loss pains us 2.25 times more than a $1 gain helps us, according to the economists Daniel Kahneman and Amos Tversky in a famous 1979 article in the journal Econometrica. This insight has implications for investing, as people tend to "overplay" the stock market by reacting more to losses than to gains. Indeed, this behavior looks irrational to traditional economists, but is consistent once we understand better how the mind works, these economists argue.

Traditional economists also assume human beings have complete self-control. But, for instance, people will buy cigarettes by the pack instead of the carton even though the carton saves them money, to keep usage down. They purchase locks for their refrigerators and overpay on taxes to force themselves to save. In other words, we protect ourselves from our worst temptations but pay a price to do so. One way behavioral economists are responding to this is by setting up ways for people to keep themselves free of these temptations. This includes what are called "nudges" toward more rational behavior rather than mandatory regulations from government. For example, up to 20 percent of new employees do not enroll in retirement savings plans immediately, because of procrastination or feeling overwhelmed by the different choices. Some companies are now moving to a new system, where employees are automatically enrolled unless they "opt out." Almost no-one opts out in this program and employees begin saving at the early years, which are most critical for retirement.

Another area that seems illogical is the idea of mental accounting, or putting dollars in different mental categories where they take different values. Economists typically consider dollars to be **fungible**, or having equal value to the individual, regardless of the situation.

You might, for instance, think of the $25 you found in the street differently from the $25 you earned from three hours working in a fast food restaurant. The street money might well be treated as "mad money" with little rational regard to getting the best value. This is in one sense strange, since it is still equivalent to three hours of hard work in the restaurant. Yet the "easy come-easy go" mentality replaces the rational economizer because of the situation, or context, in which the money was attained.

In another example of mental accounting that seems inconsistent to a traditional economist, a person could carry a credit card debt of $1,000 that has a 15% yearly interest cost, and simultaneously have a $2,000 savings account that pays only 2% per year. That means she pays $150 a year to the credit card company, while collecting only $40 annually in bank interest, so she loses $130 a year. That doesn't seem wise.

The "rational" decision would be to pay off the debt, since a $1,000 savings account with $0 in debt is the equivalent net worth, and she would now net $20 per year. But curiously, it is not uncommon for people to ignore this advice, since they will treat a loss to their savings account as higher than the benefit of paying off their credit card. The dollars are not being treated as fungible so it looks irrational to traditional economists.

Which view is right, the behavioral economists' or the traditional view? Both have their advantages, but behavioral economists have at least shed a light on trying to describe and explain behavior that has historically been dismissed as irrational. If most of us are engaged in some "irrational behavior," perhaps there are deeper underlying reasons for this behavior in the first place.

"Eeny, Meeny, Miney, Moe"—Making Choices

In what category did consumers worldwide increase their spending during the recession? Higher education. According to the United Nations Educational, Scientific, and Cultural Organization (UNESCO), enrollment in colleges and universities rose one-third in China and almost two-thirds in Saudi Arabia, nearly doubled in Pakistan, tripled in Uganda, and surged by three million—18 percent—in the United States. Why were consumers willing to spend on education during lean times? Both individuals and countries view higher education as the way to prosperity. Many feel that increased earnings are a significant benefit of attending college.

Bureau of Labor Statistics data from May 2012 supports this view, as shown in Figure 3. They show a positive correlation between earnings and education. The data also indicate that unemployment rates fall with higher levels of education and training.

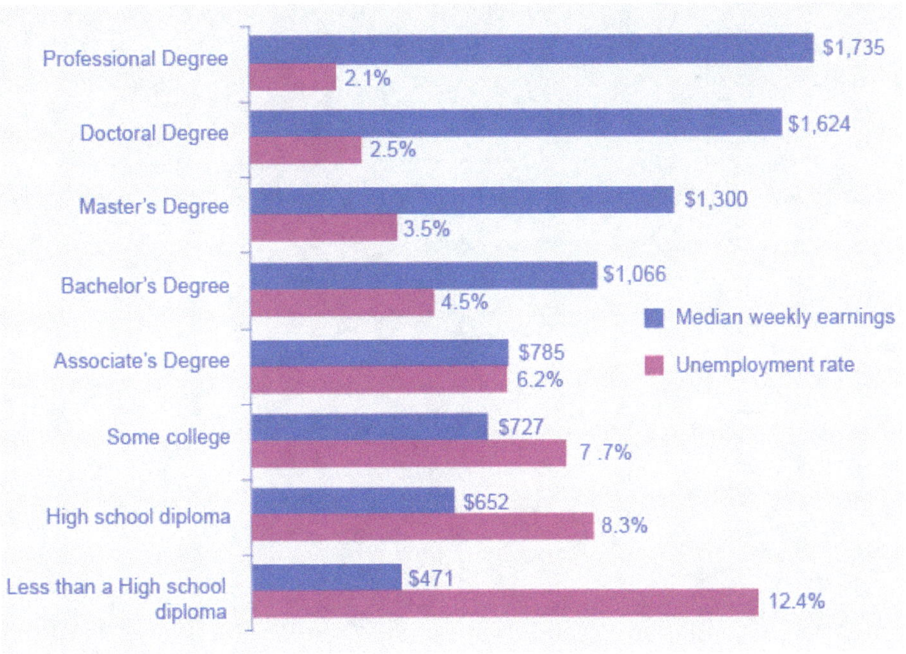

Figure 3. The Impact of Education on Earnings and Unemployment Rates, 2012. Those with the highest degrees in 2012 had substantially lower unemployment rates whereas those with the least formal education suffered from the highest unemployment rates. The national median average weekly income was $815, and the nation unemployment average in 2012 was 6.8%. (Source: Bureau of Labor Statistics, May 22, 2013)

Concepts and Summary

When making a choice along the intertemporal budget constraint, a household will choose the combination of present consumption, savings, and future consumption that provides the most utility. The result of a higher rate of return (or higher interest rates) can be a higher quantity of saving, the same quantity of saving, or a lower quantity of saving, depending on preferences about present and future consumption. Behavioral economics is a branch of economics that seeks to understand and explain the "human" factors that drive what traditional economists see as people's irrational spending decisions.

CHAPTER

8 CHALLENGING UTILITARIANISM'S IMPACT

8.1 THE VALUE OF ECONOMICS

The term value and the concept of value theory have taken on two distinct definitions in relation to economic theory. The first definition of the term value pertains to the role of normative analysis within economic theory. As discussed in chapter 1, for orthodox economic thinkers there is little room for normative thinking in the rigorous world of scientific economics. Subjective or moral judgments are discouraged in favor of utilizing a positive, value-free approach that is not a statement of anyone's value judgment or subjective feelings, but rather of what "is." By the standard orthodox textbook definition, the term "value" relates to personal biases and subjective beliefs. Also, recall from Chapter 2, the positive versus normative conflict presented by orthodox economics represents a false dichotomy. As has been discussed by non-orthodox economic theorists, subjective values tend to be present in all economic paradigms and are unavoidable.

The second definition of value that is common in economics is the one most people think of when they think of the term "value." For most people when they think of the value of something, such as a product, they are simultaneously thinking of the price of that product. Therefore, the term value and the term price tend to be used interchangeably. As a result, for many economists it is important to develop a theory of value because the theory of value provides the theorist with a sense of the origin of prices. After all, if an economist can identify the root source of value, then the same economist will also understand the root origin of prices. Since prices are incredibly important informational signals, being able to explain from where prices originate adds an important depth to economic theory.

On the surface both usages of the term "value," as described above, appear to be mutually exclusive. However, closer inspection reveals two interrelated issues. Scientists, economists included, already tend to, whether knowingly or unknowingly, assert subjective values within their theories. Values not only generate a necessary entanglement of facts and values, but they then become present throughout the very act of theorizing. In the case of economics, this means that the economic ideas that theorists present will include elements of their basic worldview or, as some would say, their philosophy.

The remainder of this chapter is laid out in such a manner as to explore the role of philosophy in economics. First, the philosophical foundation of orthodox economics, and its history, is explored. As will be shown, orthodox economics relies upon utilitarian philosophy for its value-based understanding of human action and motivation. As such, orthodox economics believes that the concept of utility holds the key to understanding the origin of prices. Additionally, utilitarianism forms the basis for the ethical perspective presented by orthodox economics. Upon closely examining the orthodox story of utility, the chapter moves on to identify important limitations that develop as a result of the use of utility. The chapter then moves on to provide alternative examples from heterodox economics, pointing out philosophical worldviews outside of utilitarianism that can form the basis of economic thought. Importantly, the alternative approaches presented do not suffer the pitfalls that are present within the orthodox, utilitarian approach.

8.2 UTILITARIANISM: THE PRINCIPLES OF ORTHODOX ECONOMICS

For those interested in the study of economics the concept of utility has a long history. Going back to the time of antiquity, great thinkers such as Aristotle made reference to the importance of the creation of use-value. From an Aristotelian standpoint use-value is the idea that human material production ought to be directed toward the creation of things that benefit human beings. Aristotle prioritized usefulness and discouraged wastefulness.

The role of the utility theory of value as a central component of the preferred ideological vision of orthodox economists of today, in some ways dates back to the time of Adam Smith. Smith, continuing the Aristotelian line of thinking, also saw significance in the concept of use-value.

Use-Value – The idea that the value of an object is based on how useful the product is to the consumer. Products have an intrinsic value to their consumers.

For Smith though, use-value represented the perceived benefit that people would derive from consumption. For Smith, consumers would be more apt to buy products that they perceived as useful as opposed to products that they believed are not useful. Still, Smith's analysis remains a long way from how utility is utilized by orthodox economists.

Although Smith does not go into much further development beyond his acknowledgement that consumers attach some kind of use-value to useful items, it is clear that Smith opens the door to the potential development of the idea that utility plays a role in determining the prices of products. Consider, if utility, or use-value, is important to consumers, then, presumably, utility must play a role in determining consumers' interest in purchasing a product. Because consumer demand is a reflection of consumer purchasing interests, consumer demand will be essential to the determination of the prices of products. It is with the evolution of economic ideas in the 19th century that the relationship between utility and prices is cemented within orthodox economic thought.

In order to understand the role of utility in contemporary orthodox economics, the place to begin is with the early 19th century philosopher and political economist Jeremy Bentham. Bentham possibly had the most prominent influence on the philosophical development of utility. Bentham's perspective is known as utilitarianism. Bentham describes utility as the cornerstone of the "Greatest Happiness Principle." In Bentham's usage, utility evolves beyond a description of usefulness into the embodiment of happiness. Utilitarianism espouses the belief that people are pleasure maximizers and pain minimizers. Therefore, any action that a person engages in must be driven by the desire either to gain happiness or to reduce pain. Taken to the field of economics, in Bentham's view, people desire products because those products bring the person happiness. Clearly, Bentham's perspective had a profound effect on orthodox economics, given the many references that this textbook has made in Chapters 2 and 6 to consumers being driven to maximize their utility.

Bentham's story, for all of its applicability to contemporary orthodox economics, is still only a partial analysis. One area in which Bentham's argument is incomplete is in his treatment of the measurability of utility. When describing how a consumer may assign utility to a product, Bentham freely employed both **cardinal** and **ordinal** measures of utility.

Cardinal utility – Is the idea that the utility a consumer assigns to a product is objective and, therefore, quantifiably measurable.

Ordinal utility – Is the idea that the utility that a consumer assigns to a product is subjective, in the mind of the consumer, and is, therefore, not directly quantifiably measurable.

As a rule Bentham seemed to generally acknowledge ordinal utility as being conceptually sound in comparison to cardinal utility. Bentham understood that cardinal utility cannot be objectively measured, a person cannot be attached to a device that measures units of happy (utils). There are, however, indirect measures that can allude to cardinal utility, such as the order in which consumers purchase products. Given two products with an identical price, if a consumer purchases one of the products prior to the other, it stands to reason that the first product purchased retain greater utility than the second product. Regardless, in absolute terms, how much utility a consumer actually assigns to a product cannot be empirically measured, rendering it subjective to the consumer. Limitations aside, Bentham frequently developed examples that required cardinal measures of utility.

Another area in which Bentham's analysis was incomplete pertained to the relationship between utility and the origins of prices of products. Recall the principle of diminishing marginal utility described in Chapter 7. Bentham anticipates the idea of diminishing marginal utility by describing instances in which a person can acquire more of something but feel less satisfaction from the additional unit than they received from earlier units. Bentham's depiction, however, remains abstract rather than appearing "scientifically" concrete.

Figure 1. Portrait of Jeremy Bentham (Source: Wellcome Images, Wikimedia, CC-BY 4.0)

Resolving some of the incomplete features of Bentham's story are the marginalists of the 1870s. Independent of one another, a group of thinkers triggered what is now referred to as the marginalist revolution. The marginalists famously apply differential calculus to utility analysis. Differential calculus focuses on rates of change between two variables. In the case of utility, differential calculus can be used to tell a story about how, as a consumer consumes more of a product, the happiness derived from that product will change. The marginalists attempted to demonstrate, in a more concrete way, the idea that as more of something is consumed, the satisfaction or utility per unit would decline. By applying calculus, and drawing pictures to reflect the conclusions drawn from the mathematical presentation, the marginalists create the appearance of a scientific advancement in the study of utility in economics. In terms of legacy, the marginalists use of calculus is a hallmark of modern orthodox economic theory.

As much as the marginalists influence the apparatus of modern orthodox economics, their analysis still remained incomplete in that the marginalists do not resolve the issue of ordinal versus cardinal utility. It is not until the 20th century that orthodox economic theorists settle on the use of ordinal utility as the foundation of their measurement of utility. The thinker most responsible for solidifying ordinal utility's place within economics is Paul Samuelson. Paul Samuelson develops a theory known as Revealed Preference. On the surface, revealed preference theory articulates the idea that the amount of utility that any one person derives from the consumption of a product is purely subjective to the consumer in question. However, once a consumer identifies that which brings them the greater happiness, the consumer then reveals their preferences to everyone by consuming the product that they desire. In this respect, revealed preference theory seeks to quantify utility by identifying utility as a consequence of a consumer's actions.

THE APPLICATION OF UTILITARIANS WITHIN ORTHODOX ECONOMICS AND ITS IMPLICATIONS

Whether an unwitting or a conscious choice, utility continues to be the preferred philosophical starting point for contemporary orthodox economists. Utility also carries with it a specific interpretation of human actions and interactions. Recall, for orthodox economics, the human being is a hedonist continually in search of greater pleasure or diminished pain. Any socially determined characteristics are given (not analyzed, merely accepted), yielding an isolated utility maximizer. Also, recall, that this notion of a hedonistic person is deeply controversial with respect to its application in economics. There simply does not exist irrefutable evidence that individuals only pursue products because those products provide the individual with pleasure. Human motive can be defined in many ways with hedonism being just one of many interpretations.

Regardless of its accuracy or inaccuracy, orthodox economists perceive that, for individuals, utility is maximized through the act of exchange. At any particular point in time, an individual, possessing an initial endowment (income), begins engaging in the act of exchange with some other individual economic agent. As all exchanges are assumed to be voluntary, any exchange that two parties are willing to engage in must be an exchange that will make both parties better off, otherwise neither party would engage in the exchange. Because being made better off means, according to orthodox economic theory, acquiring more utility, the act of exchanging is the act increasing one's holdings of utility. Any and all exchanges then must be increasing individual, and subsequently, society's total utility. Presumably, once some kind of round of exchanges is complete, any and all parties that engaged in exchanges are now better off because now they have more utility as a result of their exchanges.

Of course, no one really knows whether or not the result of these exchanges really has made the participants better off or worse off because there is no device that measures utility. Utility is purely subjective and non-empirical, which means that the revealed preference argument yields an outcome in which it must be assumed that all exchange participants are made better, otherwise they would not have participated in the exchange. Assuming people are better off does not mean that people are actually better off.

8.3 UTILITY AND PARETO OPTIMALITY: ORTHODOX ECONOMIC PERSPECTIVE ON SOCIAL WELFARE

For orthodox economists the ideal outcome for an economy is an outcome in which Pareto optimality is achieved. The concept of Pareto optimality owes its origins to a 19th century Italian mathematician Vilfredo Pareto. Stated simply, the Pareto criterion for determining whether an economy has produced the "best" or "ideal" outcome is fulfilled when economic outcomes are such that there is no way to make any one or many people better off without making any one person or many worse off.

On its own the Pareto criterion for social well-being is an attractive proposition. After all if someone is harmed in order to improve the plight of someone else or many others, then it appears obvious that someone is being granted preferential treatment at the expense of someone else or many others. The granting of preferential treatment hardly seems fair or equitable. In this context, the utilization of the Pareto criterion eliminates the need to make those choices.

Additionally, the granting of preferential treatment opens the door to a long series of ethical questions that can be avoided by applying the Pareto criterion. On what basis is the decision to harm or benefit being made? How or when are interventions that inflict harm or bestow benefits decided? If an intervention does take place, who is making the decision to inflict harm or bestow benefits? What is the degree of harm or benefit triggered by an intervention? What is the ethical basis for intervening? In many ways, whenever a government must make budgetary decisions, it is asking and answering these questions. For example, perhaps government policymakers would like to expand the size of the military. Expanding the size of the military requires that the government finance the expansion of the military. Financing military expansion may require that other government spending programs be reduced. Alternatively, perhaps taxes will be raised to pay for the military expansion. Either way, whomever is responsible for financing the military expansion is directly paying for someone else to benefit. In defense of expanding the military, policymakers may have to justify to the public why the public will, presumably, benefit from the expansion of the military. The Pareto criterion appears to clearly answer these questions. If a society knows when it is in a position of maximum benefit, then, on the basis of the Pareto criterion, no justification can be made to either harm or benefit anyone, causing all of the above questions become moot.

Something important has now been revealed. The Pareto criterion only becomes applicable when there is a measure of what it means for someone, or many, to benefit and for someone, or many, to be harmed. If some kind of metric exists, then, once measured, a society will know when no one person or many can be made better off without someone or many being harmed. Therefore, what is essential to the Pareto criterion is the mechanism a theorist uses to measure and determine a society's overall well being. For orthodox economists, the measure of individual and social well-being is the amount of utility that individuals and society has derived.

Utility Maximization and Pareto Optimality: Ethical Implications

Given the nature of utility maximization, human social interaction is reduced to exchange between individuals. Clearly the utility assumption generates a distinct depiction of human beings, human needs, and human society. The utility maximizing assumption also generates a specific conception of what is an economically "just" society. In other words, orthodox economics has a specific view of what it believes is the best way for society to be organized economically.

The orthodox worldview can be neatly summarized. If people desire utility, then people can acquire utility by exchanging with others. Once people exchange with others, the act of exchanging makes them better off. Once all exchanges are complete, all people are as well off as they can become economically. If everyone is as well off as they can become, then no one, or many, can be made better off without someone, or many, being made worse off. As far as orthodox economics is concerned, society has reached its ideal, Pareto optimal, outcome because people were free to make choices within an economy that facilitates exchanges, namely a market based economy.

At this point it should be clear that utilitarianism provides the philosophical foundation supporting orthodox economics while Pareto optimality represents the final outcome of the orthodox social welfare theory. If utility is the initial proposition on which orthodox theory is built, and Pareto optimality is the culmination of orthodox economic theory, then the utility and Pareto optimality must be intrinsically linked.

The dilemma for orthodox economics is that by accepting the utility theory of value and adopting the Pareto criterion as a social welfare measure, orthodox economics produces a very specific, and ethically limited, framework. For example, by focusing exclusively on the point of exchange, orthodox economics tends to ignore situations in which people are in disagreement with one another, circumstances of conflict. The reason why conflict is generally ignored is because the conditions of exchange are assumed in advance. For orthodox economics, the institutions of exchange, such as markets, contract law, and contract enforcement, are assumed to be in place prior to economic agents exchanging. Additionally, by assuming that initial endowments are given, orthodox economics assumes the existence of income on the part of trading parties, but generally fails to recognize where income originates.

The trouble for orthodox economics is that it is not hard to imagine a world in which one's income is affected by discriminatory factors such as racism, sexism, sexual orientation or any other divisive perception. In fact, imagination is not necessary, as the real world is filled with examples of discrimination and exploitation. Regardless of form, the outcome of discrimination is the same, some are able to exploit others by virtue of their power to discriminate. Or, in another example, it is clear that conditions of inequality can empower some relative to others. People that disproportionately benefit from economic outcomes are endowed with more income and have the power to acquire resources. In instances in which the acquisition of resources becomes concentrated in the hands of a small number of people, those with great wealth and/or income may have the power to exploit their positions of power at the expense of others. Of course, with exploitation, conditions of inequality may be worsened allowing unequal situations to become further entrenched.

Conscientious observers of a capitalist market system, including utilitarians, are aware that situations of exploitation are not only present, but virtually unavoidable. Given the existence of conflict and inherent disparities of power, it is easy to imagine that someone might want to intervene in economic affairs in order to level the playing field. For example, someone might advocate to pass laws to penalize discriminatory behavior so as to reduce its prevalence, or others might seek to impose taxes on some so as to redistribute income or wealth in the hopes of reducing inequality. The interventions in questions would certainly be designed to make someone, or many, better off at the expense of someone else, or many others. As a result, no matter how justified the interventionist actions may be, and they are certainly justifiable in the examples provided above, within the utilitarian and Pareto criterion context the interventionist actions cannot be supported!

If the significance of utilitarianism and the Pareto criterion remains obscure, then perhaps less abstract and much more obvious examples may be useful. The following situations, using subjective measures of utility, are Pareto sub-optimal and cannot be justified:

- The defeat of Nazi Germany because Adolf Hitler was made worse off.
- The end of slavery in the American South because slave owners were made worse off.

Clearly, to any reasonable observer the defeat of Nazi Germany and the end of slavery in the American South are justifiable as they ended horrible chapters in human history. However, by following the utilitarian belief and coupling it to the Pareto criterion, orthodox economics cannot really make any argument to defend the destruction of Nazi Germany and the conclusion of slavery in the American South. Subjectively speaking, Hitler's loss of utility may have more than offset the world's gain in utility and thus made the world worse off. Or, subjectively speaking, the loss of utility to slave owners in the South may have more than offset the gain in utility experienced by the former slaves. After all, if no quantifiable measure is possible it is actually impossible to know whether or not total utility has become larger or smaller so there is no way for a utilitarian to justify an intervention in the above, albeit extreme, cases. Additionally, any intervention in the above cases required someone or many being made worse off in order to make some or many better off. The utilitarian tradition has no adequate way of applying anything more than some kind of hedonistic, happiness seeking, value judgment to human action. Obviously, there are serious moral and ethical weaknesses associated with the acceptance of utilitarianism.

In summary, the significance and value-laden implications of accepting utility, appears to elude most orthodox economists. In neoclassical theory price and utility are equalized, specifically price and marginal utility. Therefore, price equals value and this concludes the story. The neoclassical oversimplification of value theory, which treats value and price as synonyms, fails to recognize that by believing in utility, the orthodox economist is believing in a set of pre-ordained value judgments. The importance of this point cannot be overstated. Observe the significance of prices in a capitalist economy as described in this textbook. Marveling at how fluidly consumers and producers respond to price changes in markets the textbook states:

"...adjustments in response to price changes happen all of the time in a market economy, often so smoothly and rapidly that we barely notice them...For both the U.S. economy and the world economy as a whole, markets – that is, demand and supply – are the primary social mechanism for answering the basic questions about what is produced, how it is produced, and for whom it is produced." (pg. 71)

Because prices send the signals that determine the allocation of resources in a market economy, and the allocation of resources has tremendous social ramifications, then the question of whether or not the allocation of resources is "socially just" must be addressed. Because value theory provides the foundation for which the quantitative origin of prices, it is value theory then that also provides the basis for the normative criterion from which prices and the allocation of resources may be interpreted. Clearly, the choice of value theory is extremely important.

Unfortunately, for orthodox economics, the normative implications of the utilitarian assumption generally lay dormant.

As non-orthodox economists are well aware, value theory acts as a cohesive, it is the glue that connects economic theory to a society's moral and ethical norms. Any complete theoretical depiction of economic interaction necessarily requires a theory of value. As such, it is important to self- reflect on what values have been adopted by a theory and how those values impact how economic outcomes are interpreted. Given the importance of value theory, the one dominant proposition presented throughout this paper is that it is absolutely necessary for any economic theorist to anchor their theoretical ideas to a theory of value. Within this context, however, the utility theory of value presents orthodox economists with a dual horned dilemma. To accept utility as the basis for their analysis means that orthodox economists are implicitly valuing any and all market driven economic outcomes, regardless of the negative impacts that those outcomes may have on large segments of the society. To the contrary, to argue against any and all market outcomes as just, an economist, orthodox or otherwise, necessarily must begin their theorizing applying a different set of values outside of the value of endless hedonism that is central to utilitarian beliefs.

8.4 RELEASE FROM THE UTILITARIANISM'S NORMATIC CONSTRAINTS

Given the limitations and challenges associated with utilitarianism, many students of economics seek out alternative approaches for measuring economic well-being and interpreting the societal implications of economic outcomes. The following describes, two alternative, heterodox, approaches for interpreting economic conditions.

TWO NORMATIVE EXAMPLES FROM HETERODOX ECONOMICS

Abandoning Utility: The Capabilities Approach and the Ethical Considerations of Amartya Sen

Where do the seeds of discontent sprout? In 1998 Amartya Sen was awarded the Nobel Prize in economics. Sen is a fascinating case study as he provides an example of an economist who is not a utilitarian. Early in his career Sen had abandoned utilitarianism. What prompted Sen to abandon utility as a first principle? The answer to this question can be found at the beginning of Sen's career when Sen encountered a utilitarian tradition in economics that had shed nearly all the conventional characteristics of ethical analysis. While the early 19th century utilitarian thinkers such as Bentham had identified and described some of the ethical issues surrounding the idea of diminishing marginal utility, by the late 20th century utilitarianism in economics had been reduced to revealed preference theory. For Sen, utilitarianism provides entirely too-narrow an assessment of what it means to be a person. The result is that there are far too many limits associated with utilitarianism for the utilitarian to be able to make effective, and informed, moral evaluations.

Taken further, Sen also recognizes the link between the moral vacuum produced by utilitarian philosophy and the neoclassical application of the Pareto criterion. For Sen, utilitarianism and the Pareto criterion are like a form of normative handcuffs. Neither the distribution of income nor initial utilities factor in to the choice making, exchange story, promoted by orthodox economics. By ignoring the initial endowments of income or utility, Sen argues that a condition of Pareto optimal may also be one of deep inequality and hardship. Those without property and with little income often times find themselves without property and little income even though they have engaged in market exchange.

Admittedly, a person's actual freedom to exchange may provide a person with a degree of additional utility. Clearly being free to make choices is empowering and valuable to individuals. However, one's freedom to act does not mean that a person is in a remotely decent position in the market. The fact is, a market outcome can be Pareto optimal and still be less than socially optimal. For example, instead of demanding change people in poor situations often simply adjust to their negative circumstances. The deprived find some area of existence that gives them pleasure and make do. The result is a disadvantaged yet acquiescent populace that not only continues to function, but may be falsely perceived as happy or not too sad. In this example, utilitarianism generates a persistently unfair outcome within a population of people ill-equipped to effectively do anything to alter that outcome. This utilitarian picture highlights a tendency to under-estimate the plight of people in negative circumstances and causes Sen to conclude that neoclassical welfare economics is incapable of addressing the ethical issues that accompany the existence of poverty and oppression.

In terms of the problems associated with the distribution of utilities, Sen criticizes the utilitarian notion that every action in life is based on pleasure or happiness. There is no equality to be found in adding up everyone's utility to find a sum of total utility. It is possible for a maximum of total social utility to be generated under a circumstance in which one person receives the largest share of the available utility while many others receive very little. Further, it is not feasible to correct for an unequal distribution of utilities generated by market outcomes. The only way to rectify the impasse requires that the theorist be able to engage in interpersonal comparisons of well-being. In other words, people need to be able to compare how well off they are relative to other people. Relative comparisons are not something to which utility is adept at explaining. Given all of the problems Sen identifies, he departs from utilitarian precepts and develops an alternative measure of economic well-being.

The Capabilities Approach

The capabilities approach represents Sen's alternative to the neoclassical welfare model. The capabilities approach is a theoretical device that allows for interpersonal welfare comparisons, while also maintaining the ability and freedom of people to make choices. For Sen, the interpersonal comparisons of well-being should be based on a group of what Sen calls "functionings."

Functionings – Represents a state of being for an individual as well as the collection of all things an individual can be doing. Functionings can be as basic as being well-nourished and properly sheltered to as challenging as flying an airplane.

In turn, the measure of social welfare is the "capability" of people to access and develop their "functionings."

Capability – Is the availability of functionings coupled with the ability of the individual to achieve a combination of functionings.

The combination of functionings that are available and the ability of an individual to achieve a combination of functionings is the measure of an individuals well-being. Consider the following table.

	Limited Capabilities	Greater Capabilities
Limited Functionings	Low Welfare	Moderate Welfare
Greater Functionings	Moderate Welfare	High Welfare

Based on the capabilities approach, having many options available, such as states of being or activities to pursue, and then having the freedom to pursue those options is the ideal. The highest social welfare is achieved when a society produces an environment that meets basic needs while also provide people with ample opportunities to pursue challenging and life enriching activities. To the contrary, having limited access to functionings, and limited freedom in the pursuit of those functionings is the least advantageous position. In the case of moderate welfare outcomes, either individuals have many possible functionings available, but a limited freedom to pursue those functionings, or a limited set of available functionings but substantial freedom to pursue those goals.

CAPABILITIES AND FUNCTIONINGS: EXAMPLES OF WELFARE OUTCOMES

Limited Functionings/Limited Capabilities

Represents a case in which a person or a group of people are living with clearly definable limits to their **functionings** as defined by abject poverty, malnourishment and/or starvation and with little to no medical care. In this scenario the person or people are simply seeking to survive from one day to the next, there is little to no long term planning or goals. Possibly the result of social and political unrest such as a civil war (the current situation in Syria for example), or a weather calamity such as a drought, or a socioeconomic order such as the slave economy of the pre-Civil War American South.

Given the horrendous living conditions and limited functioning, any person living under these conditions would likely attempt make changes in their lives in order to try and reduce their immediate suffering. The ability to make changes, their **capabilities**, may not be possible as they may be living under conditions of political, military, and economic repression. Absent the freedom to maneuver, the person or people in this circumstance are rendered virtually helpless to the situation in which they have befallen. For example, unless the slave is freed, as property, the slave simply cannot pursue other options

Limited Functionings/Greater Capabilities

Represents a case in which a person or people are again deeply limited in terms of having basic needs and few wants met. In this instance, however, the person or people in this circumstance have some options to escape their plight. For example, consider the scenario of political unrest, if greater capabilities are present, the person or people can possibly vacate the region in which the unrest in unfolding. Evacuation of refugees to other more stable regions of the world create capabilities for the now displaced residents from a place devoid of functionings to places with both functionings and resources to expand capabilities. Another example could be the freeing of slaves in the American South during the post-Civil War period.

Greater Functionings/Limited Capabilities

Represents a case in which a person or people have their basic needs and wants met, while enjoying the luxury of having many other possible functionings available within the society such as educational, health care, and employment opportunities. In this instance, however, the person or people in this circumstance do not have options available to access the abundance of functionings. For example, consider the scenario of repressive political forces that are the result of situations of patriarchal social structures, or general totalitarian principles. A society characterized by repressive political regimes will restrict the freedom of its populace to enjoy the varied functionings that exist. A historic example would be the Jewish population that was subjected to the ruling principles of Nazi Germany.

Greater Functionings/Greater Capabilities

Represents a case in which a person or people have their basic needs and wants met, while enjoying the luxury of having many other possible functionings available within the society such as educational, health care, and employment opportunities. In this instance, however, the person or people in this circumstance also have a great many options available to access the abundance of functionings. For example, consider the example of the majority of people living in economies characterized as advanced developed economies with largely democratic political institutions. Certainly there remain conditions of repression such as discrimination, sexism, racism, and any number of limiting conditions. However, given democratic political structures and civil society outlets, people are able to continue to press for ever-expanding capabilities.

The capabilities approach then is not just a story of the freedom to pursue well-being, such as is the case in the story provided by orthodox economics. Instead, the capabilities approach is asking questions about initial endowments, available functionings, as well as the distributional outcomes associated with the pursuit of those functionings. Given the capabilities approach, the social welfare analysis of economics is no longer reduced to the action of choice making, but rather to both the conditions preceding choice as well as the outcomes associated with choices. While functionings can vary for different people across social circumstances, as well as time and place, so long as people have the ability to obtain the outlined functionings then they have an opportunity to elevate their well-being. Clearly, the capabilities approach represents for Sen, and others, a framework capable of generating more ethically pleasing results than that of the utility-tainted Pareto criterion.

In conclusion, Sen has managed to escape the ethical handcuffs of utilitarianism. The capabilities approach offers Sen, and other economists interested in exploring the capabilities approach, a new ethical theory. Sen has clearly avoided the fate of many neoclassical economists, i.e. being able study economics absent ethics.

The Marxian Approach and the Labor Theory of Value

Another approach to applying normative reasoning toward economic phenomena is the Marxian labor theory of value. In stark contrast to the utility theory of value, the preanalytic vision associated with the labor theory of value produces a view of humanity and human need that is virtually antithetical to the utilitarian depiction. Rather than experiencing social interaction through exchange, within the labor theory of value human beings are presented as engaged in the act of production.

The basic proposition on which the labor theory of value is constructed is the idea that before something can be exchanged it must be produced. As a result, the value of products is generated at the point of production, where the products are created. At the point of production, labor is the essential component of production processes. While machines can enhance the productivity of human labor, machines only exist as a result of the collective accumulation of human labor over time. Importantly, machines themselves do not create labor. After all, a nail cannot hammer itself. The implication is that the process of production has always required human labor power as even the most sophisticated machines require human operators.

Additionally, production has always been a social endeavor as human beings work with one another to produce those things that satisfy the material wants of people. Consider, for example, a loaf of bread that you see on a grocery store shelf. The production and distribution process necessary to bring the loaf of bread to the grocery store shelf is extensive, requiring the contribution of a great many people. For starters, the agricultural process that provides the wheat, and/or oats, and/or grains that are the primary ingredients for making bread have to be grown by farmers. The number of farmers involved may number in the hundreds or thousands. Additionally, the farmers will use tools and other inputs provided to them by other producers. Those producer, the producers of farm equipment, will also bring together laborers and equipment in a manufacturing process that will build farm equipment. By continuation, the tools and equipment used in the manufacturing process that builds farm equipment will also have to be produced by laborers using other tools and equipment in other production processes, and so on and so forth. On the other end of the production process, after harvesting, the basic agricultural inputs used in making bread will be transported to processing facilities. The act of transportation requires that laborers operate transportation equipment like trains and trucks. Just as was the case with farm equipment, transportation equipment will be made by many laborers that will be utilizing many machines that will have been produced by many other laborers using many other machines, and so on and so forth. Of course, transportation equipment generally requires fuel. If the fuel is a petroleum byproduct, then the extraction of petroleum will once again require many laborers using significant amounts of equipment through many stages of production until a fuel is available that will be used to operate the transportation equipment. Over and over again, each element of production requires many other laborers in many other production processes in a seemingly endless and nearly incomprehensible scale of human interaction. Clearly, production is an inherently social process that only takes place when human beings apply themselves to a multitude of production processes

Because the sole universally necessary element in the production process is labor, labor becomes the only true and relevant source of value. Human history demonstrates that human survival necessitates that human beings engage first and foremost in the process of providing for material needs. If human beings exchange, it is only because they first produced an excess that they are willing to exchange. Exchange is not a necessary condition for human survival, whereas production is required for human existence.

When juxtaposed, the differences between the vision generated by the utility theory of value and the labor theory of value could not be more visible. Let's examine four primary differences.

First, orthodox economics downplays any necessary human social relationships, as individuals are viewed as isolated utility maximizers within orthodox economic thought. To the contrary, adherents to the labor theory of value see human behavior itself, including exchange relationships, as being the result of social relationships. By continuation, a strong argument can be made that there are also important historical understandings and divisions between the two value theories. For utility theorists, because human behavior is perceived as a universal constant across time, understanding economic history is not a necessary component of their theory. Labor theorists, however, must study history closely in order to attempt to understand and identify the important changes in social arrangements that have historically arisen in different socioeconomic systems.

Second, due to the fact that exchange is a voluntary form of social interaction, harmonious outcomes appear normal within utilitarian thinking. To the contrary, since labor is the source of value and production, if there are class differences in a society, those class differences will inevitably end in conflict. The result is that conflict, not harmony, is front and center for labor theorists.

Third, while neoclassical economists take as given individual preferences, and by implication assert that the act of choosing is always efficient, labor theorists argue that preferences arise from social relationships and social interactions. As such, adherents to the labor theory of value do not accept the choice-driven revealed preference argument on social welfare.

Fourth, whereas orthodox economists identify individual incomes as originating through a voluntary process of exchange between individuals whose preferences are given, the labor theorist argues that the income that flows to non-laboring classes is the byproduct of a process of **exploitation**.

Exploitation – The idea that a producer or producers of a product receive compensation that is less than the value of what the producer or producers contributed to the production process.

Clearly the utility theory of value and the labor theory of value yield two different and competing conceptions of human existence, producing two different normative criteria for evaluating human interaction.

It would appear that the choice of value theory and recognition of its normative impact should be of the utmost importance to a theorist. This is not always the case. Perhaps due to the obscure relationship between price and value in neoclassical theory, there are many neoclassical theorists who directly violate the philosophical foundations of their accepted theory of value and do so by attempting to temper the less-than-savory ethical outcomes present in a capitalist market system. Alternatively, while most heterodox thinkers openly challenge the ethical outcomes of the market system and the conclusions brought about by the use of utility, many very prominent heterodox thinkers also either reject the need for a theory of value or do not explicitly endorse a formal theory of value. Sen falls under the latter category. In both instances value theory's importance is being inadequately recognized. While continued criticism of neoclassical theory is undoubtedly warranted, heterodox economists, regardless of their lofty accomplishments, prestige, and respectability, should not be absolved of deserved criticism. Within this premise, an evaluation of the relationship between value theory and Sen's important contribution to the critique of neoclassical welfare economics will be the focus of the remainder of this paper.

8.5 AT A GLANCE

Many students of economics are drawn to the discipline out of an interest in understanding the social and moral meaning and significance of economic outcomes. Interpreting the social and moral meaning of economic outcomes, however, requires a set of philosophical beliefs that can be effectively integrated and tied to economic activity. In this chapter we have seen how orthodox economics entwines utilitarian philosophy to economic activity. We have also seen the limitations to the utilitarian approach in that it gives the adherents to this tradition little to no room to challenge the outcomes associated with market economic activity. In this chapter we have also seen how heterodox economists, by not accepting the utilitarian tradition have utilized other philosophical approaches, such as the capabilities approach or the labor theory of value, to interpret economic events. In the case of these alternative philosophical approaches, market outcomes are not assumed to be socially just. For heterodox economists, as a result of alternative philosophical visions, questions of conflict, such as exploitation and discrimination, are directly confronted and possible solutions are provided.

CHAPTER

MODERN CONSUMPTION: AN INSTITUTIONAL ANALYSIS 9

Who are we and what do we want?

One of the more notorious elements of the neoclassical perspective in economics is its treatment of people as isolated, self-interested individuals. These 'economic agents' are endowed with their own personal 'utility functions' and *de gustibus non est disputandum*: tastes are simply a matter of personal preference. The choices we make, then, are nothing more than the manifestation of our tastes as we calculate the most satisfaction we can get from our scarce resources–most importantly, our money, which we begrudgingly acquire through work.

Pause for a moment to think about the following questions: what does it mean to be human? What is our atomistic approach to utility maximizing agents saying about human nature? And finally, does this offer a complete explanation of why we consume the things we consume (and often times aspire to consume more in the future)?

The 'hedonistic man' (or *homo economicus*) of neoclassical economics is, as institutional economist Thorstein Veblen observed, a lightning calculator of pleasures and pains, who oscillates like a homogeneous globule of desire of happiness under the impulse of stimuli that shift him about the area, but leave him intact. He has neither antecedent nor consequent. ... The hedonistic man is not a prime mover. He is not the seat of a process of living...

In point of fact, however, it seems obvious that:

- People do behave deliberately and consciously, in ways that affect the world around them – that is, they *are* prime movers, not simply reacting to external changes.
- People change, they develop, in ways that cannot simply be construed as reallocations of scarce resources – that is, people *have* antecedents (where they came from) and consequents (where they're going).

And, perhaps most importantly, people are social. Homo sapiens is a species that, unlike say lumbricus terrestris (earthworms), must live in groups. This fact has been long recognized. Take, for instance, Aristotle:

Man is by nature a social animal; an individual who is unsocial naturally and not accidentally is either beneath our notice or more than human. Society is something that precedes the individual. Anyone who either cannot lead the common life or is so self-sufficient as not to need to, and therefore does not partake of society, is either a beast or a god.

While human societies are made up of individuals, any given individual must come out of a society which existed before she did. This would suggest that our approach to understanding individual behavior should start with an understanding of society, not the other way around. In this chapter you will be introduced to an alternative, heterodox analysis along these lines: the institutional approach; and you will explore the new insights that this analysis brings to the study of consumption in modern economies.

9.1 ANALYSIS OF THE INSTITUTION

An economics that treats institutions as primary is necessary to understand the economic behavior of group-dependent individuals–that is, people making decisions within the context of their families, communities, industries, and other forms of organization, formal and informal. It is these social contexts and organizations to which heterodox economists are referring when they use the term **institutions**. A broad definition of the term might be stated as follows:

Institutions are collectively shared habits of thought–of knowing, doing, and valuing–that control, expand, and liberate individual action.

As Aristotle recognized some 24 centuries ago, these institutions exist prior to the individuals born into them. They are the rules we learn that tell us what to do and what not to do. But as constricting as that may sound, institutions also constitute a powerful tool for the human race: they allow individuals to forego solving problems that others have already solved (so that we don't have to 'reinvent the wheel', as it were); and they create reasonable expectations of others' behavior, allowing us to act collectively. Take, for instance, the simple collectively shared habit of thought concerning which side of the road to drive on. Knowing ahead of time which side we're to drive on saves us from the dangerous requirement of learning through trial and error. Likewise, this simple institution doesn't just restrict our decisions; it also produces expectations of what others will be doing, allowing us to travel more safely than we could without those expectations. In this manner, our actions are expanded beyond what they could otherwise be–we would, in fact, be more limited without this institution.

Of course, individuals are not–and could not be–made to conform precisely to the institutions into which they are born–society is not a rigid mold into which each person is poured at birth. We are 'prime movers' capable of making our own decisions and, to some extent, of changing the institutions of our society. But, it is the collective power that institutions give human communities as a whole which ultimately liberates us, that allows us to shape our own destinies and to participate in the collective shaping of our community's destiny as well.

Finally, as habits, institutions clearly must stay the same over some period of time. Yet, the technologies, laws, culture, and so on–that is, the institutions–of any given society evolve over time, too. This occurs through the accidental and intentional adaptation of how we think–our 'habits of thought'–to an ever-changing world around us. But, this creates an inherent tension within the concept of institutions: as the essential means by which humans collectively survive, institutions must constantly evolve to meet the proliferating exigencies we face; yet, as habits, they must have a resilience to change, a constancy, to be of any use at all. Recognizing this tension offers an important insight into the essential nature of present institutions: our collectively shared habits of thought are always a combination of useful ways of solving problems and the useless remnants of old ways of thinking.

With the basic tools and insights of institutional analysis in hand, we turn now to analyzing consumption in modern society. As you'll see, the decisions we make when it comes to what we consume and why we make those decisions can look very different once we take this fundamentally distinct perspective as our starting point. Our understanding of how we act as consumers depends on our understanding of who we are as a species.

9.2 CONSPICUOUS CONSUMPTION

An institutional analysis of modern consumption patterns would, of course, look first and foremost to a society's institutions to explain these behaviors. Our tastes and preferences, in this view, are primarily the result, not of some abstract lightning calculation of marginal utilities per dollar, but rather of the common habits of thought shared among our peers, our family, and our society more generally. They do not emerge miraculously from each of our individual constitutions. Instead, they are the result of an institutional evolution, occurring in part by unplanned drift, and in part by intentional acts of problem solving, ceremonial observance, and persuasion.

In this view, we're consuming the things we consume today largely because we learned that those things are appropriate to consume. And, importantly, the institutions that define what is and is not appropriate do not entirely reflect what is most conducive to nurturing individual well-being, social cooperation, and sustainable uses of technology. Rather, they will reflect in part the imbecile and anachronistic habits of thought inherited from our past.

Take for instance one of Veblen's best-known concepts, conspicuous consumption: consuming goods not for their capacity to produce personal satisfaction (utility), but rather because they allow the consumer to demonstrate or enhance her prestige. Surely, a host of examples come to mind readily: designer clothing that serves no better as clothing than equivalents without the brand recognition; upscale dining establishments serving food that is no more nutritional than their more modest counterparts; sports cars that, while perhaps hypothetically capable of winning high-speed races, are no better at what they'll actually be used for (driving around town and sitting in traffic) than an ordinary automobile. What do all of these have in common?

While one could argue that each of these examples is a good or service of a higher quality than their cheaper alternatives, most people would easily recognize that there is an element in each of allowing one to conspicuously consume–to 'show off' the fact that one has the money to make purchases that others simply could not afford. The question becomes, why would someone go out of their way to spend money on things that, in fact, *don't* provide additional utility or value in use? And, as you might have guessed, answering this question requires an analysis of the institutions that guide our consumption decisions in modern society. The following breakout box points the way toward Veblen's ultimate conclusion.

Sometimes referred to as the first feminist economist, Thorstein Veblen published his "Economic Theory of Woman's Dress" in 1894, breaking down the characteristics of the apparel of his time that offered the consumer something more than simply protection from the elements. His three cardinal principles of women's dress, each of which was "advertising the fiction that they live without any gainful occupation," were:

Expensiveness: clothing "must be uneconomical"–that is, demonstrating that the wearer, or her family, has the means to waste money on items of little functional value. High-dollar brand names make this easier to recognize for the uninitiated; but ultimately the expense of the work and material that went into producing these items is a more subtle, sophisticated way of indicating the same.

- Novelty: to the extent that clothing is useful, the wearer must not get the full use value from it. She must discard articles well before even insignificant wear starts to show. Observing seasonal changes in fashion helps to coordinate and enforce this sort of consumption observance.
- Ineptitude: clothing must show that the wearer doesn't have to participate in useful work. For instance, clothing might be severely binding, or footwear might restrict movement.

Can you think of any examples of consumption goods outside of women's apparel that fit this description? My personal favorite comes from men's professional clothing: the necktie. As you're probably aware, neckties don't serve much of a function–they're certainly not providing warmth, and in fact they're not even covering up an otherwise naked part of the body. So why do some men find themselves compelled not only to buy and wear these products, but to periodically discard the old ones and purchase new ones?

A common response from students is: they make you look professional. But, that just begs the question, why do they make you look professional–that is, why do we associate neckties with professionalism? Surely men in most professions don't actually make use of the tie in their work (though I've found they make a convenient wipe for smudged eyeglasses). Consider Veblen's cardinal principles above as applied to the necktie.

Expensiveness: while presumably whatever function neckties serve could be equally well-served were they made from a relatively inexpensive material like cotton (or, for that matter, paper), they tend instead to be made of more expensive materials like silk.

- Novelty: those who follow men's fashion will know that neckties are subject to similar style changes as other types of clothing–in terms, especially, of patterns and widths. Most people are probably able to discern a tie that was purchased in the 1980s versus the 2010s, much as most people can give a rough date to when a car was produced just by looking at it.
- Ineptitude: paradoxically, to demonstrate professionalism, men are often expected to wear apparel that does more to hinder than to aid their capacity for work. The delicate and expensive fabric, for instance, indicates that the 'professional man' is not likely doing work that would involve 'getting his hands dirty' in the literal sense. Likewise, it would not typically be wise to wear a long necktie in a manufacturing context in which machines are being used, lest the tie get caught in the machine.

These are strange principles by which to guide your consumption goods, indeed; and certainly not ones that are limited to women's dress–or even clothing in general. A little reflection on modern culture and the reader could probably see these principles in much of what we consume today. But, again, why are these apparently useless and even wasteful elements so desireable to the modern consumer? Why would someone want to waste money, or to show off they they don't contribute to society? The remainder of this section will give a summary explanation.

It goes almost without saying that, as social creatures, we humans feel a sense of self-esteem based in part on how we think others see us. We strive to fit in, to avoid feeling inferior, and at times to show our superiority to others–which, of course, must make others feel inferior. But, how we do so is dictated by the accepted social norms–the institutions–that we were born into; and those institutions have mutated through generations to produce a 'strange' set of criteria for who is superior and who is inferior.

In much earlier times one's prowess, the respect afforded by one's peers, would reflect chiefly the capacity to ably accomplish something that was useful to the group. As humans' technologies improved, however, it became increasingly the case that:

- The greatest contribution to current productivity came from the countless generations of workers, inventors, engineers, and so on from whom society had inherited its industrial arts. And,
- As technologies became increasingly sophisticated, more and more people, each having increasingly specialized skills, was necessary to efficiently produce things with these more sophisticated technologies.

The problem with these developments is that it becomes very difficult to differentiate one person's contribution from another's, or, more accurately, from the general productivity of the group acting collectively.

Consequently, over a very long time the presumption developed that how much you contributed relative to others would simply be reflected in how much money you made (whether this is true or not is another matter altogether). But this presented a problem for establishing the amount of prestige others should afford you: how much you have in your bank account isn't typically public information, and politeness dictates that you shouldn't go around waving your most recent ATM account balance slip in people's faces. The solution? Demonstrate your prowess, as evidenced by your vast riches, by wasting money wherever possible.

Part of this anthropological history, which can only be given in the most rudimentary of forms here, also demonstrates a division of employments in terms of prestige. In particular, early humans garnered prestige from exercising their power over the natural world–hunting and killing large game, or controlling the floods through irrigation channels, for instance. However, once technologies improved, it became increasingly the case that demonstrating power meant controlling or extracting from the productive community itself–that is, from people–more so than from nature. As a result, the higher classes came to be associated with occupations of predation, control, and leisure–for instance, politics and war, management and finance, celebrity and fashion, . With consumption as the chief way to demonstrate, and to reinforce in the minds of one's peers, that one belongs to the 'better' class of people, our institutions began to prescribe an element of ineptitude, showing exemption from useful labor.

9.3 THE DIFFICULT WORLD OF MODERN CONSUMPTION

The institutional analysis of conspicuous consumption demonstrates the importance of moving past notions of utility maximization, and beginning to look at the historical and cultural reasons behind individual consumers' decisions. Yet, consider the following

- Americans are exposed to hundreds, perhaps thousands, of advertisements every day
- Some consumers are willing to camp outside of stores for days just to be the first to purchases a new product
- The traditional holiday of Thanksgiving has now been paired with (if not eclipsed by) the so-called 'Black Friday' it precedes

These and many other examples might be taken to suggest that it is not only the individual decisions of consumers concerning what to buy that needs to be explained. Rather, we should also be looking to understand consumer*ism*–the social preoccupation with acquiring and, most importantly, identifying with consumer goods–as well.

To understand the importance of advertising and consumerism today, the best place to start is with the work of institutional economist John Kenneth Galbraith. In The Affluent Society (1958) and later in The New Industrial State (1967), Galbraith argued forcefully that the historical conditions that classical and neoclassical economists were chiefly concerned with–namely, production of necessities amidst widespread poverty and the allocation of scarce resources–had been superseded by an age of relative affluence. Mass production, as you'll see in a later chapter of this textbook, had largely solved the problem of producing enough to adequately meet the needs of the people (though ensuring everyone has access to basic necessities remains a problem to this day). Of course, solving one problem presents new ones, and for Galbraith one of the most important problems society had come to face was how to ensure that there would be demand for what could be produced once our basic needs were met.

Enter the adman. As Galbraith argued, advertising and salesmanship became important once our basic needs were, for the most part, easily met, and our remaining desires were no long immediately evident to us. Advertising and salesmanship functioned, then, to 'synthesize, elaborate, and nurture' our desires for goods and services beyond those serving simply to keep us fed, clothed, sheltered, and so on. Another way to look at it: where businesses had come increasingly to serve customers in ways that went beyond providing the goods and services to meet basic needs, these businesses required a way to maintain demand–the willingness to buy–where hunger, cold, and so on would not. In this manner, advertising and salesmanship became a form of 'demand management', designed to keep sales up, to keep people buying even after they would have otherwise felt satisfied.

The 1959 Cadillac Eldorado, sporting the decorative tailfins that reflected the increasing influence of marketing on automobile design in the mid-20th century. (Wikimedia user Veesixteen. Public Domain)

With the ascendancy of marketing, the products we buy come to take on special characteristics as their design increasingly reflects the needs of businesses to sell as much as our own personal wants and needs. More or less superficial options for colors and frequent style changes, for instance, demonstrate that consumption is, increasingly, a conspicuous act.

But more than this, these new characteristics indicate that people are associating their very identities with the consumption choices they make. Consider, for instance, what kind of car you would prefer to drive versus what kind of car you wouldn't want to 'be caught dead in'. Or, ask yourself why it is common to see groups of people who are all dressed similarly. It's likely not difficult to see that consumption and identity have become significantly intertwined in modern culture.

But what of the rebels–the people who refuse to conform? As you might have guessed, today there are plenty of products available for her as well. Consider the New York advertising firm Doyle Dane Bernbach's campaign to sell the Volkswagen Beetle in the 1960s. The ads famously used wit and humor to target drivers who favored reliability and affordability over the increasingly common conspicuous consumption elements of American automobiles. A 1963 magazine spread, for instance, depicted 15 identical images of the Beetle with model years from 1945 to 1963 under each image, indicating the utter lack of changes in the body design over this period. With advertising like this Volkswagen was able to successfully market its products to the consumers who didn't accommodate themselves to the mainstream preferences of the time.

The Volkwagen ad campaign of the 1960s might be taken as marketing naturally restraining the potential excesses of conspicuous consumption: needless model changes and functionless decorations were explicitly rejected, even mocked, in these ads. However, the important thing to recognize is that it also allowed consumers to display their of independence from the cultural trends while still maintaining their relationship with the businesses that provide these goods.

Over the decades this form of marketing has evolved into what institutional economist Philip Mirowski calls "murketing": a form of marketing in which businesses promote the belief that consumers are 'too smart' to be fooled or persuaded by advertising, brands, and so on. With that belief firmly held, consumers are free to buy what they want, safe in the knowledge that their decisions are their own. Self-reflection becomes unnecessary, and (potentially all) differences of opinion, whether political, cultural, or otherwise, become expressible through the conspicuous consumption of goods and services. In this manner, the very concept of Self is reduced to selections from a menu of shopping opportunities; the boundaries between a person's identity and businesses' marketing become murky–hence, "murketing."

The curious result of all of this is that our consumption choices, our preferences, our very identifies seem more and more to be adjusted to fit the goods and services available for purchase, rather the reverse. To be sure, this is not a criticism of individuals who prefer one branded identity over another. It is, rather, an observation of the extent to which the complexity of the practices of conspicuous consumption and corporate demand management have coevolved.

9.4 AT A GLANCE

The neoclassical approach to understanding consumption decisions appears to make a lot of sense, given the specific (perhaps peculiar) way the question is posed. Why do people buy what they buy? Because they prefer these things over others. Of course! But how well does this approach answer the truly interesting questions of modern consumption decisions? Why, for instance, do some people buy sports cars only to park them with everyone else in rush hour traffic? Why is it that, when we go to buy clothes, we spend so little time comparing the warmth and durability of the materials, and so much time on the finer details of 'how it looks'? De gustibus non est disputandum leads the neoclassical analysis to conclude simply that these are the elements which provide the most utility, leaving the critical thinker to ask: well, why are these the major elements of utility? (Naturally, to argue that we prefer the things that give us utility, and the things that give us utility are the things we prefer, is little more than an exercise in circular reasoning after all.)

Jettisoning the overly constricting assumption of de gustibus non est disputandum allows us to move on to an institutional analysis; and with that analysis we can begin to answer the really interesting questions. Once we accept that humans are naturally, inherently social creatures, and that a society's institutions evolve over time, we can begin to understand how consumption patterns reflect partly the needs and desire of individuals, but also in part the received 'habits of thought' of the societies these individuals were born into. We can develop plausible explanations, like conspicuous consumption, for why consumers appear to be purchasing things for their disutility or their wastefulness.

Anti-consumerism graffiti in Oslo, Norway. (Wikimedia user Anne-Sofie Ofrim. CC BY-SA 3.0)

These theories, in turn, bring to light new questions. For instance, what is the relationship between the producers of consumer goods and the desires of consumers if not simply for the former to cater to the latter? What is the nature of the Self, how is that constrained by a culture of consumerism, and how might it break free of those constraints? These may be difficult questions to answer within the standard framework of neoclassical economics. Because of this, heterodox economics often turn to an institutional analysis instead.

Who are we and what do we want?

Certainly, the basic purpose of this textbook is to introduce the student to how economists explain the way our economy works. But it's worth pausing for a moment to reflect on the following question: are you, the student, being trained in something more than theories that explain the consumption, production, and distribution of goods and services? Does it go deeper than that?

In a recent interview, linguist Noam Chomsky was asked if he agreed with the view that "bedrock human nature" indicated that we, as people, are "selfish and really seeking material comfort...that we can never get away from that–that's what we are." Chomsky's response was that such a view was a product of the last century of advertising, rather than any scientific study of actual human nature. "The natural thing for humans," Chomsky argued, "is to want to be independent, creative.... People, I think, want dignity and a sense of self-worth, and a sense of creating and doing something that's important; that's what we are. I think it's taken huge efforts, enormous efforts–a huge part of the economy is devoted to trying to drive these things out of people's heads, to make you think that all you want is more commodities..."

It is worth considering where an introductory economics class (and textbook) fits into the broader culture in which we live. While economists surely strive to be objective social scientists, it is impossible for us to completely divorce ourselves from the societies in which we were brought up. Is it possible, therefore, that the stories we tell about, for instance, consumer choices have embedded in them certain assumptions about what it is to be human? And, furthermore, is it possible that those assumptions are in part a reflection of the very societies we're trying to understand? As this chapter has demonstrated, regardless of your personal beliefs about human nature, asking these questions is important if we're to properly understand our economy as it evolves through time.

CHAPTER

THE COST AND THE INDUSTRY STRUCTURE 10

10.1 ACCOUNTING, ECONOMIC PROFIT, EXPLICIT AND IMPLICIT COSTS

Private enterprise, the ownership of businesses by private individuals, is a hallmark of the U.S. economy. When people think of businesses, often giants like Wal-Mart, Microsoft, or General Motors come to mind. But firms come in all sizes, as shown in Table 1. The vast majority of American firms have fewer than 20 employees. As of 2010, the U.S. Census Bureau counted 5.7 million firms with employees in the U.S. economy. Slightly less than half of all the workers in private firms are at the 17,000 large firms, meaning they employ more than 500 workers. Another 35% of workers in the U.S. economy are at firms with fewer than 100 workers. These small-scale businesses include everything from dentists and lawyers to businesses that mow lawns or clean houses. Indeed, Table 1 does not include a separate category for the millions of small "non-employer" businesses where a single owner or a few partners are not officially paid wages or a salary, but simply receive whatever they can earn.

Table 1. Range in Size of U.S. Firms. (Source: U.S. Census, 2010 www.census.gov)

Number of Employees	Firms (% of total firms)	Number of Paid Employees (% of total employment)
Total	5,734,538	112.0 million
0–9	4,543,315 (79.2%)	12.3 million (11.0%)
10–19	617,089 (10.8%)	8.3 million (7.4%)
20–99	475,125 (8.3%)	18.6 million (16.6%)
100–499	81,773 (1.4%)	15.9 million (14.2%)
500 or more	17,236 (0.30%)	50.9 million (49.8%)

Each of these businesses, regardless of size or complexity, tries to earn a profit:

$$Profit = Total\ Revenue\ -\ Total\ Cost$$

Total revenue is the income brought into the firm from selling its products. It is calculated by multiplying the price of the product times the quantity of output sold:

$$Total\ Revenue = Price\ \times\ Quantity$$

We will see in the following chapters that revenue is a function of the demand for the firm's products.

We can distinguish between two types of cost: explicit and implicit. Explicit costs are out-of-pocket costs, that is, payments that are actually made. Wages that a firm pays its employees or rent that a firm pays for its office are explicit costs. Implicit costs are more subtle, but just as important. They represent the opportunity cost of using resources already owned by the firm. Often for small businesses, they are resources contributed by the owners; for example, working in the business while not getting a formal salary, or using the ground floor of a home as a retail store. Implicit costs also allow for depreciation of goods, materials, and equipment that are necessary for a company to operate. (See the Work it Out feature for an extended example.)

These two definitions of cost are important for distinguishing between two conceptions of profit, accounting profit and economic profit. Accounting profit is a cash concept. It means total revenue minus explicit costs—the difference between dollars brought in and dollars paid out. Economic profit is total revenue minus total cost, including both explicit and implicit costs. The difference is important because even though a business pays income taxes based on its accounting profit, whether or not it is economically successful depends on its economic profit.

Calculating Implicit Costs

Consider the following example. Fred currently works for a corporate law firm. He is considering opening his own legal practice, where he expects to earn $200,000 per year once he gets established. To run his own firm, he would need an office and a law clerk. He has found the perfect office, which rents for $50,000 per year. A law clerk could be hired for $35,000 per year. If these figures are accurate, would Fred's legal practice be profitable?

Step 1. First you have to calculate the costs. You can take what you know about explicit costs and total them:

$$\begin{array}{lr} \textit{Office rental:} & \$50,000 \\ \textit{Law clerk's salary:} & +\$35,000 \\ \hline \textit{Total explicit costs:} & \$85,000 \end{array}$$

Step 2. Subtracting the explicit costs from the revenue gives you the accounting profit.

$$\begin{array}{lr} \textit{Revenues:} & \$200,000 \\ \textit{Explicit costs:} & -\$85,000 \\ \hline \textit{Accounting profit:} & \$115,000 \end{array}$$

But these calculations consider only the explicit costs. To open his own practice, Fred would have to quit his current job, where he is earning an annual salary of $125,000. This would be an implicit cost of opening his own firm.

Step 3. You need to subtract both the explicit and implicit costs to determine the true economic profit:

$$\textit{Economic profit} \quad \textit{total revenues} - \textit{explicit costs} - \textit{implicit costs}$$

$$\$200,000 - \$85,000 - \$125,000$$

$$-\$10,000 \textit{ per year}$$

Fred would be losing $10,000 per year. That does not mean he would not want to open his own business, but it does mean he would be earning $10,000 less than if he worked for the corporate firm.

Implicit costs can include other things as well. Maybe Fred values his leisure time, and starting his own firm would require him to put in more hours than at the corporate firm. In this case, the lost leisure would also be an implicit cost that would subtract from economic profits.

Now that we have an idea about the different types of costs, let's look at cost structures. A firm's cost structure in the long run may be different from that in the short run. We turn to that distinction in the next section.

Concepts and Summary

Privately owned firms are motivated to earn profits. Profit is the difference between revenues and costs. While accounting profit considers only explicit costs, economic profit considers both explicit and implicit costs.

10.2 THE ORGANISATION OF COSTS THROUGHOUT THE SHORT TERM

The cost of producing a firm's output depends on how much labor and physical capital the firm uses. A list of the costs involved in producing cars will look very different from the costs involved in producing computer software or haircuts or fast-food meals. However, the cost structure of all firms can be broken down into some common underlying patterns. When a firm looks at its total costs of production in the short run, a useful starting point is to divide total costs into two categories: fixed costs that cannot be changed in the short run and variable costs that can be changed.

Fixed and Variable Costs

Fixed costs are expenditures that do not change regardless of the level of production, at least not in the short term. Whether you produce a lot or a little, the fixed costs are the same. One example is the rent on a factory or a retail space. Once you sign the lease, the rent is the same regardless of how much you produce, at least until the lease runs out. Fixed costs can take many other forms: for example, the cost of machinery or equipment to produce the product, research and development costs to develop new products, even an expense like advertising to popularize a brand name. The level of fixed costs varies according to the specific line of business: for instance, manufacturing computer chips requires an expensive factory, but a local moving and hauling business can get by with almost no fixed costs at all if it rents trucks by the day when needed.

Variable costs, on the other hand, are incurred in the act of producing—the more you produce, the greater the variable cost. Labor is treated as a variable cost, since producing a greater quantity of a good or service typically requires more workers or more work hours. Variable costs would also include raw materials.

As a concrete example of fixed and variable costs, consider the barber shop called "The Clip Joint" shown in Figure 1. The data for output and costs are shown in Table 2. The fixed costs of operating the barber shop, including the space and equipment, are $160 per day. The variable costs are the costs of hiring barbers, which in our example is $80 per barber each day. The first two columns of the table show the quantity of haircuts the barbershop can produce as it hires additional barbers. The third column shows the fixed costs, which do not change regardless of the level of production. The fourth column shows the variable costs at each level of output. These are calculated by taking the amount of labor hired and multiplying by the wage. For example, two barbers cost: 2 × $80 = $160. Adding together the fixed costs in the third column and the variable costs in the fourth column produces the total costs in the fifth column. So, for example, with two barbers the total cost is: $160 + $160 = $320.

Table 2. Output and Total Costs

Labor	Quantity	Fixed Cost	Variable Cost	Total Cost
1	16	$160	$80	$240
2	40	$160	$160	$320
3	60	$160	$240	$400
4	72	$160	$320	$480
5	80	$160	$400	$560
6	84	$160	$480	$640
7	82	$160	$560	$720

The relationship between the quantity of output being produced and the cost of producing that output is shown graphically in the figure. The fixed costs are always shown as the vertical intercept of the total cost curve; that is, they are the costs incurred when output is zero so there are no variable costs.

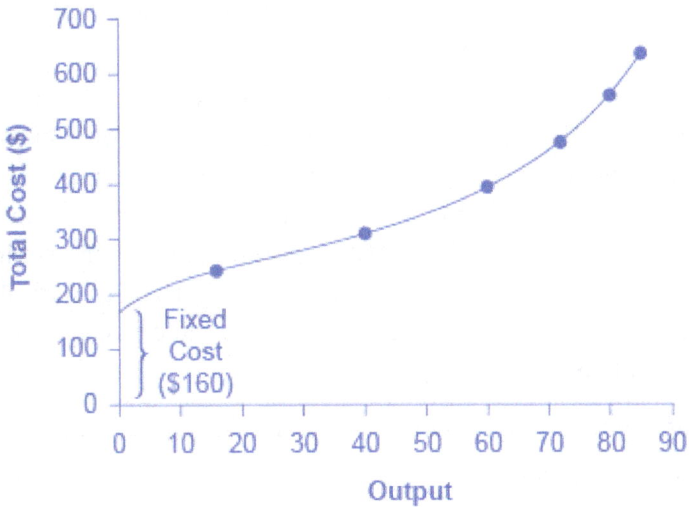

Figure 1. How Output Affects Total Costs. At zero production, the fixed costs of $160 are still present. As production increases, variable costs are added to fixed costs, and the total cost is the sum of the two.

You can see from the graph that once production starts, total costs and variable costs rise. While variable costs may initially increase at a decreasing rate, at some point they begin increasing at an increasing rate. This is caused by diminishing marginal returns, discussed in the chapter on Choice in a World of Scarcity, which is easiest to see with an example. As the number of barbers increases from zero to one in the table, output increases from 0 to 16 for a marginal gain of 16; as the number rises from one to two barbers, output increases from 16 to 40, a marginal gain of 24. From that point on, though, the marginal gain in output diminishes as each additional barber is added. For example, as the number of barbers rises from two to three, the marginal output gain is only 20; and as the number rises from three to four, the marginal gain is only 12.

To understand the reason behind this pattern, consider that a one-man barber shop is a very busy operation. The single barber needs to do everything: say hello to people entering, answer the phone, cut hair, sweep up, and run the cash register. A second barber reduces the level of disruption from jumping back and forth between these tasks, and allows a greater division of labor and specialization. The result can be greater increasing marginal returns. However, as other barbers are added, the advantage of each additional barber is less, since the specialization of labor can only go so far. The addition of a sixth or seventh or eighth barber just to greet people at the door will have less impact than the second one did. This is the pattern of diminishing marginal returns. As a result, the total costs of production will begin to rise more rapidly as output increases. At some point, you may even see negative returns as the additional barbers begin bumping elbows and getting in each other's way. In this case, the addition of still more barbers would actually cause output to decrease, as shown in the last row of Table 2.

This pattern of diminishing marginal returns is common in production. As another example, consider the problem of irrigating a crop on a farmer's field. The plot of land is the fixed factor of production, while the water that can be added to the land is the key variable cost. As the farmer adds water to the land, output increases. But adding more and more water brings smaller and smaller increases in output, until at some point the water floods the field and actually reduces output. Diminishing marginal returns occur because, at a given level of fixed costs, each additional input contributes less and less to overall production.

Average Total Cost, Average Variable Cost, Marginal Cost

The breakdown of total costs into fixed and variable costs can provide a basis for other insights as well. The first five columns of Table 3 duplicate the previous table, but the last three columns show average total costs, average variable costs, and marginal costs. These new measures analyze costs on a per-unit (rather than a total) basis and are reflected in the curves shown in Figure 2.

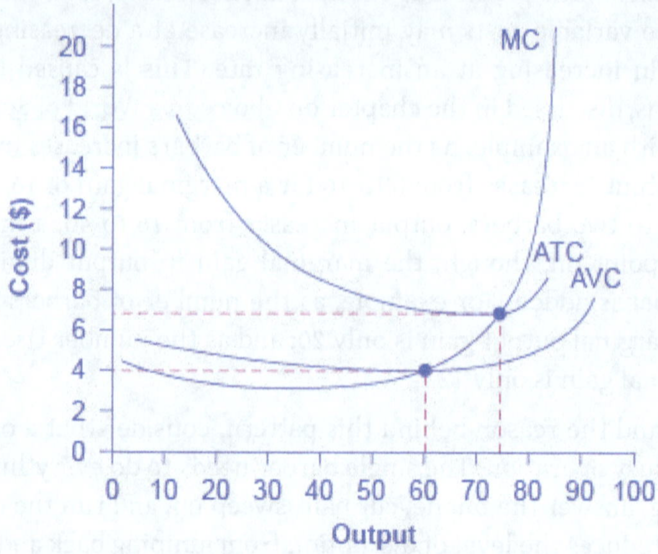

Figure 2. Cost Curves at the Clip Joint. The information on total costs, fixed cost, and variable cost can also be presented on a per-unit basis. Average total cost (ATC) is calculated by dividing total cost by the total quantity produced. The average total cost curve is typically U-shaped. Average variable cost (AVC) is calculated by dividing variable cost by the quantity produced. The average variable cost curve lies below the average total cost curve and is typically U-shaped or upward-sloping. Marginal cost (MC) is calculated by taking the change in total cost between two levels of output and dividing by the change in output. The marginal cost curve is upward-sloping.

Table 3. Different Types of Costs

Labor	Quantity	Fixed Cost	Variable Cost	Total Cost	Marginal Cost	Average Total Cost	Average Variable Cost
1	16	$160	$80	$240	$5.00	$15.00	$5.00
2	40	$160	$160	$320	$3.30	$8.00	$4.00
3	60	$160	$240	$400	$4.00	$6.60	$4.00
4	72	$160	$320	$480	$6.60	$6.60	$4.40
5	80	$160	$400	$560	$10.00	$7.00	$5.00
6	84	$160	$480	$640	$20.00	$7.60	$5.70

Average total cost (sometimes referred to simply as average cost) is total cost divided by the quantity of output. Since the total cost of producing 40 haircuts is $320, the average total cost for producing each of 40 haircuts is $320/40, or $8 per haircut. Average cost curves are typically U-shaped, as Figure 2 shows. Average total cost starts off relatively high, because at low levels of output total costs are dominated by the fixed cost; mathematically, the denominator is so small that average total cost is large. Average total cost then declines, as the fixed costs are spread over an increasing quantity of output. In the average cost calculation, the rise in the numerator of total costs is relatively small compared to the rise in the denominator of quantity produced. But as output expands still further, the average cost begins to rise. At the right side of the average cost curve, total costs begin rising more rapidly as diminishing returns kick in.

Average variable cost obtained when variable cost is divided by quantity of output. For example, the variable cost of producing 80 haircuts is $400, so the average variable cost is $400/80, or $5 per haircut. Note that at any level of output, the average variable cost curve will always lie below the curve for average total cost, as shown in Figure 2. The reason is that average total cost includes average variable cost and average fixed cost. Thus, for Q = 80 haircuts, the average total cost is $8 per haircut, while the average variable cost is $5 per haircut. However, as output grows, fixed costs become relatively less important (since they do not rise with output), so average variable cost sneaks closer to average cost.

Average total and variable costs measure the average costs of producing some quantity of output. Marginal cost is somewhat different. Marginal cost is the additional cost of producing one more unit of output. So it is not the cost per unit of all units being produced, but only the next one (or next few). Marginal cost can be calculated by taking the change in total cost and dividing it by the change in quantity. For example, as quantity produced increases from 40 to 60 haircuts, total costs rise by 400 – 320, or 80. Thus, the marginal cost for each of those marginal 20 units will be 80/20, or $4 per haircut. The marginal cost curve is generally upward-sloping, because diminishing marginal returns implies that additional units are more costly to produce. A small range of increasing marginal returns can be seen in the figure as a dip in the marginal cost curve before it starts rising. There is a point at which marginal and average costs meet, as the following Clear it Up feature discusses.

Where do marginal and average costs meet?

The marginal cost line intersects the average cost line exactly at the bottom of the average cost curve—which occurs at a quantity of 72 and cost of $6.60 in Figure 2. The reason why the intersection occurs at this point is built into the economic meaning of marginal and average costs. If the marginal cost of production is below the average cost for producing previous units, as it is for the points to the left of where MC crosses ATC, then producing one more additional unit will reduce average costs overall—and the ATC curve will be downward-sloping in this zone. Conversely, if the marginal cost of production for producing an additional unit is above the average cost for producing the earlier units, as it is for points to the right of where MC crosses ATC, then producing a marginal unit will increase average costs overall—and the ATC curve must be upward-sloping in this zone. The point of transition, between where MC is pulling ATC down and where it is pulling it up, must occur at the minimum point of the ATC curve.

This idea of the marginal cost "pulling down" the average cost or "pulling up" the average cost may sound abstract, but think about it in terms of your own grades. If the score on the most recent quiz you take is lower than your average score on previous quizzes, then the marginal quiz pulls down your average. If your score on the most recent quiz is higher than the average on previous quizzes, the marginal quiz pulls up your average. In this same way, low marginal costs of production first pull down average costs and then higher marginal costs pull them up.

The numerical calculations behind average cost, average variable cost, and marginal cost will change from firm to firm. However, the general patterns of these curves, and the relationships and economic intuition behind them, will not change.

Lessons from Alternative Measures of Costs

Breaking down total costs into fixed cost, marginal cost, average total cost, and average variable cost is useful because each statistic offers its own insights for the firm.

Whatever the firm's quantity of production, total revenue must exceed total costs if it is to earn a profit. As explored in the chapter Choice in a World of Scarcity, fixed costs are often sunk costs that cannot be recouped. In thinking about what to do next, sunk costs should typically be ignored, since this spending has already been made and cannot be changed. However, variable costs can be changed, so they convey information about the firm's ability to cut costs in the present and the extent to which costs will increase if production rises.

Why are total cost and average cost not on the same graph?

Total cost, fixed cost, and variable cost each reflect different aspects of the cost of production over the entire quantity of output being produced. These costs are measured in dollars. In contrast, marginal cost, average cost, and average variable cost are costs per unit. In the previous example, they are measured as cost per haircut. Thus, it would not make sense to put all of these numbers on the same graph, since they are measured in different units ($ versus $ per unit of output).

It would be as if the vertical axis measured two different things. In addition, as a practical matter, if they were on the same graph, the lines for marginal cost, average cost, and average variable cost would appear almost flat against the horizontal axis, compared to the values for total cost, fixed cost, and variable cost. Using the figures from the previous example, the total cost of producing 40 haircuts is $320. But the average cost is $320/40, or $8. If you graphed both total and average cost on the same axes, the average cost would hardly show.

Average cost tells a firm whether it can earn profits given the current price in the market. If we divide profit by the quantity of output produced we get **average profit**, also known as the firm's *profit margin*. Expanding the equation for profit gives:

$$\begin{aligned} \textit{average profit} \quad & \frac{\textit{profit}}{\textit{quantity produced}} \\ & \frac{\textit{total revenue} - \textit{total cost}}{\textit{quantity produced}} \\ & \frac{\textit{total revenue}}{\textit{quantity produced}} - \frac{\textit{total cost}}{\textit{quantity produced}} \\ & \textit{average revenue} - \textit{average cost} \end{aligned}$$

But note that:

$$\begin{aligned} \textit{average revenue} \quad & \frac{\textit{price} \times \textit{quantity produced}}{\textit{quantity produced}} \\ & \textit{price} \end{aligned}$$

Thus:

$$\textit{average profit} = \textit{price} - \textit{average cost}$$

This is the firm's **profit margin.** This definition implies that if the market price is above average cost, average profit, and thus total profit, will be positive; if price is below average cost, then profits will be negative.

The marginal cost of producing an additional unit can be compared with the marginal revenue gained by selling that additional unit to reveal whether the additional unit is adding to total profit—or not. Thus, marginal cost helps producers understand how profits would be affected by increasing or decreasing production.

A Variety of Cost Patterns

The pattern of costs varies among industries and even among firms in the same industry. Some businesses have high fixed costs, but low marginal costs. Consider, for example, an Internet company that provides medical advice to customers. Such a company might be paid by consumers directly, or perhaps hospitals or healthcare practices might subscribe on behalf of their patients. Setting up the website, collecting the information, writing the content, and buying or leasing the computer space to handle the web traffic are all fixed costs that must be undertaken before the site can work. However, when the website is up and running, it can provide a high quantity of service with relatively low variable costs, like the cost of monitoring the system and updating the information. In this case, the total cost curve might start at a high level, because of the high fixed costs, but then might appear close to flat, up to a large quantity of output, reflecting the low variable costs of operation. If the website is popular, however, a large rise in the number of visitors will overwhelm the website, and increasing output further could require a purchase of additional computer space.

For other firms, fixed costs may be relatively low. For example, consider firms that rake leaves in the fall or shovel snow off sidewalks and driveways in the winter. For fixed costs, such firms may need little more than a car to transport workers to homes of customers and some rakes and shovels. Still other firms may find that diminishing marginal returns set in quite sharply. If a manufacturing plant tried to run 24 hours a day, seven days a week, little time remains for routine maintenance of the equipment, and marginal costs can increase dramatically as the firm struggles to repair and replace overworked equipment.

Every firm can gain insight into its task of earning profits by dividing its total costs into fixed and variable costs, and then using these calculations as a basis for average total cost, average variable cost, and marginal cost. However, making a final decision about the profit-maximizing quantity to produce and the price to charge will require combining these perspectives on cost with an analysis of sales and revenue, which in turn requires looking at the market structure in which the firm finds itself. Before we turn to the analysis of market structure in other chapters, we will analyze the firm's cost structure from a long-run perspective.

CONCEPTS AND SUMMARY

In a short-run perspective, a firm's total costs can be divided into fixed costs, which a firm must incur before producing any output, and variable costs, which the firm incurs in the act of producing. Fixed costs are sunk costs; that is, because they are in the past and cannot be altered, they should play no role in economic decisions about future production or pricing. Variable costs typically show diminishing marginal returns, so that the marginal cost of producing higher levels of output rises.

Marginal cost is calculated by taking the change in total cost (or the change in variable cost, which will be the same thing) and dividing it by the change in output, for each possible change in output. Marginal costs are typically rising. A firm can compare marginal cost to the additional revenue it gains from selling another unit to find out whether its marginal unit is adding to profit.

Average total cost is calculated by taking total cost and dividing by total output at each different level of output. Average costs are typically U-shaped on a graph. If a firm's average cost of production is lower than the market price, a firm will be earning profits.

Average variable cost is calculated by taking variable cost and dividing by the total output at each level of output. Average variable costs are typically U-shaped. If a firm's average variable cost of production is lower than the market price, then the firm would be earning profits if fixed costs are left out of the picture.

10.3 THE STRUCTURE OF COSTS IN THE LONG RUN

The long run is the period of time when all costs are variable. The long run depends on the specifics of the firm in question—it is not a precise period of time. If you have a one-year lease on your factory, then the long run is any period longer than a year, since after a year you are no longer bound by the lease. No costs are fixed in the long run. A firm can build new factories and purchase new machinery, or it can close existing facilities. In planning for the long run, the firm will compare alternative **production technologies** (or processes).

In this context, technology refers to all alternative methods of combining inputs to produce outputs. It does not refer to a specific new invention like the tablet computer. The firm will search for the production technology that allows it to produce the desired level of output at the lowest cost. After all, lower costs lead to higher profits—at least if total revenues remain unchanged. Moreover, each firm must fear that if it does not seek out the lowest-cost methods of production, then it may lose sales to competitor firms that find a way to produce and sell for less.

Choice of Production Technology

Many tasks can be performed with a range of combinations of labor and physical capital. For example, a firm can have human beings answering phones and taking messages, or it can invest in an automated voicemail system. A firm can hire file clerks and secretaries to manage a system of paper folders and file cabinets, or it can invest in a computerized recordkeeping system that will require fewer employees. A firm can hire workers to push supplies around a factory on rolling carts, it can invest in motorized vehicles, or it can invest in robots that carry materials without a driver. Firms often face a choice between buying a many small machines, which need a worker to run each one, or buying one larger and more expensive machine, which requires only one or two workers to operate it. In short, physical capital and labor can often substitute for each other.

Consider the example of a private firm that is hired by local governments to clean up public parks. Three different combinations of labor and physical capital for cleaning up a single average-sized park appear in Table 6. The first production technology is heavy on workers and light on machines, while the next two technologies substitute machines for workers. Since all three of these production methods produce the same thing—one cleaned-up park—a profit-seeking firm will choose the production technology that is least expensive, given the prices of labor and machines.

Production technology 1	10 workers	2 machines
Production technology 2	7 workers	4 machines
Production technology 3	3 workers	7 machines
Table 6. Three Ways to Clean a Park		

Production technology 1 uses the most labor and least machinery, while production technology 3 uses the least labor and the most machinery. Table 7 outlines three examples of how the total cost will change with each production technology as the cost of labor changes. As the cost of labor rises from example A to B to C, the firm will choose to substitute away from labor and use more machinery.

This example shows that as an input becomes more expensive (in this case, the labor input), firms will attempt to conserve on using that input and will instead shift to other inputs that are relatively less expensive. This pattern helps to explain why the demand curve for labor (or any input) slopes down; that is, as labor becomes relatively more expensive, profit-seeking firms will seek to substitute the use of other inputs. When a multinational employer like Coca-Cola or McDonald's sets up a bottling plant or a restaurant in a high-wage economy like the United States, Canada, Japan, or Western Europe, it is likely to use production technologies that conserve on the number of workers and focuses more on machines. However, that same employer is likely to use production technologies with more workers and less machinery when producing in a lower-wage country like Mexico, China, or South Africa.

Table 7. Total Cost with Rising Labor Costs

Example A: Workers cost $40, machines cost $80			
	Labor Cost	**Machine Cost**	**Total Cost**
Cost of technology 1	10 × $40 = $400	2 × $80 = $160	$560
Cost of technology 2	7 × $40 = $280	4 × $80 = $320	$600
Cost of technology 3	3 × $40 = $120	7 × $80 = $560	$680
Example B: Workers cost $55, machines cost $80			
	Labor Cost	**Machine Cost**	**Total Cost**
Cost of technology 1	10 × $55 = $550	2 × $80 = $160	$710
Cost of technology 2	7 × $55 = $385	4 × $80 = $320	$705
Cost of technology 3	3 × $55 = $165	7 × $80 = $560	$725
Example C: Workers cost $90, machines cost $80			
	Labor Cost	**Machine Cost**	**Total Cost**
Cost of technology 1	10 × $90 = $900	2 × $80 = $160	$1,060
Cost of technology 2	7 × $90 = $630	4 × $80 = $320	$950
Cost of technology 3	3 × $90 = $270	7 × $80 = $560	$830

Example A shows the firm's cost calculation when wages are $40 and machines costs are $80. In this case, technology 1 is the low-cost production technology. In example B, wages rise to $55, while the cost of machines does not change, in which case technology 2 is the low-cost production technology. If wages keep rising up to $90, while the cost of machines remains unchanged, then technology 3 clearly becomes the low-cost form of production, as shown in example C.

Economies of Scale

Once a firm has determined the least costly production technology, it can consider the optimal scale of production, or quantity of output to produce. Many industries experience economies of scale. Economies of scale refers to the situation where, as the quantity of output goes up, the cost per unit goes down. This is the idea behind "warehouse stores" like Costco or Walmart. In everyday language: a larger factory can produce at a lower average cost than a smaller factory.

Figure 1 illustrates the idea of economies of scale, showing the average cost of producing an alarm clock falling as the quantity of output rises. For a small-sized factory like S, with an output level of 1,000, the average cost of production is $12 per alarm clock. For a medium-sized factory like M, with an output level of 2,000, the average cost of production falls to $8 per alarm clock. For a large factory like L, with an output of 5,000, the average cost of production declines still further to $4 per alarm clock.

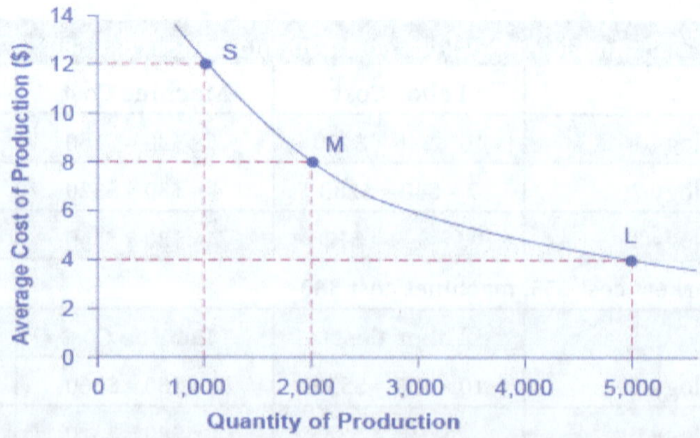

Figure 1. Economies of Scale. A small factory like S produces 1,000 alarm clocks at an average cost of $12 per clock. A medium factory like M produces 2,000 alarm clocks at a cost of $8 per clock. A large factory like L produces 5,000 alarm clocks at a cost of $4 per clock. Economies of scale exist because the larger scale of production leads to lower average costs.

The average cost curve in Figure 1 may appear similar to the average cost curves presented earlier in this chapter, although it is downward-sloping rather than U-shaped. But there is one major difference. The economies of scale curve is a long-run average cost curve, because it allows all factors of production to change. The short-run average cost curves presented earlier in this chapter assumed the existence of fixed costs, and only variable costs were allowed to change.

One prominent example of economies of scale occurs in the chemical industry. Chemical plants have a lot of pipes. The cost of the materials for producing a pipe is related to the circumference of the pipe and its length. However, the volume of chemicals that can flow through a pipe is determined by the cross-section area of the pipe. The calculations in Table 8 show that a pipe which uses twice as much material to make (as shown by the circumference of the pipe doubling) can actually carry four times the volume of chemicals because the cross-section area of the pipe rises by a factor of four (as shown in the Area column).

Table 8. Comparing Pipes: Economies of Scale in the Chemical Industry

	Circumference (2πr2πr)	Area (πr2πr2)
4-inch pipe	12.5 inches	12.5 square inches
8-inch pipe	25.1 inches	50.2 square inches
16-inch pipe	50.2 inches	201.1 square inches

A doubling of the cost of producing the pipe allows the chemical firm to process four times as much material. This pattern is a major reason for economies of scale in chemical production, which uses a large quantity of pipes. Of course, economies of scale in a chemical plant are more complex than this simple calculation suggests. But the chemical engineers who design these plants have long used what they call the "six-tenths rule," a rule of thumb which holds that increasing the quantity produced in a chemical plant by a certain percentage will increase total cost by only six-tenths as much.

Shapes of Long-Run Average Cost Curves

While in the short run firms are limited to operating on a single average cost curve (corresponding to the level of fixed costs they have chosen), in the long run when all costs are variable, they can choose to operate on any average cost curve. Thus, the long-run average cost (LRAC) curve is actually based on a group of short-run average cost (SRAC) curves, each of which represents one specific level of fixed costs. More precisely, the long-run average cost curve will be the least expensive average cost curve for any level of output. Figure 2 shows how the long-run average cost curve is built from a group of short-run average cost curves. Five short-run-average cost curves appear on the diagram. Each SRAC curve represents a different level of fixed costs. For example, you can imagine SRAC1 as a small factory, SRAC2 as a medium factory, SRAC3 as a large factory, and SRAC4 and SRAC5 as very large and ultra-large. Although this diagram shows only five SRAC curves, presumably there are an infinite number of other SRAC curves between the ones that are shown. This family of short-run average cost curves can be thought of as representing different choices for a firm that is planning its level of investment in fixed cost physical capital—knowing that different choices about capital investment in the present will cause it to end up with different short-run average cost curves in the future.

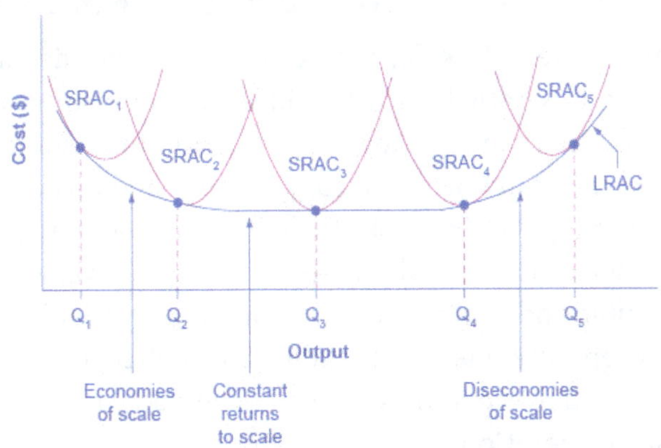

Figure 2. From Short-Run Average Cost Curves to Long-Run Average Cost Curves. The five different short-run average cost (SRAC) curves each represents a different level of fixed costs, from the low level of fixed

costs at SRAC1 to the high level of fixed costs at SRAC5. Other SRAC curves, not shown in the diagram, lie between the ones that are shown here. The long-run average cost (LRAC) curve shows the lowest cost for producing each quantity of output when fixed costs can vary, and so it is formed by the bottom edge of the family of SRAC curves. If a firm wished to produce quantity Q3, it would choose the fixed costs associated with SRAC.

The long-run average cost curve shows the cost of producing each quantity in the long run, when the firm can choose its level of fixed costs and thus choose which short-run average costs it desires. If the firm plans to produce in the long run at an output of Q3, it should make the set of investments that will lead it to locate on SRAC3, which allows producing q3 at the lowest cost. A firm that intends to produce Q3 would be foolish to choose the level of fixed costs at SRAC2 or SRAC4. At SRAC2 the level of fixed costs is too low for producing Q3 at lowest possible cost, and producing q3 would require adding a very high level of variable costs and make the average cost very high. At SRAC4, the level of fixed costs is too high for producing q3 at lowest possible cost, and again average costs would be very high as a result.

The shape of the long-run cost curve, as drawn in Figure 2, is fairly common for many industries. The left-hand portion of the long-run average cost curve, where it is downward- sloping from output levels Q_1 to Q_2 to Q_3, illustrates the case of economies of scale. In this portion of the long-run average cost curve, larger scale leads to lower average costs. This pattern was illustrated earlier in Figure 1.

In the middle portion of the long-run average cost curve, the flat portion of the curve around Q_3, economies of scale have been exhausted. In this situation, allowing all inputs to expand does not much change the average cost of production, and it is called **constant returns to scale**. In this range of the LRAC curve, the average cost of production does not change much as scale rises or falls. The following Clear it Up feature explains where diminishing marginal returns fit into this analysis.

How do economies of scale compare to diminishing marginal returns?

The concept of economies of scale, where average costs decline as production expands, might seem to conflict with the idea of diminishing marginal returns, where marginal costs rise as production expands. But diminishing marginal returns refers only to the short-run average cost curve, where one variable input (like labor) is increasing, but other inputs (like capital) are fixed. Economies of scale refers to the long-run average cost curve where all inputs are being allowed to increase together. Thus, it is quite possible and common to have an industry that has both diminishing marginal returns when only one input is allowed to change, and at the same time has increasing or constant economies of scale when all inputs change together to produce a larger-scale operation.

Finally, the right-hand portion of the long-run average cost curve, running from output level Q_4 to Q_5, shows a situation where, as the level of output and the scale rises, average costs rise as well. This situation is called **diseconomies of scale.** A firm or a factory can grow so large that it becomes very difficult to manage, resulting in unnecessarily high costs as many layers of management try to communicate with workers and with each other, and as failures to communicate lead to disruptions in the flow of work and materials. Not many overly large factories exist in the real world, because with their very high production costs, they are unable to compete for long against plants with lower average costs of production. However, in some planned economies, like the economy of the old Soviet Union, plants that were so large as to be grossly inefficient were able to continue operating for a long time because government economic planners protected them from competition and ensured that they would not make losses.

Diseconomies of scale can also be present across an entire firm, not just a large factory. The leviathan effect can hit firms that become too large to run efficiently, across the entirety of the enterprise. Firms that shrink their operations are often responding to finding itself in the diseconomies region, thus moving back to a lower average cost at a lower output level.

The Size and Number of Firms in an Industry

The shape of the long-run average cost curve has implications for how many firms will compete in an industry, and whether the firms in an industry have many different sizes, or tend to be the same size. For example, say that one million dishwashers are sold every year at a price of $500 each and the long-run average cost curve for dishwashers is shown in Figure 3 (a). In Figure 3 (a), the lowest point of the LRAC curve occurs at a quantity of 10,000 produced. Thus, the market for dishwashers will consist of 100 different manufacturing plants of this same size. If some firms built a plant that produced 5,000 dishwashers per year or 25,000 dishwashers per year, the average costs of production at such plants would be well above $500, and the firms would not be able to compete.

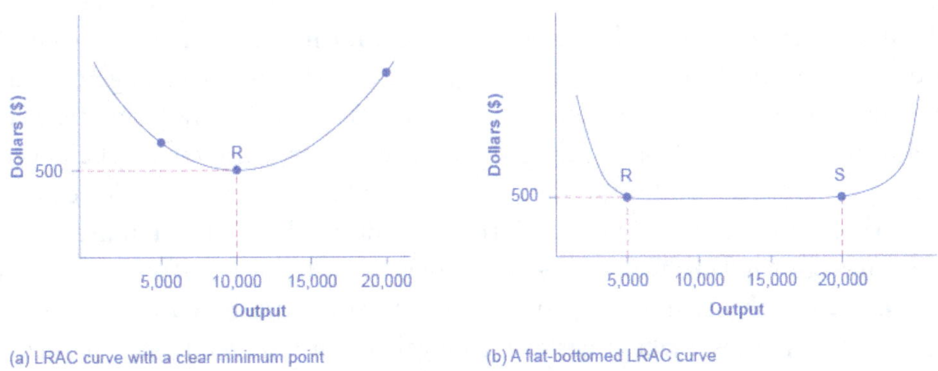

Figure 3. The LRAC Curve and the Size and Number of Firms. (a) Low-cost firms will produce at output level R. When the LRAC curve has a clear minimum point, then any firm producing a different quantity

will have higher costs. In this case, a firm producing at a quantity of 10,000 will produce at a lower average cost than a firm producing, say, 5,000 or 20,000 units. (b) Low-cost firms will produce between output levels R and S. When the LRAC curve has a flat bottom, then firms producing at any quantity along this flat bottom can compete. In this case, any firm producing a quantity between 5,000 and 20,000 can compete effectively, although firms producing less than 5,000 or more than 20,000 would face higher average costs and be unable to compete.

How can cities be viewed as examples of economies of scale?

Why are people and economic activity concentrated in cities, rather than distributed evenly across a country? The fundamental reason must be related to the idea of economies of scale—that grouping economic activity is more productive in many cases than spreading it out. For example, cities provide a large group of nearby customers, so that businesses can produce at an efficient economy of scale. They also provide a large group of workers and suppliers, so that business can hire easily and purchase whatever specialized inputs they need. Many of the attractions of cities, like sports stadiums and museums, can operate only if they can draw on a large nearby population base. Cities are big enough to offer a wide variety of products, which is what many shoppers are looking for.

These factors are not exactly economies of scale in the narrow sense of the production function of a single firm, but they are related to growth in the overall size of population and market in an area. Cities are sometimes called "agglomeration economies."

These agglomeration factors help to explain why every economy, as it develops, has an increasing proportion of its population living in urban areas. In the United States, about 80% of the population now lives in metropolitan areas (which include the suburbs around cities), compared to just 40% in 1900. However, in poorer nations of the world, including much of Africa, the proportion of the population in urban areas is only about 30%. One of the great challenges for these countries as their economies grow will be to manage the growth of the great cities that will arise.

If cities offer economic advantages that are a form of economies of scale, then why don't all or most people live in one giant city? At some point, agglomeration economies must turn into diseconomies. For example, traffic congestion may reach a point where the gains from being geographically nearby are counterbalanced by how long it takes to travel. High densities of people, cars, and factories can mean more garbage and air and water pollution. Facilities like parks or museums may become overcrowded. There may be economies of scale for negative activities like crime, because high densities of people and businesses, combined with the greater impersonality of cities, make it easier for illegal activities as well as legal ones. The future of cities, both in the United States and in other countries around the world, will be determined by their ability to benefit from the economies of agglomeration and to minimize or counterbalance the corresponding diseconomies.

A more common case is illustrated in Figure 3 (b), where the LRAC curve has a flat-bottomed area of constant returns to scale. In this situation, any firm with a level of output between 5,000 and 20,000 will be able to produce at about the same level of average cost. Given that the market will demand one million dishwashers per year at a price of $500, this market might have as many as 200 producers (that is, one million dishwashers divided by firms making 5,000 each) or as few as 50 producers (one million dishwashers divided by firms making 20,000 each). The producers in this market will range in size from firms that make 5,000 units to firms that make 20,000 units. But firms that produce below 5,000 units or more than 20,000 will be unable to compete, because their average costs will be too high. Thus, if we see an industry where almost all plants are the same size, it is likely that the long-run average cost curve has a unique bottom point as in Figure 3 (a). However, if the long-run average cost curve has a wide flat bottom like Figure 3 (b), then firms of a variety of different sizes will be able to compete with each other.

The flat section of the long-run average cost curve in Figure 3 (b) can be interpreted in two different ways. One interpretation is that a single manufacturing plant producing a quantity of 5,000 has the same average costs as a single manufacturing plant with four times as much capacity that produces a quantity of 20,000. The other interpretation is that one firm owns a single manufacturing plant that produces a quantity of 5,000, while another firm owns four separate manufacturing plants, which each produce a quantity of 5,000. This second explanation, based on the insight that a single firm may own a number of different manufacturing plants, is especially useful in explaining why the long-run average cost curve often has a large flat segment—and thus why a seemingly smaller firm may be able to compete quite well with a larger firm. At some point, however, the task of coordinating and managing many different plants raises the cost of production sharply, and the long-run average cost curve slopes up as a result.

In the examples to this point, the quantity demanded in the market is quite large (one million) compared with the quantity produced at the bottom of the long-run average cost curve (5,000, 10,000 or 20,000). In such a situation, the market is set for competition between many firms. But what if the bottom of the long-run average cost curve is at a quantity of 10,000 and the total market demand at that price is only slightly higher than that quantity—or even somewhat lower?

Return to Figure 3 (a), where the bottom of the long-run average cost curve is at 10,000, but now imagine that the total quantity of dishwashers demanded in the market at that price of $500 is only 30,000. In this situation, the total number of firms in the market would be three. A handful of firms in a market is called an "oligopoly," and the chapter on Monopolistic Competition and Oligopoly will discuss the range of competitive strategies that can occur when oligopolies compete.

Alternatively, consider a situation, again in the setting of Figure 3 (a), where the bottom of the long-run average cost curve is 10,000, but total demand for the product is only 5,000. (For simplicity, imagine that this demand is highly inelastic, so that it does not vary according to price.) In this situation, the market may well end up with a single firm—a monopoly—producing all 5,000 units. If any firm tried to challenge this monopoly while producing a quantity lower than 5,000 units, the prospective competitor firm would have a higher average cost, and so it would not be able to compete in the longer term without losing money. The chapter on Monopoly discusses the situation of a monopoly firm.

Thus, the shape of the long-run average cost curve reveals whether competitors in the market will be different sizes. If the LRAC curve has a single point at the bottom, then the firms in the market will be about the same size, but if the LRAC curve has a flat-bottomed segment of constant returns to scale, then firms in the market may be a variety of different sizes.

The relationship between the quantity at the minimum of the long-run average cost curve and the quantity demanded in the market at that price will predict how much competition is likely to exist in the market. If the quantity demanded in the market far exceeds the quantity at the minimum of the LRAC, then many firms will compete. If the quantity demanded in the market is only slightly higher than the quantity at the minimum of the LRAC, a few firms will compete. If the quantity demanded in the market is less than the quantity at the minimum of the LRAC, a single-producer monopoly is a likely outcome.

Shifting Patterns of Long-Run Average Cost

New developments in production technology can shift the long-run average cost curve in ways that can alter the size distribution of firms in an industry.

For much of the twentieth century, the most common change has been to see alterations in technology, like the assembly line or the large department store, where large-scale producers seemed to gain an advantage over smaller ones. In the long-run average cost curve, the downward-sloping economies of scale portion of the curve stretched over a larger quantity of output.

However, new production technologies do not inevitably lead to a greater average size for firms. For example, in recent years some new technologies for generating electricity on a smaller scale have appeared. The traditional coal-burning electricity plants needed to produce 300 to 600 megawatts of power to exploit economies of scale fully. However, high-efficiency turbines to produce electricity from burning natural gas can produce electricity at a competitive price while producing a smaller quantity of 100 megawatts or less. These new technologies create the possibility for smaller companies or plants to generate electricity as efficiently as large ones.

Another example of a technology-driven shift to smaller plants may be taking place in the tire industry. A traditional mid-size tire plant produces about six million tires per year. However, in 2000, the Italian company Pirelli introduced a new tire factory that uses many robots. The Pirelli tire plant produced only about one million tires per year, but did so at a lower average cost than a traditional mid-sized tire plant.

Controversy has simmered in recent years over whether the new information and communications technologies will lead to a larger or smaller size for firms. On one side, the new technology may make it easier for small firms to reach out beyond their local geographic area and find customers across a state, or the nation, or even across international boundaries. This factor might seem to predict a future with a larger number of small competitors. On the other side, perhaps the new information and communications technology will create "winner-take-all" markets where one large company will tend to command a large share of total sales, as Microsoft has done in the production of software for personal computers or Amazon has done in online bookselling. Moreover, improved information and communication technologies might make it easier to manage many different plants and operations across the country or around the world, and thus encourage larger firms. This ongoing battle between the forces of smallness and largeness will be of great interest to economists, businesspeople, and policymakers.

AMAZON

Traditionally, bookstores have operated in retail locations with inventories held either on the shelves or in the back of the store. These retail locations were very pricey in terms of rent. Amazon has no retail locations; it sells online and delivers by mail. Amazon offers almost any book in print, convenient purchasing, and prompt delivery by mail. Amazon holds its inventories in huge warehouses in low-rent locations around the world. The warehouses are highly computerized using robots and relatively low-skilled workers, making for low average costs per sale. Amazon demonstrates the significant advantages economies of scale can offer to a firm that exploits those economies.

CONCEPTS AND SUMMARY

A production technology refers to a specific combination of labor, physical capital, and technology that makes up a particular method of production.

In the long run, firms can choose their production technology, and so all costs become variable costs. In making this choice, firms will try to substitute relatively inexpensive inputs for relatively expensive inputs where possible, so as to produce at the lowest possible long-run average cost.

Economies of scale refers to a situation where as the level of output increases, the average cost decreases. Constant returns to scale refers to a situation where average cost does not change as output increases. Diseconomies of scale refers to a situation where as output increases, average costs increase also.

The long-run average cost curve shows the lowest possible average cost of production, allowing all the inputs to production to vary so that the firm is choosing its production technology. A downward-sloping LRAC shows economies of scale; a flat LRAC shows constant returns to scale; an upward-sloping LRAC shows diseconomies of scale. If the long-run average cost curve has only one quantity produced that results in the lowest possible average cost, then all of the firms competing in an industry should be the same size. However, if the LRAC has a flat segment at the bottom, so that a range of different quantities can be produced at the lowest average cost, the firms competing in the industry will display a range of sizes. The market demand in conjunction with the long-run average cost curve determines how many firms will exist in a given industry.

If the quantity demanded in the market of a certain product is much greater than the quantity found at the bottom of the long-run average cost curve, where the cost of production is lowest, the market will have many firms competing. If the quantity demanded in the market is less than the quantity at the bottom of the LRAC, there will likely be only one firm.

CHAPTER

PERFECT COMPETITION IN ECONOMICS 11

11.1 COMPETITION IN PERFECTS AND WHY IT MATTERS

Firms are said to be in perfect competition when the following conditions occur: (1) many firms produce identical products; (2) many buyers are available to buy the product, and many sellers are available to sell the product; (3) sellers and buyers have all relevant information to make rational decisions about the product being bought and sold; and (4) firms can enter and leave the market without any restrictions—in other words, there is free entry and exit into and out of the market.

A **perfectly competitive firm** is known as a **price taker**, because the pressure of competing firms forces them to accept the prevailing equilibrium price in the market. If a firm in a perfectly competitive market raises the price of its product by so much as a penny, it will lose all of its sales to competitors. When a wheat grower, as discussed in the Bring it Home feature, wants to know what the going price of wheat is, he or she has to go to the computer or listen to the radio to check. The market price is determined solely by supply and demand in the entire market and not the individual farmer. Also, a perfectly competitive firm must be a very small player in the overall market, so that it can increase or decrease output without noticeably affecting the overall quantity supplied and price in the market.

A perfectly competitive market is a hypothetical extreme; however, producers in a number of industries do face many competitor firms selling highly similar goods, in which case they must often act as price takers. Agricultural markets are often used as an example. The same crops grown by different farmers are largely interchangeable. According to the United States Department of Agriculture monthly reports, in 2015, U.S. corn farmers received an average price of $6.00 per bushel and wheat farmers received an average price of $6.00 per bushel. A corn farmer who attempted to sell at $7.00 per bushel, or a wheat grower who attempted to sell for $8.00 per bushel, would not have found any buyers. A perfectly competitive firm will not sell below the equilibrium price either. Why should they when they can sell all they want at the higher price? Other examples of agricultural markets that operate in close to perfectly competitive markets are small roadside produce markets and small organic farmers.

This chapter examines how profit-seeking firms decide how much to produce in perfectly competitive markets. Such firms will analyze their costs as discussed in the chapter on Cost and Industry Structure. In the short run, the perfectly competitive firm will seek the quantity of output where profits are highest or, if profits are not possible, where losses are lowest. In this example, the "short run" refers to a situation in which firms are producing with one fixed input and incur fixed costs of production. (In the real world, firms can have many fixed inputs.)

In the long run, perfectly competitive firms will react to profits by increasing production. They will respond to losses by reducing production or exiting the market. Ultimately, a long-run *equilibrium* will be attained when no new firms want to enter the market and existing firms do not want to leave the market, as economic profits have been driven down to zero.

Concepts and Summary

A perfectly competitive firm is a price taker, which means that it must accept the equilibrium price at which it sells goods. If a perfectly competitive firm attempts to charge even a tiny amount more than the market price, it will be unable to make any sales. In a perfectly competitive market there are thousands of sellers, easy entry, and identical products. A short-run production period is when firms are producing with some fixed inputs. Long-run equilibrium in a perfectly competitive industry occurs after all firms have entered and exited the industry and seller profits are driven to zero.

Perfect competition means that there are many sellers, there is easy entry and exiting of firms, products are identical from one seller to another, and sellers are price takers.

Determining the Highest Profit by Comparing Total Revenue and Total Cost

A perfectly competitive firm can sell as large a quantity as it wishes, as long as it accepts the prevailing market price. Total revenue is going to increase as the firm sells more, depending on the price of the product and the number of units sold. If you increase the number of units sold at a given price, then total revenue will increase. If the price of the product increases for every unit sold, then total revenue also increases. As an example of how a perfectly competitive firm decides what quantity to produce, consider the case of a small farmer who produces raspberries and sells them frozen for $4 per pack. Sales of one pack of raspberries will bring in $4, two packs will be $8, three packs will be $12, and so on. If, for example, the price of frozen raspberries doubles to $8 per pack, then sales of one pack of raspberries will be $8, two packs will be $16, three packs will be $24, and so on.

Total revenue and total costs for the raspberry farm, broken down into fixed and variable costs, are shown in Table 1 and also appear in Figure 1. The horizontal axis shows the quantity of frozen raspberries produced in packs; the vertical axis shows both total revenue and total costs, measured in dollars. The total cost curve intersects with the vertical axis at a value that shows the level of fixed costs, and then slopes upward. All these cost curves follow the same characteristics as the curves covered in the Cost and Industry Structure chapter.

Figure 1. Total Cost and Total Revenue at the Raspberry Farm. Total revenue for a perfectly competitive firm is a straight line sloping up. The slope is equal to the price of the good. Total cost also slopes up, but with some curvature. At higher levels of output, total cost begins to slope upward more steeply because of diminishing marginal returns. The maximum profit will occur at the quantity where the gap of total revenue over total cost is largest.

Table 1. Total Cost and Total Revenue at the Raspberry Farm

Quantity (Q)	Total Cost (TC)	Fixed Cost (FC)	Variable Cost (VC)	Total Revenue (TR)	Profit
0	$62	$62	–	$0	-$62
10	$90	$62	$28	$40	-$50
20	$110	$62	$48	$80	-$30
30	$126	$62	$64	$120	-$6
40	$144	$62	$82	$160	$16
50	$166	$62	$104	$200	$34
60	$192	$62	$130	$240	$48
70	$224	$62	$162	$280	$56

Quantity (Q)	Total Cost (TC)	Fixed Cost (FC)	Variable Cost (VC)	Total Revenue (TR)	Profit
80	$264	$62	$202	$320	$56
90	$324	$62	$262	$360	$36
100	$404	$62	$342	$400	-$4

Based on its total revenue and total cost curves, a perfectly competitive firm like the raspberry farm can calculate the quantity of output that will provide the highest level of profit. At any given quantity, total revenue minus total cost will equal profit. One way to determine the most profitable quantity to produce is to see at what quantity total revenue exceeds total cost by the largest amount. On Figure 1, the vertical gap between total revenue and total cost represents either profit (if total revenues are greater that total costs at a certain quantity) or losses (if total costs are greater that total revenues at a certain quantity). In this example, total costs will exceed total revenues at output levels from 0 to 40, and so over this range of output, the firm will be making losses. At output levels from 50 to 80, total revenues exceed total costs, so the firm is earning profits. But then at an output of 90 or 100, total costs again exceed total revenues and the firm is making losses. Total profits appear in the final column of Table 1. The highest total profits in the table, as in the figure that is based on the table values, occur at an output of 70–80, when profits will be $56.

A higher price would mean that total revenue would be higher for every quantity sold. A lower price would mean that total revenue would be lower for every quantity sold. What happens if the price drops low enough so that the total revenue line is completely below the total cost curve; that is, at every level of output, total costs are higher than total revenues? In this instance, the best the firm can do is to suffer losses. But a profit-maximizing firm will prefer the quantity of output where total revenues come closest to total costs and thus where the losses are smallest.

(Later we will see that sometimes it will make sense for the firm to shutdown, rather than stay in operation producing output.)

Comparing Marginal Revenue and Marginal Costs

Firms often do not have the necessary data they need to draw a complete total cost curve for all levels of production. They cannot be sure of what total costs would look like if they, say, doubled production or cut production in half, because they have not tried it. Instead, firms experiment. They produce a slightly greater or lower quantity and observe how profits are affected. In economic terms, this practical approach to maximizing profits means looking at how changes in production affect marginal revenue and marginal cost.

Figure 2 presents the marginal revenue and marginal cost curves based on the total revenue and total cost in Table 1. The marginal revenue curve shows the additional revenue gained from selling one more unit. As mentioned before, a firm in perfect competition faces a perfectly elastic demand curve for its product—that is, the firm's demand curve is a horizontal line drawn at the market price level. This also means that the firm's marginal revenue curve is the same as the firm's demand curve: Every time a consumer demands one more unit, the firm sells one more unit and revenue goes up by exactly the same amount equal to the market price. In this example, every time a pack of frozen raspberries is sold, the firm's revenue increases by $4. Table 2 shows an example of this. This condition only holds for price taking firms in perfect competition where:

$$marginal\ revenue = price$$

The formula for marginal revenue is:

$$marginal\ revenue = \frac{change\ in\ total\ revenue}{change\ in\ quantity}$$

Table 2. Marginal Revenue

Price	Quantity	Total Revenue	Marginal Revenue
$4	1	$4	–
$4	2	$8	$4
$4	3	$12	$4
$4	4	$16	$4

Notice that marginal revenue does not change as the firm produces more output. That is because the price is determined by supply and demand and does not change as the farmer produces more (keeping in mind that, due to the relative small size of each firm, increasing their supply has no impact on the total market supply where price is determined).

Since a perfectly competitive firm is a price taker, it can sell whatever quantity it wishes at the market-determined price. Marginal cost, the cost per additional unit sold, is calculated by dividing the change in total cost by the change in quantity. The formula for marginal cost is:

$$marginal\ cost = \frac{change\ in\ total\ cost}{change\ in\ quantity}$$

Ordinarily, marginal cost changes as the firm produces a greater quantity.

In the raspberry farm example, shown in Figure 2, Figure 3 and Table 3, marginal cost at first declines as production increases from 10 to 20 to 30 packs of raspberries—

which represents the area of increasing marginal returns that is not uncommon at low levels of production. But then marginal costs start to increase, displaying the typical pattern of diminishing marginal returns. If the firm is producing at a quantity where MR > MC, like 40 or 50 packs of raspberries, then it can increase profit by increasing output because the marginal revenue is exceeding the marginal cost. If the firm is producing at a quantity where MC > MR, like 90 or 100 packs, then it can increase profit by reducing output because the reductions in marginal cost will exceed the reductions in marginal revenue. The firm's profit-maximizing choice of output will occur where MR = MC (or at a choice close to that point). You will notice that what occurs on the production side is exemplified on the cost side. This is referred to as duality.

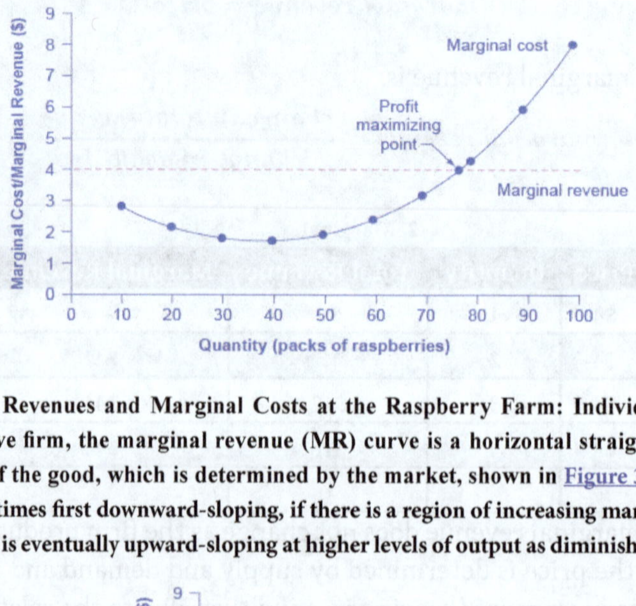

Figure 2. Marginal Revenues and Marginal Costs at the Raspberry Farm: Individual Farmer. For a perfectly competitive firm, the marginal revenue (MR) curve is a horizontal straight line because it is equal to the price of the good, which is determined by the market, shown in Figure 3. The marginal cost (MC) curve is sometimes first downward-sloping, if there is a region of increasing marginal returns at low levels of output, but is eventually upward-sloping at higher levels of output as diminishing marginal return

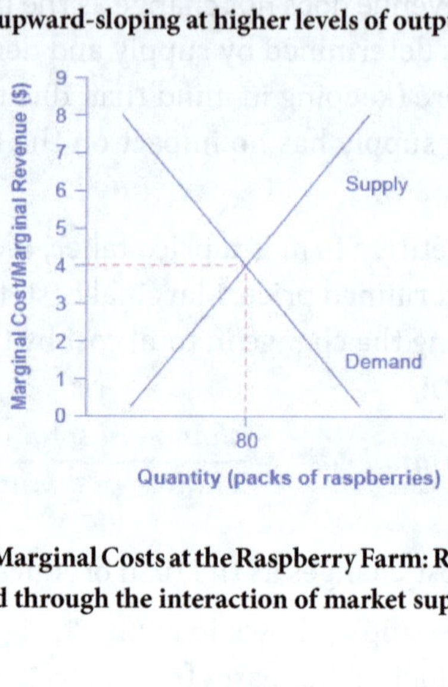

Figure 3. Marginal Revenues and Marginal Costs at the Raspberry Farm: Raspberry Market. The equilibrium price of raspberries is determined through the interaction of market supply and market demand at $4.00.

Table 3. Marginal Revenues and Marginal Costs at the Raspberry Farm

Quantity	Total Cost	Fixed Cost	Variable Cost	Marginal Cost	Total Revenue	Marginal Revenue
0	$62	$62	–	–	–	–
10	$90	$62	$28	$2.80	$40	$4.00
20	$110	$62	$48	$2.00	$80	$4.00
30	$126	$62	$64	$1.60	$120	$4.00
40	$144	$62	$82	$1.80	$160	$4.00
50	$166	$62	$104	$2.20	$200	$4.00
60	$192	$62	$130	$2.60	$240	$4.00
70	$224	$62	$162	$3.20	$280	$4.00
80	$264	$62	$202	$4.00	$320	$4.00
90	$324	$62	$262	$6.00	$360	$4.00
100	$404	$62	$342	$8.00	$400	$4.00

In this example, the marginal revenue and marginal cost curves cross at a price of $4 and a quantity of 80 produced. If the farmer started out producing at a level of 60, and then experimented with increasing production to 70, marginal revenues from the increase in production would exceed marginal costs—and so profits would rise. The farmer has an incentive to keep producing. From a level of 70 to 80, marginal cost and marginal revenue are equal so profit doesn't change. If the farmer then experimented further with increasing production from 80 to 90, he would find that marginal costs from the increase in production are greater than marginal revenues, and so profits would decline.

The profit-maximizing choice for a perfectly competitive firm will occur where marginal revenue is equal to marginal cost—that is, where MR = MC. A profit-seeking firm should keep expanding production as long as MR > MC. But at the level of output where MR = MC, the firm should recognize that it has achieved the highest possible level of economic profits. (In the example above, the profit maximizing output level is between 70 and 80 units of output, but the firm will not know they've maximized profit until they reach 80, where MR = MC.) Expanding production into the zone where MR < MC will only reduce economic profits. Because the marginal revenue received by a perfectly competitive firm is equal to the price P, so that P = MR, the profit-maximizing rule for a perfectly competitive firm can also be written as a recommendation to produce at the quantity where P = MC.

Profits and Losses with the Average Cost Curve

Does maximizing profit (producing where MR = MC) imply an actual economic profit? The answer depends on the relationship between price and average total cost. If the price that a firm charges is higher than its average cost of production for that quantity produced, then the firm will earn profits. Conversely, if the price that a firm charges is lower than its average cost of production, the firm will suffer losses. You might think that, in this situation, the farmer may want to shut down immediately. Remember, however, that the firm has already paid for fixed costs, such as equipment, so it may continue to produce and incur a loss. Figure 4 illustrates three situations: (a) where price intersects marginal cost at a level above the average cost curve, (b) where price intersects marginal cost at a level equal to the average cost curve, and (c) where price intersects marginal cost at a level below the average cost curve.

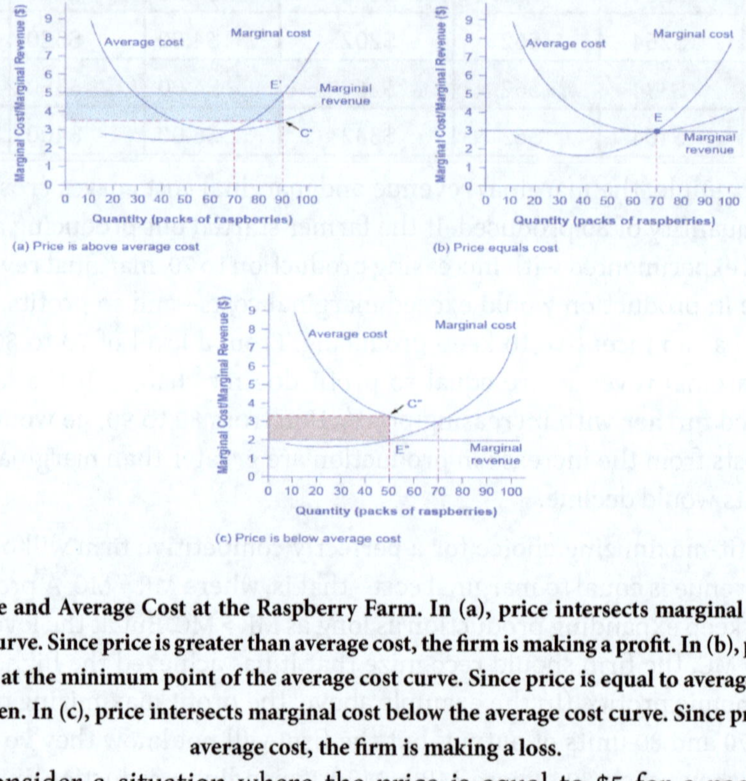

Figure 4. Price and Average Cost at the Raspberry Farm. In (a), price intersects marginal cost above the average cost curve. Since price is greater than average cost, the firm is making a profit. In (b), price intersects marginal cost at the minimum point of the average cost curve. Since price is equal to average cost, the firm is breaking even. In (c), price intersects marginal cost below the average cost curve. Since price is less than average cost, the firm is making a loss.

First consider a situation where the price is equal to $5 for a pack of frozen raspberries. The rule for a profit-maximizing perfectly competitive firm is to produce the level of output where Price= MR = MC, so the raspberry farmer will produce a quantity of 90, which is labeled as e in Figure 4 (a). Remember that the area of a rectangle is equal to its base multiplied by its height. The farm's total revenue at this price will be shown by the large shaded rectangle from the origin over to a quantity of 90 packs (the base) up to point E' (the height), over to the price of $5, and back to the origin. The average cost of producing 80 packs is shown by point C or about $3.50.

Total costs will be the quantity of 80 times the average cost of \$3.50, which is shown by the area of the rectangle from the origin to a quantity of 90, up to point C, over to the vertical axis and down to the origin. It should be clear from examining the two rectangles that total revenue is greater than total cost. Thus, profits will be the blue shaded rectangle on top.

It can be calculated as:

It can be calculated as:

$$\textit{profit} \quad \textit{total revenue} - \textit{total cost}$$

$$(90)(\$5.00) - (90)(\$3.50)$$

$$\$135$$

Or, it can be calculated as:

$$\textit{profit} \quad (\textit{price} - \textit{average cost}) \times \textit{quantity}$$

$$(\$5.00 - \$3.50) \times 90$$

$$\$135$$

Now consider Figure 4 (b), where the price has fallen to \$3.00 for a pack of frozen raspberries. Again, the perfectly competitive firm will choose the level of output where Price = MR = MC, but in this case, the quantity produced will be 70. At this price and output level, where the marginal cost curve is crossing the average cost curve, the price received by the firm is exactly equal to its average cost of production.

The farm's total revenue at this price will be shown by the large shaded rectangle from the origin over to a quantity of 70 packs (the base) up to point E (the height), over to the price of \$3, and back to the origin. The average cost of producing 70 packs is shown by point C'. Total costs will be the quantity of 70 times the average cost of \$3.00, which is shown by the area of the rectangle from the origin to a quantity of 70, up to point E, over to the vertical axis and down to the origin. It should be clear from that the rectangles for total revenue and total cost are the same. Thus, the firm is making zero profit. The calculations are

$$\textit{profit} \quad \textit{total revenue} - \textit{total cost}$$

$$(70)(\$3.00) - (70)(\$3.00)$$

$$\$0$$

Or, it can be calculated as:

$$\textit{profit} \quad (\textit{price} - \textit{average cost}) \times \textit{quantity}$$

$$(\$3.00 - \$3.00) \times 70$$

$$\$0$$

In Figure 4 (c), the market price has fallen still further to \$2.00 for a pack of frozen raspberries. At this price, marginal revenue intersects marginal cost at a quantity of 50. The farm's total revenue at this price will be shown by the large shaded rectangle from the origin over to a quantity of 50 packs (the base) up to point E" (the height), over to the price of \$2, and back to the origin. The average cost of producing 50 packs is shown by point C" or about \$3.30. Total costs will be the quantity of 50 times the average cost of \$3.30, which is shown by the area of the rectangle from the origin to a quantity of 50, up to point C", over to the vertical axis and down to the origin. It should be clear from examining the two rectangles that total revenue is less than total cost. Thus, the firm is losing money and the loss (or negative profit) will be the rose-shaded rectangle.

The calculations are:

$$\textit{profit} \quad \textit{total revenue} - \textit{total cost}$$

$$(50)(\$2.00) - (50)(\$3.30)$$

$$-\$77.50$$

Or:

$$\textit{profit} \quad (\textit{price} - \textit{average cost}) \times \textit{quantity}$$

$$(\$1.75 - \$3.30) \times 50$$

$$-\$77.50$$

If the market price received by a perfectly competitive firm leads it to produce at a quantity where the price is greater than average cost, the firm will earn profits. If the price received by the firm causes it to produce at a quantity where price equals average cost, which occurs at the minimum point of the AC curve, then the firm earns zero profits. Finally, if the price received by the firm leads it to produce at a quantity where the price is less than average cost, the firm will earn losses. This is summarized in Table 4.

Table 4.

If...	Then...
Price > ATC	Firm earns an economic profit
Price = ATC	Firm earns zero economic profit
Price < ATC	Firm earns a loss

The Shutdown Point

The possibility that a firm may earn losses raises a question: Why can the firm not avoid losses by shutting down and not producing at all? The answer is that shutting down can reduce variable costs to zero, but in the short run, the firm has already paid for fixed costs. As a result, if the firm produces a quantity of zero, it would still make losses because it would still need to pay for its fixed costs. So, when a firm is experiencing losses, it must face a question: should it continue producing or should it shut down?

As an example, consider the situation of the Yoga Center, which has signed a contract to rent space that costs $10,000 per month. If the firm decides to operate, its marginal costs for hiring yoga teachers is $15,000 for the month. If the firm shuts down, it must still pay the rent, but it would not need to hire labor. Table 5 shows three possible scenarios. In the first scenario, the Yoga Center does not have any clients, and therefore does not make any revenues, in which case it faces losses of $10,000 equal to the fixed costs. In the second scenario, the Yoga Center has clients that earn the center revenues of $10,000 for the month, but ultimately experiences losses of $15,000 due to having to hire yoga instructors to cover the classes. In the third scenario, the Yoga Center earns revenues of $20,000 for the month, but experiences losses of $5,000.

In all three cases, the Yoga Center loses money. In all three cases, when the rental contract expires in the long run, assuming revenues do not improve, the firm should exit this business. In the short run, though, the decision varies depending on the level of losses and whether the firm can cover its variable costs. In scenario 1, the center does not have any revenues, so hiring yoga teachers would increase variable costs and losses, so it should shut down and only incur its fixed costs. In scenario 2, the center's losses are greater because it does not make enough revenue to offset the increased variable costs plus fixed costs, so it should shut down immediately. If price is below the minimum average variable cost, the firm must shut down. In contrast, in scenario 3 the revenue that the center can earn is high enough that the losses diminish when it remains open, so the center should remain open in the short run.

Table 5. Should the Yoga Center Shut Down Now or Later?

$$\textit{profit} \quad \textit{total revenue} - (\textit{fixed costs} + \textit{variable cost})$$

$$0 - \$10,000$$

$$-\$10,000$$

Scenario 2

The center earns revenues of $10,000, and variable costs are $15,000. The center should shut down now.

$$\textit{profit} \quad \textit{total revenue} - (\textit{fixed costs} + \textit{variable cost})$$

$$\$10,000 - (\$10,000 + \$15,000)$$

$$-\$15,000$$

Scenario 3

The center earns revenues of $20,000, and variable costs are $15,000. The center should continue in business.

$$\begin{aligned} \textit{profit} &= \textit{total revenue} - (\textit{fixed costs} + \textit{variable cost}) \\ &= \$20,000 - (\$10,000 + \$15,000) \\ &= -\$5,000 \end{aligned}$$

This example suggests that the key factor is whether a firm can earn enough revenues to cover at least its variable costs by remaining open. Let's return now to our raspberry farm. Figure 5 illustrates this lesson by adding the average variable cost curve to the marginal cost and average cost curves. At a price of $2.20 per pack, as shown in Figure 5 (a), the farm produces at a level of 50. It is making losses of $56 (as explained earlier), but price is above average variable cost and so the firm continues to operate. However, if the price declined to $1.80 per pack, as shown in Figure 5 (b), and if the firm applied its rule of producing where P = MR = MC, it would produce a quantity of 40. This price is below average variable cost for this level of output. If the farmer cannot pay workers (the variable costs), then it has to shut down. At this price and output, total revenues would be $72 (quantity of 40 times price of $1.80) and total cost would be $144, for overall losses of $72. If the farm shuts down, it must pay only its fixed costs of $62, so shutting down is preferable to selling at a price of $1.80 per pack.

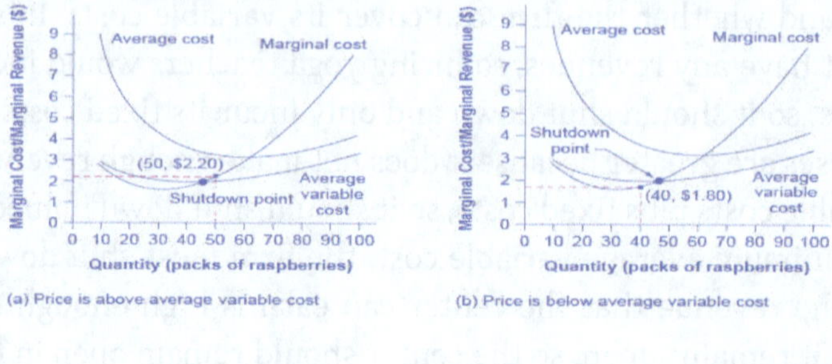

Figure 5. The Shutdown Point for the Raspberry Farm. In (a), the farm produces at a level of 50. It is making losses of $56, but price is above average variable cost, so it continues to operate. In (b), total revenues are $72 and total cost is $144, for overall losses of $72. If the farm shuts down, it must pay only its fixed costs of $62. Shutting down is preferable to selling at a price of $1.80 per pack.

Looking at Table 6, if the price falls below $2.05, the minimum average variable cost, the firm must shut down.

Table 6. Cost of Production for the Raspberry Farm

Quantity	Total Cost	Fixed Cost	Variable Cost	Marginal Cost	Average Cost	Average Variable Cost
0	$62	$62	–	–	–	–
10	$90	$62	$28	$2.80	$9.00	$2.80
20	$110	$62	$48	$2.00	$5.50	$2.40
30	$126	$62	$64	$1.60	$4.20	$2.13
40	$144	$62	$82	$1.80	$3.60	$2.05
50	$166	$62	$104	$2.20	$3.32	$2.08
60	$192	$62	$130	$2.60	$3.20	$2.16
70	$224	$62	$162	$3.20	$3.20	$2.31
80	$264	$62	$202	$4.00	$3.30	$2.52
90	$324	$62	$262	$6.00	$3.60	$2.91
100	$404	$62	$342	$8.00	$4.04	$3.42

The intersection of the average variable cost curve and the marginal cost curve, which shows the price where the firm would lack enough revenue to cover its variable costs, is called the **shutdown point**. If the perfectly competitive firm can charge a price above the shutdown point, then the firm is at least covering its average variable costs. It is also making enough revenue to cover at least a portion of fixed costs, so it should limp ahead even if it is making losses in the short run, since at least those losses will be smaller than if the firm shuts down immediately and incurs a loss equal to total fixed costs. However, if the firm is receiving a price below the price at the shutdown point, then the firm is not even covering its variable costs. In this case, staying open is making the firm's losses larger, and it should shut down immediately. To summarize, if:

- price < minimum average variable cost, then firm shuts down
- price = minimum average variable cost, then firm stays in business

Short-Run Outcomes for Perfectly Competitive Firms

The average cost and average variable cost curves divide the marginal cost curve into three segments, as shown in Figure 6. At the market price, which the perfectly competitive firm accepts as given, the profit-maximizing firm chooses the output level where price or marginal revenue, which are the same thing for a perfectly competitive firm, is equal to marginal cost: P = MR = MC.

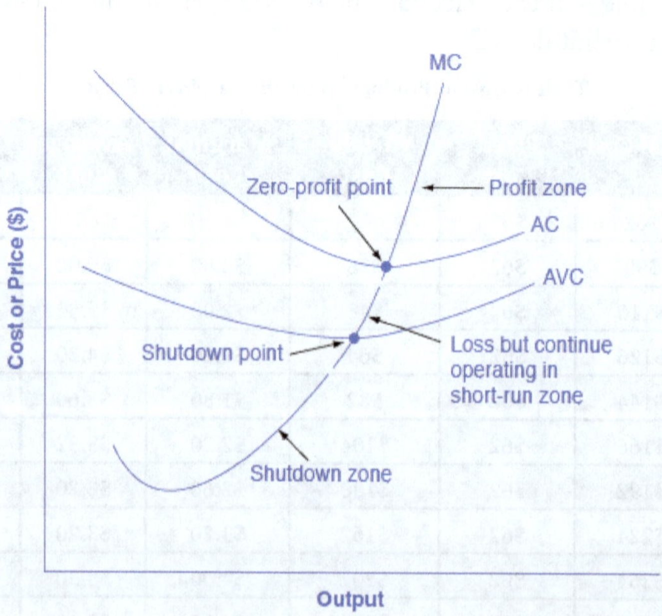

Figure 6. Profit, Loss, Shutdown. The marginal cost curve can be divided into three zones, based on where it is crossed by the average cost and average variable cost curves. The point where MC crosses AC is called the zero-profit point. If the firm is operating at a level of output where the market price is at a level higher than the zero-profit point, then price will be greater than average cost and the firm is earning profits. If the price is exactly at the zero-profit point, then the firm is making zero profits. If price falls in the zone between the shutdown point and the zero-profit point, then the firm is making losses but will continue to operate in the short run, since it is covering its variable costs. However, if price falls below the price at the shutdown point, then the firm will shut down immediately, since it is not even covering its variable costs.

First consider the upper zone, where prices are above the level where marginal cost (MC) crosses average cost (AC) at the zero profit point. At any price above that level, the firm will earn profits in the short run. If the price falls exactly on the zero profit point where the MC and AC curves cross, then the firm earns zero profits. If a price falls into the zone between the zero profit point, where MC crosses AC, and the shutdown point, where MC crosses AVC, the firm will be making losses in the short run—but since the firm is more than covering its variable costs, the losses are smaller than if the firm shut down immediately. Finally, consider a price at or below the shutdown point where MC crosses AVC. At any price like this one, the firm will shut down immediately, because it cannot even cover its variable costs.

Marginal Cost and the Firm's Supply Curve

For a perfectly competitive firm, the marginal cost curve is identical to the firm's supply curve starting from the minimum point on the average variable cost curve. To understand why this perhaps surprising insight holds true, first think about what the supply curve means. A firm checks the market price and then looks at its supply curve to decide what quantity to produce. Now, think about what it means to say that a firm will maximize its profits by producing at the quantity where P = MC. This rule means that the firm checks the market price, and then looks at its marginal cost to determine the quantity to produce—and makes sure that the price is greater than the minimum average variable cost. In other words, the marginal cost curve above the minimum point on the average variable cost curve becomes the firm's supply curve.

Watch this video that addresses how drought in the United States can impact food prices across the world. (Note that the story on the drought is the second one in the news report; you need to let the video play through the first story in order to watch the story on the drought.)

As discussed in the chapter on Demand and Supply, many of the reasons that supply curves shift relate to underlying changes in costs. For example, a lower price of key inputs or new technologies that reduce production costs cause supply to shift to the right; in contrast, bad weather or added government regulations can add to costs of certain goods in a way that causes supply to shift to the left. These shifts in the firm's supply curve can also be interpreted as shifts of the marginal cost curve. A shift in costs of production that increases marginal costs at all levels of output—and shifts MC to the left—will cause a perfectly competitive firm to produce less at any given market price. Conversely, a shift in costs of production that decreases marginal costs at all levels of output will shift MC to the right and as a result, a competitive firm will choose to expand its level of output at any given price. The following Work It Out feature will walk you through an example.

At What Price Should the Firm Continue Producing in the Short Run?

To determine the short-run economic condition of a firm in perfect competition, follow the steps outlined below. Use the data shown in Table 7.

Table 7.

Q	P	TFC	TVC	TC	AVC	ATC	MC	TR	Profits
0	$28	$20	$0	–	–	–	–	–	–
1	$28	$20	$20	–	–	–	–	–	–
2	$28	$20	$25	–	–	–	–	–	–
3	$28	$20	$35	–	–	–	–	–	–
4	$28	$20	$52	–	–	–	–	–	–
5	$28	$20	$80	–	–	–	–	–	–

Step 1. Determine the cost structure for the firm. For a given total fixed costs and variable costs, calculate total cost, average variable cost, average total cost, and marginal cost. Follow the formulas given in the Cost and Industry Structure chapter. These calculations are shown in Table 8.

Table 8.

Q	P	TFC	TVC	TC (TFC+TVC)	AVC (TVC/Q)	ATC (TC/Q)	MC (TC2-TC1)/ (Q2-Q1)
0	$28	$20	$0	$20+$0=$20	–	–	–
1	$28	$20	$20	$20+$20=$40	$20/1=$20.00	$40/1=$40.00	($40-$20)/ (1-0)= $20
2	$28	$20	$25	$20+$25=$45	$25/2=$12.50	$45/2=$22.50	($45-$40)/ (2-1)= $5
3	$28	$20	$35	$20+$35=$55	$35/3=$11.67	$55/3=$18.33	($55-$45)/ (3-2)= $10
4	$28	$20	$52	$20+$52=$72	$52/4=$13.00	$72/4=$18.00	($72-$55)/ (4-3)= $17
5	$28	$20	$80	$20+$80=$100	$80/5=$16.00	$100/5=$20.00	($100-$72)/ (5-4)= $28

Step 2. Determine the market price that the firm receives for its product. This should be given information, as the firm in perfect competition is a price taker. With the given price, calculate total revenue as equal to price multiplied by quantity for all output levels produced. In this example, the given price is $30. You can see that in the second column of Table 9.

Table 9.

Quantity	Price	Total Revenue (P × Q)
0	$28	$28×0=$0
1	$28	$28×1=$28
2	$28	$28×2=$56
3	$28	$28×3=$84
4	$28	$28×4=$112
5	$28	$28×5=$140

Step 3. Calculate profits as total cost subtracted from total revenue, as shown in Table 10.

Table 10.

Quantity	Total Revenue	Total Cost	Profits (TR-TC)
0	$0	$20	$0-$20=-$20
1	$28	$40	$28-$40=-$12
2	$56	$45	$56-$45=$11
3	$84	$55	$84-$55=$29
4	$112	$72	$112-$72=$40
5	$140	$100	$140-$100=$40

Step 4. To find the profit-maximizing output level, look at the Marginal Cost column (at every output level produced), as shown in Table 11, and determine where it is equal to the market price. The output level where price equals the marginal cost is the output level that maximizes profits.

Table 11.

Q	P	TFC	TVC	TC	AVC	ATC	MC	TR	Profits
0	$28	$20	$0	$20	–	–	–	$0	-$20
1	$28	$20	$20	$40	$20.00	$40.00	$20	$28	-$12
2	$28	$20	$25	$45	$12.50	$22.50	$5	$56	$11
3	$28	$20	$35	$55	$11.67	$18.33	$10	$84	$29
4	$28	$20	$52	$72	$13.00	$18.00	$17	$112	$40
5	$28	$20	$80	$100	$16.40	$20.40	$30	$140	$40

Step 5. Once you have determined the profit-maximizing output level (in this case, output quantity 5), you can look at the amount of profits made (in this case, $40).

Step 6. If the firm is making economic losses, the firm needs to determine whether it produces the output level where price equals marginal revenue and equals marginal cost or it shuts down and only incurs its fixed costs.

Step 7. For the output level where marginal revenue is equal to marginal cost, check if the market price is greater than the average variable cost of producing that output level.

- If P > AVC but P < ATC, then the firm continues to produce in the short-run, making economic losses.
- If P < AVC, then the firm stops producing and only incurs its fixed costs.

- In this example, the price of $28 is greater than the AVC ($16.40) of producing 5 units of output, so the firm continues producing.

Concepts and Summary

As a perfectly competitive firm produces a greater quantity of output, its total revenue steadily increases at a constant rate determined by the given market price. Profits will be highest (or losses will be smallest) at the quantity of output where total revenues exceed total costs by the greatest amount (or where total revenues fall short of total costs by the smallest amount). Alternatively, profits will be highest where marginal revenue, which is price for a perfectly competitive firm, is equal to marginal cost. If the market price faced by a perfectly competitive firm is above average cost at the profit-maximizing quantity of output, then the firm is making profits. If the market price is below average cost at the profit-maximizing quantity of output, then the firm is making losses.

If the market price is equal to average cost at the profit-maximizing level of output, then the firm is making zero profits. The point where the marginal cost curve crosses the average cost curve, at the minimum of the average cost curve, is called the "zero profit point." If the market price faced by a perfectly competitive firm is below average variable cost at the profit-maximizing quantity of output, then the firm should shut down operations immediately. If the market price faced by a perfectly competitive firm is above average variable cost, but below average cost, then the firm should continue producing in the short run, but exit in the long run. The point where the marginal cost curve crosses the average variable cost curve is called the shutdown point.

11.3 DECISIONS ON ENTRY AND EXIT IN THE LONG RUN

The line between the short run and the long run cannot be defined precisely with a stopwatch, or even with a calendar. It varies according to the specific business. The distinction between the short run and the long run is therefore more technical: in the short run, firms cannot change the usage of fixed inputs, while in the long run, the firm can adjust all factors of production.

In a competitive market, profits are a red cape that incites businesses to charge. If a business is making a profit in the short run, it has an incentive to expand existing factories or to build new ones. New firms may start production, as well. When new firms enter the industry in response to increased industry profits it is called **entry**.

Losses are the black thundercloud that causes businesses to flee. If a business is making losses in the short run, it will either keep limping along or just shut down, depending on whether its revenues are covering its variable costs. But in the long run, firms that are facing losses will shut down at least some of their output, and some firms will cease production altogether. The long-run process of reducing production in response to a sustained pattern of losses is called **exit**. The following Clear It Up feature discusses where some of these losses might come from, and the reasons why some firms go out of business.

Why do firms cease to exist?

Can we say anything about what causes a firm to exit an industry? Profits are the measurement that determines whether a business stays operating or not. Individuals start businesses with the purpose of making profits. They invest their money, time, effort, and many other resources to produce and sell something that they hope will give them something in return. Unfortunately, not all businesses are successful, and many new startups soon realize that their "business adventure" must eventually end.

In the model of perfectly competitive firms, those that consistently cannot make money will "exit," which is a nice, bloodless word for a more painful process. When a business fails, after all, workers lose their jobs, investors lose their money, and owners and managers can lose their dreams. Many businesses fail. The U.S. Small Business Administration indicates that in 2011, 409,040 new firms "entered," and 470,376 firms failed.

Sometimes a business fails because of poor management or workers who are not very productive, or because of tough domestic or foreign competition. Businesses also fail from a variety of causes that might best be summarized as bad luck. For example, conditions of demand and supply in the market shift in an unexpected way, so that the prices that can be charged for outputs fall or the prices that need to be paid for inputs rise. With millions of businesses in the U.S. economy, even a small fraction of them failing will affect many people—and business failures can be very hard on the workers and managers directly involved. But from the standpoint of the overall economic system, business exits are sometimes a necessary evil if a market-oriented system is going to offer a flexible mechanism for satisfying customers, keeping costs low, and inventing new products.

How Entry and Exit Lead to Zero Profits in the Long Run

No perfectly competitive firm acting alone can affect the market price. However, the combination of many firms entering or exiting the market will affect overall supply in the market. In turn, a shift in supply for the market as a whole will affect the market price. Entry and exit to and from the market are the driving forces behind a process that, in the long run, pushes the price down to minimum average total costs so that all firms are earning a zero profit.

To understand how short-run profits for a perfectly competitive firm will evaporate in the long run, imagine the following situation. The market is in **long-run equilibrium**, where all firms earn zero economic profits producing the output level where P = MR = MC and P = AC. No firm has the incentive to enter or leave the market. Let's say that the product's demand increases, and with that, the market price goes up. The existing firms in the industry are now facing a higher price than before, so they will increase production to the new output level where P = MR = MC.

This will temporarily make the market price rise above the average cost curve, and therefore, the existing firms in the market will now be earning economic profits. However, these economic profits attract other firms to enter the market. Entry of many new firms causes the market supply curve to shift to the right. As the supply curve shifts to the right, the market price starts decreasing, and with that, economic profits fall for new and existing firms. As long as there are still profits in the market, entry will continue to shift supply to the right. This will stop whenever the market price is driven down to the zero-profit level, where no firm is earning economic profits.

Short-run losses will fade away by reversing this process. Say that the market is in long-run equilibrium. This time, instead, demand decreases, and with that, the market price starts falling. The existing firms in the industry are now facing a lower price than before, and as it will be below the average cost curve, they will now be making economic losses. Some firms will continue producing where the new P = MR = MC, as long as they are able to cover their average variable costs. Some firms will have to shut down immediately as they will not be able to cover their average variable costs, and will then only incur their fixed costs, minimizing their losses. Exit of many firms causes the market supply curve to shift to the left. As the supply curve shifts to the left, the market price starts rising, and economic losses start to be lower. This process ends whenever the market price rises to the zero-profit level, where the existing firms are no longer losing money and are at zero profits again. Thus, while a perfectly competitive firm can earn profits in the short run, in the long run the process of entry will push down prices until they reach the zero-profit level. Conversely, while a perfectly competitive firm may earn losses in the short run, firms will not continually lose money. In the long run, firms making losses are able to escape from their fixed costs, and their exit from the market will push the price back up to the zero-profit level. In the long run, this process of entry and exit will drive the price in perfectly competitive markets to the zero-profit point at the bottom of the AC curve, where marginal cost crosses average cost.

The Long-Run Adjustment and Industry Types

Whenever there are expansions in an industry, costs of production for the existing and new firms could either stay the same, increase, or even decrease. Therefore, we can categorize an industry as being (1) a constant cost industry (as demand increases, the cost of production for firms stays the same), (2) an increasing cost industry (as demand increases, the cost of production for firms increases), or (3) a decreasing cost industry (as demand increases the costs of production for the firms decreases).

For a **constant cost industry**, whenever there is an increase in market demand and price, then the supply curve shifts to the right with new firms' entry and stops at the point where the new long-run equilibrium intersects at the same market price as before. But why will costs remain the same? In this type of industry, the supply curve is very elastic. Firms can easily supply any quantity that consumers demand. In addition, there is a perfectly elastic supply of inputs—firms can easily increase their demand for employees, for example, with no increase to wages. Tying in to our Bring it Home discussion, an increased demand for ethanol in recent years has caused the demand for corn to increase. Consequently, many farmers switched from growing wheat to growing corn. Agricultural markets are generally good examples of constant cost industries.

For an **increasing cost industry**, as the market expands, the old and new firms experience increases in their costs of production, which makes the new zero-profit level intersect at a higher price than before. Here companies may have to deal with limited inputs, such as skilled labor. As the demand for these workers rise, wages rise and this increases the cost of production for all firms. The industry supply curve in this type of industry is more inelastic.

For a **decreasing cost industry**, as the market expands, the old and new firms experience lower costs of production, which makes the new zero-profit level intersect at a lower price than before. In this case, the industry and all the firms in it are experiencing falling average total costs. This can be due to an improvement in technology in the entire industry or an increase in the education of employees. High tech industries may be a good example of a decreasing cost market.

Figure 1 (a) presents the case of an adjustment process in a constant cost industry. Whenever there are output expansions in this type of industry, the long-run outcome implies more output produced at exactly the same original price. Note that supply was able to increase to meet the increased demand. When we join the before and after long-run equilibriums, the resulting line is the long run supply (LRS) curve in perfectly competitive markets. In this case, it is a flat curve. Figure 1 (b) and Figure 1 (c) present the cases for an increasing cost and decreasing cost industry, respectively. For an increasing cost industry, the LRS is upward sloping, while for a decreasing cost industry, the LRS is downward sloping.

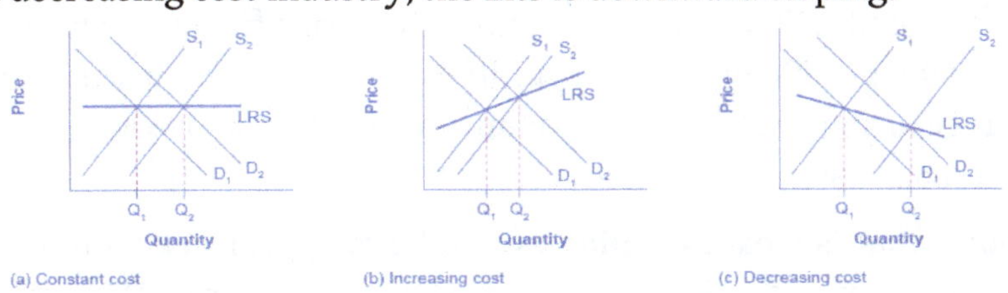

Figure 1. Adjustment Process in a Constant-Cost Industry. In (a), demand increased and supply met it. Notice that the supply increase is equal to the demand increase. The result is that the equilibrium price

stays the same as quantity sold increases. In (b), notice that sellers were not able to increase supply as much as demand. Some inputs were scarce, or wages were rising. The equilibrium price rises. In (c), sellers easily increased supply in response to the demand increase. Here, new technology or economies of scale caused the large increase in supply, resulting in declining equilibrium price.

CONCEPTS AND SUMMARY

In the long run, firms will respond to profits through a process of entry, where existing firms expand output and new firms enter the market. Conversely, firms will react to losses in the long run through a process of exit, in which existing firms reduce output or cease production altogether. Through the process of entry in response to profits and exit in response to losses, the price level in a perfectly competitive market will move toward the zero-profit point, where the marginal cost curve crosses the AC curve, at the minimum of the average cost curve.

The long-run supply curve shows the long-run output supplied by firms in three different types of industries: constant cost, increasing cost, and decreasing cost.

11.4 EFFICIENCY IN PERFECTLY COMPETITIVE MARKETS

When profit-maximizing firms in perfectly competitive markets combine with utility-maximizing consumers, something remarkable happens: the resulting quantities of outputs of goods and services demonstrate both productive and allocative efficiency (terms that were first introduced in (Choice in a World of Scarcity) .

Productive efficiency means producing without waste, so that the choice is on the production possibility frontier. In the long run in a perfectly competitive market, because of the process of entry and exit, the price in the market is equal to the minimum of the long-run average cost curve. In other words, goods are being produced and sold at the lowest possible average cost.

Allocative efficiency means that among the points on the production possibility frontier, the point that is chosen is socially preferred—at least in a particular and specific sense. In a perfectly competitive market, price will be equal to the marginal cost of production. Think about the price that is paid for a good as a measure of the social benefit received for that good; after all, willingness to pay conveys what the good is worth to a buyer. Then think about the marginal cost of producing the good as representing not just the cost for the firm, but more broadly as the social cost of producing that good. When perfectly competitive firms follow the rule that profits are maximized by producing at the quantity where price is equal to marginal cost, they are thus ensuring that the social benefits received from producing a good are in line with the social costs of production.

To explore what is meant by **allocative efficiency**, it is useful to walk through an example. Begin by assuming that the market for wholesale flowers is perfectly competitive, and so P = MC. Now, consider what it would mean if firms in that market produced a lesser quantity of flowers. At a lesser quantity, marginal costs will not yet have increased as much, so that price will exceed marginal cost; that is, P > MC. In that situation, the benefit to society as a whole of producing additional goods, as measured by the willingness of consumers to pay for marginal units of a good, would be higher than the cost of the inputs of labor and physical capital needed to produce the marginal good. In other words, the gains to society as a whole from producing additional marginal units will be greater than the costs.

Conversely, consider what it would mean if, compared to the level of output at the allocatively efficient choice when P = MC, firms produced a greater quantity of flowers. At a greater quantity, marginal costs of production will have increased so that P < MC. In that case, the marginal costs of producing additional flowers is greater than the benefit to society as measured by what people are willing to pay. For society as a whole, since the costs are outstripping the benefits, it will make sense to produce a lower quantity of such goods.

When perfectly competitive firms maximize their profits by producing the quantity where P = MC, they also assure that the benefits to consumers of what they are buying, as measured by the price they are willing to pay, is equal to the costs to society of producing the marginal units, as measured by the marginal costs the firm must pay—and thus that allocative efficiency holds.

The statements that a perfectly competitive market in the long run will feature both productive and allocative efficiency do need to be taken with a few grains of salt. Remember, economists are using the concept of "efficiency" in a particular and specific sense, not as a synonym for "desirable in every way." For one thing, consumers' ability to pay reflects the income distribution in a particular society. Thus, a homeless person may have no ability to pay for housing because they have insufficient income.

Perfect competition, in the long run, is a hypothetical benchmark. For market structures such as monopoly, monopolistic competition, and oligopoly, which are more frequently observed in the real world than perfect competition, firms will not always produce at the minimum of average cost, nor will they always set price equal to marginal cost. Thus, these other competitive situations will not produce productive and allocative efficiency.

Moreover, real-world markets include many issues that are assumed away in the model of perfect competition, including pollution, inventions of new technology, poverty which may make some people unable to pay for basic necessities of life, government programs like national defense or education, discrimination in labor markets, and buyers and sellers who must deal with imperfect and unclear information. These issues are explored in other chapters. However, the theoretical efficiency of perfect competition does provide a useful benchmark for comparing the issues that arise from these real-world problems.

A Dime a Dozen

A quick glance at Table 14 reveals the dramatic increase in North Dakota corn production—more than double. Taking into consideration that corn typically yields two to three times as many bushels per acre as wheat, it is obvious there has been a significant increase in bushels of corn. Why the increase in corn acreage? Converging prices.

Table 14. (Source: USDA National Agricultural Statistics Service)

Year	Corn (millions of acres)	Wheat (millions of acres)
2014	91.6	56.82

Historically, wheat prices have been higher than corn prices, offsetting wheat's lower yield per acre. However, in recent years wheat and corn prices have been converging. In April 2013, Agweek reported the gap was just 71 cents per bushel. As the difference in price narrowed, switching to the production of higher yield per acre of corn simply made good business sense. Erik Younggren, president of the National Association of Wheat Growers said in the Agweek article, "I don't think we're going to see mile after mile of waving amber fields [of wheat] anymore." (Until wheat prices rise, we will probably be seeing field after field of tasseled corn.)

Concepts and Summary

Long-run equilibrium in perfectly competitive markets meets two important conditions: allocative efficiency and productive efficiency. These two conditions have important implications. First, resources are allocated to their best alternative use. Second, they provide the maximum satisfaction attainable by society.

References

IndexMundi. n.d. "Wheat Monthly Price—U.S. Dollars per Metric Ton." Accessed March 11, 2015. http://www.indexmundi.com/commodities/?commodity=wheat.

Knutson, J. "Wheat on the Defensive in the Northern Plains." *Agweek, Associated Press State Wire: North Dakota (ND)*. April 14, 2013.

SBA Office of Advocacy. 2014. "Frequently Asked Questions: Advocacy: the voice of small business in government." Accessed March 11, 2015. https://www.sba.gov/sites/default/files/advocacy/FAQ_March_2014_0.pdf.

CHAPTER

THE MONOPOLY AND ITS KIND 12

12.1 THE FORMATION OF MONOPOLIES: BARRIERS TO ENTRY

Because of the lack of competition, monopolies tend to earn significant economic profits. These profits should attract vigorous competition as described in Perfect Competition, and yet, because of one particular characteristic of monopoly, they do not. Barriers to entry are the legal, technological, or market forces that discourage or prevent potential competitors from entering a market. Barriers to entry can range from the simple and easily surmountable, such as the cost of renting retail space, to the extremely restrictive. For example, there are a finite number of radio frequencies available for broadcasting. Once the rights to all of them have been purchased, no new competitors can enter the market.

In some cases, barriers to entry may lead to monopoly. In other cases, they may limit competition to a few firms. Barriers may block entry even if the firm or firms currently in the market are earning profits. Thus, in markets with significant barriers to entry, it is not true that abnormally high profits will attract new firms, and that this entry of new firms will eventually cause the price to decline so that surviving firms earn only a normal level of profit in the long run.

There are two types of monopoly, based on the types of barriers to entry they exploit. One is **natural monopoly**, where the barriers to entry are something other than legal prohibition. The other is **legal monopoly**, where laws prohibit (or severely limit) competition.

Natural Monopoly

Economies of scale can combine with the size of the market to limit competition. (This theme was introduced in Cost and Industry Structure). Figure 1 presents a long-run average cost curve for the airplane manufacturing industry. It shows economies of scale up to an output of 8,000 planes per year and a price of P0, then constant returns to scale from 8,000 to 20,000 planes per year, and diseconomies of scale at a quantity of production greater than 20,000 planes per year.

Now consider the market demand curve in the diagram, which intersects the long-run average cost (LRAC) curve at an output level of 6,000 planes per year and at a price P_1, which is higher than P_0. In this situation, the market has room for only one producer. If a second firm attempts to enter the market at a smaller size, say by producing a quantity of 4,000 planes, then its average costs will be higher than the existing firm, and it will be unable to compete. If the second firm attempts to enter the market at a larger size, like 8,000 planes per year, then it could produce at a lower average cost—but it could not sell all 8,000 planes that it produced because of insufficient demand in the market.

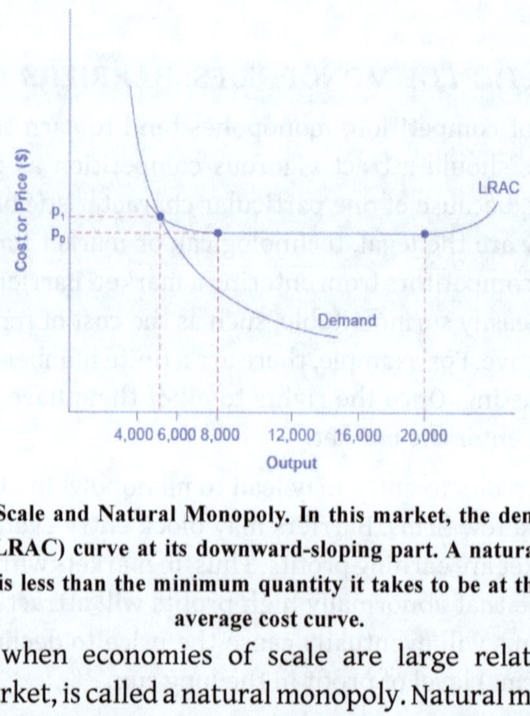

Figure 1. Economies of Scale and Natural Monopoly. In this market, the demand curve intersects the long-run average cost (LRAC) curve at its downward-sloping part. A natural monopoly occurs when the quantity demanded is less than the minimum quantity it takes to be at the bottom of the long-run average cost curve.

This situation, when economies of scale are large relative to the quantity demanded in the market, is called a natural monopoly. Natural monopolies often arise in industries where the marginal cost of adding an additional customer is very low, once the fixed costs of the overall system are in place. Once the main water pipes are laid through a neighborhood, the marginal cost of providing water service to another home is fairly low. Once electricity lines are installed through a neighborhood, the marginal cost of providing additional electrical service to one more home is very low. It would be costly and duplicative for a second water company to enter the market and invest in a whole second set of main water pipes, or for a second electricity company to enter the market and invest in a whole new set of electrical wires. These industries offer an example where, because of economies of scale, one producer can serve the entire market more efficiently than a number of smaller producers that would need to make duplicate physical capital investments.

A natural monopoly can also arise in smaller local markets for products that are difficult to transport. For example, cement production exhibits economies of scale, and the quantity of cement demanded in a local area may not be much larger than what a single plant can produce. Moreover, the costs of transporting cement over land are high, and so a cement plant in an area without access to water transportation may be a natural monopoly.

CONTROL OF A PHYSICAL RESOURCE

Another type of natural monopoly occurs when a company has control of a scarce physical resource. In the U.S. economy, one historical example of this pattern occurred when ALCOA—the Aluminum Company of America—controlled most of the supply of bauxite, a key mineral used in making aluminum. Back in the 1930s, when ALCOA controlled most of the bauxite, other firms were simply unable to produce enough aluminum to compete.

As another example, the majority of global diamond production is controlled by DeBeers, a multi-national company that has mining and production operations in South Africa, Botswana, Namibia, and Canada. It also has exploration activities on four continents, while directing a worldwide distribution network of rough cut diamonds. Though in recent years they have experienced growing competition, their impact on the rough diamond market is still considerable.

Legal Monopoly

For some products, the government erects barriers to entry by prohibiting or limiting competition. Under U.S. law, no organization but the U.S. Postal Service is legally allowed to deliver first-class mail. Many states or cities have laws or regulations that allow households a choice of only one electric company, one water company, and one company to pick up the garbage. Most legal monopolies are considered utilities—products necessary for everyday life—that are socially beneficial to have. As a consequence, the government allows producers to become regulated monopolies, to insure that an appropriate amount of these products is provided to consumers. Additionally, legal monopolies are often subject to economies of scale, so it makes sense to allow only one provider.

Promoting Innovation

Innovation takes time and resources to achieve. Suppose a company invests in research and development and finds the cure for the common cold. In this world of near ubiquitous information, other companies could take the formula, produce the drug, and because they did not incur the costs of research and development (R&D), undercut the price of the company that discovered the drug. Given this possibility, many firms would choose not to invest in research and development, and as a result, the world would have less innovation. To prevent this from happening, the

Constitution of the United States specifies in Article I, Section 8: "The Congress shall have Power . . . To Promote the Progress of Science and Useful Arts, by securing for limited Times to Authors and Inventors the Exclusive Right to their Writings and Discoveries." Congress used this power to create the U.S. Patent and Trademark Office, as well as the U.S. Copyright Office. A patent gives the inventor the exclusive legal right to make, use, or sell the invention for a limited time; in the United States, exclusive patent rights last for 20 years. The idea is to provide limited monopoly power so that innovative firms can recoup their investment in R&D, but then to allow other firms to produce the product more cheaply once the patent expires.

A trademark is an identifying symbol or name for a particular good, like Chiquita bananas, Chevrolet cars, or the Nike "swoosh" that appears on shoes and athletic gear. Roughly 1.9 million trademarks are registered with the U.S. government. A firm can renew a trademark over and over again, as long as it remains in active use.

A **copyright**, according to the U.S. Copyright Office, "is a form of protection provided by the laws of the United States for 'original works of authorship' including literary, dramatic, musical, architectural, cartographic, choreographic, pantomimic, pictorial, graphic, sculptural, and audiovisual creations." No one can reproduce, display, or perform a copyrighted work without permission of the author. Copyright protection ordinarily lasts for the life of the author plus 70 years.

Roughly speaking, patent law covers inventions and copyright protects books, songs, and art. But in certain areas, like the invention of new software, it has been unclear whether patent or copyright protection should apply. There is also a body of law known as **trade secrets**. Even if a company does not have a patent on an invention, competing firms are not allowed to steal their secrets. One famous trade secret is the formula for Coca-Cola, which is not protected under copyright or patent law, but is simply kept secret by the company.

Taken together, this combination of patents, trademarks, copyrights, and trade secret law is called **intellectual property**, because it implies ownership over an idea, concept, or image, not a physical piece of property like a house or a car. Countries around the world have enacted laws to protect intellectual property, although the time periods and exact provisions of such laws vary across countries. There are ongoing negotiations, both through the World Intellectual Property Organization (WIPO) and through international treaties, to bring greater harmony to the intellectual property laws of different countries to determine the extent to which patents and copyrights in one country will be respected in other countries.

Government limitations on competition used to be even more common in the United States. For most of the twentieth century, only one phone company—AT&T—was legally allowed to provide local and long distance service. From the 1930s to the 1970s, one set of federal regulations limited which destinations airlines could choose to fly to and what fares they could charge; another set of regulations limited the interest rates that banks could pay to depositors; yet another specified what trucking firms could charge customers.

What products are considered utilities depends, in part, on the available technology. Fifty years ago, local and long distance telephone service was provided over wires. It did not make much sense to have multiple companies building multiple systems of wiring across towns and across the country. AT&T lost its monopoly on long distance service when the technology for providing phone service changed from wires to microwave and satellite transmission, so that multiple firms could use the same transmission mechanism. The same thing happened to local service, especially in recent years, with the growth in cellular phone systems.

The combination of improvements in production technologies and a general sense that the markets could provide services adequately led to a wave of **deregulation**, starting in the late 1970s and continuing into the 1990s. This wave eliminated or reduced government restrictions on the firms that could enter, the prices that could be charged, and the quantities that could be produced in many industries, including telecommunications, airlines, trucking, banking, and electricity.

Around the world, from Europe to Latin America to Africa and Asia, many governments continue to control and limit competition in what those governments perceive to be key industries, including airlines, banks, steel companies, oil companies, and telephone companies.

Intimidating Potential Competition

Businesses have developed a number of schemes for creating barriers to entry by deterring potential competitors from entering the market. One method is known as **predatory pricing**, in which a firm uses the threat of sharp price cuts to discourage competition. Predatory pricing is a violation of U.S. antitrust law, but it is difficult to prove.

Consider a large airline that provides most of the flights between two particular cities. A new, small start-up airline decides to offer service between these two cities. The large airline immediately slashes prices on this route to the bone, so that the new entrant cannot make any money. After the new entrant has gone out of business, the incumbent firm can raise prices again.

After this pattern is repeated once or twice, potential new entrants may decide that it is not wise to try to compete. Small airlines often accuse larger airlines of predatory pricing: in the early 2000s, for example, ValuJet accused Delta of predatory pricing, Frontier accused United, and Reno Air accused Northwest. In 2015, the Justice Department ruled against American Express and Mastercard for imposing restrictions on retailers who encouraged customers to use lower swipe fees on credit transactions.

In some cases, large advertising budgets can also act as a way of discouraging the competition. If the only way to launch a successful new national cola drink is to spend more than the promotional budgets of Coca-Cola and Pepsi Cola, not too many companies will try. A firmly established brand name can be difficult to dislodge.

Summing Up Barriers to Entry

Table 1 lists the barriers to entry that have been discussed here. This list is not exhaustive, since firms have proved to be highly creative in inventing business practices that discourage competition. When barriers to entry exist, perfect competition is no longer a reasonable description of how an industry works. When barriers to entry are high enough, monopoly can result.

Table 1. Barriers to Entry

Barrier to Entry	Government Role?	Example
Natural monopoly	Government often responds with regulation (or ownership)	Water and electric companies
Control of a physical resource	No	DeBeers for diamonds
Legal monopoly	Yes	Post office, past regulation of airlines and trucking
Patent, trademark, and copyright	Yes, through protection of intellectual property	New drugs or software
Intimidating potential competitors	Somewhat	Predatory pricing; well-known brand names

Concepts and Summary

Barriers to entry prevent or discourage competitors from entering the market. These barriers include: economies of scale that lead to natural monopoly; control of a physical resource; legal restrictions on competition; patent, trademark and copyright protection; and practices to intimidate the competition like predatory pricing. Intellectual property refers to legally guaranteed ownership of an idea, rather than a physical item. The laws that protect intellectual property include patents, copyrights, trademarks, and trade secrets. A natural monopoly arises when economies of scale persist over a large enough range of output that if one firm supplies the entire market, no other firm can enter without facing a cost disadvantage.

12.2 HOW A PROFIT-MAXIMIZING MONOPOLY CHOOSES OUTPUT AND PRICE

Consider a monopoly firm, comfortably surrounded by barriers to entry so that it need not fear competition from other producers. How will this monopoly choose its profit-maximizing quantity of output, and what price will it charge? Profits for the monopolist, like any firm, will be equal to total revenues minus total costs. The pattern of costs for the monopoly can be analyzed within the same framework as the costs of a **perfectly competitive firm**—that is, by using total cost, fixed cost, variable cost, marginal cost, average cost, and average variable cost. However, because a monopoly faces no competition, its situation and its decision process will differ from that of a perfectly competitive firm. (The Clear it Up feature discusses how hard it is sometimes to define "market" in a monopoly situation.)

Demand Curves Perceived by a Perfectly Competitive Firm and by a Monopoly

A perfectly competitive firm acts as a price taker, so its calculation of total revenue is made by taking the given market price and multiplying it by the quantity of output that the firm chooses. The demand curve as it is perceived by a perfectly competitive firm appears in Figure 1 (a). The flat perceived demand curve means that, from the viewpoint of the perfectly competitive firm, it could sell either a relatively low quantity like Ql or a relatively high quantity like Qh at the market price P.

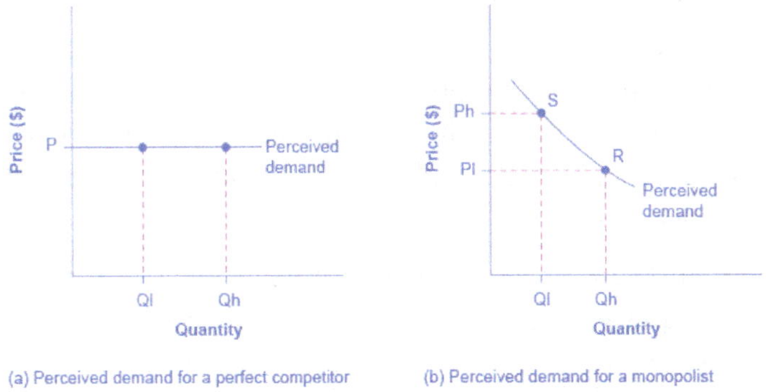

Figure 1. The Perceived Demand Curve for a Perfect Competitor and a Monopolist. (a) A perfectly competitive firm perceives the demand curve that it faces to be flat. The flat shape means that the firm can sell either a low quantity (Ql) or a high quantity (Qh) at exactly the same price (P). (b) A monopolist perceives the demand curve that it faces to be the same as the market demand curve, which for most goods is downward-sloping. Thus, if the monopolist chooses a high level of output (Qh), it can charge only a relatively low price (Pl); conversely, if the monopolist chooses a low level of output (Ql), it can then charge a higher price (Ph). The challenge for the monopolist is to choose the combination of price and quantity that maximizes profits.

What defines the market?

A monopoly is a firm that sells all or nearly all of the goods and services in a given market. But what defines the "market"?

In a famous 1947 case, the federal government accused the DuPont company of having a monopoly in the cellophane market, pointing out that DuPont produced 75% of the cellophane in the United States. DuPont countered that even though it had a 75% market share in cellophane, it had less than a 20% share of the "flexible packaging materials," which includes all other moisture-proof papers, films, and foils. In 1956, after years of legal appeals, the U.S. Supreme Court held that the broader market definition was more appropriate, and the case against DuPont was dismissed.

Questions over how to define the market continue today. True, Microsoft in the 1990s had a dominant share of the software for computer operating systems, but in the total market for all computer software and services, including everything from games to scientific programs, the Microsoft share was only about 14% in 2014. The Greyhound bus company may have a near-monopoly on the market for intercity bus transportation, but it is only a small share of the market for intercity transportation if that market includes private cars, airplanes, and railroad service. DeBeers has a monopoly in diamonds, but it is a much smaller share of the total market for precious gemstones and an even smaller share of the total market for jewelry. A small town in the country may have only one gas station: is this gas station a "monopoly," or does it compete with gas stations that might be five, 10, or 50 miles away?

In general, if a firm produces a product without close substitutes, then the firm can be considered a monopoly producer in a single market. But if buyers have a range of similar—even if not identical—options available from other firms, then the firm is not a monopoly. Still, arguments over whether substitutes are close or not close can be controversial.

While a monopolist can charge any price for its product, that price is nonetheless constrained by demand for the firm's product. No monopolist, even one that is thoroughly protected by high barriers to entry, can require consumers to purchase its product. Because the monopolist is the only firm in the market, its demand curve is the same as the market demand curve, which is, unlike that for a perfectly competitive firm, downward-sloping.

Figure 1 illustrates this situation. The monopolist can either choose a point like R with a low price (Pl) and high quantity (Qh), or a point like S with a high price (Ph) and a low quantity (Ql), or some intermediate point. Setting the price too high will result in a low quantity sold, and will not bring in much revenue. Conversely, setting the price too low may result in a high quantity sold, but because of the low price, it will not bring in much revenue either. The challenge for the monopolist is to strike a profit-maximizing balance between the price it charges and the quantity that it sells. But why isn't the perfectly competitive firm's demand curve also the market demand curve? See the following Clear it Up feature for the answer to this question.

The difference between perceived demand and market demand.

The demand curve as perceived by a perfectly competitive firm is not the overall market demand curve for that product. However, the firm's demand curve as perceived by a monopoly is the same as the market demand curve. The reason for the difference is that each perfectly competitive firm perceives the demand for its products in a market that includes many other firms; in effect, the demand curve perceived by a perfectly competitive firm is a tiny slice of the entire market demand curve. In contrast, a monopoly perceives demand for its product in a market where the monopoly is the only producer.

Total Cost and Total Revenue for a Monopolist

Profits for a monopolist can be illustrated with a graph of total revenues and total costs, as shown with the example of the hypothetical HealthPill firm in Figure 2. The total cost curve has its typical shape; that is, total costs rise and the curve grows steeper as output increases.

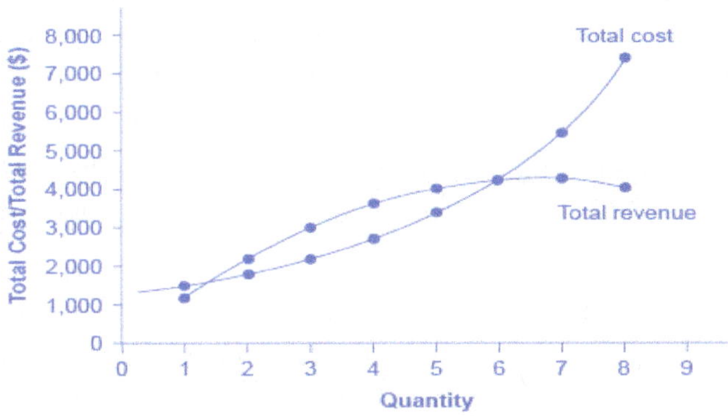

Figure 2. Total Revenue and Total Cost for the HealthPill Monopoly.

Total revenue for the monopoly firm called HealthPill first rises, then falls. Low levels of output bring in relatively little total revenue, because the quantity is low. High levels of output bring in relatively less revenue, because the high quantity pushes down the market price. The total cost curve is upward-sloping. Profits will be highest at the quantity of output where total revenue is most above total cost. Of the choices in Table 2, the highest profits happen at an output of 4. The profit-maximizing level of output is not the same as the revenue-maximizing level of output, which should make sense, because profits take costs into account and revenues do not.

Table 2. Total Costs and Total Revenues of HealthPill

Quantity	Total Cost	Quantity	Price	Total Revenue	Profit = Total Revenue – Total Cost
1	1,500	1	1,200	1,200	–300
2	1,800	2	1,100	2,200	400
3	2,200	3	1,000	3,000	800
4	2,800	4	900	3,600	800
5	3,500	5	800	4,000	500
6	4,200	6	700	4,200	0
7	5,600	7	600	4,200	–1,400
8	7,400	8	500	4,000	–3,400

To calculate total revenue for a monopolist, start with the demand curve perceived by the monopolist. Table 2 shows quantities along the demand curve and the price at each quantity demanded, and then calculates total revenue by multiplying price times quantity at each level of output. (In this example, the output is given as 1, 2, 3, 4, and so on, for the sake of simplicity. If you prefer a dash of greater realism, you can imagine that these output levels and the corresponding prices are measured per 1,000 or 10,000 pills.) As the figure illustrates, total revenue for a monopolist rises, flattens out, and then falls. In this example, total revenue is highest at a quantity of 6 or 7.

Clearly, the total revenue for a monopolist is not a straight upward-sloping line, in the way that total revenue was for a perfectly competitive firm. The different total revenue pattern for a monopolist occurs because the quantity that a monopolist chooses to produce affects the market price, which was not true for a perfectly competitive firm. If the monopolist charges a very high price, then quantity demanded drops, and so total revenue is very low. If the monopolist charges a very low price, then, even if quantity demanded is very high, total revenue will not add up to much. At some intermediate level, total revenue will be highest.

However, the monopolist is not seeking to maximize revenue, but instead to earn the highest possible profit. Profits are calculated in the final row of the table. In the HealthPill example in Figure 2, the highest profit will occur at the quantity where total revenue is the farthest above total cost. Of the choices given in the table, the highest profits occur at an output of 4, where profit is 800.

Marginal Revenue and Marginal Cost for a Monopolist

In the real world, a monopolist often does not have enough information to analyze its entire total revenues or total costs curves; after all, the firm does not know exactly what would happen if it were to alter production dramatically. But a monopolist often has fairly reliable information about how changing output by small or moderate amounts will affect its marginal revenues and marginal costs, because it has had experience with such changes over time and because modest changes are easier to extrapolate from current experience. A monopolist can use information on marginal revenue and marginal cost to seek out the profit-maximizing combination of quantity and price.

The first four columns of Table 3 use the numbers on total cost from the HealthPill example in the previous exhibit and calculate marginal cost and average cost. This monopoly faces a typical upward-sloping marginal cost curve, as shown in Figure 3. The second four columns of Table 3 use the total revenue information from the previous exhibit and calculate marginal revenue.

Notice that marginal revenue is zero at a quantity of 7, and turns negative at quantities higher than 7. It may seem counterintuitive that marginal revenue could ever be zero or negative: after all, does an increase in quantity sold not always mean more revenue? For a perfect competitor, each additional unit sold brought a positive marginal revenue, because marginal revenue was equal to the given market price. But a monopolist can sell a larger quantity and see a decline in **total revenue**. When a monopolist increases sales by one unit, it gains some marginal revenue from selling that extra unit, but also loses some marginal revenue because every other unit must now be sold at a lower price. As the quantity sold becomes higher, the drop in price affects a greater quantity of sales, eventually causing a situation where more sales cause marginal revenue to be negative.

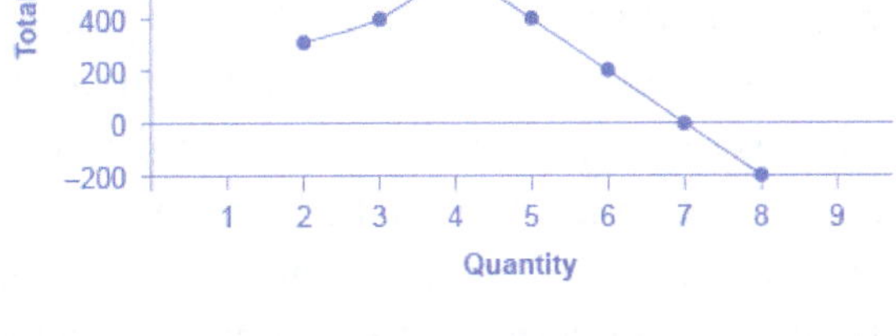

Figure 3. Marginal Revenue and Marginal Cost for the HealthPill Monopoly.

For a monopoly like HealthPill, marginal revenue decreases as additional units are sold. The marginal cost curve is upward-sloping. The profit-maximizing choice for the monopoly will be to produce at the quantity where marginal revenue is equal to marginal cost: that is, MR = MC. If the monopoly produces a lower quantity, then MR > MC at those levels of output, and the firm can make higher profits by expanding output. If the firm produces at a greater quantity, then MC > MR, and the firm can make higher profits by reducing its quantity of output.

Table 3. Costs and Revenues of HealthPill

Cost Information				Revenue Information			
Quantity	**Total Cost**	**Marginal Cost**	**Average Cost**	**Quantity**	**Price**	**Total Revenue**	**Marginal Revenue**
1	1,500	1,500	1,500	1	1,200	1,200	1,200
2	1,800	300	900	2	1,100	2,200	1,000
3	2,200	400	733	3	1,000	3,000	800
4	2,800	600	700	4	900	3,600	600
5	3,500	700	700	5	800	4,000	400
6	4,200	700	700	6	700	4,200	200
7	5,600	1,400	800	7	600	4,200	0
8	7,400	1,800	925	8	500	4,000	–200

A monopolist can determine its profit-maximizing price and quantity by analyzing the marginal revenue and marginal costs of producing an extra unit. If the marginal revenue exceeds the marginal cost, then the firm should produce the extra unit.

For example, at an output of 3 in Figure 3, marginal revenue is 800 and marginal cost is 400, so producing this unit will clearly add to overall profits. At an output of 4, marginal revenue is 600 and marginal cost is 600, so producing this unit still means overall profits are unchanged. However, expanding output from 4 to 5 would involve a marginal revenue of 400 and a marginal cost of 700, so that fifth unit would actually reduce profits. Thus, the monopoly can tell from the marginal revenue and marginal cost that of the choices given in the table, the profit-maximizing level of output is 4.

Indeed, the monopoly could seek out the profit-maximizing level of output by increasing quantity by a small amount, calculating marginal revenue and marginal cost, and then either increasing output as long as marginal revenue exceeds marginal cost or reducing output if marginal cost exceeds marginal revenue. This process works without any need to calculate total revenue and total cost. Thus, a profit-maximizing monopoly should follow the rule of producing up to the quantity where marginal revenue is equal to marginal cost—that is, MR = MC.

MAXIMIZING PROFITS

If you find it counterintuitive that producing where marginal revenue equals marginal cost will maximize profits, working through the numbers will help.

Step 1. Remember that marginal cost is defined as the change in total cost from producing a small amount of additional output.

$$MC = \frac{change\ in\ total\ cost}{change\ in\ quantity\ produced}$$

Step 2. Note that in Table 3, as output increases from 1 to 2 units, total cost increases from \$1500 to \$1800. As a result, the marginal cost of the second unit will be:

$$MC = \frac{\$1800 - \$1500}{1}$$
$$= \$300$$

Step 3. Remember that, similarly, marginal revenue is the change in total revenue from selling a small amount of additional output.

$$MR = \frac{change\ in\ total\ revenue}{change\ in\ quantity\ sold}$$

Step 4. Note that in Table 3, as output increases from 1 to 2 units, total revenue increases from \$1200 to \$2200. As a result, the marginal revenue of the second unit will be:

$$MR = \frac{\$2200 - \$1200}{1}$$
$$= \$1000$$

Table 4. Marginal Revenue, Marginal Cost, Marginal and Total Profit

Quantity	Marginal Revenue	Marginal Cost	Marginal Profit	Total Profit
1	1,200	1,500	–300	–300
2	1,000	300	700	400
3	800	400	400	800
4	600	600	0	800
5	400	700	–300	500
6	200	700	-500	0
7	0	1,400	–1,400	–1,400

Table 4 repeats the marginal cost and marginal revenue data from Table 3, and adds two more columns: Marginal profit is the profitability of each additional unit sold. It is defined as marginal revenue minus marginal cost. Finally, total profit is the sum of marginal profits. As long as marginal profit is positive, producing more output will increase total profits. When marginal profit turns negative, producing more output will decrease total profits. Total profit is maximized where marginal revenue equals marginal cost. In this example, maximum profit occurs at 4 units of output.

A perfectly competitive firm will also find its profit-maximizing level of output where MR = MC. The key difference with a perfectly competitive firm is that in the case of perfect competition, marginal revenue is equal to price (MR = P), while for a monopolist, marginal revenue is not equal to the price, because changes in quantity of output affect the price.

Illustrating Monopoly Profits

It is straightforward to calculate profits of given numbers for total revenue and total cost. However, the size of monopoly profits can also be illustrated graphically with Figure 4, which takes the marginal cost and marginal revenue curves from the previous exhibit and adds an average cost curve and the monopolist's perceived demand curve.

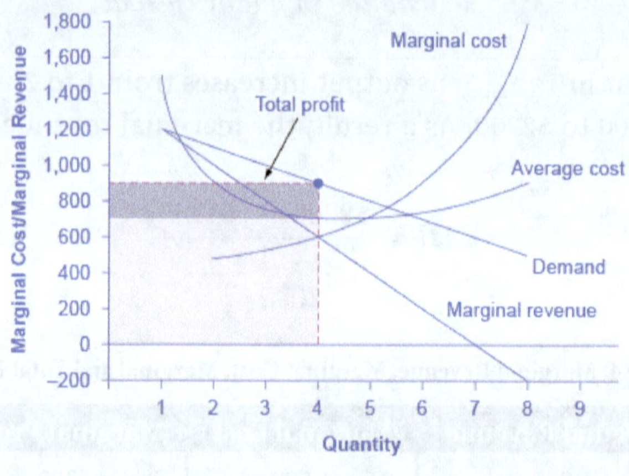

Figure 4. Illustrating Profits at the HealthPill Monopoly.

This figure begins with the same marginal revenue and marginal cost curves from the HealthPill monopoly presented in Figure 3. It then adds an average cost curve and the demand curve faced by the monopolist. The HealthPill firm first chooses the quantity where MR = MC; in this example, the quantity is 4. The monopolist then decides what price to charge by looking at the demand curve it faces. The large box, with quantity on the horizontal axis and marginal revenue on the vertical axis, shows total revenue for the firm. Total costs for the firm are shown by the lighter-shaded box, which is quantity on the horizontal axis and marginal cost of production on the vertical axis. The large total revenue box minus the smaller total cost box leaves the darkly shaded box that shows total profits. Since the price charged is above average cost, the firm is earning positive profits.

Figure 5 illustrates the three-step process where a monopolist: selects the profit-maximizing quantity to produce; decides what price to charge; determines total revenue, total cost, and profit.

Step 1: The Monopolist Determines Its Profit-Maximizing Level of Output

The firm can use the points on the demand curve D to calculate total revenue, and then, based on total revenue, calculate its marginal revenue curve. The profit-maximizing quantity will occur where MR = MC—or at the last possible point before marginal costs start exceeding marginal revenue. On Figure 4, MR = MC occurs at an output of 4.

Step 2: The Monopolist Decides What Price to Charge

The monopolist will charge what the market is willing to pay. A dotted line drawn straight up from the profit-maximizing quantity to the demand curve shows the profit-maximizing price. This price is above the average cost curve, which shows that the firm is earning profits.

Step 3: Calculate Total Revenue, Total Cost, and Profit

Total revenue is the overall shaded box, where the width of the box is the quantity being sold and the height is the price. In Figure 4, the bottom part of the shaded box, which is shaded more lightly, shows total costs; that is, quantity on the horizontal axis multiplied by average cost on the vertical axis. The larger box of total revenues minus the smaller box of total costs will equal profits, which is shown by the darkly shaded box. In a perfectly competitive market, the forces of entry would erode this profit in the long run. But a monopolist is protected by barriers to entry. In fact, one telltale sign of a possible monopoly is when a firm earns profits year after year, while doing more or less the same thing, without ever seeing those profits eroded by increased competition.

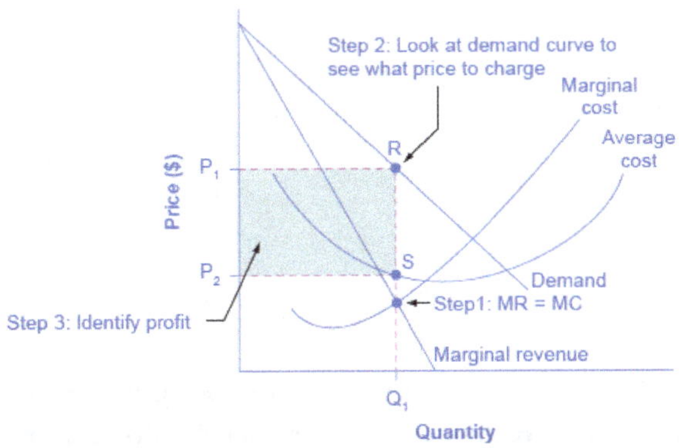

Figure 5. How a Profit-Maximizing Monopoly Decides Price In Step 1, the monopoly chooses the profit-maximizing level of output Q1, by choosing the quantity where MR = MC. In Step 2, the monopoly decides

how much to charge for output level 1 by drawing a line straight up from Q1 to point R on its perceived demand curve. Thus, the monopoly will charge a price (P1). In Step 3, the monopoly identifies its profit. Total revenue will be Q1 multiplied by P1. Total cost will be Q1 multiplied by the average cost of producing Q1, which is shown by point S on the average cost curve to be P2. Profits will be the total revenue rectangle minus the total cost rectangle, shown by the shaded zone in the figure.

Why is a monopolist's marginal revenue always less than the price?

The marginal revenue curve for a monopolist always lies beneath the market demand curve. To understand why, think about increasing the quantity along the demand curve by one unit, so that you take one step down the demand curve to a slightly higher quantity but a slightly lower price. A demand curve is not sequential: It is not that first we sell Q1 at a higher price, and then we sell Q2 at a lower price. Rather, a demand curve is conditional: If we charge the higher price, we would sell Q1. If, instead, we charge a lower price (on all the units that we sell), we would sell Q2.

So when we think about increasing the quantity sold by one unit, marginal revenue is affected in two ways. First, we sell one additional unit at the new market price. Second, all the previous units, which could have been sold at the higher price, now sell for less. Because of the lower price on all units sold, the marginal revenue of selling a unit is less than the price of that unit—and the marginal revenue curve is below the demand curve. *Tip*: For a straight-line demand curve, MR and demand have the same vertical intercept. As output increases, marginal revenue decreases twice as fast as demand, so that the horizontal intercept of MR is halfway to the horizontal intercept of demand. You can see this in the Figure 6.

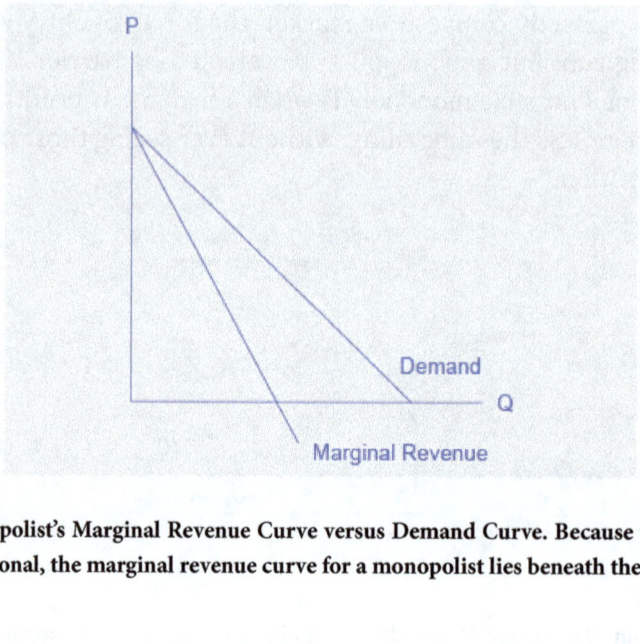

Figure 6. The Monopolist's Marginal Revenue Curve versus Demand Curve. Because the market demand curve is conditional, the marginal revenue curve for a monopolist lies beneath the demand curve.

THE INEFFICIENCY OF MONOPOLY

Most people criticize monopolies because they charge too high a price, but what economists object to is that monopolies do not supply enough output to be allocatively efficient. To understand why a monopoly is inefficient, it is useful to compare it with the benchmark model of perfect competition.

Allocative efficiency is a social concept. It refers to producing the optimal quantity of some output, the quantity where the marginal benefit to society of one more unit just equals the marginal cost. The rule of profit maximization in a world of perfect competition was for each firm to produce the quantity of output where P = MC, where the price (P) is a measure of how much buyers value the good and the marginal cost (MC) is a measure of what marginal units cost society to produce. Following this rule assures allocative efficiency. If P > MC, then the marginal benefit to society (as measured by P) is greater than the marginal cost to society of producing additional units, and a greater quantity should be produced. But in the case of monopoly, price is always greater than marginal cost at the profit-maximizing level of output, as can be seen by looking back at Figure 4. Thus, consumers will suffer from a monopoly because a lower quantity will be sold in the market, at a higher price, than would have been the case in a perfectly competitive market.

The problem of inefficiency for monopolies often runs even deeper than these issues, and also involves incentives for efficiency over longer periods of time. There are counterbalancing incentives here. On one side, firms may strive for new inventions and new intellectual property because they want to become monopolies and earn high profits—at least for a few years until the competition catches up. In this way, monopolies may come to exist because of competitive pressures on firms. However, once a barrier to entry is in place, a monopoly that does not need to fear competition can just produce the same old products in the same old way—while still ringing up a healthy rate of profit. John Hicks, who won the Nobel Prize for economics in 1972, wrote in 1935: "The best of all monopoly profits is a quiet life." He did not mean the comment in a complimentary way. He meant that monopolies may bank their profits and slack off on trying to please their customers.

When AT&T provided all of the local and long-distance phone service in the United States, along with manufacturing most of the phone equipment, the payment plans and types of phones did not change much. The old joke was that you could have any color phone you wanted, as long as it was black. But in 1982, AT&T was split up by government litigation into a number of local phone companies, a long-distance phone company, and a phone equipment manufacturer. An explosion of innovation followed. Services like call waiting, caller ID, three-way calling, voice mail though the phone company, mobile phones, and wireless connections to the Internet all became available. A wide range of payment plans was offered, as well. It was no longer true that all phones were black; instead, phones came in a wide variety of shapes and colors. The end of the telephone monopoly brought lower prices, a greater quantity of services, and also a wave of innovation aimed at attracting and pleasing customers.

THE REST IS HISTORY

In the opening case, the East India Company and the Confederate States were presented as a monopoly or near monopoly provider of a good. Nearly every American schoolchild knows the result of the 'unwelcome visit' the 'Mohawks' bestowed upon Boston Harbor's tea-bearing ships—the Boston Tea Party. Regarding the cotton industry, we also know Great Britain remained neutral during the Civil War, taking neither side during the conflict.

Did the monopoly nature of these business have unintended and historical consequences? Might the American Revolution have been deterred, if the East India Company had sailed the tea-bearing ships back to England? Might the southern states have made different decisions had they not been so confident "King Cotton" would force diplomatic recognition of the Confederate States of America? Of course, it is not possible to definitively answer these questions; after all we cannot roll back the clock and try a different scenario. We can, however, consider the monopoly nature of these businesses and the roles they played and hypothesize about what might have occurred under different circumstances.

Perhaps if there had been legal free tea trade, the colonists would have seen things differently; there was smuggled Dutch tea in the colonial market. If the colonists had been able to freely purchase Dutch tea, they would have paid lower prices and avoided the tax.

What about the cotton monopoly? With one in five jobs in Great Britain depending on Southern cotton and the Confederate States nearly the sole provider of that cotton, why did Great Britain remain neutral during the Civil War? At the beginning of the war, Britain simply drew down massive stores of cotton. These stockpiles lasted until near the end of 1862. Why did Britain not recognize the Confederacy at that point? Two reasons: The Emancipation Proclamation and new sources of cotton. Having outlawed slavery throughout the United Kingdom in 1833, it was politically impossible for Great Britain, empty cotton warehouses or not, to recognize, diplomatically, the Confederate States. In addition, during the two years it took to draw down the stockpiles, Britain expanded cotton imports from India, Egypt, and Brazil.

Monopoly sellers often see no threats to their superior marketplace position. In these examples did the power of the monopoly blind the decision makers to other possibilities? Perhaps. But, as they say, the rest is history.

Concepts and Summary

A monopolist is not a price taker, because when it decides what quantity to produce, it also determines the market price. For a monopolist, total revenue is relatively low at low quantities of output, because not much is being sold. Total revenue is also relatively low at very high quantities of output, because a very high quantity will sell only at a low price. Thus, total revenue for a monopolist will start low, rise, and then decline. The marginal revenue for a monopolist from selling additional units will decline. Each additional unit sold by a monopolist will push down the overall market price, and as more units are sold, this lower price applies to more and more units.

The monopolist will select the profit-maximizing level of output where MR = MC, and then charge the price for that quantity of output as determined by the market demand curve. If that price is above average cost, the monopolist earns positive profits.

Monopolists are not productively efficient, because they do not produce at the minimum of the average cost curve. Monopolists are not allocatively efficient, because they do not produce at the quantity where P = MC. As a result, monopolists produce less, at a higher average cost, and charge a higher price than would a combination of firms in a perfectly competitive industry. Monopolists also may lack incentives for innovation, because they need not fear entry.

CHAPTER

COMPETITION IN MONOPOLISTS AND OLIGOPOLY 13

13.1 AN INTRODUCTION TO MONOPOLISTIC COMPETITION

Monopolistic competition involves many firms competing against each other, but selling products that are distinctive in some way. Examples include stores that sell different styles of clothing; restaurants or grocery stores that sell different kinds of food; and even products like golf balls or beer that may be at least somewhat similar but differ in public perception because of advertising and brand names. There are over 600,000 restaurants in the United States. When products are distinctive, each firm has a mini-monopoly on its particular style or flavor or brand name. However, firms producing such products must also compete with other styles and flavors and brand names. The term "monopolistic competition" captures this mixture of mini-monopoly and tough competition, and the following Clear It Up feature introduces its derivation.

Who invented the theory of imperfect competition?

The theory of imperfect competition was developed by two economists independently but simultaneously in 1933. The first was Edward Chamberlin of Harvard University who published The Economics of Monopolistic Competition. The second was Joan Robinson of Cambridge University who published The Economics of Imperfect Competition. Robinson subsequently became interested in macroeconomics where she became a prominent Keynesian, and later a post-Keynesian economist. (See the Welcome to Economics! and The Keynesian Perspective chapters for more on Keynes.)

Differentiated Products

A firm can try to make its products different from those of its competitors in several ways: physical aspects of the product, location from which the product is sold, intangible aspects of the product, and perceptions of the product. Products that are distinctive in one of these ways are called **differentiated products**.

Physical aspects of a product include all the phrases you hear in advertisements: unbreakable bottle, nonstick surface, freezer-to-microwave, non-shrink, extra spicy, newly redesigned for your comfort. The location of a firm can also create a difference between producers. For example, a gas station located at a heavily traveled intersection can probably sell more gas, because more cars drive by that corner. A supplier to an automobile manufacturer may find that it is an advantage to locate close to the car factory.

Intangible aspects can differentiate a product, too. Some intangible aspects may be promises like a guarantee of satisfaction or money back, a reputation for high quality, services like free delivery, or offering a loan to purchase the product. Finally, product differentiation may occur in the minds of buyers. For example, many people could not tell the difference in taste between common varieties of beer or cigarettes if they were blindfolded but, because of past habits and advertising, they have strong preferences for certain brands. Advertising can play a role in shaping these intangible preferences.

The concept of differentiated products is closely related to the degree of variety that is available. If everyone in the economy wore only blue jeans, ate only white bread, and drank only tap water, then the markets for clothing, food, and drink would be much closer to perfectly competitive. The variety of styles, flavors, locations, and characteristics creates product differentiation and monopolistic competition.

Perceived Demand for a Monopolistic Competitor

A monopolistically competitive firm perceives a demand for its goods that is an intermediate case between monopoly and competition. Figure 1 offers a reminder that the demand curve as faced by a perfectly competitive firm is perfectly elastic or flat, because the perfectly competitive firm can sell any quantity it wishes at the prevailing market price. In contrast, the demand curve, as faced by a monopolist, is the market demand curve, since a monopolist is the only firm in the market, and hence is downward sloping.

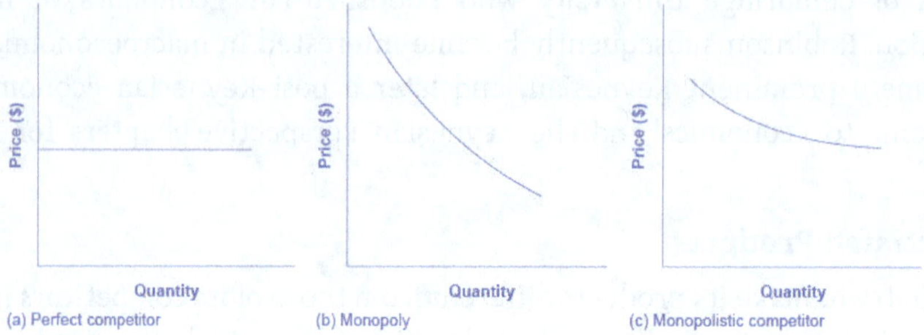

Figure 1. Perceived Demand for Firms in Different Competitive Settings. The demand curve faced by a perfectly competitive firm is perfectly elastic, meaning it can sell all the output it wishes at the prevailing

market price. The demand curve faced by a monopoly is the market demand. It can sell more output only by decreasing the price it charges. The demand curve faced by a monopolistically competitive firm falls in between.

The demand curve as faced by a monopolistic competitor is not flat, but rather downward-sloping, which means that the monopolistic competitor can raise its price without losing all of its customers or lower the price and gain more customers. Since there are substitutes, the demand curve facing a monopolistically competitive firm is more elastic than that of a monopoly where there are no close substitutes. If a monopolist raises its price, some consumers will choose not to purchase its product—but they will then need to buy a completely different product. However, when a monopolistic competitor raises its price, some consumers will choose not to purchase the product at all, but others will choose to buy a similar product from another firm. If a monopolistic competitor raises its price, it will not lose as many customers as would a perfectly competitive firm, but it will lose more customers than would a monopoly that raised its prices.

At a glance, the demand curves faced by a monopoly and by a monopolistic competitor look similar—that is, they both slope down. But the underlying economic meaning of these perceived demand curves is different, because a monopolist faces the market demand curve and a monopolistic competitor does not. Rather, a monopolistically competitive firm's demand curve is but one of many firms that make up the "before" market demand curve. Are you following? If so, how would you categorize the market for golf balls? Take a swing, then see the following Clear It Up feature.

Are golf balls really differentiated products?

Monopolistic competition refers to an industry that has more than a few firms, each offering a product which, from the consumer's perspective, is different from its competitors. The U.S. Golf Association runs a laboratory that tests 20,000 golf balls a year. There are strict rules for what makes a golf ball legal. The weight of a golf ball cannot exceed 1.620 ounces and its diameter cannot be less than 1.680 inches (which is a weight of 45.93 grams and a diameter of 42.67 millimeters, in case you were wondering). The balls are also tested by being hit at different speeds. For example, the distance test involves having a mechanical golfer hit the ball with a titanium driver and a swing speed of 120 miles per hour. As the testing center explains: "The USGA system then uses an array of sensors that accurately measure the flight of a golf ball during a short, indoor trajectory from a ball launcher. From this flight data, a computer calculates the lift and drag forces that are generated by the speed, spin, and dimple pattern of the ball. ... The distance limit is 317 yards."

Over 1800 golf balls made by more than 100 companies meet the USGA standards. The balls do differ in various ways, like the pattern of dimples on the ball, the types of plastic used on the cover and in the cores, and so on. Since all balls need to conform to the USGA tests, they are much more alike than different. In other words, golf ball manufacturers are monopolistically competitive.

However, retail sales of golf balls are about $500 million per year, which means that a lot of large companies have a powerful incentive to persuade players that golf balls are highly differentiated and that it makes a huge difference which one you choose. Sure, Tiger Woods can tell the difference. For the average duffer (golf-speak for a "mediocre player") who plays a few times a summer—and who loses a lot of golf balls to the woods and lake and needs to buy new ones—most golf balls are pretty much indistinguishable.

How a Monopolistic Competitor Chooses Price and Quantity

The monopolistically competitive firm decides on its profit-maximizing quantity and price in much the same way as a monopolist. A monopolistic competitor, like a monopolist, faces a downward-sloping demand curve, and so it will choose some combination of price and quantity along its perceived demand curve.

As an example of a profit-maximizing monopolistic competitor, consider the Authentic Chinese Pizza store, which serves pizza with cheese, sweet and sour sauce, and your choice of vegetables and meats. Although Authentic Chinese Pizza must compete against other pizza businesses and restaurants, it has a differentiated product. The firm's perceived demand curve is downward sloping, as shown in Figure 2 and the first two columns of Table 1.

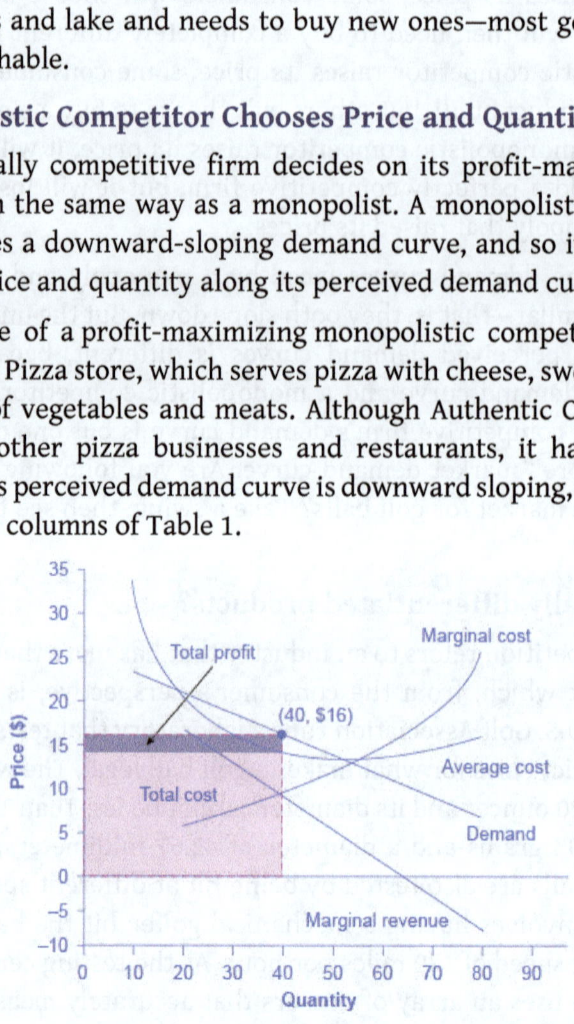

Figure 2. How a Monopolistic Competitor Chooses its Profit Maximizing Output and Price. To maximize profits, the Authentic Chinese Pizza shop would choose a quantity where marginal revenue equals marginal cost, or Q where MR = MC. Here it would choose a quantity of 40 and a price of $16.

Table 1. Revenue and Cost Schedule

Quantity	Price	Total Revenue	Marginal Revenue	Total Cost	Marginal Cost	Average Cost
10	$23	$230	–	$340	–	$34
20	$20	$400	$17	$400	$6	$20
30	$18	$540	$14	$480	$8	$16
40	$16	$640	$10	$580	$10	$14.50
50	$14	$700	$6	$700	$12	$14
60	$12	$720	$2	$840	$14	$14
70	$10	$700	–$2	$1,020	$18	$14.57
80	$8	$640	–$6	$1,280	$26	$16

The combinations of price and quantity at each point on the demand curve can be multiplied to calculate the total revenue that the firm would receive, which is shown in the third column of Table 1. The fourth column, marginal revenue, is calculated as the change in total revenue divided by the change in quantity. The final columns of Table 1 show total cost, marginal cost, and average cost. As always, marginal cost is calculated by dividing the change in total cost by the change in quantity, while average cost is calculated by dividing total cost by quantity. The following Work It Out feature shows how these firms calculate how much of its product to supply at what price.

How a Monopolistic Competitor Determines How Much to Produce and at What Price

The process by which a monopolistic competitor chooses its profit-maximizing quantity and price resembles closely how a monopoly makes these decisions process. First, the firm selects the profit-maximizing quantity to produce. Then the firm decides what price to charge for that quantity.

Step 1. The monopolistic competitor determines its profit-maximizing level of output. In this case, the Authentic Chinese Pizza company will determine the profit-maximizing quantity to produce by considering its marginal revenues and marginal costs. Two scenarios are possible:

- If the firm is producing at a quantity of output where marginal revenue exceeds marginal cost, then the firm should keep expanding production, because each marginal unit is adding to profit by bringing in more revenue than its cost. In this way, the firm will produce up to the quantity where MR = MC.
- If the firm is producing at a quantity where marginal costs exceed marginal revenue, then each marginal unit is costing more than the revenue it brings

in, and the firm will increase its profits by reducing the quantity of output until MR = MC.

In this example, MR and MC intersect at a quantity of 40, which is the profit-maximizing level of output for the firm.

Step 2. The monopolistic competitor decides what price to charge. When the firm has determined its profit-maximizing quantity of output, it can then look to its perceived demand curve to find out what it can charge for that quantity of output. On the graph, this process can be shown as a vertical line reaching up through the profit-maximizing quantity until it hits the firm's perceived demand curve. For Authentic Chinese Pizza, it should charge a price of $16 per pizza for a quantity of 40.

Once the firm has chosen price and quantity, it's in a position to calculate total revenue, total cost, and profit. At a quantity of 40, the price of $16 lies above the average cost curve, so the firm is making economic profits. From Table 1 we can see that, at an output of 40, the firm's total revenue is $640 and its total cost is $580, so profits are $60. In Figure 2, the firm's total revenues are the rectangle with the quantity of 40 on the horizontal axis and the price of $16 on the vertical axis. The firm's total costs are the light shaded rectangle with the same quantity of 40 on the horizontal axis but the average cost of $14.50 on the vertical axis. Profits are total revenues minus total costs, which is the shaded area above the average cost curve.

Although the process by which a monopolistic competitor makes decisions about quantity and price is similar to the way in which a monopolist makes such decisions, two differences are worth remembering. First, although both a monopolist and a monopolistic competitor face downward-sloping demand curves, the monopolist's perceived demand curve is the market demand curve, while the perceived demand curve for a monopolistic competitor is based on the extent of its product differentiation and how many competitors it faces. Second, a monopolist is surrounded by barriers to entry and need not fear entry, but a monopolistic competitor who earns profits must expect the entry of firms with similar, but differentiated, products.

Monopolistic Competitors and Entry

If one monopolistic competitor earns positive economic profits, other firms will be tempted to enter the market. A gas station with a great location must worry that other gas stations might open across the street or down the road—and perhaps the new gas stations will sell coffee or have a carwash or some other attraction to lure customers. A successful restaurant with a unique barbecue sauce must be concerned that other restaurants will try to copy the sauce or offer their own unique recipes. A laundry detergent with a great reputation for quality must be concerned that other competitors may seek to build their own reputations.

The entry of other firms into the same general market (like gas, restaurants, or detergent) shifts the demand curve faced by a monopolistically competitive firm. As more firms enter the market, the quantity demanded at a given price for any particular firm will decline, and the firm's perceived demand curve will shift to the left. As a firm's perceived demand curve shifts to the left, its marginal revenue curve will shift to the left, too. The shift in marginal revenue will change the profit-maximizing quantity that the firm chooses to produce, since marginal revenue will then equal marginal cost at a lower quantity.

Figure 3 (a) shows a situation in which a monopolistic competitor was earning a profit with its original perceived demand curve (D0). The intersection of the marginal revenue curve (MR0) and marginal cost curve (MC) occurs at point S, corresponding to quantity Q0, which is associated on the demand curve at point T with price P0. The combination of price P0 and quantity Q0 lies above the average cost curve, which shows that the firm is earning positive economic profits.

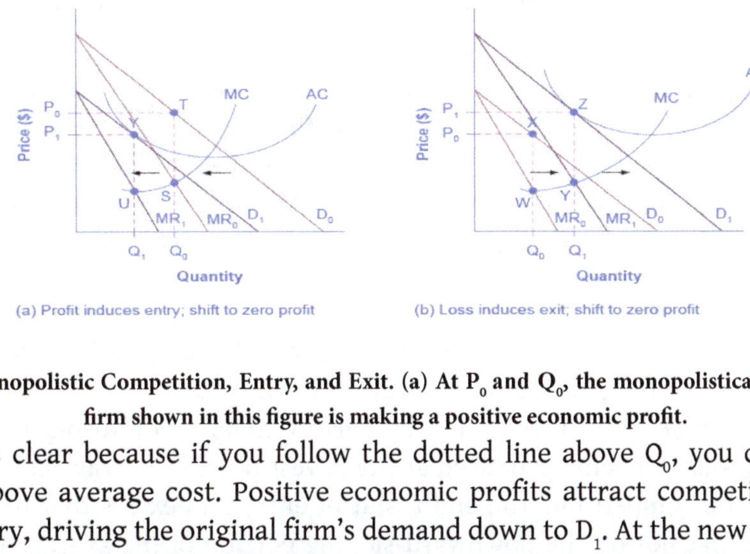

Figure 3. Monopolistic Competition, Entry, and Exit. (a) At P_0 and Q_0, the monopolistically competitive firm shown in this figure is making a positive economic profit.

This is clear because if you follow the dotted line above Q_0, you can see that price is above average cost. Positive economic profits attract competing firms to the industry, driving the original firm's demand down to D_1. At the new equilibrium quantity (P_1, Q_1), the original firm is earning zero economic profits, and entry into the industry ceases. In (b) the opposite occurs. At P_0 and Q_0, the firm is losing money. If you follow the dotted line above Q_0, you can see that average cost is above price. Losses induce firms to leave the industry. When they do, demand for the original firm rises to D_1, where once again the firm is earning zero economic profit.

Unlike a monopoly, with its high barriers to entry, a monopolistically competitive firm with positive economic profits will attract competition. When another competitor enters the market, the original firm's perceived demand curve shifts to the left, from D_0 to D_1, and the associated marginal revenue curve shifts from MR_0 to MR_1. The new profit-maximizing output is Q_1, because the intersection of the MR_1 and MC now occurs at point U. Moving vertically up from that quantity on the new demand curve, the optimal price is at P_1.

As long as the firm is earning positive economic profits, new competitors will continue to enter the market, reducing the original firm's demand and marginal revenue curves. The long-run equilibrium is shown in the figure at point Y, where the firm's perceived demand curve touches the average cost curve. When price is equal to average cost, economic profits are zero. Thus, although a monopolistically competitive firm may earn positive economic profits in the short term, the process of new entry will drive down economic profits to zero in the long run. Remember that zero economic profit is not equivalent to zero accounting profit. A zero economic profit means the firm's accounting profit is equal to what its resources could earn in their next best use. Figure 3 (b) shows the reverse situation, where a monopolistically competitive firm is originally losing money. The adjustment to long-run equilibrium is analogous to the previous example. The economic losses lead to firms exiting, which will result in increased demand for this particular firm, and consequently lower losses. Firms exit up to the point where there are no more losses in this market, for example when the demand curve touches the average cost curve, as in point Z.

Monopolistic competitors can make an economic profit or loss in the short run, but in the long run, entry and exit will drive these firms toward a zero economic profit outcome. However, the zero economic profit outcome in monopolistic competition looks different from the zero economic profit outcome in perfect competition in several ways relating both to efficiency and to variety in the market.

Monopolistic Competition and Efficiency

The long-term result of entry and exit in a perfectly competitive market is that all firms end up selling at the price level determined by the lowest point on the average cost curve. This outcome is why perfect competition displays **productive efficiency**: goods are being produced at the lowest possible average cost. However, in monopolistic competition, the end result of entry and exit is that firms end up with a price that lies on the downward-sloping portion of the average cost curve, not at the very bottom of the AC curve. Thus, monopolistic competition will not be productively efficient.

In a perfectly competitive market, each firm produces at a quantity where price is set equal to marginal cost, both in the short run and in the long run. This outcome is why perfect competition displays allocative efficiency: the social benefits of additional production, as measured by the marginal benefit, which is the same as the price, equal the marginal costs to society of that production. In a monopolistically competitive market, the rule for maximizing profit is to set MR = MC—and price is higher than marginal revenue, not equal to it because the demand curve is downward sloping. When P > MC, which is the outcome in a monopolistically competitive market, the benefits to society of providing additional quantity, as measured by the price that people are willing to pay, exceed the marginal costs to society of producing those units. A monopolistically competitive firm does not produce more, which means that society loses the net benefit of those extra units. This is the same argument we made about monopoly, but in this case to a lesser degree. Thus, a monopolistically competitive industry will produce a lower quantity of a good and charge a higher price for it than would a perfectly competitive industry. See the following Clear It Up feature for more detail on the impact of demand shifts.

Why does a shift in perceived demand cause a shift in marginal revenue?

The combinations of price and quantity at each point on a firm's perceived demand curve are used to calculate total revenue for each combination of price and quantity. This information on total revenue is then used to calculate marginal revenue, which is the change in total revenue divided by the change in quantity. A change in perceived demand will change total revenue at every quantity of output and in turn, the change in total revenue will shift marginal revenue at each quantity of output. Thus, when entry occurs in a monopolistically competitive industry, the perceived demand curve for each firm will shift to the left, because a smaller quantity will be demanded at any given price. Another way of interpreting this shift in demand is to notice that, for each quantity sold, a lower price will be charged. Consequently, the marginal revenue will be lower for each quantity sold—and the marginal revenue curve will shift to the left as well. Conversely, exit causes the perceived demand curve for a monopolistically competitive firm to shift to the right and the corresponding marginal revenue curve to shift right, too.

A monopolistically competitive industry does not display productive and allocative efficiency in either the short run, when firms are making economic profits and losses, nor in the long run, when firms are earning zero profits.

The Benefits of Variety and Product Differentiation

Even though monopolistic competition does not provide productive efficiency or allocative efficiency, it does have benefits of its own. Product differentiation is based on variety and innovation. Many people would prefer to live in an economy with many kinds of clothes, foods, and car styles; not in a world of perfect competition where everyone will always wear blue jeans and white shirts, eat only spaghetti with plain red sauce, and drive an identical model of car. Many people would prefer to live in an economy where firms are struggling to figure out ways of attracting customers by methods like friendlier service, free delivery, guarantees of quality, variations on existing products, and a better shopping experience.

Economists have struggled, with only partial success, to address the question of whether a market-oriented economy produces the optimal amount of variety. Critics of market-oriented economies argue that society does not really need dozens of different athletic shoes or breakfast cereals or automobiles. They argue that much of the cost of creating such a high degree of product differentiation, and then of advertising and marketing this differentiation, is socially wasteful—that is, most people would be just as happy with a smaller range of differentiated products produced and sold at a lower price. Defenders of a market-oriented economy respond that if people do not want to buy differentiated products or highly advertised brand names, no one is forcing them to do so. Moreover, they argue that consumers benefit substantially when firms seek short-term profits by providing differentiated products. This controversy may never be fully resolved, in part because deciding on the optimal amount of variety is very difficult, and in part because the two sides often place different values on what variety means for consumers. Read the following Clear It Up feature for a discussion on the role that advertising plays in monopolistic competition.

How does advertising impact monopolistic competition?

The U.S. economy spent about $180.12 billion on advertising in 2014, according to eMarketer.com. Roughly one third of this was television advertising, and another third was divided roughly equally between Internet, newspapers, and radio. The remaining third was divided up between direct mail, magazines, telephone directory yellow pages, and billboards. Mobile devices are increasing the opportunities for advertisers.

Advertising is all about explaining to people, or making people believe, that the products of one firm are differentiated from the products of another firm. In the framework of monopolistic competition, there are two ways to conceive of how advertising works: either advertising causes a firm's perceived demand curve to become more inelastic (that is, it causes the perceived demand curve to become steeper); or advertising causes demand for the firm's product to increase (that is, it causes the firm's perceived demand curve to shift to the right). In either case, a successful advertising campaign may allow a firm to sell either a greater quantity or to charge a higher price, or both, and thus increase its profits.

However, economists and business owners have also long suspected that much of the advertising may only offset other advertising. Economist A. C. Pigou wrote the following back in 1920 in his book, *The Economics of Welfare*:

> It may happen that expenditures on advertisement made by competing monopolists [that is, what we now call monopolistic competitors] will simply neutralise one another, and leave the industrial position exactly as it would have been if neither had expended anything. For, clearly, if each of two rivals makes equal efforts to attract the favour of the public away from the other, the total result is the same as it would have been if neither had made any effort at all.

Concepts and Summary

Monopolistic competition refers to a market where many firms sell differentiated products. Differentiated products can arise from characteristics of the good or service, location from which the product is sold, intangible aspects of the product, and perceptions of the product.

The perceived demand curve for a monopolistically competitive firm is downward-sloping, which shows that it is a price maker and chooses a combination of price and quantity. However, the perceived demand curve for a monopolistic competitor is more elastic than the perceived demand curve for a monopolist, because the monopolistic competitor has direct competition, unlike the pure monopolist. A profit-maximizing monopolistic competitor will seek out the quantity where marginal revenue is equal to marginal cost. The monopolistic competitor will produce that level of output and charge the price that is indicated by the firm's demand curve.

If the firms in a monopolistically competitive industry are earning economic profits, the industry will attract entry until profits are driven down to zero in the long run. If the firms in a monopolistically competitive industry are suffering economic losses, then the industry will experience exit of firms until economic profits are driven up to zero in the long run.

A monopolistically competitive firm is not productively efficient because it does not produce at the minimum of its average cost curve. A monopolistically competitive firm is not allocatively efficient because it does not produce where P = MC, but instead produces where P > MC. Thus, a monopolistically competitive firm will tend to produce a lower quantity at a higher cost and to charge a higher price than a perfectly competitive firm.

Monopolistically competitive industries do offer benefits to consumers in the form of greater variety and incentives for improved products and services. There is some controversy over whether a market-oriented economy generates too much variety.

13.2 INTRODUCTION TO OLIGOPOLY

Many purchases that individuals make at the retail level are produced in markets that are neither perfectly competitive, monopolies, nor monopolistically competitive. Rather, they are oligopolies. Oligopoly arises when a small number of large firms have all or most of the sales in an industry. Examples of oligopoly abound and include the auto industry, cable television, and commercial air travel. Oligopolistic firms are like cats in a bag. They can either scratch each other to pieces or cuddle up and get comfortable with one another. If oligopolists compete hard, they may end up acting very much like perfect competitors, driving down costs and leading to zero profits for all. If oligopolists collude with each other, they may effectively act like a monopoly and succeed in pushing up prices and earning consistently high levels of profit. Oligopolies are typically characterized by mutual interdependence where various decisions such as output, price, advertising, and so on, depend on the decisions of the other firm(s). Analyzing the choices of oligopolistic firms about pricing and quantity produced involves considering the pros and cons of competition versus collusion at a given point in time.

Why Do Oligopolies Exist?

A combination of the barriers to entry that create monopolies and the product differentiation that characterizes monopolistic competition can create the setting for an oligopoly. For example, when a government grants a patent for an invention to one firm, it may create a monopoly. When the government grants patents to, for example, three different pharmaceutical companies that each has its own drug for reducing high blood pressure, those three firms may become an oligopoly.

Similarly, a natural monopoly will arise when the quantity demanded in a market is only large enough for a single firm to operate at the minimum of the long-run average cost curve. In such a setting, the market has room for only one firm, because no smaller firm can operate at a low enough average cost to compete, and no larger firm could sell what it produced given the quantity demanded in the market.

Quantity demanded in the market may also be two or three times the quantity needed to produce at the minimum of the average cost curve—which means that the market would have room for only two or three oligopoly firms (and they need not produce differentiated products). Again, smaller firms would have higher average costs and be unable to compete, while additional large firms would produce such a high quantity that they would not be able to sell it at a profitable price. This combination of economies of scale and market demand creates the barrier to entry, which led to the Boeing-Airbus oligopoly for large passenger aircraft.

The product differentiation at the heart of monopolistic competition can also play a role in creating oligopoly. For example, firms may need to reach a certain minimum size before they are able to spend enough on advertising and marketing to create a recognizable brand name. The problem in competing with, say, Coca-Cola or Pepsi is not that producing fizzy drinks is technologically difficult, but rather that creating a brand name and marketing effort to equal Coke or Pepsi is an enormous task.

Collusion or Competition?

When oligopoly firms in a certain market decide what quantity to produce and what price to charge, they face a temptation to act as if they were a monopoly. By acting together, oligopolistic firms can hold down industry output, charge a higher price, and divide up the profit among themselves. When firms act together in this way to reduce output and keep prices high, it is called **collusion**. A group of firms that have a formal agreement to collude to produce the monopoly output and sell at the monopoly price is called a **cartel**. See the following Clear It Up feature for a more in-depth analysis of the difference between the two.

Collusion versus cartels: How can I tell which is which?

In the United States, as well as many other countries, it is illegal for firms to collude since collusion is anti-competitive behavior, which is a violation of antitrust law. Both the Antitrust Division of the Justice Department and the Federal Trade Commission have responsibilities for preventing collusion in the United States.

The problem of enforcement is finding hard evidence of collusion. Cartels are formal agreements to collude. Because cartel agreements provide evidence of collusion, they are rare in the United States. Instead, most collusion is tacit, where firms implicitly reach an understanding that competition is bad for profits.

The desire of businesses to avoid competing so that they can instead raise the prices that they charge and earn higher profits has been well understood by economists. Adam Smith wrote in Wealth of Nations in 1776: "People of the same trade seldom meet together, even for merriment and diversion, but the conversation ends in a conspiracy against the public, or in some contrivance to raise prices."

Even when oligopolists recognize that they would benefit as a group by acting like a monopoly, each individual oligopoly faces a private temptation to produce just a slightly higher quantity and earn slightly higher profit—while still counting on the other oligopolists to hold down their production and keep prices high. If at least some oligopolists give in to this temptation and start producing more, then the market price will fall. Indeed, a small handful of oligopoly firms may end up competing so fiercely that they all end up earning zero economic profits—as if they were perfect competitors.

The Prisoner's Dilemma

Because of the complexity of oligopoly, which is the result of mutual interdependence among firms, there is no single, generally-accepted theory of how oligopolies behave, in the same way that we have theories for all the other market structures. Instead, economists use **game theory**, a branch of mathematics that analyzes situations in which players must make decisions and then receive payoffs based on what other players decide to do. Game theory has found widespread applications in the social sciences, as well as in business, law, and military strategy.

The prisoner's dilemma is a scenario in which the gains from cooperation are larger than the rewards from pursuing self-interest. It applies well to oligopoly. The story behind the prisoner's dilemma goes like this:

Two co-conspiratorial criminals are arrested. When they are taken to the police station, they refuse to say anything and are put in separate interrogation rooms. Eventually, a police officer enters the room where Prisoner A is being held and says: "You know what? Your partner in the other room is confessing. So your partner is going to get a light prison sentence of just one year, and because you're remaining silent, the judge is going to stick you with eight years in prison. Why don't you get smart? If you confess, too, we'll cut your jail time down to five years, and your partner will get five years, also." Over in the next room, another police officer is giving exactly the same speech to Prisoner B. What the police officers do not say is that if both prisoners remain silent, the evidence against them is not especially strong, and the prisoners will end up with only two years in jail each.

The game theory situation facing the two prisoners is shown in Table 3. To understand the dilemma, first consider the choices from Prisoner A's point of view. If A believes that B will confess, then A ought to confess, too, so as to not get stuck with the eight years in prison. But if A believes that B will not confess, then A will be tempted to act selfishly and confess, so as to serve only one year. The key point is that A has an incentive to confess regardless of what choice B makes! B faces the same set of choices, and thus will have an incentive to confess regardless of what choice A makes. Confess is considered the dominant strategy or the strategy an individual (or firm) will pursue regardless of the other individual's (or firm's) decision. The result is that if prisoners pursue their own self-interest, both are likely to confess, and end up doing a total of 10 years of jail time between them.

Table 3. The Prisoner's Dilemma Problem

Remain Silent (cooperate with other prisoner)		Prisoner B Confess (do not cooperate with other prisoner)	
Prisoner A	Remain Silent (cooperate with other prisoner)	A gets 2 years, B gets 2 years	A gets 8 years, B gets 1 year
	Confess (do not cooperate with other prisoner)	A gets 1 year, B gets 8 years	A gets 5 years B gets 5 years

The game is called a dilemma because if the two prisoners had cooperated by both remaining silent, they would only have had to serve a total of four years of jail time between them. If the two prisoners can work out some way of cooperating so that neither one will confess, they will both be better off than if they each follow their own individual self-interest, which in this case leads straight into longer jail terms.

The Oligopoly Version of the Prisoner's Dilemma

The members of an oligopoly can face a prisoner's dilemma, also. If each of the oligopolists cooperates in holding down output, then high monopoly profits are possible. Each oligopolist, however, must worry that while it is holding down output, other firms are taking advantage of the high price by raising output and earning higher profits. Table 4 shows the prisoner's dilemma for a two-firm oligopoly—known as a **duopoly**. If Firms A and B both agree to hold down output, they are acting together as a monopoly and will each earn $1,000 in profits. However, both firms' dominant strategy is to increase output, in which case each will earn $400 in profits.

Table 4. A Prisoner's Dilemma for Oligopolists

Hold Down Output (cooperate with other firm)		Firm B	Increase Output (do not cooperate with other firm)
Firm A	Hold Down Output (cooperate with other firm)	A gets $1,000, B gets $1,000	A gets $200, B gets $1,500
	Increase Output (do not cooperate with other firm)	A gets $1,500, B gets $200	A gets $400, B gets $400

Can the two firms trust each other? Consider the situation of Firm A:

- If A thinks that B will cheat on their agreement and increase output, then A will increase output, too, because for A the profit of $400 when both firms increase output (the bottom right-hand choice in Table 4) is better than a profit of only $200 if A keeps output low and B raises output (the upper right-hand choice in the table).
- If A thinks that B will cooperate by holding down output, then A may seize the opportunity to earn higher profits by raising output. After all, if B is going to hold down output, then A can earn $1,500 in profits by expanding output (the bottom left-hand choice in the table) compared with only $1,000 by holding down output as well (the upper left-hand choice in the table).

Thus, firm A will reason that it makes sense to expand output if B holds down output and that it also makes sense to expand output if B raises output. Again, B faces a parallel set of decisions.

The result of this prisoner's dilemma is often that even though A and B could make the highest combined profits by cooperating in producing a lower level of output and acting like a monopolist, the two firms may well end up in a situation where they each increase output and earn only $400 each in profits. The following Clear It Up feature discusses one cartel scandal in particular.

Lysine cartel

Lysine, a $600 million-a-year industry, is an amino acid used by farmers as a feed additive to ensure the proper growth of swine and poultry. The primary U.S. producer of lysine is Archer Daniels Midland (ADM), but several other large European and

Japanese firms are also in this market. For a time in the first half of the 1990s, the world's major lysine producers met together in hotel conference rooms and decided exactly how much each firm would sell and what it would charge. The U.S. Federal Bureau of Investigation (FBI), however, had learned of the cartel and placed wire taps on a number of their phone calls and meetings.

From FBI surveillance tapes, following is a comment that Terry Wilson, president of the corn processing division at ADM, made to the other lysine producers at a 1994 meeting in Mona, Hawaii:

I wanna go back and I wanna say something very simple. If we're going to trust each other, okay, and if I'm assured that I'm gonna get 67,000 tons by the year's end, we're gonna sell it at the prices we agreed to . . . The only thing we need to talk about there because we are gonna get manipulated by these [expletive] buyers—they can be smarter than us if we let them be smarter. . . . They [the customers] are not your friend. They are not my friend. And we gotta have 'em, but they are not my friends. You are my friend. I wanna be closer to you than I am to any customer. Cause you can make us ... money. ... And all I wanna tell you again is let's—let's put the prices on the board. Let's all agree that's what we're gonna do and then walk out of here and do it.

The price of lysine doubled while the cartel was in effect. Confronted by the FBI tapes, Archer Daniels Midland pled guilty in 1996 and paid a fine of $100 million. A number of top executives, both at ADM and other firms, later paid fines of up to $350,000 and were sentenced to 24–30 months in prison.

In another one of the FBI recordings, the president of Archer Daniels Midland told an executive from another competing firm that ADM had a slogan that, in his words, had "penetrated the whole company." The company president stated the slogan this way: "Our competitors are our friends. Our customers are the enemy." That slogan could stand as the motto of cartels everywhere.

How to Enforce Cooperation

How can parties who find themselves in a prisoner's dilemma situation avoid the undesired outcome and cooperate with each other? The way out of a prisoner's dilemma is to find a way to penalize those who do not cooperate.

Perhaps the easiest approach for colluding oligopolists, as you might imagine, would be to sign a contract with each other that they will hold output low and keep prices high. If a group of U.S. companies signed such a contract, however, it would be illegal. Certain international organizations, like the nations that are members of the **Organization of Petroleum Exporting Countries (OPEC)**, have signed international agreements to act like a monopoly, hold down output, and keep prices high so that all of the countries can make high profits from oil exports. Such agreements, however, because they fall in a gray area of international law, are not legally enforceable. If Nigeria, for example, decides to start cutting prices and selling more oil, Saudi Arabia cannot sue Nigeria in court and force it to stop.

Because oligopolists cannot sign a legally enforceable contract to act like a monopoly, the firms may instead keep close tabs on what other firms are producing and charging. Alternatively, oligopolists may choose to act in a way that generates pressure on each firm to stick to its agreed quantity of output.

One example of the pressure these firms can exert on one another is the **kinked demand curve**, in which competing oligopoly firms commit to match price cuts, but not price increases. This situation is shown in Figure 1. Say that an oligopoly airline has agreed with the rest of a cartel to provide a quantity of 10,000 seats on the New York to Los Angeles route, at a price of $500. This choice defines the kink in the firm's perceived demand curve. The reason that the firm faces a kink in its demand curve is because of how the other oligopolists react to changes in the firm's price. If the oligopoly decides to produce more and cut its price, the other members of the cartel will immediately match any price cuts—and therefore, a lower price brings very little increase in quantity sold.

If one firm cuts its price to $300, it will be able to sell only 11,000 seats. However, if the airline seeks to raise prices, the other oligopolists will not raise their prices, and so the firm that raised prices will lose a considerable share of sales. For example, if the firm raises its price to $550, its sales drop to 5,000 seats sold. Thus, if oligopolists always match price cuts by other firms in the cartel, but do not match price increases, then none of the oligopolists will have a strong incentive to change prices, since the potential gains are minimal. This strategy can work like a silent form of cooperation, in which the cartel successfully manages to hold down output, increase price, and share a monopoly level of profits even without any legally enforceable agreement.

Consider a member firm in an oligopoly cartel that is supposed to produce a quantity of 10,000 and sell at a price of $500. The other members of the cartel can encourage this firm to honor its commitments by acting so that the firm faces a kinked demand curve. If the oligopolist attempts to expand output and reduce price slightly, other firms also cut prices immediately—so if the firm expands output to 11,000, the price per unit falls dramatically, to $300. On the other side, if the oligopoly attempts to raise its price, other firms will not do so, so if the firm raises its price to $550, its sales decline sharply to 5,000. Thus, the members of a cartel can discipline each other to stick to the pre-agreed levels of quantity and price through a strategy of matching all price cuts but not matching any price increases.

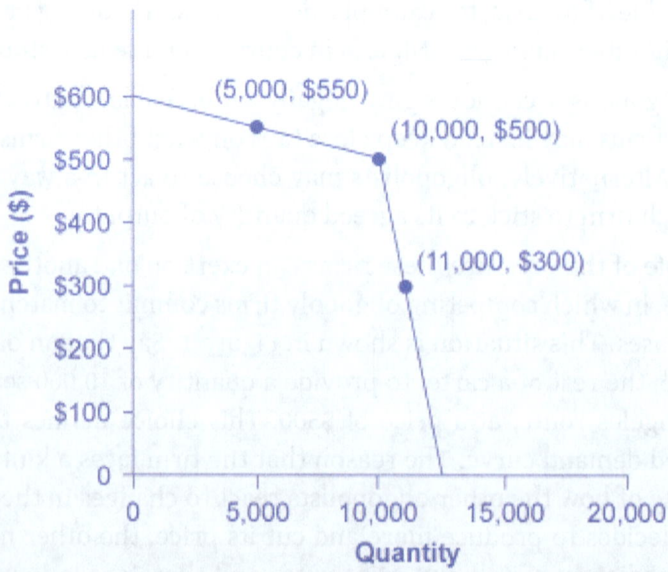

Figure 1. A Kinked Demand Curve.

Many real-world oligopolies, prodded by economic changes, legal and political pressures, and the egos of their top executives, go through episodes of cooperation and competition. If oligopolies could sustain cooperation with each other on output and pricing, they could earn profits as if they were a single monopoly. However, each firm in an oligopoly has an incentive to produce more and grab a bigger share of the overall market; when firms start behaving in this way, the market outcome in terms of prices and quantity can be similar to that of a highly competitive market.

Tradeoffs of Imperfect Competition

Monopolistic competition is probably the single most common market structure in the U.S. economy. It provides powerful incentives for innovation, as firms seek to earn profits in the short run, while entry assures that firms do not earn economic profits in the long run. However, monopolistically competitive firms do not produce at the lowest point on their average cost curves. In addition, the endless search to impress consumers through product differentiation may lead to excessive social expenses on advertising and marketing.

Oligopoly is probably the second most common market structure. When oligopolies result from patented innovations or from taking advantage of economies of scale to produce at low average cost, they may provide considerable benefit to consumers. Oligopolies are often buffeted by significant barriers to entry, which enable the oligopolists to earn sustained profits over long periods of time. Oligopolists also do not typically produce at the minimum of their average cost curves. When they lack vibrant competition, they may lack incentives to provide innovative products and high-quality service.

The task of public policy with regard to competition is to sort through these multiple realities, attempting to encourage behavior that is beneficial to the broader society and to discourage behavior that only adds to the profits of a few large companies, with no corresponding benefit to consumers. Monopoly and Antitrust Policy discusses the delicate judgments that go into this task.

The Temptation to Defy the Law

Oligopolistic firms have been called "cats in a bag," as this chapter mentioned. The French detergent makers chose to "cozy up" with each other. The result? An uneasy and tenuous relationship. When the Wall Street Journal reported on the matter, it wrote: "According to a statement a Henkel manager made to the [French anti-trust] commission, the detergent makers wanted 'to limit the intensity of the competition between them and clean up the market.' Nevertheless, by the early 1990s, a price war had broken out among them." During the soap executives' meetings, which sometimes lasted more than four hours, complex pricing structures were established. "One [soap] executive recalled 'chaotic' meetings as each side tried to work out how the other had bent the rules." Like many cartels, the soap cartel disintegrated due to the very strong temptation for each member to maximize its own individual profits.

How did this soap opera end? After an investigation, French antitrust authorities fined Colgate-Palmolive, Henkel, and Proctor & Gamble a total of €361 million ($484 million). A similar fate befell the icemakers. Bagged ice is a commodity, a perfect substitute, generally sold in 7- or 22-pound bags. No one cares what label is on the bag. By agreeing to carve up the ice market, control broad geographic swaths of territory, and set prices, the icemakers moved from perfect competition to a monopoly model. After the agreements, each firm was the sole supplier of bagged ice to a region; there were profits in both the long run and the short run. According to the courts: "These companies illegally conspired to manipulate the marketplace." Fines totaled about $600,000—a steep fine considering a bag of ice sells for under $3 in most parts of the United States.

Even though it is illegal in many parts of the world for firms to set prices and carve up a market, the temptation to earn higher profits makes it extremely tempting to defy the law.

Concepts and Summary

An oligopoly is a situation where a few firms sell most or all of the goods in a market. Oligopolists earn their highest profits if they can band together as a cartel and act like a monopolist by reducing output and raising price. Since each member of the oligopoly can benefit individually from expanding output, such collusion often breaks down—especially since explicit collusion is illegal.

The prisoner's dilemma is an example of game theory. It shows how, in certain situations, all sides can benefit from cooperative behavior rather than self-interested behavior. However, the challenge for the parties is to find ways to encourage cooperative behavior.

CHAPTER

THE GROWTH OF BIG BUSINESS 14

14.1 THE HISTORY OF BIG BUSINESS IN AMERICA

The history of the American experience tends to be viewed as exceptional relative to Europe. The tradition has generally been to view the course of American development as unique and separate from the antecedent European history that America originates from. One consequence of this ideological tradition has been to view corporate power as an anomaly to an otherwise well-functioning system, in which unfettered market forces generally produce highly competitive, small firms that do not possess effective market power. The actual history is quite different.

From the very foundation of the American colonies big business has been the rule, not the exception. The Virginia Company, a joint-stock company that enjoyed an exclusive patent on very large swathes of land (see figure 1 below), established the first British colony at Jamestown in 1607. A patent is taken here to mean an exclusive grant by the sovereign with respect to a particular land tract, and establishes a fundamental claim to ownership and disposal of that land.

The managerial class vested with the power of the charter administered all aspects of colonial life. Virtually all of the land that makes up the area that is described as the original thirteen colonies was held in ownership by a small set of individuals vested with property rights derived from monarchical legal traditions, granted with an exclusive patent for private development.

Business Enterprise and Property Rights

The corporate firm and the legal structure of property rights coevolved in the course of US economic history. When we examine the going concern with an emphasis on its proprietary relationships with other aspects of the economy this codevelopment appears all the more transparent. That is, the firm is the site of a great many transactions in the economic system. Monetary transactions in which the firm makes a claim to resources generated in the economy involve rules governing the proprietary relationships between the transacting party and the resources in question. In order to secure exclusive and steady claim to a set of resources the firm must be contractually entitled to the resources as private property. Hence, it is important to study the codevelopment between firms and the legal framework on the matter of property.

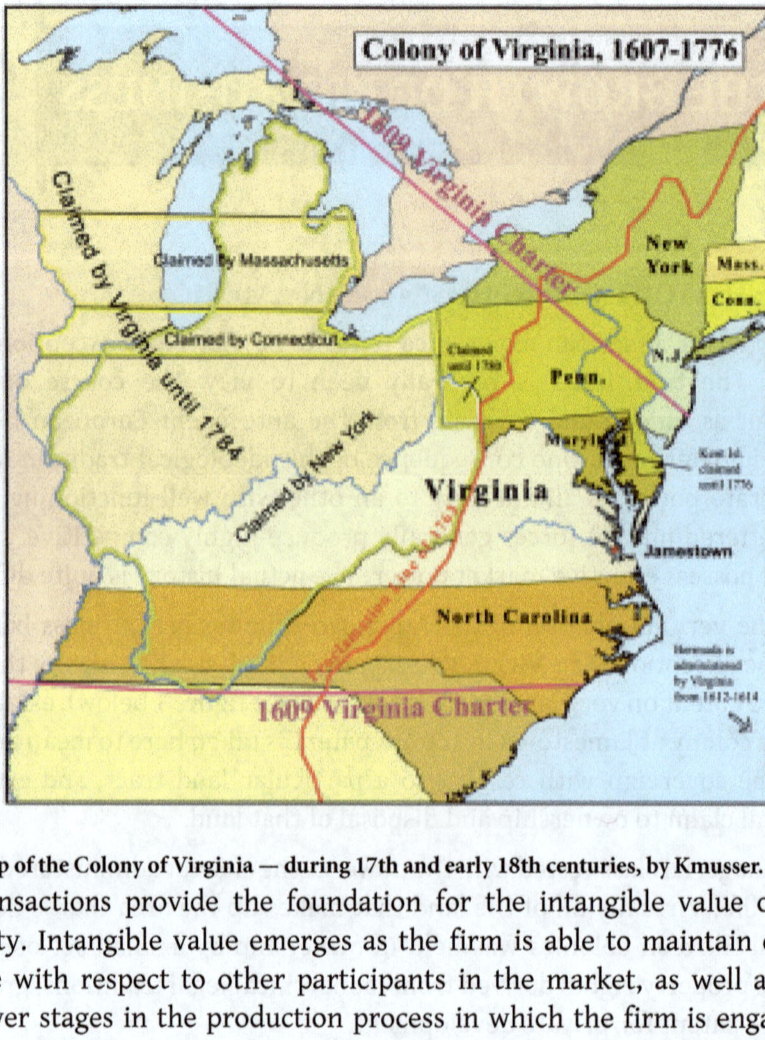

Figure 1. Map of the Colony of Virginia — during 17th and early 18th centuries, by Kmusser. CC BY SA 2.5

These transactions provide the foundation for the intangible value of the firm as property. Intangible value emerges as the firm is able to maintain differential advantage with respect to other participants in the market, as well as maintain control over stages in the production process in which the firm is engaged, while exerting its influence over matters of market governance. Precisely how society chooses to assign rights to such property is a matter of primary importance from the standpoint of determining the status of vestiture. Hence, insofar as firms embody the creation of property and affect existing claims to property, it is necessary to adjust the legal framework to establish a coherent system of property rights. By setting up the problem as essentially a relationship between the law and the corporation, we can appreciate the importance of the corporation in the development of American capitalism.

Colonial legal institutions

Colonial America borrowed its legal framework from the English common law system. The common law tradition allows for judges to freely interpret new laws in light of old ones, suggesting that judges take an active role in shaping the subsequent development of legal institutions. This legal tradition of judicial instrumentalism will be important as we examine the changing nature of property and the firm.

Real Property Rights

The colonists derived their property rights as privileges of the king. Since colonists were subjects of the king, they enjoyed all the rights to property that citizens in London enjoyed. The Crown permitted the free and common socage system of land tenure in the American colonies, as opposed to other land tenure systems that reflected the myriad feudal relations and systems of mutual obligation. Free and common socage is described by the following features:

- Perpetual ownership
- Transmissible to heirs.
- Free disposal of property
- Alienable

The fee simple system, as Americans would come to know it, embodies a set of rights. Property is often thought of as a "bundle of rights" for this reason. Accompanying these bundles of rights are a set of rents due the donor of the land, the king. Quit rents, then, represent the debt the holder of real property owes to the sovereign for the right to remain at liberty with the property. If the landholder defaults on this obligation by failing to make the quit rent payment, ownership reverts to the sovereign. Modern observers may look to a city like Kansas City, Missouri which possesses a large inventory of housing whose landlords are not current in their tax liability to the local government. Eventually, the state takes possession of the real property and all rights associated with ownership are revoked, until the property is disposed of again as private property.

Police Power

One of the principal legal developments in American economic history is that the state holds broad powers to establish and define markets, or otherwise exercise its police powers toward some economic end. This power allows the state to establish special privileges to private entities so that it may collect rents by controlling access to resources. For example, suppose a local municipality wished to transform a waterfall into a lock & canal system in order to facilitate inland navigation via steamship. The state may grant a franchise to a firm for exclusive use of the public right of way, thereby entitling the owner of the concern to a rent. Alternatively, the state may attempt to directly develop the falls to remove the impediment to navigation. In either case, the extent to which income is transferred from the community as a result of the establishment of a lock & canal depends entirely upon the discretion of those in control of the property, who must decide whether and to what extent they will charge rents. In general, the firm must earn revenues from its ongoing marketing activity in order to remain a going concern.

EMERGENCE OF PRIORITY RIGHTS

One peculiarity of English common law was the institution of granting existing property holders protections against a future neighbor who may impose costs upon on them in their own pursuits regarding their property. The doctrine of ancient lights, as it was known, is the underlying concept of the practice of establishing a basis for prescriptive rights in common law. This common law principle suggests that the long tenured holders of property rights are protected from new developments that would diminish or impede upon their property, in an absolute sense. For example, a property holder who enjoys the benefit of, say, unimpeded sunlight would have the reasonable expectation that rival parties who wish to construct a home adjacent to their property would not be able to do so if it resulted in blocking such daylight. But, the doctrine of ancient lights was not restricted solely to the issue of sunlight, but more broadly as referring to general benefits to property ownership. In effect, the doctrine of ancient lights imputes a conservative bias in the course of development in such a way that favors temporal or generation advantage to prior property holders.

As the American economy developed, this doctrine was tested in court and found to obstruct the economic development of urban areas. Prescriptive rights were found to be inconsistent with the social conditions in which American economic development was embedded. In 1838, a case in New York state, *Parker v. Foote,* established precedent for overturning the institution of prescriptive rights, wherein the judge ruled that the doctrine of ancient lights cannot be applied without inhibiting the growth of cities and internal improvements. Hence, the law was adjusted by judicial instrumentalism to accommodate and legitimate negative externalities as a byproduct of economic development. When economists refer to negative externalities they are describing costs that impact third parties as a result of some economic process not born by the agents principally engaged in such activity.

The validity of contracts between unequals

Under English contract law, contracts were held as valid only when struck on an equitable basis. That contract validity rested upon notions of equity was vestigial to feudal institutions. Contracts were not considered valid if they were struck between two parties that were viewed as too unequal. For example, contracts between someone of sound mind and one that is mentally impaired would be considered invalid on the premise that the two parties were not equal in their contracting ability. It follows that based upon this equity consideration in the common-law tradition contracts between, say, a factory owner and an individual laborer would not be valid. In American capitalism, such an idea is anachronistic and incompatible with the manner in which value is extracted, appropriated and capitalized. While the equity tradition remained central to American contract law throughout the 18th century, four important changes to contract law would emerge in the course of American development.

First, in the 19th century the courts interpreted contracts struck between free persons without compulsions as valid, on the principle that mutual assent generally implied validity irrespective of equity. For example, if a factory owner made the terms of employment known to the public and workers accepted a labor contract in exchange for wages, then the contract is valid whether or not the individual worker stands on equitable terms with her employer. In this circumstance equity refers to the balance of bargaining power between parties in transaction with each other. It would be absurd to think that a factory owner possesses the same bargaining power as an individual worker, for the owner controls and exercises their discretion over the the production process. Despite this lack of equity, the labor contract is considered valid so long as the worker knows in advance what she signing up for.

Second, the rule embodied above, that of mutual assent or "meeting of the wills" as it is referred to in contract law, applied to transactions in markets. Provided the buyer is free to inspect the quality of the goods, then any asymmetry of knowledge regarding its quality or serviceability does not impair the validity of the contract in exchange.

Third, contracts were struck in terms of market prices, as opposed to customary prices that ensure equity through time. That is to say, if the prices of the goods changed from the time the contract is struck and the buyer takes delivery, then the contracted price remains valid. This institutional change facilitated the development of futures contracts. A futures contract is nothing more than a promise to pay at a later date for delivery of some good, where the contracted price is settled in current market prices. The following breakout box provides a simply example to illustrate how they work.

How Futures Contracts Work

Suppose I am in the wheat milling business. I know that I need 100 bushels of wheat so that I can mill all of the meal I expect to sell next month. I have a feeling that next month the price of wheat is going to increase, so I decide to lock in today's prices on the wheat that I'll receive next month. I can do this by buying a futures contract from a wheat farmer for delivery of her wheat in a month, but at today's price.

Futures contracts are the foundation of a whole class of financial instruments called options, which are ubiquitous in modern American capitalism as they are used to provide risk hedging positions for firms that have an interest in the commodities that undergird the futures contract in question. They are also a means of speculating in financial markets, but that is a topic we shall avoid for now. The main point to remember here, is that changing from customary to market prices in contract law opened up space for the financialized firm to thrive and grow, essential to the development of the modern corporation.

Fourth, the courts began to interpret contract law such that employer liability for hazards incurred by workers was limited. The presumption that, with the principle of mutual assent, dangers and risks associated with the workplace were encapsulated in the wage, implied that workers that agreed to the terms of employment absolved employers' liability of injury. Additionally, the "fellow servant doctrine" suggested that employers were further limited in liability where injuries to an employee resulted from negligence on the part of his coworkers. Given the nature of production, it is common to expect that contributory negligence plays some part in the hazards, making it difficult for workers to establish negligence and liability on the part of their employer.

The Supreme Court

Since John Marshall's tenure as Chief Justice (1801- 1835), the Supreme Court has exercised considerable power in the shaping of American economic legal institutions. In the 1819 case McCullough v. Maryland, Chief Justice Marshall established the implied powers of the court in engaging in judicial review and revision of the legal framework as the court sees fit. The basic premise was that the constitution was intended to be robust through the ages to changes in the technical and social character of the nation. Accordingly, the court reserved the right and asserted its power to interpret its scope broadly; subsequent rulings would be made in light of new economic and social developments, while preserving the legitimacy of the constitution. In McCullough v. Maryland, the constitutional legitimacy of the Second Bank of the United States was under question. Marshall ruled that since the bank was chartered with the purpose of effecting the ends of the constitution itself, namely regulation of interstate commerce, then it was legitimate despite no specific provision in the constitution for a central bank.

Several antebellum cases before the Supreme Court helped establish the power of the federal government to regulate interstate commerce via the Commerce Clause of the Constitution, superseding state and local desires for the same. In Gibbons v. Ogden (1824), the court overturned a monopoly granted by the state of New York to a steamship concern because its business involved traffic in New Jersey, ruling that individual states do not have the authority to regulate interstate commerce.

While the powers of the port of Philadelphia were upheld in the service of regulating commerce for its municipal needs, Chief Justice Tawney in Cooley v. Board of Wardens (1851) held that where such regulation touched upon issues of national importance, particularly involving its seaport, those regulatory powers were reserved for Congress. Brown v. Maryland (1827) ruled that no state had the power to license and tax importers.

While the Supreme Court was laying the foundation for federal regulation of business enterprise, the immediate impact following *Gibbons v. Ogden* was the liberation of private corporations from state regulation. Not until 1887 with the establishment of the Interstate Commerce Commission, which emerged in response to problems associated with market governance in railroads, did the federal government assert itself on matters of regulation. As a consequence, corporations were free to grow and pursue national markets without the interference of local intervention.

Recall, this discussion of the history of changing legal institutions is in regards to the proprietary nature of corporations. Perhaps the most important case governing the subsequent development of the legal foundations of corporate property and futurity in America economic is Dartmouth College v. Woodward (1819). Again, Justice Marshall plays a pivotal role in the coevolution of property law and corporations. The direct issue at stake was the legitimacy of Dartmouth's corporate charter as it rested upon a grant from King George III, prior to the establishment of the United States. Indirectly, all patents granted by the King prior to the revolution were called into question if the court ruled the proprietary basis for Dartmouth's charter to be invalid following the American Revolution. Marshall ruled that revolutions do not inherently undermine vested property rights. This granted legitimacy by judicial review to all original patents by the King, including the original Virginia Company patent, which accounted for a considerable portion of all land in the United State. Nearly all of the areas affected by the Northwest Ordinances were derived from the original crown patents, suggesting that overturning the Dartmouth charter could undermine the legitimacy of all American real property rights.

Canals, Steamboats and Railroads

The canalization of the America's inland waterways, a period spanning 1815 – 1843, marks an important moment in the development of the corporation. Particularly, the canal building era laid the foundations for a newfound importance for corporations and the ability for private citizens to control the development of the social provisioning process. In short, society's relationship with corporations changed as it used them as institutions for the development of large-scale public works projects.

As the US grew westward, institutions were established to facilitate inter-regional trade, and bring to eastern markets the product of the hinterland. State governments issued franchises to concerns that incorporated on the premise that they would improve waterways in the interior watersheds of the nation. In return, the corporation was entitled to revenues associated with control over the canals. Similarly, firms were incorporated to engage in inland navigation along the canalized waterways and establish rates sufficient to cover their costs and in accordance with the principle of *charging what the market may bear*. That is to say, firms set prices and administer them to the market, allowing the firm to capture quasi-rents and accumulate monetary claims on its balance sheet. Firms are limited in the extent to which such rents may be appropriated from the public, which includes factors such as the ability to pay from participants in the market as well as rules, formal and informal, that may provide a governance structure to the market. For instance, an association may exist between navigation concerns that facilitate the orderly division of the market, which may impose limits on the pricing discretion of its members. In other situations, the market may be divided between firms with different cost structures. In the event that the firms with lowest cost structure establishes a market price, less efficient firms will be limited in their ability to capture quasi-rents from the public due to pressure to retain market share.

The enterprises that were incorporated for the purposes of building and operating the canals were large. The engineering challenges before them required the organizational capacity to administer the provisioning of resources and labor that spanned whole regions. The firm was faced with planning challenges that exceeded the scope and capacity of small-scale proprietors. Consequently, most enterprises engaged in the canal business were cooperative ventures between private interests and the state. Private interests included merchants who wished to lower transport costs and grow the market for their trade, capitalists vested in navigation companies, as well as land speculators, who believed that improvements following canalization of waterways would increase the salable value of land held adjacent to the improvement. The state became the financial partner in the venture, providing institutional means for generating revenue through tax levies and bond issues, and remaining ultimately responsible for financing its ongoing maintenance. Notably, the Erie Canal, constructed between 1817 and 1825, was a landmark achievement of the cooperation between private interests and the State of New York toward the end of transforming economic relationships, such that corporations become a central site of social provisioning in the development of the American economy.

Figure 2. Workers operating a lock at Lockport, New York ca. 1839 along the Erie Canal. Engraving by W. H. Bartlett. Public Domain.

To better understand how large scale public works projects, like the Erie Canal, were so transformative consider the financial and organizational implications of its development. First, the Erie Canal was financed largely through the issuance of bonds. Such bonds were held as wealth by private citizens who became vested in the interests of the canal as a going concern. To remain a going concern, the canal required the establishment of rates sufficient to cover its costs as well as sufficient traffic to provide revenues to support its financial liabilities. As a result, those financially vested in the canal as bondholders were compelled to take an interest in the development of the economic space as a whole such that the canal remained viable, to include promotion of settlement in regions adjacent to the canal and its feeder lines. The grandness of the venture required a further elaboration of the large-scale, economic interdependence in which national markets became increasingly important. Second, given the extent of private, monied interests vested in the canal, an administrative structure was required in order to ensure the orderly operation of the canal and its finances. In the case of the Erie Canal, such an administrative framework was established by legislature and structured as a commission, whose leadership were drawn from the business communities affected by the existence of the canal.

As America's inland waterways were improved through lock and canal systems, the steamship became increasingly important to the social provisioning process. For some communities, navigation companies engaged in the steamer trade emerged as its first large, powerful corporations. For example, consider the Oregon Steam Navigation Company (OSN) whose business was centered in Portland, Oregon in the mid to late 19th century. While small compared to East Coast metropoles, Portland was the most important city on the West Coast after San Francisco, until the 1890s when Seattle was connected with the transcontinental rail system via the Northern Pacific. The OSN was Oregon's first, great monopoly whose **intangible value** provided the basis for wealth for many of the region's "founding fathers." The intangible value of the corporation lied in:

- the exclusive rights of way that the firm enjoyed in Portland.
- ownership and control over key portages along the Columbia River, and.
- access to the state legislature via the social networks of its owners and agents.

In 1866 efforts to extend a regional trunk of the nascent transcontinental railway system into Portland from the Sacramento Valley in California involved courting the owners of the Oregon Steamship Navigation Company (OSN) on the presumption that their political connections would ensure special acts of incorporation from the Oregon legislature favorable to the Californian interests. Initially, such owners attempted to block the advance of the railroad promoters for threat of the viability of the going business of the OSN. However, later that year, perhaps hedging against the threat of eventual encroachment on their business, members of the OSN leadership sought to secure the franchise for the Oregon section of the regional trunk of the transcontinental, thereby securing associated land grants and privileges from the state, which set off a race between two competing concerns to build a railroad through the Willamette Valley in Oregon that would connect Portland with a road from California. The ultimate objective lied in establishing legitimate claim to the exclusive charter, ostensibly by demonstrating commitment to actually build the road and fulfill the spirit of the charter, while undermining the legitimacy of the rival concern through the courts and in the public mind through influence of the press. The outcome was mutual insolvency between the two parties, who had each incorporated variants on the name Oregon Central Railroad.

In the late 1860s, the stagecoach magnate Ben Holladay resolved the conflict by purchasing control of one of the firms, persuading the legislature to reassign the charter to the concern he had acquired, and acquiring controlling stake in his rivals. Holladay reorganized his newly acquired railway assets under a new name, California & Oregon Railroad, together with some steamship ventures that he had established or acquired in order to provide a revenue source while he developed his railway aspirations. To finance this consolidation scheme Holladay floated a considerable amount of bonds to counterparties in Europe, who were falsely led to believe that the market in the Willamette Valley in Oregon was capable of supporting the revenue requirements of his steamship and railway concerns. The balance sheet of the Oregon and California Railroad relied upon lines of credit extended from speculative financiers to remain solvent.

The Panic of 1873 undermined the solvency of the Oregon and California, as Holladay did not earn enough through revenues from his properties to service his debt obligations without the ability to issue new debt to refinance old. During a financial panic, creditors tend to stop lending, preferring instead to hold more liquid assets on their balance sheet for fear of becoming insolvent themselves, resulting in a vicious cycle of asset value deflation. The response by Holladay's creditor's was to install an agent to take receivership of Holladay's properties and reorganize his properties on a sounder basis. The surest way to achieve this end was to buy out Holladay's interests, thereby preventing him from exerting any control over the enterprises.

Over the next decade, Henry Villard, agent for German bondholders would proceed to establish new market governance institutions in the Pacific Northwest such that economic activity adjacent to the railroads would be harmonized or rationalized, with the ultimate end of servicing the debt obligations to foreign creditors. Villard's aspirations were grander than the German bondholders: Villard wanted to engage in thoroughgoing economic development and population growth. Villard wanted to build an empire on the Columbia River. A central problem facing Villard was maintaining control over the market for railroad traffic in the face of the encroaching Northern Pacific, the main northern line of the transcontinental system. The directors of the Northern Pacific wanted to run the line to Tacoma or Seattle, where the natural deepwater harbors would facilitate better access to international markets. Yet, Villard was vested in properties centered on Portland and its hinterlands. Villard organized a holding company in 1879, the Oregon Railway & Navigation Company that consolidated his railroads and steamships in the Willamette with his acquisition of controlling stake in the OSN. Initially, Villard sought order in the market along the Columbia River via traffic sharing agreements with the directors of the Northern Pacific. However, the Northern Pacific was determined to build toward the Puget Sound. In order to protect the intangible value embodied in the corporations that he had come to control, he engineered a financial takeover of the Northern Pacific, through the use of another holding company, the Oregon and Transcontinental Company incorporated in 1881, which allowed Villard to pool funds to acquire control in the Northern Pacific. Once in control of the Northern Pacific, Villard connected the Northern Pacific with the Oregon Railway and Navigation Company, ensuring that any traffic destined for the Pacific would pass through Portland.

It is important to note that holding companies are essentially financial corporations chartered for the purpose of acquiring majority ownership in another corporation, with a minimum outlay of cash. Holding companies can be layered, such that several holding companies stand between a given set of capitalists and the actual underlying corporations that the holding companies are designed to facilitate control. This can be illustrated with a simple example: suppose that a simple majority of stock ownership is sufficient to control a railroad corporation. If there are 200 shares of stock outstanding in the corporation, then it would be necessary to acquire 101 shares to ensure control. Now, suppose that a holding company can be incorporated and capitalized by issuing 101 shares of stocks and assuming parity value between the two stocks. If the holding company is sufficiently capitalized and has access to credit, it is possible that by owning a simple majority in the holding company allows one to effectively control the first corporation if the holding company is able to acquire a simple majority of its stock, for half the ownership requirement (see Figure 5 below). With each layer of holding companies between the capitalist and the firm he wishes to control, the ownership stake required for control is halved. In this way, great corporations may be brought under control of a single individual with relatively little personal outlay involved. This has been a common theme in the area of corporate control since the second half of the 19th century, and continued well into the 20th century.

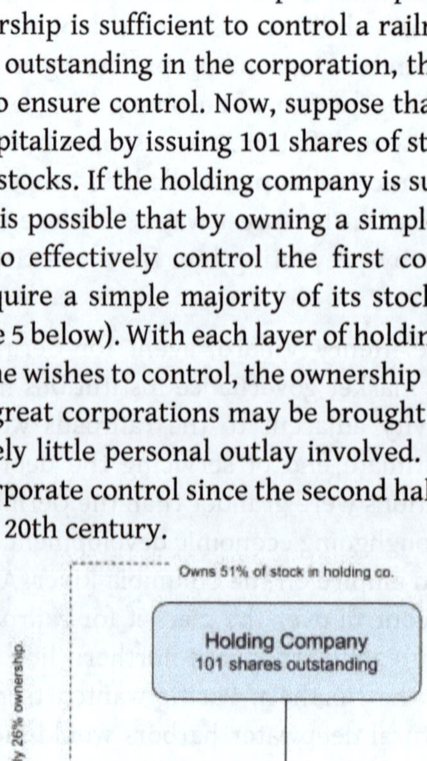

Figure 3.

14.2 THE FACTORY AND INDUSTRIALIZATION

After the Civil War, the United States economy passed into an era of rapid industrialization. The term industrialization is used here to describe a process of development that reorganizes productive activities such that they conform to a machine logic, as opposed to a handicraft logic. That is, the economy becomes increasingly constituted by a series of interconnected machine processes. When we think of the United States undergoing industrialization we are really envisioning its economy becoming a large-scale machine, capable of churning out all of the goods required to sustain the community efficiently and to sustain the machine itself, through production of intermediate goods. When we think of the economy as industrializing we are actually considering a qualitative change in the economic system. To better understand what a qualitative change in the economic system entails, consider the following key features of an industrialized, machine process economy.

Large-scale technologies that make up the core of the economic system

Particular combinations of technology incorporated into the economic system were massive in scale. For example, consider again the case of the railroads. We have previously discussed why railroads required administration from the managerial bodies of corporate entities capable of organizing the business over the scale and scope of its activities. The technology itself was massive – establishment of steam powered with a rail and car transportation system over vast geographical areas was quite literally the greatest engineering marvel that humans had achieved to date. With the railroads came the telegraph, which created the possibility for transnational and interregional rapid communication. Other hallmark technologies of an industrializing 19th century American economy include: electric light and power, streetcars, improvements in steel production, and petroleum refining.

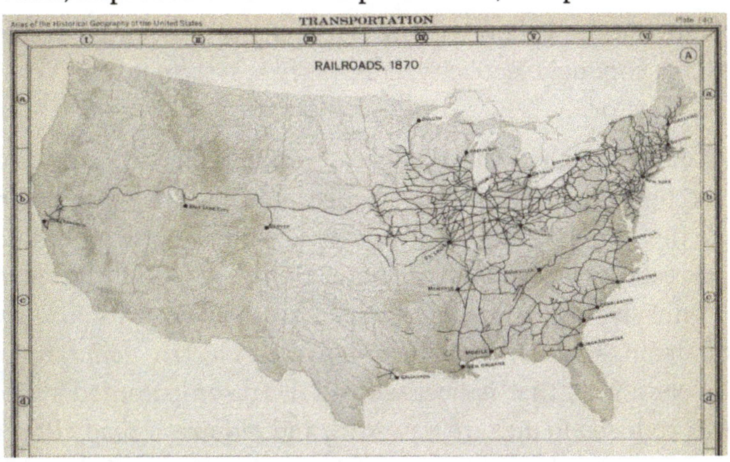

Figure 4. Atlas of the Historical Geography of the United States, Plate 140 by Charles O. Paullin. Curated by the Carnegie Institution of Science

Integrated chains of production that link markets and industries

The largeness of the business enterprise implies a high degree of interconnectedness between different stages in the production of the social product. To illustrate our point, consider the generation and provisioning of electric power. We can envision a simplified model of electric generation by breaking the whole production process into four stages:

- Production of fuel source. In this example, we will assume we're talking about a coal fired power plant. This is a good choice, because coal served as the primary fuel source for electric generating during its advent in the United States. Coal is produced by mining and is subject to geological processes that have resulted in an uneven spatial allocation of coal in the earth's crust. Therefore, coal can only be mined in certain areas. The story of coal in America begins in Pennsylvania.
- Energy conversion. The chemical energy embodied in coal must be converted into mechanical energy before it may be used to generate electricity. This conversion process is accomplished by burning the coal to transform water into steam, which creates the necessary pressure to power an engine. The engine now embodies some of the energy that existed in the coal, less losses due to inefficiencies in the conversion process. The steam engine itself is the product of a set of interconnected production processes.
- Electric Generation. The mechanical energy of the steam engine is then used to power an electric generator. Electric generators require steel, copper, and most importantly, a patent to produce.
- Distribution. Once generated, the electricity is distributed to the end user via cables that conduct electricity. Edison's first system in New York used copper as its conductor.

If you think about each of these stages of production occurring as a production process that occupies a different space geographically, then you begin to see how something like the provisioning of electricity is really a network of interdependent production processes that establishes connections between different regions. Coal is mined in Pennsylvania, and then shipped to New York for use as fuel in the production of steam. A boiler and steam-powered electric generator is purchased from a firm in New York that is licensed to sell Edison patented systems. Edison's generators are produced in upstate New York and require a steady flow of steel from Pennsylvania and copper from Michigan for ongoing production. And so on. Every single economic activity is the product of an orchestra of interconnected production processes. To function efficiently those interdependencies must be managed so that they they function as a whole machine. This is what we mean when we describe the economy as industrialized.

14.3 ORGANIZED LABOR AND BIG BUSINESS

As the business enterprise becomes large it operates on a scale of production that requires the labor of a proportionally large number of workers. The managers of the firm must ensure that they reliably and efficiently meet their production goals. To achieve this end, managers established methods for controlling their labor force so that rate of production remains within their full discretion. Introduction of mechanization into the production process serves as one historical example of the methods of controlling labor. Mechanization establishes the pace of production, by powering machine technology. For example, an assembly line sets the rate at which workers must labor. In this sense, workers on an assembly line must work at roughly the same pace, harmonizing their collected labor. By adjusting the speed of the machine, worker productivity may be adjusted across the board as desired, subject to physical limits of the labor force. Similarly, the machine process results in a "deskilling" process, which tends to homogenize the labor requirements for production. Deskilling transforms the labor process by removing the power that workers enjoy via their specialized knowledge of craft production. Machine production depends, to a much lesser degree, on the specialized knowledge of workers. Instead, this knowledge is transferred to the managerial class, who may possess knowledge of the machine and its technical requirements or retain the expertise of an engineer.

Loss of worker control over the production process results in the ability for the managerial class to retain a larger share of the monetary value of the output of the labor process. Managerial focus on cost efficiency and meeting its production targets, coupled with control over the labor process, resulted in dangerous and poor working conditions. The large business enterprise, by exercising its control over the labor process in order to exploit its workers, created the conditions for the emergence for an organized labor movement.

An exhaustive review of the labor history in the United States is beyond our reach, however, we may highlight some of the major themes and events that helped shape its development.

The Knights of Labor

Organized in 1869 by tailors in Pennsylvania, the secret organization named the Noble Order of the Knights of Labor would serve as an organizational body for workers seeking collective action following the Panic of 1873. Coal miners helped drive membership growth in the Knights of Labor through the depression of the 1870s. By 1884 there were 70,000 members of the Knights of Labor. By 1886 this figure exploded to 700,000.

The Knights of Labor participated in strikes in order to achieve their primary goal of an 8 hour workday. Most notably, the Knights of Labor won a struggle against Jay Gould over a dispute concerning the Wabash Railroad in 1885.

The Great Railway Strike of 1877

Railroads figure prominently in the course of American economic history for they have left lasting and transformative imprints on the course of development. It is natural, then, to link a major moment in the history of the labor movement to consequences of railroad speculation and administration. The economic depression of the 1870's was global in nature and was caused largely by a financial crisis related to the value of railroad securities. The Panic of 1873 emerged from a financial system that had become increasingly fragile during the speculative episode in railroad securities, mostly bonds, following the Civil War. Jay Cooke, a major US banker during the latter part of the 19th century, was heavily vested in the market for Northern Pacific bonds to interests in Europe. During the 1870s Europeans were less keen to accept the risk associated with holding American railroad bonds. In turn, this led to the inability for Cooke to continue issuing debt and ultimately resulted in his firm becoming insolvent. The failure of Jay Cooke & Company set off a wave of bank failures and a closure of the New York Stock Exchange. The result of this financial panic was a nearly decade long depression.

As a result, railroads were under pressure to cut their labor costs. Notable railroads such as the Pennsylvania and Baltimore & Ohio Railroads had administered waves of wage cuts. Railroad workers organized themselves in the summer of 1877 and succeeded in bringing the railroad system in the eastern part of the United States to a grinding halt. Striking railroad workers were joined by sympathetic workers in other mining and manufacturing sectors, which resulted in fears on the part of the state and business interests that labor was growing into a coherent and powerful countervailing force. To quell the strikers, initially local militias were deployed. However, local militias were ineffective due to their propensity to defect and join the strikers, as they found themselves in common interest with their fellow members of the community. Consequently, National Guard and federal troops were brought into cities under the control of the strikers and were far more effective, because the soldiers were not particularly vested with the interests of the community and more likely to follow the orders of their commanding officers.

Figure 5. Maryland National Guard Sixth Regiment fighting to suppress strikers in Baltimore. Harper's Weekly, Journal of Civilization, Vol XXL, No. 1076, New York. Public domain.

The strikes of 1877 serve as an important moment in the development of the political economy of the labor situation in the United States. Following the strikes, membership in labor organizations increased substantially. Likewise, more national guard units were established with an eye toward checking the power of labor going forward. In the realm of economic theory, the struggle between big business and big labor was taken as a serious matter of consideration. The development of neoclassical economics owes much of its theory of distribution to the international labor struggle that reached a fever pitch in the 1870s. For example, John Bates Clark, the father of the marginal product theory of distribution, was working out a theory of distribution that sought to move consideration of the distribution of the social product away from conflict between social classes, toward one based upon marginal contributions of each ***factor*** of production (land, labor, capital) in the production process. The result, is a theoretical system that finds fairness in an unequal distribution of income and wealth. Bates' theory was a direct response to the class conflict embodied in events like the Great Strikes of 1877.

While it is not possible to give the history of the labor movement in the United States a thorough treatment here, we can summarize some of central implications and consequences:

- Ongoing coherence and emphasize around the demand for an 8 hour working day.
- Development of systems of administration and organization capable of exerting a countervailing force against big business.
- Formation of institutions capable of allowing workers to regain some of the control over production that was lost with the demise of handicraft production as a result of industrialization.

14.4 LARGE-SCALE BUSINESS REGULATION

A central problem facing the business enterprise is maintaining the orderly governance of the markets in which they operate. The going concern wishes to form stable expectations over the viability of its business through time. An industrialized economics system means that firms are embedded in networks of interdependent financial flows, which suggests that firms must find mechanisms to coordinate their operations and establish norms governing how other participants in the markets will behave, especially via their pricing policy. Formal and informal cartel systems were frequently established in an attempt to bring harmony to markets. Earlier we have referred to these arrangements as **restrictive trade practices**, due to their objective of avoiding price competition between firms over market share. Recall, the business enterprise must ensure that it is capable of administering a price to the market that embodies a sufficient markup that recovers their costs over some defined period. Prices must be also provide a flow of income to its shareholders as profits, as well as a means of accumulating funds for investment purposes. If firms engage in a price war to capture a larger share of the market, they will undermine their revenue streams and have difficulty achieving their desired cash flows. The solution is to institute controls on individual firms so that they are properly incentivized to cooperate.

Market governance institutions are best viewed as efforts on the part of the business community to socialize the risks and rewards to individual firms. However, voluntary and privately organized market governance institutions were not terribly stable. There was always the risk that some participants would defect and undermine the cooperative agreement, resulting in a newfound round of ruinous competition.

A solution to the instability of private market governance structures was found in the federal government. The Interstate Commerce Commission (ICC) was established in 1887 in order to provide regulation over railroad rates, and emerged largely as a result of lobbying efforts by the railroads themselves. Government regulation over markets was not new to the American economic history. However, establishment of the ICC resulted in the federal government exercising its discretion over of the development of economic affairs, by instituting a new form of market governance by regulatory commission. With a standing commission now responsible for authorizing proposed rate schedules the problem of coordinating and enforcing voluntary rate design policies solved by outsourcing this function to the federal government.

The Interstate Commerce Commission emerged as a result of two political processes. On one hand, agricultural interests organized through the Grange, Patrons of Husbandry, and the like, viewed railroads as monopolies that extracted unfair monetary flows from them by charging exorbitant rates, and administering differential rate schedules that had the effect of advantaging some ratepayers at the expense of others, and undermining the ability for some farmers to bring their goods to market. These agricultural interests tended to view their monopoly power as the primary concern, and sought to compel railroads to act as if they were competitive and thereby undermine their ability to capture rents. Businessmen in the railroad and finance industry sought regulation as a means to ensure coordination between competitors, but held different views about how such regulation should be structured. Ultimately, the railway interests embraced the ICC for it helped to quell anti-monopolist agitated while preserving private control and ownership of the railway system.

The Sherman Act

The 1890s mark a turning point in American economic history. Historians generally mark 1890 as the close of the frontier, as the transcontinental railways had linked the Pacific with the Atlantic and allowed for rapid and low cost transportation and communication. In the 1890s cities in the United States began electrifying. By the 1890s, big business had become a powerful and central organizing institution in the American economy. Passage of the Sherman Act in 1890 serves as an important landmark in the history of big business and provides a useful bookend for delineating a new phase in the American economic development.

The Sherman Act of 1890 sought to prohibit behavior that may be construed as acting in restraint of trade. The anti-trust act makes illegal cartels and conspiracies to engage in price fixing. Consequently, some mechanisms that firms relied upon previously to govern markets were no longer legal, such as pooling arrangements and cartels. While the Sherman Act was seldom applied in earnest as a means to restrain corporate power, it did encourage the practice of firms attempting to consolidate control through mergers and acquisitions of their competitors.

The first great merger wave occurs between 1895 and 1904 and represents the effect of the Sherman Act on the methods by which firms attempted to control markets in the wake of the Panic of 1893. Efforts by firms to capture more market share in order to spread their fixed costs more widely, led to ruinous price wars. Since previous forms of market governance had been largely prohibited by law in the Sherman Act, firms responded by consolidating in order to eliminate the costs associated with redundant capacity in light of the depressed economic conditions of the early 1890s. Between 1895 and 1904 roughly 300 firms disappeared on an annual average basis. From 1898 to 1902 this wave of mergers was particularly acute, with 1028 firms lost to consolidation in 1899 alone. The 1890s merger movement produced some of the more notable monopolies in American history, such as U.S. Steel, American Tobacco, Du Pont, and International Harvester.

The Sherman Act, when measured by its efficacy in preventing the consolidation of corporate control, was a total failure. However, it is important to note its foundational importance to subsequent processes of coevolution between the going concern as big business and the legal framework. Extensive revision of the laws governing corporate behavior would occur in the 20th century. Nevertheless, the Sherman Act serves as a an excellent reference point for a turning point in the history of the corporation in American and closing our discussion of the history of big business.

14.5 CONCISE SUMMARY

This chapter has sought to provide a broad outline for understanding some of the more important themes that contextualize the big business in American history. The history is expansive, and so we have held a fairly narrow view of the going concern in a limited period of American history. The value in this approach, however, has been to focus on a foundational period in American economic history, the 19th century, and explore how the interaction between corporations under the control of members of the business community and legal frameworks established a course of development in which big business becomes a normal feature of capitalism in the United States. By tracing the corporation from its roots in colonial Virginia to the landmark Sherman Act in 1890, we have taken care to view the firm as a vehicle for institutional change and the locus of cumulative causation. Therefore, we walk away from this reading of American economic history with the understanding that thinking about the firm as a site of institutional capacity facilitates a more dynamic understanding of economic development. We see that power, control and influence matter in formulating a rich understanding of why the United States economy developed as it did, rather than following some other technical possibility.

CHAPTER

PRICING AND COSTS: THE EVIDENCE 15

15.1 NEOCLASSICAL THEORY OF THE FIRM TESTING

Let's review the basic properties of the neoclassical theory of the firm as given in previous chapters ("Cost and Industry Structure," "Perfect Competition," and "Monopoly"). To keep things simple, we'll focus on the short run behavior of a single firm, and we'll look to the similarities of this behavior regardless of whether the market is competitive or monopolistic. First, the firm is portrayed as a functional relationship between inputs (factors) and outputs (products). Because we're considering the short run, there are variable and fixed inputs, and therefore variable and fixed costs.

Second, the firm accepts the demand for its product as given and determines how much it should produce–its quantity of output (Q)–so that its profits are maximized where the cost of producing the last unit equals the revenue from selling it–that is, where marginal cost (MC) equals marginal revenue (MR). We assume that the firm is subject to diminishing marginal returns. Therefore marginal costs will always eventually rise to meet marginal revenue and will cause average total cost (ATC) to eventually rise (giving it its 'U' shape). Hence, the very simple **Hypothesis 1**: over some short-run period, managers are aware of their firms' marginal costs associated with increasing (or decreasing) their production, and they generally find that marginal cost increases over a relevant range of production.

Now, consider the conditions presented in the chapters "Cost and Industry Structure" and "Perfect Competition":

- If MC < ATC, then ATC is decreasing (marginal cost is 'dragging down' average total cost the same way a low test score would drag down your course grade). Therefore, if ATC is decreasing, it must be the case that MC < ATC.
- Profits = Q(P-ATC), where P represents price. Therefore, firms make losses when P < ATC, break even when P = ATC, and make profits when P > ATC.
- Profit maximizing firms under perfect competition produce where MC = MR = P.

We can read these three conditions in reverse to establish a necessary condition for firms to avoid making a loss. Plugging (3) into (2), it should be clear that, since the firm will produce where P = MC, the profit equation can be restated as Profits = Q(MC – ATC) under perfect competition. Hence, if the firm is going to break even or make a profit then MC must be ≥ ATC. Taking this back to (1), then, for MC to be equal to or greater than ATC, ATC must either be constant or increasing at some reasonable level of output.

Hence, **Hypothesis 2**: if firms maximize profits by producing a quantity where marginal cost equals marginal revenue, then under competitive conditions firms must normally be producing in a situation in which average total cost is either constant or increasing. Really, this is just an extension of hypothesis one which allows us to test our theory by looking at average total costs rather than marginal costs.

Testing the Theory

It is generally held that a developed science should be capable of expressing ideas about how the world works in hypotheses, and that these hypotheses should be compared with actual observations to determine how well the theory explains what we see in the real world. Fortunately (and perhaps surprisingly), a considerable number of studies on both costs and prices have been produced going back over 100 years. Saving the reader a laborious trek through all of them, we'll just look at a couple to test the validity of our hypotheses.

In 1998 Alan Blinder and colleagues published a book, Asking About Prices, which was not actually concerned with microeconomics (it was concerned with testing theories of macroeconomic price 'stickiness'), but just the same can help us test our hypotheses [1]. Their approach was somewhat uncommon to mainstream economics at the end of the 20th century: they simply asked business people about how they did things. For our purposes, their work (see p. 103) sheds light on hypothesis 1. Asking business executives about the shape of their marginal cost curve was apparently a bit tricky. Evidently, most do not normally consider the concept of marginal cost, so the surveyors had to repeat, rephrase, and further explain the question before a response could be given.

And the responses were not encouraging for the neoclassical theory of the firm. Firms representing only 11% of GDP were believed to have upward sloping marginal costs curves. Nearly half reported constant marginal costs, and, almost shockingly, 41% reported decreasing marginal costs (suggesting increasing returns). Evidently, the 'law' of diminishing marginal returns is more like a local custom, appropriate to only a small part (about 11%) of the US economy.

In fact, similar findings had been reported over 50 years ago. In an article published in the American Economic Review in 1952, Wilford Eitemen and Glenn

Guthrie reported their findings from a survey of manufacturing companies across the US. Specifically, they found that only 5% of the goods produced conformed to the standard 'U'-shaped depiction of average total costs. The majority (60%) of products were reported as having average total cost curves which simply declined as output increased up to maximum capacity. (Almost all remaining products were reported as similar but with a slight rise in average total costs just before capacity was reached.)

Designing the Average Total Cost Curve

Eitemen offered a simple, intuitive reason why we should expect that most average total cost curves would always decline with increased output. One way to look at the matter is in terms of the percentage of designed maximum capacity output at which you would want your production process to operate most efficiently. To give an example, imagine you're an engineer and you have been tasked with designing a machine (or a factory, or the layout of an office) that can produce some maximum number of units in a given day. In designing the machine, you find that it will have to operate more or less efficiently depending on how heavily it's being used. Would you design it to operate most efficiently when it's only running at 20% capacity? Maybe 60%? Perhaps 99%?

Most would say that a production process should work best when it's operating somewhere near the level of output it was designed to be capable of producing–otherwise, why should it be made to produce so much output in the first place? Translate 'work best' into 'operate at lowest average total cost' and the implication should be clear: a 'U'-shaped average total cost curve indicates a production process that was designed to be capable of producing up to some maximum amount inefficiently. In contrast, a declining average total cost curve indicates that the production process was made to work best when it's producing as much as it was designed to be capable of producing–the most efficient, lowest average total cost point being at or near 100% of maximum capacity output.

Returning to the three postulates we used to develop hypothesis 2, Eitemen and Guthrie's findings indicate a clear departure from the standard model of firm behavior. If most firms believe their average total costs decline as output increases, then mathematically their marginal cost curves must be below ('dragging down') their average total costs. (Perhaps in many cases, the firm's marginal costs are constant as Blinder et al. indicate is common throughout the economy.) Now, if marginal costs are always less than average total costs, then there are only two possible conclusions to be drawn:

- Firms produce a quantity where MC = MR. But, since MC is always < ATC, and under perfect competition profits = Q(MC-ATC), then firms in perfectly competitive markets will always make a loss. This doesn't seem like an attractive conclusion–surely we can find firms in competitive markets that manage to make a profit. So it's worth considering the alternative:

- Firms do not produce a quantity where MC = MR. That is, under the cost structure that most firms report, the standard profit maximization behavior postulated in the neoclassical theory of the firm is not only unrealistic, it's impossible.

Clearly, the implications of these findings do not bode well for the neoclassical theory of the firm presented in earlier chapters. The preponderance of evidence may not wholly refute the neoclassical model, but it does expose severe limitations. In the breakout box below, two additional hypotheses are examined, giving greater reason to abandon the neoclassical theory of the firm. The section that follows then introduces a few basic concepts from an alternative, heterodox viewpoint.

Two More Hypotheses

From the neoclassical perspective, we can imagine a firm incrementally increasing its, say, weekly output, and continuing to do so as long as its marginal revenue is greater than its marginal cost. Once the additional revenue of one additional unit of output just covers the cost of that unit's production, the firm settles on that level of output–profit maximizing equilibrium has been reached where MC = MR. Assuming that marginal cost must be positive (most workers won't pay their boss to let them work more hours, but perhaps there are exceptions), then marginal revenue must also be positive.

Now, refer back to chapter "Elasticity," specifically the section asking "Does Raising Price Bring in More Revenue." There you learned that a firm that is able to set its own price can increase revenues by cutting prices if demand is elastic. If on the other hand demand is inelastic, cutting your price will increase your sales (that's the law of demand after all), but the lower price will weigh heavier on your revenues than the gained sales, and your revenues will actually decline. Mathematically, this works out to a simple rule: if demand is elastic then selling more will increase revenues–which is to say that marginal revenue is positive when the elasticity of demand > 1 (and MR is zero when the elasticity of demand = 1, and negative when elasticity of demand is < 1). Hence, **hypothesis 3**: If firms produce where MC = MR, then MR must be positive, and therefore demand must be elastic.

Blinder et al. (1998 p. 99) found some support for this–but not much. While noting many businesses do not actually calculate or even think along these lines, the authors found that, among those that could give an answer, 84% believed demand to be inelastic (and, by implication, negative revenues). In fact, 41% believed that the elasticity of demand was zero–that is, a price cut would not increase sales at all.

Now consider a more general issue. In chapter "Supply and Demand" you were introduced to the centerpiece of neoclassical economics: the market model. The chief argument of that model is that prices in the market will adjust to bring supply and demand into an equilibrium in which the quantity people wish to sell is equal to the quantity people wish to purchase–that is, the price mechanism acts to clear markets. This model fits into the broader narrative of neoclassical thought which holds that capitalist economies are organized by price adjustments in the complex network of markets that make up these economies. Therefore, Hypothesis 4: unless the world changes very seldom or very slowly, leaving most markets in their previously established equilibria for long stretches of time, prices should be changing rapidly with frequent bidding, as in an auction market.

Figure 2 - Left: Auctioneer does brisk business at the Hickman Saturday Auction, 15 miles south of Lincoln, NE. (O'Rear, Public Domain). Right: Stock brokers on the New York Stock Exchange, 1963. (US News & World Report, Public Domain). Price bidding is essential to auction markets like the ones depicted above. But, of the things you've purchased in the last month, for how many of them did you bid–or even negotiate–a price?

By now you could probably predict what the evidence was going to tell us about this important part of standard neoclassical theory: throughout most of the modern US economy, prices change relatively infrequently. Blinder et al. (1998, p. 84) find that 49% of responding firms change their prices no more than once in a year or even longer. Indeed, only 22% reprice daily, weekly, or monthly. The auction market model at the core of neoclassical economics exists, indeed; but, it would appear that it lies somewhere between minor and insignificant in today's economy.

The evidence reviewed above suggests that basic ideas from neoclassical microeconomics about how businesses, markets, and capitalist economies function have, at best, very limited application to the real world. While the evidence doesn't necessarily deliver a fatal blow to the neoclassical theory of the firm, it should be disconcerting to find so many businesses viewing their world and their work in a fundamentally contradictory way. Likewise, the prevalence of yearly price changes doesn't invalidate the auction model of markets you learned in an earlier chapter; but it does raise questions as to its usefulness, and to whether an alternative model should take priority in our understanding of modern capitalist economies.

15.2 PRICES AND COSTS: A HETERODOX OPTION

The empirical findings presented in the previous section suggest that our standard models of how firms behave and what determines prices are not appropriate for understanding today's economies. Choosing the profit maximizing level of output does not appear to be relevant to firm behavior in the short run. Likewise, frequent price adjustments 'in the market' are not characteristic of most real-world markets, in which prices are clearly determined by producers and maintained over relatively long periods of time. All of this suggests that a deeper look into the actual nature of firms' costs and the actual manner in which prices are determined is necessary. Fortunately, ample information about these processes is available, and it comes from the costing practices of accountants and the pricing practices of management.

Costing is the process of estimating the costs of production before production actually takes place–and, hence, before the actual costs of production are known with certainty. To do this, of course, it would be necessary to have some idea of how much output the business will be producing and the direct and indirect expenses that will be involved at that level of production. Making such calculations may involve a simple, educated guess or a sophisticated process of research, experiment, and forecast. What is important, from a theoretical standpoint, is that it is a fundamentally uncertain task which takes place before exchanges occur in the market. This view is consistent with what was suggested above, that firms plan their production processes before, a topic discussed further in chapter "The Megacorp."

Depreciation and the Going Concern

A complete review of cost accounting isn't necessary here, but one particular type of cost, depreciation, is of particular historical and conceptual significance. Depreciation is a way of accounting for the expense of an asset–say, a machine press–over the life of the asset. For instance, suppose your machine shop purchases a press (a machine that does exactly what it sounds like it does) for $20,000. If you expect that the press will be in use for the next 10 years you might account for a depreciation expense of $2,000 per year for the next decade.

To understand the significance of depreciation, consider how businesses usually calculated income before the late 1800s. Before then, business enterprise was often treated as a terminal venture, having a clearly defined beginning and end date. Investors would pool money to start a business, purchase materials and capital (say, a ship and local goods to be traded abroad), and hire workers (the ship's crew). At some predetermined date (perhaps when the ship returned to port) the business would be liquidated: its crew would be paid and any remaining assets would be sold off. The resulting profit to the investors would, in essence, simply be whatever money was leftover. In this approach, what was the relationship between the productive asset (the ship) and profit?

Profits were simply decreased by the cost of the ship, but increased by whatever price could be fetched by selling the ship at the end of the venture.

But, accountants in the late 1800s asked, is that an appropriate way to think of, say, a railroad company? Will a railroad lay thousands of miles of line, run trains across it for some predetermined number of years, and then pull up the line to be sold for scrap metal? Clearly not. Instead, fixed assets like a railroad's line, or an airline's planes, or a law firm's office building are depreciated over the course of their useful life. Conceptually, this is simply the recognition of the role those assets play in allowing these businesses to generate an income into the foreseeable future. Most importantly, this accounting method reflects the fact that these businesses are not treated as terminal ventures. Rather, they, as nearly all businesses today, are considered **going concerns**: organizations which are expected to continue to exist into the foreseeable future.

Prices from Pricing

Similar to costing, pricing refers to procedures businesses use to determine, beforehand, the price at which they will sell their product once production is up and running and sales can be made. While modern pricing procedures can be complex and will vary widely across different businesses and industries, two basic methods should be understood: full cost pricing and target rate of return pricing. Both are instances of markup (or cost-plus) pricing: setting the price of a business enterprise's product by adding some dollar amount over and above average costs of production.

Full cost pricing (sometimes called normal cost pricing) is the simpler of the two methods. It can be written as

$$P = (ATC)(1 + r)$$

Where:

P is the price at which the business plans to sell its product

ATC is the average total (or per-unit) cost determined in the costing process

r is the predetermined markup

Target rate of return pricing is similar, but a bit more complicated. Here the price is being set, not to achieve a particular percentage profit above costs, but to earn a desired return on the money invested into the business. The formula can be written as

$$P = ATC + \frac{ROI(IC)}{Q}$$

Where:

ROI is desired return on invested capital

IC is invested capital–that is, money invested into producing the product

Q is the expected quantity of output sold

Calculating Prices

To illustrate both approaches, consider a business that invests $10 million into a plant designed to manufacture inexpensive steak knives. It expects that over some relevant period it will be able to produce and sell 2 million knives; and, at that level of production, its per-unit costs will be $1.80 per knife. The calculated prices using our two pricing procedures are given below (assuming that in the first case the desired markup is 10% (or 0.1), and in the second the desired return on invested capital is also 10%).

Full cost price: $P = (1.80)(1 + 0.1) = \$1.98$

Target rate of return price: $$P = (1.80) + \frac{(0.1)(10,000,000)}{2,000,000} = \$2.30$$

Notice also that, even though the markup and desired return on invested capital are both 0.1 (10%), the resulting markups and hence the prices are not the same. This is because, although both procedures are essentially marking the price up over costs, the treatment of the costs being marked up are different.

It is worth reflecting on the significance of these insights into cost accounting and markup pricing, as they represent important general concepts in heterodox economics which are usually neglected in standard neoclassical theory. First, they suggest that business enterprises are making decisions before anything is even produced, let alone 'brought to market'. In particular, pricing practices (and the intended quantity of output and corresponding cost estimates on which pricing is based) are a component of the planning process which takes place within the business enterprise. Contrary to the axiom that firms cannot recover fixed costs in the short run and therefore should ignore them in making short run decisions, it is long run planning driving short run behavior that is most important for understanding what determines prices.

Second, to acknowledge costing and pricing as it actually occurs is to acknowledge that the future is fundamentally unknowable. While standard (neoclassical) models assume that firms know their production costs and, typically, also the amount they can sell and the resulting revenues they can expect to take in, actual firms face uncertainty in how their plans will work out. A particular implication of this reality: since firms set prices based on estimated average total costs at an expected level of output, a change in the actual quantity of production/sales is unlikely to affect the predetermined price. This suggests that price and quantity supplied are determined completely separately, which in turn means that there is no such thing as a supply curve.

The Illusory Supply Curve

Recall from the basics of the neoclassical market model that a supply schedule (and its corresponding supply curve) simply shows the relationship between how much a firm (or firms) would be willing to supply at various market prices. That is, supply simply refers to the functional relationship between quantity supplied and the market price, with the market price determining the quantity supplied. If, however, the two are determined separately then there's no way around the implication: quantity supplied is not functionally related to the market price–that is, there is no supply curve.

The astute reader may have already realized the impossibility of supply curves under certain conditions from the failed hypotheses discussed earlier in this chapter. Referring back to chapter "Perfect Competition," specifically the section titled "Marginal Cost and the Firm's Supply Curve," you'll recall that a firm's marginal cost curve (above minimum average variable cost) is its supply curve. (This is because quantity supplied is determined where MC = MR and, under competitive conditions, MR = P. Hence, quantity supplied is determined by P = MC.) Now, as was shown with the test of hypothesis 2 above, firms simply couldn't determine their quantity supplied this way–at least not under competitive conditions and having the empirically typical average total cost curves. This, of course, means that the neoclassical theory of supply must be rejected for these cases.

This doesn't mean that the basic ideas of supply–higher prices leading to higher output and vice versa, for instance–are completely absent in the real world. Some industries–particularly, those related to mining and agriculture–do in fact see diminishing returns. In these (albeit limited) parts of modern economies upward-sloping supply curves may be found. However, as our examination of the cost structures of actual firms suggested earlier in this chapter, this relegates what is considered the normal case in neoclassical economics to a special–and pretty rare–case.

Third and finally, a review of the evidence and history of actual businesses reveals an anachronism within the neoclassical theory of the firm. As you learned in chapter "Perfect Competition," the firm chooses the most profitable line of business (and appropriate production technique) in the long run, and the profit maximizing quantity to produce in the short run. If, in the short run, the firm is making a loss it will choose to shut down (if its fixed cost losses would be lower than the losses on continuing production). In an abstract, but important way the business enterprise this theory is describing is a terminal venture. Yet, beyond the halls and offices of economics departments, firms are generally seen as going concerns. This is reflected, for instance, in the accounting practices discussed above, as well as in the relationships firms maintain with customers. Blinder et al. (1998, pp. 96-7) found that 85% of all sales in the economy are made to regular customers whom the business expects to sell to in the future. In manufacturing and wholesale trade that number is over 90%.

As will be explored in more depth in the chapter "The Megacorp," the idea that businesses are organized and run as going concerns is a significant theoretical innovation over the standard neoclassical theory of the firm. For now, we only need to consider what it means for prices. The role of the price mechanism–the 'invisible hand of the market'–in neoclassical economics cannot be overstated. It is the process by which self-interested people (consumers, workers, entrepreneurs, landlords, and all the rest) are brought together in exchange for their mutual benefit. It is the mechanism that allows economists to believe in a (potentially) optimal equilibrium state–in an individual market, and in a capitalist economy as a whole.

In contrast, what is being argued in this section is that prices–at least those prices not actually determined through an auction–are set by businesses themselves as part of their planning process. The reader may have noticed that in the markup pricing introduced above a glaring question was ignored: namely, what determines the markup? A succinct, if incomplete answer can now be given: if the firm is to be a going concern, the markup, as well as the procedures that determined costs, will reflect the needs of the firm to continue to do business into the foreseeable future. For most firms there will also be plans to grow. Hence, from this view, prices are not exchange-based, market clearing values at all. They are, rather, reproduction prices–allowing the firm to reproduce itself through time–and, typically, also growth prices–ensuring the firm brings in the earnings necessary to expand. To use a now-familiar term, the vast majority of the prices we see in actual capitalist economies today might best be called **going concern prices.**

15.3 NEOCLASSICAL AND HETERODOX THEORY COMPARISON

For quick reference, a table contrasting general views from neoclassical and heterodox economics on firms, costs, and prices is provided below. The student should be aware that we are painting in broad strokes here. Both neoclassical and heterodox economics include a variety of sophisticated models and theories, some of which would contradict the characterizations made below. However, as an introduction to microeconomics this table should suffice as a reflection of the core positions and standard ideas within these two camps.

	Neoclassical	Heterodox
Prices are determined in...	the market	the planning processes of the business enterprise
Prices function to...	clear markets	ensure the reproduction and growth of business enterprises
As production increases, average total costs...	first decline to some minimum (or efficient) point and then start to rise again (that is, ATC is 'U'-shaped)	typically decline up to (or very near) the maximum output at which the production process was designed to operate
Marginal costs...	eventually rise with higher levels of production due to the law of diminishing returns	are not generally contemplated by business executives and are not relevant to microeconomic theory, in part because firms don't (and couldn't) typically produce according marginal costs and revenues.
Price and quantity supplied...	are functionally related– that is, when price changes quantity will generally change	are, in most instances, determined completely separately
Firms are viewed as...	terminal ventures, always and everywhere maximizing profits	going concerns, organized and operated to (try to) stay in business into the foreseeable future
Firms make short-run decisions...	ignoring fixed costs, because by definition these cannot be changed	typically in accordance with the long-run strategies determined through their long-run planning process

www.ingramcontent.com/pod-product-compliance
Lightning Source LLC
LaVergne TN
LVHW062219200926
848484LV00006B/1435

* 9 7 8 1 7 8 7 1 5 1 7 8 9 *